RACE AND
THE FOUNDATIONS
OF KNOWLEDGE

T0287990

Race and the Foundations of Knowledge

Cultural Amnesia in the Academy

Edited by

JOSEPH YOUNG AND
JANA EVANS BRAZIEL

UNIVERSITY OF ILLINOIS PRESS

URBANA AND CHICAGO

© 2006 by the Board of Trustees
of the University of Illinois
All rights reserved
Manufactured in the United States of America
1 2 3 4 5 C P 5 4 3 2 1
∞ This book is printed on acid-free paper.

Library of Congress Cataloging-in-Publication Data
Race and the foundations of knowledge : cultural amnesia in the
academy / edited by Joseph Young and Jana Evans Braziel.
 p.   cm.
Includes bibliographical references and index.
ISBN-13: 978-0-252-03012-3 (cloth : alk. paper)
ISBN-10: 0-252-03012-5 (cloth : alk. paper)
ISBN-13: 978-0-252-07256-7 (paper : alk. paper)
ISBN-10: 0-252-07256-1 (paper : alk. paper)
1. Discrimination in higher education—United States.
2. Prejudices—United States. 3. Minority college teachers—
United States. 4. Educational sociology—United States.
5. Race relations. 6. Racism. I. Young, Joseph A. II. Braziel,
Jana Evans, 1967–
LC212.42.R32   2006
378.1'9829—dc22   2005011372

CONTENTS

ACKNOWLEDGMENTS

First and foremost, we thank our families for their love, support, and commitment: thank you, Diane, Jennifer, Jim, Jessi, Maddie, and Dylan. For editorial expertise, we also extend our appreciation to Laurie Matheson and the staff at the University of Illinois Press. For sponsoring the Race in the Humanities conference (University of Wisconsin–La Crosse, November 2001), we thank the following: the University of Wisconsin System Office of Multicultural Affairs; University of Wisconsin Extension Office of Equal Opportunity and Diversity Programs; University of Wisconsin System Institute on Race and Ethnicity; University of Wisconsin–Milwaukee Office of Multicultural Affairs and Department of Student Academic Development; University of Wisconsin–Stout Student Support Services; the University of Wisconsin–La Crosse Office of Affirmative Action and Diversity; the University of Wisconsin–La Crosse Provost's Office; the University of Wisconsin–La Crosse Chancellor's Office; the University of Wisconsin–La Crosse Foundation; the Noel J. Richards Fund; the Allan Birchler Fund; the College of Liberal Studies at the University of Wisconsin–La Crosse; the Institute for Ethnic and Racial Studies at the University of Wisconsin–La Crosse; and the following University of Wisconsin–La Crosse departments: English, Philosophy, Foreign Languages, History, Political Science/Public Administration, Sociology/Archaeology, and Women's Studies. An earlier version of James W. Perkinson's chapter appeared in the *Journal of the American Academy of Religion,* volume 72, number 3 (2004), and is reprinted here by permission of Oxford University Press.

RACE AND
THE FOUNDATIONS
OF KNOWLEDGE

Cultural Amnesia and the Academy— Why the Problem of the Twenty-first Century Is Still the "Problem of the Color Line"

Joseph Young and Jana Evans Braziel

We begin by evoking the words of the prescient W. E. B. Du Bois, who first wrote that "the problem of the Twentieth Century is the problem of the color line" in an article entitled "The Freedmen's Bureau," which was published in the *Atlantic Monthly* in 1901 and republished as "The Forethought" of *The Souls of Black Folk* in 1903. Echoing Du Bois's words and sentiments in 2005, a little more than one hundred years after the publication of *The Souls of Black Folk,* we assert (yet are disheartened that we must) that the problem of the twenty-first century remains the "problem of the color line": moreover, the institutionalized foundations of race and racialized ways of knowing and the resolute cultural amnesia within the academy, even from within the most unexpected halls of that institution, have perpetuated, not solved, resolved, or even tepidly confronted this centuries-old problem. Cultural amnesia about the structuring forces of race, racialization, and even overt racism within the academy thus make it impossible to imagine "political culture beyond the color line," though some have admonished those who refuse to surrender that battle.[1] We thus also borrow and echo sentiments from Charles W. Mills, who pointedly critiques the often vapid intellectual gymnastics of postmodernity in the concluding chapter of *The Racial Contract:* while we are sympathetic to some of the political ends of postmodernism, "ultimately, [we] see it as an epistemological and theoretical dead end, itself symptomatic rather than diagnostic of the problems of the globe as we [have] enter[ed] the new millennium" (129).

Race and the Foundations of Knowledge: Cultural Amnesia in the Academy offers both deliberate critical resistance to the historical erasures of public memory— most profoundly, perhaps, in the academy itself—and revisionist attempts to restore what has been erased within the cultural memory of the Americas. More specifically, it addresses race and the multitude of roles that race and racialization have played in the formation of academic disciplines and knowledge. Of all social sectors and public institutions, the academy most resolutely perpetuates a core set of ideas and foundations of knowledge (indeed, many hold this aspect to be its very principle and defining mission), and while it is a malleable, evolving body, it remains intractable in its racialized foundations, witnessed perhaps most visibly in recent debates and Supreme Court decisions about affirmative action, but no less palpably in its formation of disciplines and its constructions of knowledge. The modernist era, as Mills pointedly reveals in his contribution to this volume, has been plagued by contradictions of equality and disparity, personhood and subpersonhood, revolution and enslavement; rather than being exceptional to modernity, these contradictions are rather constitutive of it. One of the most devastating effects and consequences of dominant forms of cultural experience in the Americas has been the political subordination and cultural erasures experienced by African diasporic subjects in the so-called "New World." For African Americans hemispherically, Édouard Glissant explains, "There was the drawn-out damnation of the loss of family heritage, the erasure of collective memory, the initial trauma of the Middle Passage, the belly of the slave ship, the agonizing obliteration of old and familiar objects, and the need to master a plethora of new and frustrating tools. . . . And then there were all the forbidden tools: guns and other weapons, books, pencils, and notebooks" (*Faulkner, Mississippi* 162). Glissant's passage reveals the active forms of political subjugation and the pervasive forms of historical erasure that were part and parcel of the African diasporic experiences in the "New World." In this sentiment, Glissant echoes an earlier anticolonialist writer also from Martinique, Frantz Fanon, who wrote in *The Wretched of the Earth,* "Colonization is not satisfied merely with holding a people in its grip and emptying the native's brain of all form and content. By a kind of perverted logic, it turns to the past of the oppressed people, and distorts, disfigures and destroys it" (170). Likewise, the Americas have distorted or erased their own Africanist presences.

The Americas still suffer from historical amnesia, a deep unwillingness to face and confront the inflicted wounds of the past: the legacies of genocide, slavery, and colonialism committed against indigenous or native Americans and enslaved Africans. And these wounds have been academic, intellectual, and ontological as well as material or physical. To heal, we must remember, we must never forget. Above all, this is why reparations and debates over reparations are so vital to the present and the future, as much as they historically redress the violences of the past. African American scholars such as Robert O'Meally, Geneviève Fabre, David Blight, and others (in *History and Memory in African-American Culture*) have theorized the importance of historical memory, and their efforts parallel the work of Caribbean scholars Édouard Glissant, Edward Baugh, Derek Walcott, Stuart Hall, and others who have entered into Antillean "quarrels with history" (particularly history as defined within a Hegelian worldview). The work of historical remembrance, however, though clearly about the wounds of the past, is also about the present and the future. As Hall rhetorically asks in his essay "Cultural

Identity and Diaspora": "Is it only a matter of unearthing that which the colonial experience buried and overlaid, bringing to light the hidden communities it suppressed? Or is a quite different practice entailed—not the rediscovery but the *production* of identity? Not an identity grounded in the archeology, but in the *retelling* of the past?" (235). Within Hall's diasporic framework, historical remembrance is present- and future-, as well as past-, oriented; it remembers the past—however fractured, fragmented, or impartial—as an act of survival in the present and for the future.

History and memory are entangled ideas, not separate ones with the first belonging ostensibly to public culture and the second to individual psyche; both are interwoven in the African "American" imagination as it reflects on nature and remembers subterranean and submarine histories. This interweaving is a *genesis* of future spaces and times, as well as the creative remembrance of past spaces and times. Memory, Glissant muses, "is not a calendar memory; our experience of time does not keep company with the rhythms of month and year alone; it is aggravated by the void, the final sentence of the Plantation" (*Poetics* 72). But this touching upon the void, this experience of the abyss that is the inheritance of the Middle Passage (or "the final sentence of the Plantation") is also genesis, creation—"the infinite abyss, in the end became knowledge" (*Poetics* 8). To counter the erasures of History (capital H), it is necessary to unravel other submerged histories through an imaginative, if not literal, "effort of memory."

Regrettably, the historical erasures of public memory persist in many critical domains that should resist: notably in poststructuralist approaches to African American studies that deconstruct race and ignore the perpetuation of racism, despite their theoretical disavowals of the analytical category of race. In contrast to this willful denial of race and racialization historically—itself a form of cultural amnesia that merely perpetuates racist historical elision—the contributors to *Race and the Foundations of Knowledge* seek to understand and probe the ways in which race has been formative in thought itself, structurally inherent to the formation of knowledge and academic disciplines. As a preface to those aims, this introduction offers three specific arguments: first, that poststructuralist deconstructions of race are merely apolitical intellectual exercises—mental gymnastics, if you will—if they do not also offer solid ground for eradicating the political, material consequences of race and racism; second, that critical race theorists, whose interventions have had profound and radical effects on the fields of legal studies and political science, and more recently (and surprisingly) philosophy, offer a more viable critical approach for thinking through the legacies of race within the Americas, not only in legal studies but also within academic fields of study; and third, that our very understanding of modes and methods (i.e., disciplines) for understanding have been, and continue to be, racially inflected.

This book, then, is unapologetically about race. This book is about race and the role that race has played in the formation of knowledge, generally, and the role (or myriad and nuanced, often contradictory, roles) it has played in the construction of humanistic disciplines, specifically: their content of study, as well as methods, methodologies, theoretical presuppositions, disciplinary boundaries, the exclusions such boundaries enact, and the inclusions these boundaries are predicated and built upon. We understand, of course, that in foregrounding race and its multiple locations in the humanities, this book and our focus run counter to most contemporary discursive formations around race in the humanities. Many scholars will resolutely and emphatically state that "race does not exist." For many, perhaps most saliently those who rely on poststructuralist (by now pedestrian) dismissals of race, the idea of a "color-blind" world is stressed without any attention to history, historical injustice, or continued forms of racial oppression. As Tony Zaragoza reminds us in his contribution, however, "color-blind" rhetorics inflect, and often determine, racialized and racist practices and, more disconcertingly, public policies. Similarly, Matthew Abraham trenchantly examines the racialized cultures of academic and judicial institutions—as well as their mutual sustenance through law schools—wherein institutional forms of socialization perpetuate white privilege and race-biased interpretations of the law and legal discourses. Derrick E. White further explores how public policies become race-inflected and addresses the detrimental impact of these policies on minority communities. All these scholars pointedly reveal how the rhetoric of color blindness places us squarely in the vise of an insidious racial bind. For individuals who insist on color blindness, it remains an uninterrogated common knowledge that "race does not exist." Yes, race is a cultural construct. Yet why insist on and persist in thinking that cultural constructs "do not exist"? Not only do they exist, but they are encoded with real material, political, and social forms of power. This anthology not only argues that race exists but also examines the centuries-long and multiply coded manifestations of race in the humanities: as ground of possibility, as *a priori* concept, as a point of differential knowledge, or even as a mark of foundational exclusion. We therefore agree with Howard Winant in his assessment of race in a contemporary cultural context:

> Today the theory of race has been utterly transformed. The socially constructed status of the concept of race, which I have labeled the racial formation process, is widely recognized (Omi and Winant 1986), so much so that it is now often conservatives who argue that race is an illusion. The main task facing racial theory today, in fact, is no longer to critique the seemingly "natural" or "commonsense" concept of race—although that effort has not by any means been entirely completed. Rather, the central task is to focus attention on the continuing significance and changing meaning of race. It is to argue against the recent discovery of the illusory nature of race; against the supposed contemporary transcendence of race; against the widely reported death of the concept of race; and against the replacement of the category of race by other, supposedly more objective, categories like ethnicity, nationality, or class. All these initiatives are mistaken at best, and intellectually dishonest at worst. (181–82)

To theorize alternative ways of knowing and being, we must probe and rigorously analyze (think *through*, not over, if you will) the deeply embedded structures of race and racialization—manifest in myriad, even contradictory, forms—in academic disciplines and knowledge, as well as in societal, political, or other cultural terrains. What Winant identifies as the dangerous "'natural' or 'commonsense' concept of race" becomes the primary focus of the chapter in this volume by Alexis Shotwell, who examines the mechanisms by which race and racism are propagated by uninterrogated notions of "common sense" and everyday practices of racial privilege.

That being said, we do not define race, though we recognize that historically it has been defined in such ways, as any of the following: an ontological category, a biological or psychological essence, a fixed or unchanging category of uncomplicated belonging, a genetically determined classification with presumed intrinsic epistemological interpretations. Like the scholars who insist that race does not (or should not) exist (Anthony Kwame Appiah, Houston Baker Jr., Henry Louis Gates Jr., Paul Gilroy, and others), we too recognize race as a historical category defined through biologistic reductivism, a political classification intended to define individuals through difference in oppressive ways, a social and cultural construct, a discursive formation. It is not, however, an "empty" category or a "free-floating signifier," as some would have it. If nothing else, history proves, and regrettably, contemporary forms of racist and racial oppression demonstrate, that race exists; it has real material, political, social, and, we would argue, intellectual and academic consequences; it continues to occupy numerous (and perhaps even unconscious and systemic) places in our social imaginary; and it remains embedded within our ways of knowing, thinking, learning, and producing knowledge. To deconstruct race does not render it nonexistent in its social and political forms, will never erase its historical and even humanistic legacies, nor will it undo its effects or legibility. This book intends to examine the effects (the afterlife, if you will) of race (in all its legible forms) within the humanities. By so doing, it also rethinks and renegotiates the innumerable roles race has played not only in forming the *object,* but also, and more significantly, in formulating (and severely delimiting) the *subjects* of academic disciplines and knowledge-based enterprises (intending, of course, the full resonances, including the capitalistic ones, of that word). As Lewis Gordon suggests (*Existentia Africana* 102), it would be a mistake "to claim that social phenomena are invalid because of their 'social' status"; or as Mills pointedly writes, "race is sociopolitical rather than biological, but it is nonetheless real" (*Racial Contract* 126).

Mills argues that, although the racial contract has been the most devastating contract in history, it is not unique. "All peoples can fall into Whiteness under the appropriate circumstances as shown by the ('White') black Hutus' 1994 massacre of half a million to a million inferior black Tutsis" (*Racial Contract* 128–29). This observation may be the aporia, the very site at which Mills's excellent treatise on the Racial Contract becomes problematic (why criticize whites for employing a racial contract if humankind is intrinsically racist?). As Gatsinzi Basaninyenzi reveals, however, in "Dark-Faced Europeans," his contribution to this book, the situation was far more complicated than was obvious and was historically implicated in colonialist perspectives of race: Rwandese society, Basaninyenzi argues, had institutionalized Eurocentric, colonialist notions of race from nineteenth-century racialized sciences that deemed the Hutus farther removed from Caucasian features and thus racially inferior. Nevertheless, if Mills's conclusions are indicative of all humanity, then such a declaration is reflective of having arrived at the deepest level of the racial discourse, of having arrived at the understanding of the multiplicity of destructive discourses as Derrida (251) might put it. Mills embraces a pragmatist conception of truth: truth as consisting only of what can be established within a conventional framework as opposed to a nonprepositional truth that possesses a relentless suppleness, of being both what can be verified and what fundamentally is the case, whether or not anyone could assume or authenticate it (Culler 155). At this point, Mills's analysis is a kind of destruction of metaphysics, an elimination of metaphysical oppositions, an erasing of difference. Though we may have arrived at the ultimate implication of poststructuralist theory, such a location offers only incoherent insight. Yet for the sake of argument, let us accept for the moment the proposition that nonwhites can be racists before the fact of "Whiteness" (before exposure to the West), that because of Darwinian epigenesis, or of evolution, human nature, like the human species, is not static but given to change multidirectionally stimulated by a combination of human genes and whatever environmental stimuli (that there is no fixed, ahistorical human essence). Heidegger's insight is noteworthy in commenting on the direction that bewitched Europe. Modern civilization's turn to an epistemological subject and foundational imperatives for thought proved insufficient for a true disclosure of being, yielding instead a hegemonic engagement with the world that provides aggressive, territorial, opportunistic selves a somewhat guaranteed historicity and sociality. "We are," as Heidegger says (*Poetry, Language, Thought*), "too late for the gods and too early for Being."

We thus begin with our critiques of poststructuralist deconstructions of race, before addressing what we see as the promising political imports of a critical race approach to literary and cultural studies in order to expose the racialized formations of humanistic and social science disciplines.

Deconstructing the "Deconstructionist (Race) Machine"

Although the essentialist vision of "race" as a permanent, unambiguous, and objective set of biological characteristics has been dismissed by an antiessentialist view as mere chimera or as a cultural and "ideological construction designed to secure the interests of racists" (Bernasconi and Lott xvii), both individuals and groups still face, in a postmodernist milieu, racialized transcendental and public spheres. This anthology addresses that problematic. Race is more than merely a fiction or scientific myth eradicable by the verbal fiat of a momentary academic disciplinary practice of a few theorists. As a concept, race, because of its centuries-long practice of hierarchically structuring peoples globally from a European-centered perspective (Bernasconi and Lott), has become determinative of understanding and conceptualization at the most fundamental levels of modification and abstraction in human thought. Racialized residue has infected ontology and epistemology, the very basis of meaning. Reason itself (if one abstracts this as a necessary ontology in opposition to views of reason as rationalizations of authoritarian tendencies in cultures) is infected with racism. The antirace discourses of Anthony Kwame Appiah, Houston Baker Jr., Henry Louis Gates Jr., Paul Gilroy, and Cornel West, while adopting utopic liberal idealism, reject the concept of race as fictitious and therefore irrelevant in their quest for the value-neutral, tolerance-spirited individual (Gordon, *Existentia Africana*). As James W. Perkinson and Joseph Young differently reveal in their respective chapters, however, race inflects not only literary genres (as Young shows) and theological presuppositions (as Perkinson demonstrates), but also notions of subjectivity, objectivity, individualism, and even reason or rationality.

As a further enhancement of these efforts, the contributors to *Race and the Foundations of Knowledge: Cultural Amnesia in the Academy* believe that we need not be seduced by theory; we need to make it useful in the Foucaultian sense of obtaining a vehicle for the imbrication of power by widening the discourse on race and disabling those who may dominate the field and who limit discussion only to a textual or tropological theory of race. The problematics of signification need not be our only battleground, either. The contributors to this volume directly engage the gaps, fissures, and often cataclysmic theoretical intersections of poststructuralist and political economic approaches to race analyses, rather than valorizing one approach over and to the exclusion or refusal of the other. Nor need we wait for Bhabha's time lag between event and enunciation to recover space for postcolonial agency. Unplugging the racialized circuitry may be a function of suspending a certain kind of judgment, bracketing the duality that creates the reciprocating ontological vectors of Manichean delirium, producing a European-designed human reality based on white privilege. To be rigorous, theory must be instructive and radical in the Husserlian sense (Gordon, *Fanon* 6–12). We must decenter the white subject as transcendental ego, recovering an altogether new structure to mediate things of our consciousness that produce meaning and designate reality. Radically different structures that mediate an alternate reality would result in a challenge to those "white Lockean, Kantian, Millian persons who own themselves and their efficient nature-appropriating labor, who are rational noumenal duty-respecting beings, whose individuality must be respected by the modernist liberal state, [and who] emerge not merely in contrast to but to a certain extent on the backs of nonwhite subpersons thousands of miles away, whose self-ownership is qualified and whose labor is inefficient, whose phenomenal traits limit their rationality and consequent moral autonomy, and for whom, accordingly, slavery and despotic colonial rule are appropriate" (Mills, *Racial Contract,* 128). A practice that investigates and abstracts the racialized structures of such a conceptualization of reality is the purpose of this anthology. The contributors to this volume would agree that disconnecting a racialized circuitry in the *a priori* network (which would be a radical form of self-reflection and was arguably an indispensable objective of Black Aestheticians, however their homophobia and misogyny were misappropriated) is more meaningful than valorizing the indeterminacy of verbal play for theory's sake. It is at the provocative, often volatile, intersections of poststructuralism and political economy, then, that our contributors wage their intellectual and material battles. The problematic self-construction of 1960s Black Power critics in analytical projects like Houston Baker Jr.'s "anthropology of art" (*Journey Back*) and vernacular theory (*Blues, Ideology, and Afro-American Literature*), and like Henry Louis Gates Jr.'s microanalysis of African American figurative language in search of structure (*"Race," Writing, and Difference; Figures in Black; Signifying Monkey*) are apparently efforts that substitute analysis, theoretical rigor, and sophistication for the supposedly dreaded racial polemics in the reading of African American texts. Given to conclusions that are self-referential and evasive, however, Gates and Baker dismiss the efforts of Black Aestheticians as merely self-conscious glorification of black separatism that attempts to secure a utopic vision by literary decree. A comparable kind of ideological/formalistic distortion Gates engages in is his article "Critical Fanonism" (1991); it is a project designed to decenter Frantz Fanon in colonial and post-colonial studies, and it reflects the kind of analysis that Appiah's essay "The Uncompleted Argument: Du Bois and the Illusion of Race" (1986) posits with the argument that Du Bois was a racist for not repudiating race altogether. Appiah's *In My Father's House* (1992) endeavors to situate all discussions about race within a Western discourse on liberation that discredits any use of race, even as an interrogative tool. As Hussain importantly demonstrates in chapter 7 of this book, purely discursive approaches may create a virtually "textual Fanon" divorced from the "revolutionary Fanon" of race- and class-based anticolonial struggles. Again, we do not reject poststructural approaches to race analysis, but only insist that these approaches be critically situated with respect to urgent material problems within the political economy of race.

How can we achieve rigorous theory if some theorists attempt to ontologize their disciplinary and methodological approaches as a means of preempting theoretical praxis altogether (Gordon, *Fanon*)? What function is there in framing black cultural artifacts like "blues" as paradigmatic linguistic discourse if such expressions can be read as possessing at least a double logic at the textual level? What is the status of the subversive elements of a particular blues song? The hybridity latent in these cultural forms would not permit Baker to isolate, with his structuralist methodology, expressive manifestations of black American culture uncontaminated by a white imaginary that would racialize the foundation of these systems. Baker's supposedly more theoretically sophisticated study of black cultural expression may not possess an authentic center. Without the Hegelian contrariness of the self, or more appropriately the Husserlian transcendental ego intending a reality for historically located black subjects, there is no "I" that seeks to establish itself as the subject of its own discourse. There is only a disembodied, passive gaze that easily can be forced into the object slot of a phenomenological bipolarity.

Why does Gates ontologize structure in a search for structure when there is always a deeper structure or an inevitable moment of referentiality that betrays an opposing structure? Perhaps more basic than linguistic meaning in this particular and the source of all structure is the understanding that consciousness is an act constitutive of the world (Karl Otto Apel, Husserl, and Merleau-Ponty). Without a microanalysis of intentionality and the a priori network of both artist and critic, all our conclusions are well less than tentative. Why not microanalyze literature as an embodied subjectivity and as a matrix of our experience of a not too fully determinate but ambiguous world (Merleau-Ponty)? Gates's and Baker's misreadings and misappropriations of black culture in a theory-inflected academic reality represent not so much a move toward theoretical thoroughness, but rather a move toward the thorough decentering of black antiestablishment thinkers by situating them in self-referential signifying systems of a tropological and textual theory of race where language (or the code) speaks the subject, revealing more a problematics of signification than showing signifyin(g) as both desirable and observable verbal play.

Appiah's critique of Du Bois's use of "a biological notion of race to pursue an antiracist political agenda" betrays an unsophisticated confrontation of Du Bois's complexity and an ignorance of the context in which he wrote (Bernasconi and Lott). Racial classification, however much a biological fiction, was being used to justify stratifications of social privilege and the foundation of much social injustice. Ironically, "in declaring biological and essential conceptions of race useless and dangerous," as critical race theorist and legal scholar Jayne Chong-Soon Lee astutely writes in her important article "Navigating the Topology of Race," Appiah "fails to recognize that race is defined *not* by its inherent content, but by the social relations that construct it" (443, emphasis added); ultimately, Appiah himself ends up reifying race as an unchanging, fixed, and predetermined ontological category. Chong-Soon Lee's article, as the editors of *Critical Race Theory: The Key Writings That Formed the Movement* explain, challenges Appiah's argument "that the concept of race, of racial difference, has no ground to give it meaning except in racist motivation" (440); Chong-Soon Lee demonstrates, rather, how race may also be the contingent foundation for collective aspirations and political struggle. (Gilroy, regrettably, falls prey to the same intellectual trap as Appiah.) Postcolonial theorist Robert Young further argues that Appiah's critiques of Pan-Africanism sorely miss the mark, and Young persuasively demonstrates that Pan-Africanism was less a movement grounded in essentialist ideas about race, origin, and "homeland" (Africa) than it was a powerful transnational political coalition that was grounded in anti-imperialist and anticolonialist mobilization: "The greatness and the grandeur of the transcontinental Pan-African project has been lost [in critiques such as Appiah's]. As a common strategy against white European oppression (whether anti-colonial or domestic, as in the case of the US), African and American Pan-Africanism gave both constituencies particular strength by virtue of a combined international solidarity and common political programme demanding representation, land rights, education, economic reconstruction, and an end to racism and institutionalized racist practices. Moreover, it developed as an independent project beholden to neither of the great world powers or their ideologies" (*Postcolonialism* 237).

Similarly, the contributors to *Race and the Foundations of Knowledge: Cultural Amnesia in the Academy* see our efforts as ones grounded in anti-imperialist and antiracist political alliances in the Americas that want to unmoor myths of universalized aesthetics free of materialist political implications; our efforts then are not ones predicated on "race" as the violent and racist perpetuation of racialized sciences and knowledges. In our readings, then, the analytical projects of Appiah, Baker, Gates, and Gilroy initiate a paradigmatic shift and become a kind of Foucaultian episteme: an unconscious, regulating, hegemonic structure that limits what can be written in the coming epoch (Foucault, *Order of Things*). It is a forced systemic adjustment of certain kinds of intellectual dissent, a shift toward epistemic closure, a locking out of the voice of the oppressed; but it does achieve for its elucidators a form of agency, a privileged space within the academy.

As domestic species of neocolonialism or methodologies recoverable in the colonialist/racist discourse, Baker's and Gates's analytical projects serve an ideological function. Gates's fascination with and fetish for the vernacular and figures of signification function to explain such artifacts as full of the rhetoricity and representation of the indigenous culture and oral discourse of African Americans. Baker's "anthropology of art" as a scientific method of studying the status of and the relationship among art objects confirms a mature creativity from a developed cultural context. For both, and rightly so, vernacular black literature is as intricate a tradition as that of the ambient logocentric, text-centered traditions of Europe and Anglo/Euro-America. Abdul JanMohamed would note that this is an example of internalization of Western culture, that such obsession with articulating the richness of African American culture is a manifestation of the hegemonic phase of colonialism. Gates's and Baker's efforts to demonstrate the engaging tapestry and complexity of the black oral tradition (and their own abilities, especially Gates's skill in developing an empiricism of sensibility that served as the foundation for his perspective, enabling him to isolate signifyin(g), a poststructuralist concept of intertexuality as a formal structure in African American literature) are like the Wheatleys' efforts to prove that Phillis actually wrote those poems, representing for all concerned that she was in possession of "the most salient repository of 'genius,' the visible sign of reason itself" (Gates 9), and therefore, a human unworthy of slavery. Such demonstrations are intrinsic to the authority of the hegemonic discourses they profess to critique. The efforts of Gates, Baker, and Phillis Wheatley to prove the humanity of Africans and their descendants or the richness of their indigenous cultures begs the question of the humanity of whites and their use of "reason" as the repository of genius. By suggesting that a demonstration of African literacy in English is enough to convince the enlightened white of the African's humanity is to privilege this aspect of the ideology of the colonial/racial discourse, as Ngugi wa Thiong'o powerfully indicts, to the foreclosure of other material concerns.

Such projects, subsumed by an antirace rhetoric and inflected by a postmodern, anti-Fanonian need to theorize race out of existence, suggest hostility toward radical liberationist criticism designed to create *theoria* and *praxis* that do not ignore but root out mutated and subtler forms of racism and its effects. Paul Gilroy called for just such critical interventions in his 1993 *Black Atlantic: Modernity and Double Consciousness,* writing, "In these embattled circumstances it is regrettable that questions of 'race' and representation have been so regularly banished from orthodox histories of Western aesthetic judgment, taste, and cultural value. There is a plea here that further inquiries should be made into precisely how discussion of 'race,' beauty, ethnicity, and culture have contributed to the critical thinking that eventually gave rise to cultural studies" (56). In an odd reversal, however, Gilroy's most recent book, *Against Race,* though motivated by a desire to embrace a "planetary humanism" or global cosmopolitanism, opposes the continued use of race as an analytical category; in outlining what Gilroy sees as a "crisis of raciology," he insinuates that race as racism will cease to exist when pan-Africanists and African Americans loosen their hold on such illusory moorings.

We reject these premises as both based on erroneous assumptions—in actuality, race and racism will end when the powers and privileges of whiteness are no more—and directed toward dangerous rhetorical and political ends. The perils of Gilroy's argument are strikingly clear in a passage from the chapter "The Tyrannies of Unanism," the final chapter in a section of the book entitled "Fascism, Embodiment, and Revolutionary Conservatism," wherein Gilroy affiliates black nationalists with and defines them as fascists. In the passage, Gilroy writes, "For politically opposed groups to discover common cause, things have to happen—meetings must be conducted, language adjusted, objectives redefined, and purpose and solidarity reconfigured. I am asking you to venture into the unstable location where white supremacists and black nationalists, Klansmen, Nazis, neo-Nazis and ethnic absolutists, Zionists and anti-semites have been able to encounter each other as potential allies rather than sworn foes" (*Against Race* 219). While a structural relation undeniably exists here—one politics forged in opposition to the other—one must never forget, as Gilroy seems to do, that the counterpolitics emerged against oppression, violence, even death for purposes of survival. Such historical "encounters"—as Gilroy benignly, speciously, and bafflingly refers to them—have had, we must never forget, violent, even genocidal outcomes! By what means, measures, and motives can Klansmen ever be potential allies with black nationalists, or Nazis with Jews? Particularly as the sole intent of the nefarious, dominant groups—whether Klansmen, anti-Semites, Nazis, or neo-Nazis—has been structurally, even constitutionally predicated on the violent, brutal, and resolved eradication of the minority groups—whether African American or Jewish. These are questions, disappointingly, that Gilroy never answers. We are speechless in response to such a statement; but then again, Gilroy's words really require no further comment; they speak for themselves. We just don't happen to like, or agree with, the message they convey. We elect to give Gilroy the benefit of the doubt in assuming that he is seriously confused in his thinking, rather than the other, less generous, yet still logically coherent, alternatives.[2]

With sleight-of-hand, "against race" acrimony becomes a kind of ersatz solution for a "color-blind" society. What is targeted as a goal, however, is not even the elimination of the continued effects of racism but a commitment to a utopic vision of ending all race thinking even where "race-thinking" is a challenge to or endeavor to understand racism in all its transformative manifestations. Gilroy's utopic vision is committed to a kind of politeness and civility that betrays its goal of inducing a form of cultural stupefaction and historical petrifaction (JanMohamed's *Manichean Aesthetics*), a kind of arrested interiority or psychological paralysis among critics who also summon Fanon and his analyses of epidermal schematization not as a way to end such discussions, but as a way of exposing "white moral cognitive dysfunction" in such practices (Mills, *Racial Contract,* 95).

Gilroy thus misappropriates Fanon's phenomenological insight by suggesting "that the 'epidermalization' of difference operates only on one scale which will not always claim priority over other less visible modes of differentiation" (*Against Race* 217). For the subject contaminated by the Manichean aesthetics and victimized by a sublimated Manichean allegory, epidermalization mutates all scales and subsumes all morphologies. By arguing, for example, that multidimensional medical imaging is transforming the old, modern representations of race (*Against Race* 43), which becomes a kind of deontologizing of "race," Gilroy begs the question that a new benign postracial science will appear as a result of the influence of new scientific directions like the human genome projects as confessor of the ultimate signifier of human distinctiveness. We concur with Gordon that "'scientific' society has not proven to be less racist historically than 'lay' society. . . . That same community is dominated in spirit by a form of physicalist naturalism and biological determinism that underlay various forms of racist intellectualism from the advancement of quantitative intelligence testing to insidious racist Darwinism. One wonders how far and wide are the distances between phrenologists of the nineteenth century and recent gene detectives who seek 'artistic' and 'rational' genes" (*Existentia Africana* 101). Gilroy believes that "race"-entrenching pragmatism should be theorized out of sight (*Against Race* 42). We believe that a "race"-liberating practice should be fostered to address the harm caused by theories that attempt to hide mutated forms of racism by claiming that to ignore racism is to force it to go away. Deontologizing race is of little use if the *a priori* intuitive network of the colonial/settler/master is not cleansed of the grammar of meaning of the grotesqueries of the semiotics of blackness (see Habib's *Shakespeare and Race*) that privileges the white subject at the expense of all other subjects. For the native/domestic racial other, rooting out racism comes from a kind of metaphysical, ontological, epistemological purging. The colonial master has to confront the absurdity of his postulations, elucidations, and assertions in all their transformations; must confront the racial other recreating himself/herself. Joseph Young, Gatsinzi Basaninyenzi, Azfar Hussain, and S. Lily Mendoza all analyze and attempt to displace the colonialist legacies of racialized knowledges in the fields of literary and postcolonial studies, revising purely discursive approaches to race analysis through careful readings of the political economic ramifications of such purely discursive approaches. Sartre's appropriation of Fanon is also instructive here. As opposed to blinding one's self to colonialism or the racist ideology that legitimizes it in hopes of a cure of its effects, one must remember "that no gentleness can efface the marks of violence. . . . The native cures himself of colonial neurosis by thrusting out the settler through force of arms" (Sartre 21).

Perhaps the impracticality of Gilroy's utopic vision is superseded by the pragmatism of contending, coexisting visions as mutually assured destruction or mutually assuring ethical conduct. Without the balance that occurs from the scrutiny of contending ideological, epistemological, ontological gazes, the racial other could ignore racism and tolerate the distortion of its effects, thereby encouraging academic projects that willfully confuse 1960s evening news Kodak moments of Black Panther party paramilitary posturing as fascism (as apposed to a belligerent self-defense). The racial other could stand mute in the face of a willy-nilly equating of the stylized bravadoes of sexual and violent narrative conquests of rap and hip-hop vernacular fads with the violence of Western imperialism (that the harsh language of vernacular street cultures is somehow equal in violence to the millions exterminated during the Age of Imperialism). Of course, the racial other would have to develop a technology of suppression to resist criticizing projects that dismiss the subordinate's rage and indignation in the face of his or her victimization as somehow an aberration from normal standards of conduct and judgment and affected by the victim's own racism. Although in the white social imaginary, such projects would be the assumption of a morally unimpeachable position, we contend, however, that such projects and their academic wide support are indicative of a struggle over "right remembering" and a disguising, by those who would curry favor from those who dominate, the ferocity of the master's domination (slavery, colonialism, post-Reconstruction repression, Jim Crow, neocolonialism, and the translucent racism of race-implicated epistemological closures), making white civility and the assumption of moral unimpeachability possible.

Gilroy's utopian project substitutes the discredited discourse of the imperial dream, the essentialist racism inherent in positing differential race variation as a function of fundamental biological inequality and justification for expropriating the racial other, with a more fashionable and politically viable discourse energized by "against race" rhetoric, "color blindness" and "essential sameness," "'a color-evasive and power-evasive' language that asserts that 'we are all the same under the skin,' which in ignoring the 'structural and institutional dimensions of racism' implies that 'materially, we have the same chances in US society,' so that 'any failure to achieve is therefore the fault of people of color themselves'" (Mills, *Racial Contract*, 153, n. 5). Not being grounded in a factual/statistical heuristic, Gilroy's argument ignores the devastating details of structural and institutional racism that reveal patterns of a racialized society and the basic aggregate arrangements of power and privilege that aggressively oppress blacks and other minorities (Marable, *Great Wells*, and *How Capitalism*). Similarly, institutional biases of the academy are equally observable in established boundaries and subdivisions that obstruct certain trajectories of intellectual thought, scholarship, or pedagogy that would not privilege the kind of subject historically peripheralized at the academy. Such hegemonic conceptualizations of inquiry and discourse, we believe, are examples of the continued commitment to race as an ontological category and antithetical to an emancipatory function of the university. As Molefi Kete Asante expressly states in his chapter in this volume, *Against Race* "is not a book against *racism*, as perhaps it ought to be, but a book against the *idea of race* as an organizing theme in human relations," further charging that "Gilroy has lost sight of the central problem of white racial hierarchy and therefore can concentrate on the inadequacies of the oppressed." Even more pointedly, Asante asks, "Why should African-descended scholars be promoted for advancing ethnic abstractness?" With the historically persistent trafficking in black men's and women's bodies first through the transatlantic slave trade, and later through brutal forms of racial violence, abhorrent political segregation, Jim Crowism, capitalist labor structures, the international division of labor, housing and employment discrimination, maligning media representations, the racially targeted "drug war," and now the racially targeted "war on terror," pervasive acts of urban and rural police brutality, all-too-common and unjust incarceration, continued lack of "due process" and jury of "one's peers," and all-too-frequent death row confinement, as well as military forms of U.S. imperialism in Haiti, the Caribbean, and Latin America (with the U.S. Marines penetrating the interior territories of "third world" countries), we might well ask Professor Gilroy, Aren't there more urgent battles to fight, more dangerous, far more insidious enemies to defeat?

To conclude this section, we also highlight some of the disruptive contradictions that emerge from Gilroy's position. To exemplify this point, we focus on Gilroy's reading of the absence of race in Foucault's writings. Foucault's omission (that of race) is, according to Gilroy, a blind spot in the French philosopher's ideas about power, subjectivity, and bodies.[3] "For all of his great theoretical insight into the problem of the individual observer as a locus of knowledge," Gilroy laments, "he seems to have been insufficiently attuned to the significance of protracted struggles over the raciological disunity of mankind that attended the emergence of biopolitics" (*Against Race* 44). Gilroy continues, explaining that "the human and the infrahuman emerged together, and 'race' was the line between them" (*Against Race* 44). This oversight, in Gilroy's estimation, taints Foucault's thinking ("Regrettably," writes Gilroy, "Foucault was not really interested in the meaning of racial differences or in the tests that they produced for eighteenth-century 'nomination of the visible,'" and he further notes that "although his analysis, which witnesses the birth of biopower, seems ripe for a decisive confrontation with the idea of 'race,' this never happens" [*Against Race* 44]); tellingly, though, Gilroy fails to see how this blind spot or foundational absence shapes the sum total or remainder of Foucault's entire enterprise. And moreover, Foucault's fundamental absence only mirrors and perpetuates the invisible role race played (and continues to play) in the construction of the modern world: It (the absence of race) does not, then, merely taint or mar Foucault's thinking, it is foundational and thus requisite to it. Gilroy does, though, see this line of inquiry as "a new and urgent need for future work" (*Against Race* 45)—and yet, such a conclusion only disproves Gilroy's overarching thesis "against race" and actually demands further academic inquiries into race as a vital category of political, epistemological analysis. That work, we agree, is urgent: It must shape our future intellectual and political endeavors, not foreclose new antiracist possibilities in the present and in the future by deeming race and race analyses irredeemably a matter of the past, a closed historical chapter. This book (*Race and the Foundations of Knowledge: Cultural Amnesia in the Academy*) is at its heart, at its moral base, and in its intellectual inquiries against "*against race*"; and ironically, it furthers the "new and urgent need for future work" that Gilroy himself earlier called for, even as it positions itself in opposition to Gilroy's most recent "against race" thesis. *Race and the Foundations of Knowledge: Cultural Amnesia in the Academy* serves both as a response to Gilroy's earlier plea and as a rejoinder to his later (seeming) retraction and renunciation of the viability of such critical, theoretical efforts.

This collection is, in fact, an urgent critical rejoinder to Gilroy's provocative, yet deeply disconcerting *Against Race,* which argues that ideas about race and identity politics only reiterate the racialized and racist sciences of the nineteenth century. Gilroy's premises fly in the face of the materialist, political critiques of critical race theorists who have persuasively, discursively, and materially demonstrated that not only does race exist, but that it continues to structure American law, legal studies, politics, and more unsettlingly, our very foundations and ways of knowing the world; hence, academic disciplines *are* racially inflected thought systems that are in need of racialized unmooring, a fact that Gilroy either dismisses or ignores.

The Racialized Foundations of Knowledges:
What the Contributors Have to Say

Influenced by the interventions made by critical race theorists, who offer a far more profoundly hybrid, discursive-materialist mode of racial-historical analysis, the contributors to *Race and the Foundations of Knowledge: Cultural Amnesia in the Academy* redress historical forms of race and racialization. Critical race theory emerged from the intersections of law, legal studies, political science, literature, and ethnic studies over the last decade to fifteen years but also evolved from earlier twentieth-century writings on race and racism, as well as antiracist political movements. Some of the key texts in the field of critical race theory include Derrick Bell's *And We Are Not Saved: The Elusive Quest for Racial Justice* (1989); Patricia J. Williams's *Alchemy of Race and Rights* (1992); Neil Gotanda's groundbreaking essay "A Critique of 'Our Constitution Is Not Color-Blind'"; Kimberlé Crenshaw's "Race, Reform, and Retrenchment"; Cheryl I. Harris's "Whiteness As Property"; and other essays from Crenshaw and colleagues' *Critical Race Theory: The Key Writings That Formed the Movement* (1996). Exploring the insights of critical race theorists and legal scholars for other humanistic and social science disciplines, such as literary studies, gender studies, anthropology, sociology, and philosophy, *Race and the Foundations of Knowledge: Cultural Amnesia in the Academy* is a collection of diverse, yet politically engaged and allied, essays that expose the racialization of knowledge, the perpetuation of race and racism in the academy, and its concomitant cultural amnesia about race and the formation of academic disciplines and methodologies.

Charles W. Mills's *Racial Contract* (1997) is equally a pathbreaking text in its historical, political, cultural, and philosophical analyses of the multiple roles that race has played in structuring social relations around an unacknowledged foundation of white privilege. And Mills's insights have been extended and critiqued in David Theo Goldberg's *Racial State* (2001), particularly as it relates to the political constructions of the modern nation-state. Other important interventions have been made by scholars working on issues of multiraciality—essays collected in Naomi Zack's *Race and Mixed Race* (1993) and G. Reginald Daniel's recent *More Than Black?* (2001)—and whiteness studies, though we offer overdue and necessary critiques of the latter area, which has been too quickly celebrated and has frequently digressed into popular cultural studies of "whiteness" (most notably, some of the essays in Mike Hill's collection, *Whiteness: A Critical Reader*), though important contributions have been made by Ruth Frankenberg in *White Women, Race Matters* (1993) and *Displacing Whiteness* (1997), by George Lipsitz in *The Possessive Investment in Whiteness* (1998), and by Richard Delgado and Jean Stefanic's edited collection *Critical White Studies* (1997).

Critical race theorists have radically challenged the by-now more pedestrian and prosaic deconstructions of race offered by poststructuralist literary critics, even those clearly embedded within the African, African American, or African Caribbean traditions such as Henry Louis Gates Jr., Anthony Kwame Appiah, Houston Baker Jr., and most recently, Paul Gilroy. Again, it is necessary to underscore that we do not reject poststructuralist approaches and the important insights, however limited or at times depoliticized, that are effectuated by such theoretical or methodological approaches; rather, we insist that such theoretical and methodological apparati must be materially recontextualized within the political economy of race in the Americas *or* risk institutional reification as the "deconstructionist (race) machine," as we have coined it, an academic, institutionalized, and institutionalizing machine that may resolutely ignore racism while happily going about the business—or rewarding enterprise—of "deconstructing race" (again, see R. Young and Hussain, this volume, on the hazards of not theorizing race materially and class racially). The interventions made by critical race theorists, specifically, and by critical legal theorists, more generally, have opened new paths for thinking about the social, cultural, historical, and legal constructions of race as well as the perpetuation of racialized foundations and parameters in law, politics, and academic disciplines. In a groundbreaking article, "A Critique of 'Our Constitution Is Color-Blind,'" Neil Gotanda has radically discarded the worn-out and tired idea that American law and constitutionality have been race-free foundations. In the current volume, Tony Zaragoza, Matthew Abraham, and Derrick E. White all further analyze the problematics of "color-blind" constitutionality and its negative consequences in still recalcitrantly race-inflected public policies legislated by predominantly white-privileged policymakers. Other pioneering efforts within the field of critical race studies have been forged by scholars such as Cheryl I. Harris, whose article "Whiteness as Property" (in Crenshaw et al.) demonstrates that race and racialized privilege are at the heart not only of U.S. notions of constitutionality and citizenship but of ideas about property and the very evolution of property law in this country: Such work makes it impossible to ignore the ways in which race, racial privilege, and conversely racial disenfranchisement have redounding material consequences in American history, law, and culture. On this issue, the chapters by Robert Young and Azfar Hussain further Harris's provocative insights. In their respective contributions to the collection, Young seeks to establish a materialist analysis of race, while Hussain theorizes the crucialness of a race analysis of class. Tony Zaragoza, Matthew Abraham, and Derek E. White all also offer insightful analyses of juridical and economic discourses that are imbued with racialized notions and racist premises and are moreover often determinative in formulating public policy. Alexis Shotwell, theorizing how race becomes a sort of "commonsense" proposition, deftly demonstrates how the intellectual and academic may perilously suffuse public sectors, trickling down to a false but firmly held conventional wisdom that reflects racial privilege and racial disenfranchisement. On a symbolic level, Joseph Young, Molefi Kete Asante, and James Perkinson all elucidate the race-infused ideals of literature, history, academia, theology, reason, rationality, and even knowledge itself, showing that the metaphoric representations of race *matter* and have real, lived, material consequences. Combining race analyses with postcolonialist theories, Gatsinzi Basaninyenzi and S. Lily Mendoza both further demonstrate the resiliency of race-based discourses and methodologies that govern both academic disciplines—literature and communication, respectively—but more dangerously also often determine heinous forms of public policy and thus construct unjust political realities. And Charles W. Mills, in the final chapter in this volume, strikingly elucidates how the structures of modernity—in entirety, part and parcel—are inflected and marred by the consequences of the "racial contract," contractually defining select (white) individuals as free and others (racially marked) as enslaved; defining some as persons, others as subpersons.

Race and the Foundations of Knowledge: Cultural Amnesia in the Academy examines the constitutive role that race has played in the formation of humanistic disciplines. As a transracial effort by scholars from diverse fields and disciplines to foreground the historical locations and legacies of race in the construction of knowledge, *Race and the Foundations of Knowledge: Cultural Amnesia in the Academy* is not driven by a false belief in "ethnic absolutism," as Gilroy might have it, nor is it driven by separatist ideologies about race. This book—along with the scores of other important academic contributions by scholars committed to unearthing the geological and systemic places of race—demonstrates that the continued project of understanding how race has formed modernity and modern ideals and ideologies is not complete; indeed, such interdisciplinary, comparative ethnic, and archaeological work has only just begun. This book then joins the efforts of many other scholars committed to understanding the continued, often invisible, presence of race; it joins the works of Asian Americanists (David Eng, Neil Gotanda, Lisa Lowe, Dorine Kondo, Michael Omi, and R. Radhakrishnan), Latin Americanists (Gloria Anzaldúa, José David Saldívar, Ramón Saldívar, Sonia Saldívar, and George Sanchez), and Caribbeanists (Hillary Beckles, Carole Boyce Davies, Lewis Gordon, Paget Henry, Charles W. Mills, Hilbourne Watson, and others), as well as countless African Americanists—indeed too many to numerate, though we will mention a few of the most notable voices: Molefi Kete Asante, Derrick Bell, Patricia Hill Collins, Kimberlé Crenshaw, Angela Davis, Chester J. Fontenot Jr., Cheryl I. Harris, bell hooks, Wahneema Lubiano, Manning Marable, Ishmael Reed, Randall Robinson, Mason Stokes, Patricia Williams. Like Gilroy, we are—and this book is—driven not by separatism but by a belief in "planetary humanism," to use one of Gilroy's useful terms; at the same time, though, we decisively reject—and this book also expressly and vehemently rejects—a "humanism" that refuses to confront the wounds of the past or that fails to examine the historical, racialized inflections of the "human" and "humanistic." Those are, ultimately, the *real* deleterious legacies of racialized thinking—not as Gilroy falsely assumes and insensitively charges—the collective aspirations of the racially oppressed.

Toward these ends, Robert Young warns of the dangers implicit in criticizing racism without condemning capitalistic exploitation, the foundation upon which racism emerges. In "Putting Materialism Back into Race Theory: Toward a Transformative Theory of Race," Young advances a materialist theory of race by suggesting how humanist and poststructualist views on race conspire in redirecting attention away from a critique of capitalism—defined as a totalizing system that mixes apparently diverse constituents of the social milieu through a matrix of exploitation—to bourgeois-acclaimed cultural questions. By recovering the authority of race as an instrument of the subordinate's resistance, the humanists manipulate the perplexities of black subjectivity to overcome materialist notions of race. Far from advancing a distinctive Afrocentric, black feminist, or black idealistic epistemology, however, Asante, Collins, and McGary respectively share a philosophical/ideological commitment to an empiricism of the subject, which is firmly rooted in mainstream philosophical tradition. Postmodernists, Young insists, draw upon the ambiguities of signification to deconstruct materialism. Poststructuralist narratives of race mark a paradigm shift, a discrete ontological reversal, from a centered black subject to a decentered subject achieved through an anticipated language as the code speaking the subject. The chief architects of this textualization of race are Baker and Gates among others, whose linguistic project—providing a modality of empowerment—reclaims the autonomy of race, which as a free-floating social theory and reified discourse can embrace both reductionist (applied to culture, politics, or desire) and antireductionist (opposition to its reduction to class) views of race.

These antireductionist pedagogues, according to Young, supplant a critique of the structure of exploitation with a discourse of autonomy. Important among these pedagogues is Gilroy, who in manipulating the problematics of race in *Against Race*, mystifies our understanding of the concept, Young argues, by separating it from deeper social structures like class and ideology. Gilroy's "postrace," a kind of "cultural cosmopolitanism," is as idealistic as his "post-Marxism" (inaugurated in the earlier work *There Ain't No Black in the Union Jack*) and constitutes his facile solution to what he calls a crisis in racial representation. These pedagogues' goals are not the revolutionary transformation of contemporary capitalist society; rather, Young argues, they desire autonomy within the current system. "In other words, they do not want to change an exploitative system, they merely want a little more (discursive) freedom within it, and this (reformist) project signals agency for Gilroy."

In "Commonsense Racial Formation: Wahneema Lubiano, Antonio Gramsci, and the Importance of the Nonpropositional," Alexis Shotwell reveals that disembodied modes of thinking like common sense are informative in our understanding of race and in the hegemonic formation of racism. "[P]erhaps even more important than ideologies at the explicit and articulated level . . . are ideologies in the more primeval sense of underlying patterns and matrices of belief" (Mills, *Blackness Visible*, 34). Shotwell appreciates the nonpropositionality of an ideologically derived concept of common sense and of race (both foundationally void, inarticulate forms of knowledge that do not embrace the classical form of propositions), but she also recognizes the tremendous durability and flexibility of both concepts in human thinking (relevant to a critique of Gilroy's attempts to eliminate through troping and reifying certain stabilizations of race and common sense as he tracks their movement through culture, inflecting into fertile terrains of growth and struggle, of inchoateness, of differing frameworks and embodiedness, of contradiction and possibility). Using Gramsci's formulation of common sense as the "folklore of philosophy," Shotwell argues that one's common sense does not need to maintain standards of logical consistency, that its very nature resists the critical propositional view, and that commonsense philosophy is the philosophy of nonphilosophers, a "conception of the world that is uncritically absorbed by the various social and cultural environments in which the moral individuality of the average person is developed."

Equally important as a consideration is what are we omitting by excluding nonpropositional modes of knowing. Shotwell relies on Wahneema Lubiano's "Black Nationalism and Black Common Sense" as a way of explaining the importance of an apparent species of nonpropositional understanding: expedient black "racial" behavior derived as it were ideologically from the African American cultural experience in the United States. Maneuvering as a form of antithetical logic (the common sense of which is realized in living in a world one understands and rejects), black nationalism, a form of inestimable ideological common sense, functions among other things as a "narrative of black history," as an explanation of "what is good and beautiful," as "rallying cry," as "style," and as "critical analysis." The importance of Shotwell's analysis in linking common sense and race or in providing a commonsense analysis of race is, as she states, "that having an articulation of race as implicit knowledge helps to describe the mechanism of 'race' in its continued creation and development in this world." As Shotwell insightfully concludes, privileging propositionality as the only ground for race precludes other significant aspects of lived experiences, which may include potentially "liberatory spaces." Shotwell's insights are relevant to those of Matthew Abraham, whose chapter sounds a necessary caveat or crucial warning that commonsense approaches to race pervade all social strata and political terrains—even, or perhaps especially, those of government institutions—even, or perhaps especially, the Supreme Court.

Matthew Abraham in "Supreme Rhetoric: The Supreme Court, Veiled Majoritarianism, and the Enforcement of the Racial Contract" contests the mythos surrounding the U.S. Supreme Court "as the great protector of the unheard and the unseen because of the supposed principled approach it brings to the assessment of competing group claims for valuable societal resources." Charged with a kind of countermajoritarianism as a function of the decision in *Marbury v. Madison* (1803), Supreme Court justices as a result of life tenure and salary protection have the liberty to hold against the interests of majorities if in so ruling the interests of "discrete and insular" minorities are protected. Yet—because of a socialization process of legal training—justices are chosen by a majority-elected president, confirmed by a Senate representative of the majority, and before these two decisive majoritarian interventions, justices are scrutinized by licensing procedures of majoritarian institutions to gain entrance to the bar, as well as to gain clerkships and tenure as federal judges—Supreme Court justices become "the most majoritarian-serving agents imaginable." What accounts for the illusion of a court that functions as a check on the tyranny of the majority is, as Abraham explains, a veiled majoritarianism, the advancement of majority interests through avowedly impartial principles. Such principles, Stanley Fish observes in *The Trouble with Principle,* are miraculous and insidious entities, for only as an illusory standpoint could they escape the material constraints of a material world; and as their foundational gist will always be infused and dominated by someone's bias perspective, justices anointed by the apparent saving grace of principles can inscribe discretely their socialized belief systems as inscriptions of disinterested adjudication.

Furthering Abraham's juridical analysis of race, Tony Zaragoza argues in "Legal Lines: Defining Racism in a Flexibility Matrix" that race and racism are still pervasive, systematic elements defining American society or culture. Zaragoza's target audience are white liberals, academics, politicians, public administrators, and the general (white) public, who commonly hold the view that race no longer exists and that racism is a social ill of the past, and he powerfully deconstructs some of that group's most cherished notions: individualism and the American dream; the misguided and racist belief in financial success being ineluctably linked to "work ethic"; and the false beliefs in a color-blind democracy, a color-blind constitution, and a color-blind legal system. Drawing his intellectual armament from critical race theorists such as Charles Mills, Cheryl I. Harris, Edouardo Bonilla-Silva, and Tyrone Forman, Zaragoza takes aim at cultural racism in the United States and at a wide range of political discourses that have become increasingly racialized in their rhetorical formations—affirmative action, college admissions, the insidious bell curve (Herrnstein and Murray *The Bell Curve*), welfare "reform," the War on Drugs—as well as issues such as hate crimes legislation and voter fraud in the 2000 presidential elections.

Moving from the legal-political to the imbricated terrains of legal-political-textual, or a complex discursive and material nexus, Joseph Young argues in "A Reversal of the Racialization of History in Hegel's Master/Slave Dialectic (Douglass's 'Heroic Slave' and Melville's 'Benito Cereno')" that the nineteenth-century narratives of Douglass and Melville reverse the Hegelian master/slave dialectic, making the slave-revolt leaders heroic and brave freedom fighters and thus breaking with stereotypical notions of slave as cowering, cowardly, and passive. Grounding his insightful literary analyses of Douglass's and Melville's texts within nineteenth-century abolitionist history, focusing specifically on the abolitionist struggles of African Americans (in literature, journalism, political movements, and the Underground Railroad), Young deconstructs reductive and dehumanizing misperceptions of African Americans at the time and demonstrates that "gains in personal freedom" for African American individuals were regarded as "threatening to the southern way of life."

Focusing on the radical, humanizing, heroic slave-revolt leaders—Madison Washington in Douglass's "Heroic Slave" and Babo in Melville's "Benito Cereno"—Joseph Young powerfully demonstrates the ways in which Douglass and Melville presciently reversed the Hegelian dialectic of master/slave and, thereby, the racialization of history by the West. Young incisively argues that this reversal was, for Douglass and Melville, more urgent than a transcendence of that dialectic: These authors were, as Young notes, "more concerned with overthrowing the Western notion that a black slave was ontologically antithetical to the hero" than in transcending Hegelian dualities. Douglass and Melville, "informed by a liberated vision of the slave's humanity and quickened by the ever-increasing number of slave revolts," Young astutely writes, "responded to the necessity for a dialectic of master and slave, a dialectic that depended on the African American composing his own discourse and becoming a force in his own fate." Young also demonstrates, however, that both the Hegelian dialectic and its literary adoption by Douglass and Melville were predicated on destructive notions of binarized racial difference.

Cognizant of this problematic, Gatsinzi Basaninyenzi warns us, in "'Dark-Faced Europeans': The Nineteenth-Century Colonial Travelogue and the Invention of the Hima Race," against ignoring the potential dissension between groups like the Hutu and Tutsi, who, instead of analyzing the lingering effects of European racism and colonialism, internalized the colonial ideology of racial inequality and thus created a "racial" time bomb that started exploding in 1957. Basaninyenzi explains the origin of the conflict between the groups less from a supposed human propensity to be intrinsically racist and more as a result of the century-old European project to establish a rationale for appropriating specific locals in, to use an already racialized hierarchical construction, Subsaharan Africa. Basaninyenzi both elucidates and challenges, in his thoughtful analyses of colonialist travel literature and of Tutsi-adopted societal paradigms of racial difference, the persistence of obsessive fetish of exoticism, the irrationality, circular logic, the incoherence, and the tragic consequences of nineteenth-century racial discourse—features of race thinking that should not be dismissed lightly. As a basis for postulating an "objective" theory about the place of the "Negro race" in nature, Georges Cuvier, credited as the father of paleontology, dissects the genitalia of Saartjie Baartman (the "celebrated" Bushwoman of South Africa exhibited in London and Paris) and concluded that blacks were just above beasts. This theory, Basaninyenzi explains, influenced and inscribed the composition of colonial travelogues that served as the foundation of nineteenth-century "scientific" racial discourse.

In his colonial travelogue, *The Lake Region of Central Africa* (1860), which is fraught with both the racial discourse of otherness and with the contradictions and incoherence of such a concept, Richard F. Burton invents the Hima race, a "Caucasian tribe" in this part of Africa, the objective of which was to gain acceptance to intellectual societies in England by contributing to its mercantile projects and "science" of race. Although Burton's Afro-Caucasian tribe contradicts the nineteenth-century racial essentialism and environmental determinism, it influenced John Hanning Speke (Burton's protégé, and because of an ideological break with his mentor, cited more by scholars when discussing the Hutu–Tutsi conflict) and Henry Morton Stanley (Speke's heir and ideological compatriot who played a major role in spreading the myth of the Hima, as he was the most widely read of the three) both of whom in writing their own colonial travelogues (*Journal of the Discovery of the Source of the Nile* and *Through the Dark Continent,* respectively) racialized the Hima for the purported objective of assuming what would become known as the "white man's burden" of regenerating Africa through the dissemination of Christianity and Western civilization. The Hima—being the link between the "pure African" and the other two so-termed superior races (the Caucasoid and the Mongoloid) and being both the promise of Africa and the rationale of European presence there—are described by Burton as possessing reflective faculties, not deficient in intelligence, "superior in civilization and social constitution to the other tribes of Eastern and Central Africa" (391). Burton also considers the Tutsi of the same racial stock as the Hima. The "pure African" type is marked by stagnation of mind, sensual indolence, moral deficiency and is wholly unfitted by nature for intellectual labor (*Lake Regions* 43, 490). When the Germans and later the Belgians colonized Rwanda, both regimes set up structures whose hierarchies reflected the prevailing racial notions. The Tutsi held positions of power next to those of whites. The Hutu, who were characterized as less intelligent, were forced to do all of the manual labor under strict supervision of the Tutsi chiefs. This hierarchy was legitimated by a racial ideology and normalized with its canonization in school textbooks and enshrined in Rwandese society as the groups internalized the colonial ideology until the beginning of the racial time bomb in 1957, when Hutu intellectuals denounced the racial monopoly of the Mututsi.

In "Toward a Political Economy of Racism and Colonialism: A Rereading of Frantz Fanon's *Wretched of the Earth*," Azfar Hussain also reminds us that while Marx and Marxism superficially, sporadically and perfunctorily stalk the halls of the social sciences, "'race'—and racism as a deeply *localized* yet profoundly *world-systemic* material-discursive phenomenon—turns out to be a blank." Hussain registers his reaction against the direction of specific discourse practices of what he calls "metropolitan humanities" ("ethnic studies," culturalist postcolonial hermeneutics, postcolonial critics, and French poststructuralists) that invoke the importance of Fanon and provide some instructive proprieties of reading but remain committed to sustaining the governing textual culture of the metropolitan academy, which is to ignore and remain indifferent to conceptual/analytical resources of Fanon's political economy. But Hussain reminds us that the revolutionary Fanon of political economic race-class discourses does not abandon Marx. In an effort to gain insights into the structure of capital in the colonial framework and into the structure of colonialism and racism, Fanon expands Marxist analysis to link the categories of race and class into a dialectically energetic interaction instructive for devising a race theory of class. Hussain explains "that production relations under capitalism have historically remained race relations in such a way that race itself comes to constitute class." Hussain's argument reads, then, as a compelling counterpoint to R. Young's, and though their insights move in different directions, they are not mutually exclusive or incompatible, but rather complementary.

While remaining politically and materially grounded, Molefi Kete Asante's essay probes the symbolic and ideational problems of institutionalized academic Eurocentrism *as* universalism. In "Afrocentricity and the Eurocentric Hegemony of Knowledge: Contradictions of Place," Asante argues against the overdetermination of knowledge according to narrow, ethnocentric parameters in which the unacknowledged specific standpoint (i.e., European) falsely masquerades as universal and aborts all other standpoints. Asserting the need for a corrective to the deleterious one-sided history that erased and destroyed all others, Asante contends that an Afrocentric perspective readdresses the erasures and violences of history and knowledge as constructed within Western traditions and speaks to the lived historical and experiential knowledge of those who are African. Asante also resists those who would blindly reassert the Eurocentric as universal, newly cloaked as Anglo-African or Afro-Saxon, and he offers a powerful critique of Gilroy's *Against Race* as predicated on unacknowledged Eurocentric ideals.

"New Frameworks in Philippine Postcolonial Historiography: Decolonizing a Discipline," is S. Lily Mendoza's examination of the historical necessity and ideological foundations for Pantayong Pananaw, an indigenous, knowledge-based, theoretical framework both for deconstructing the politics of information forma-tion in the former colonized academies of the Philippines (during U.S. occupa-tion) and for engendering new cultural initiatives for self-agency and collective empowerment. Mendoza observes that subject peoples are not only forced to submit to colonial masters but swayed to willingly acquiesce with the employment of "discursively inscribed mechanisms of control" such as mythical narratives and a totalizing discourse that not only secures their bodies, but when internalized, transports them to a more total subjective capitulation. Identifying an inextricable correlation between knowledge, discourse, and the construction of subjectivity, Mendoza shows us how through an examination of the mechanism of ideologi-cal formation what has been constructed as given, necessary, or natural can be exposed as ideologically fabricated. A deconstructive rereading of the colonial rulers' ideological discursive formations, using the cultural circuitry and insight of an indigenous theorizing perspective such as Pantayong Pananaw (a "for-us" perspective based on the discourses of the ethnolinguistic communities of the Philippines), Mendoza argues, can explode the fixity and naturalness of the he-gemonic schema containing the subjugated by dislodging the semantic anchors that hold the colonial ideology in place. Mendoza recognizes, following Gramsci, that hegemony is an active process exerted through the polemic of ideas and battle over meaning and signification; hence effective resistance may be achieved best through a counterideology (such as the "indigenization movement," starting in the early 1900s, generated from various factions of the intelligentsia inspired by a nationalist [anticolonial] mandate) that would both yield a liberation psychol-ogy (like the concept develop by Virgilio Enriquez, *Sikolohiyang Pilipino*) and prepare the subjugated for seizing an epistemic space of indigenous theorizing not always implicated in the very ideology the subjugated seeks to overturn.

In conceptualizing race in terms of "indigenous ritual," James W. Perkinson ("Between Unconsciously White and Mythically Black: European Race Discourse as Modern Witchcraft Practice") also achieves a more human-meaning specific explanation of the "metabolic violence" that aboriginal cultures the world over had to endure as a result of contact with the West than the objectified othering offered by scientific/humanitarian discourse. Metabolic violence, is, according to Perkinson, the explosion of entire cosmograms of native forms of intelligence resulting in a postcontact renegotiated comprehension of the cosmos and find-ing expression, for example, in the Native American "Ghost Dance," African millenarian prophetism, Haitian *vodun,* or other Afrodiasporic religions in the Caribbean and the Americas, the black church in the United States, and Jamaican Rastafari, to name only a few. Perkinson relativizes the scientific ideal of the West and its allied followers in other disciplines, such as the humanities discourses, that have embraced that self-same ideal. Perkinson's investigation of the historical growth of white supremacist practice reveals a kind of modernist incarnation of "witchcraft discourse" that discovers its antagonists, the renegotiated understanding of the cosmos by the native, at the exact moment of looking for them. It is a hyper-fetish confirmation engendering the problematic for Perkinson: "which 'which' is witch?" Perkinson contends that race and racism were and continue to be fundamental to the construction of the humanities in the European and Euro-American academies that found among rationales for its existence a project to repudiate domestic religious superstition, together with sorcery and magic in the colonies. Eliciting the "great chain of being" as a historical metaphor detailing how European colonialism and imperialism organized its others into a serviceable taxonomy, Perkinson also advises that analogous discourse formations are still at work and at play in contemporary social structures that have as their motivation "the stealing and consumption of the substance of others in a now global enterprise of capitalist appropriation and accumulation [that] masks its own avaricious and rapacious potency under the naturalizing function of a cultural 'common sense' that until recently could claim authoritative backing by way of philosophy and the social sciences."

Turning from cosmological rationales to political, economic structures informed by race and racism, Derrick E. White also suggests, if differently, that the racialized ruses of the past continue to ensnare us in the present. In "'Blacks Who Had Not Themselves Personally Suffered Illegal Discrimination': The Symbolic Incorporation of the Black Middle Class," White argues that social, cultural, and economic shifts in the past few decades have divided the black middle class (a class of individuals that have been symbolically incorporated into mainstream America) from the black "underclass" (which has been pathologized racially through discourses around welfare, crime, and drug use). White argues that the effect of this discursive and cultural division is twofold: one, it divorces individuals perceived to be in the "middle class" from the historical legacies of discrimination, oppression, and inequity; and two, it deracializes the "black middle class" while pathologically (and indirectly) hyperracializing the black underclass, leaving those individuals even more vulnerable to social injustice and racist oppression. White's argument also importantly points us back toward the political economic nexus of race-class that is as much at the heart of humanistic disciplines, the hierarchical nature of the academy and its racialized foundations of knowledge, as it is at the heart of public institutions. Contentious public (and media-fed) debates and judicial Supreme Court decisions over affirmative action cases brought against the University of Michigan—but with nationwide ramifications for college admissions, faculty hiring, and corporate employment across the country—pointedly reveal that the academy and other public institutions, as well as the "truths" they legislate, interpret, and implement, remain inextricably bound within racialized foundations that are invisibly configured as a priori givens, even as they are rendered transparent and remain unquestioned, uninterrogated.

Allowing the ever-wise and always politically astute Charles W. Mills to have the final word in this collection—if not in intellectual debates over race, debates

that should begin now in earnest, not paradoxically end in resolute incomple-
tion, as Gilroy may have it—we thus close with Mills's thoughtful and incisive
reflection on the inherent contradictions that are constitutive of, not exceptional
to, modernity and the modern world. In "Modernity, Persons, and Subpersons,"
Mills rereads myriad "modern" philosophical and political texts, such as Thomas
Jefferson's Declaration of Independence, Thomas Hobbes's *Leviathan* and *On the
Citizen,* John Locke's *Two Treatises of Government,* John Stuart Mill's *On Liberty,*
John Rawls's *Theory of Justice,* and other texts. Examining these key texts of the
so-called Age of Enlightenment, Mills explores how each of these thinkers' ideas
about equality, liberty, and fraternity are subtended by defining ideas about race
and racial difference. Rather than asserting that these thinkers' writings were
merely racially tainted by the cultural milieu of the times (of slavery, colonialism,
and conquest), Mills more provocatively contends that *in*equality supported,
structured, and made possible ideas about equality for the inheritors and bearers
of white privilege. This argument runs counter to most scholarly interpretations
of modern philosophical thought. "[W]hen racism is conceded, and discussed,"
Mills explains, "it tends to be within the official framework of egalitarian assumptions, generating a language of 'deviations,' 'anomalies,' 'contradictions,'
and 'ironies'. It is (reluctantly) admitted that these theorists may have been racist,
but this concession is not taken to challenge the logic of the basic framework
itself. . . . Thus one speaks of the 'irony' of Jefferson's having been a slaveholder,
or the 'contradiction' of the need for black Jacobins to carry out a separate Haitian Revolution." Further expanding the term *subperson,* first introduced in *The
Racial Contract* and *Blackness Visible,* Mills demonstrates that we need to rethink
the very philosophical conceptualizations of freedom itself: "instead of seeing
these theorists as spokesmen for equality *simpliciter,*" Mills argues, "we need to
start seeing them as spokesmen for a racialized *white* equality."

Moving from trenchant analyses of academic formations and disciplinary
boundaries to the urgent discussions of continued legal, social, and material
impacts of race, racism, and institutional forms of racialization, the contributors
demonstrate that race *persists*: it persists as a social, cultural, and historical reality
constructed over centuries; it persists as a pervasive social fabric, an intellectual
structure, that informs our ways of thinking, knowing, possessing, and legislat-
ing. As all the contributors demonstrate, then, this book is against *"against race"*
and refuses to allow Gilroy's words to be the final thought or closing statement
on race in the twenty-first century. As we demonstrated above in our analysis of
Gilroy's readings of Foucault (and the absence of race in his philosophical project
about power, subjectivity, and bodies), Gilroy's argument unravels and fails to
cohere; ultimately, Gilroy's argument—ostensibly "against race"—itself reveals
the necessity of continued thought and analysis with respect to race and its historical, intellectual, and political locations. If we have framed this introduction,
specifically, and the collection, more diffusely, as a polemic *contra* Gilroy, it is not

without urgent cause and pressing reason. Gilroy's *Against Race,* reflecting the culmination of a decade-long or longer move in its perilous, apolitical direction by African American literary and cultural critics, sadly threatens to abort the very kind of analyses of race that we believe are so vital to antiracist struggle: those that may heal historical racial wounds and expose the cultural amnesia of race "forgetting"—that has been at the heart of the academy and of other public institutions—throughout the Americas.

Notes

1. We quote this phrase from the subtitle of Paul Gilroy's *Against Race: Imagining Political Culture beyond the Color Line.* Evoking Du Bois's most famous of lines in the subtitle to the introduction, we hope to establish a necessary intellectual battle line for future academic inquiries that will move against the current "against race" tide; we too hope to one day imagine "political culture beyond the color line," but we cannot simply will it so, particularly since the wounding fractures and deeply embedded divisions of racism still haunt almost every sector of contemporary American society, including the academy.

We also intend the subtitle as a response to the facile critiques of Du Bois by Anthony Kwame Appiah in "The Uncompleted Argument" (1986) and *In My Father's House* (1992). Appiah is correct on at least one account: The argument is not over yet! Critical race theorists, whom we discuss in greater length below, also offer strategic and lively resistance to the cultural stream of "against race" intellectual thought. See also Thomas C. Holt's courageous *Problem of Race in the Twenty-first Century* and Azfar Hussain's "Color Line: The Problem of the Twenty-first Century."

2. Although we invited Professor Gilroy to respond to our critiques of *Against Race* and hoped to have include his written response in the current volume, we never received a response to the invitation that we extended.

3. For a more extensive examination of race in Foucault's thought, see Ann Laura Stoler's *Race and the Education of Desire.*

Works Cited

Apel, Karl-Otto. *Towards a Transformation of Philosophy.* Trans. Glyn Adey and David Frisby. London: Routledge and Kegan Paul, 1980.

Appiah, A. Kwame. *In My Father's House: Africa in the Philosophy of Culture.* New York: Oxford University Press, 1992.

———. "The Uncompleted Argument: Du Bois and the Illusion of Race." In Henry Louis Gates Jr., ed., *"Race," Writing, and Difference.* Chicago: University of Chicago Press, 1986. 21–37.

Baker, Houston, Jr. *Blues, Ideology, and Afro-American Literature: A Vernacular Theory.* Chicago: University of Chicago Press, 1984.

———. *The Journey Back: Issues in Black Literature and Criticism.* Chicago: University of Chicago Press, 1980.

Bhabha, Homi K. "Signs Taken for Wonders: Questions of Ambivalence and Authority under a Tree outside Delhi, May 1817." In Henry Louis Gates Jr., ed., *"Race," Writing, and Difference.* Chicago: University of Chicago Press, 1986. 163–84.

Bell, Derrick. *And We Are Not Saved: The Elusive Quest for Racial Justice.* Basic Books, 1989.

Bernasconi, Robert, and Tommy L. Lott, eds. *The Idea of Race.* Indianapolis: Hackett, 2000.

Blight, David W. *Beyond the Battlefield: Race, Memory, and the American Civil War.* Amherst: University of Massachusetts Press, 2002.

———. *Race and Reunion: The Civil War in American Memory.* Cambridge, Mass.: Belknap Press, 2001.

———. "W. E. B. Du Bois and the Struggle for American Historical Memory." In Robert O'Meally and Geneviève Fabre, eds., *History and Memory in African-American Culture.* New York: Oxford University Press, 1994. 45–71.

Burton, Richard F. *First Footsteps in East Africa; or, An Exploration of Harar.* New York: Dover, 1987.

Chong-Soon Lee, Jayne. "Navigating the Topology of Race." In Kimberlé Crenshaw, Neil Gotanda, Gary Peller, and Kendall Thomas, eds., *Critical Race Theory: The Key Writings That Formed the Movement.* New York: New Press, 1995. 441–48.

Crenshaw, Kimberlé, Neil Gotanda, Gary Peller, Kendall Thomas, eds. *Critical Race Theory: The Key Writings That Formed the Movement.* New York: New Press, 1995.

———. "Preface to Part Seven: Race and Postmodernism." In Kimberlé Crenshaw, Neil Gotanda, Gary Peller, and Kendall Thomas, eds., *Critical Race Theory: The Key Writings That Formed the Movement.* New York: New Press, 1995. 440.

Culler, Jonathan. *On Deconstruction: Theory and Criticism after Structuralism.* Ithaca, N.Y.: Cornell University Press, 1982.

Daniel, G. Reginald. *More Than Black? Multiracial Identity and the New Racial Order.* Philadelphia: Temple University Press, 2001.

Delgado, Richard, and Jean Stefancic, eds. *Critical Race Theory: The Cutting Edge.* Philadelphia: Temple University Press, 1999.

———. *Critical White Studies: Looking behind the Mirror.* Philadelphia: Temple University Press, 1997.

Delgado, Richard, Jean Stefancic, and Angela Harris, eds. *Critical Race Theory: An Introduction.* New York: New York University Press, 2001.

Derrida, Jacques. "Structure, Sign, and Play in the Discourse of the Human Sciences." In Richard Macksey and Eugenio Donato, eds., *The Structuralist Controversy: The Languages of Criticism and the Sciences of Man.* Baltimore: Johns Hopkins University Press, 1972. 247–65.

Fanon, Frantz. *The Wretched of the Earth.* Preface by Jean-Paul Sartre. Trans. Constance Farrington. New York: Grove Press, 1963.

Fish, Stanley. *The Trouble with Principle.* Cambridge, Mass.: Harvard University Press, 1999.

Foucault, Michel. *The Order of Things: An Archaeology of the Human Sciences.* New York: Vintage Books, 1994.

Frankenberg, Ruth. *White Women, Race Matters: The Social Construction of Whiteness.* Minneapolis: University of Minnesota Press, 1993.

———, ed. *Displacing Whiteness: Essays in Social and Cultural Criticism.* Durham, N.C.: Duke University Press, 1997.

Gates, Henry Louis, Jr. "Critical Fanonism." *Critical Inquiry* 17 (1991): 457–78.

———. *Figures in Black: Words, Signs, and the "Racial" Self.* New York: Oxford University Press, 1987.

————. *The Signifying Monkey: A Theory of African American Literary Criticism.* New York: Oxford University Press, 1988.

————, ed. *"Race," Writing, and Difference.* Chicago: University of Chicago Press, 1986.

Gates, Henry Louis, Jr., and Cornel West. *The Future of the Race.* New York: Knopf, 1996.

Gilroy, Paul. *Against Race: Imagining Political Culture beyond the Color Line.* Cambridge, Mass.: Belknap Press, 2000.

————. *The Black Atlantic: Modernity and Double Consciousness.* Cambridge, Mass.: Belknap Press, 1993.

————. *"There Ain't No Black in the Union Jack": The Cultural Politics of Race and Nation.* Chicago: University of Chicago Press, 1991.

Glissant, Édouard. *Caribbean Discourse.* Trans. J. Michael Dash. Charlottesville: University of Virginia Press, 1999.

————. *Faulkner, Mississippi.* Trans. Barbara Lewis and Thomas C. Spear. New York: Farrar, Straus, and Giroux, 1999.

————. *Poetics of Relation.* Trans. Betsy Wing. Ann Arbor: University of Michigan Press, 1997.

Goldberg, David Theo. *The Racial State.* Malden, Mass.: Blackwell, 2001.

Gordon, Lewis R. *Existentia Africana: Understanding Africana Existential Thought.* New York: Routledge, 2000.

————. *Fanon and the Crisis of the European Man: An Essay on Philosophy and the Human Sciences.* New York: Routledge, 1995.

Habib, Imtiaz. *Shakespeare and Race: Postcolonial Praxis in the Early Modern Period.* New York: University Press of America, 1999.

Hall, Stuart. "Cultural Identity and Diaspora." In Jana Evans Braziel and Anita Mannur, eds., *Theorizing Diaspora.* Malden, Mass.: Blackwell, 2003. 233–46.

Hegel, Georg W. F. *The Philosophy of History.* Trans. J. Sibree. New York: Dover Publications, 1956. [Originally published in 1892.]

Heidegger, Martin. *Poetry, Language, Thought.* Trans. Albert Hofstadter. New York: Harper and Row, 1971.

Herrnstein, Richard J., and Charles Murray. *The Bell Curve: Intelligence and Class Structure in American Life.* New York: Free Press, 1994.

Hill, Mike, ed. *Whiteness: A Critical Reader.* New York: New York University Press, 1997.

Holt, Thomas C. *The Problem of Race in the Twenty-first Century.* Cambridge, Mass.: Harvard University Press, 2001.

Hussain, Azfar. "The Color Line: The Problem of the Twenty-first Century." *dis/content* 3.2 (2000): 1–4.

Husserl, Edmund. *Cartesian Meditations: An Introduction to Phenomenology.* Trans. Dorion Cairns. The Hague: Martinus Nijhoff, 1960.

————. *Ideas: General Introduction to Pure Phenomenology.* Trans. W. R. Boyce Gibson. New York: Macmillan, 1931.

JanMohamed, Abdul R. "The Economy of Manichean Allegory: The Function of Racial Difference in Colonialist Literature." In Henry Louis Gates Jr., ed., *"Race," Writing, and Difference.* Chicago: University of Chicago Press, 1986. 78–106 [Rpt. from *Critical Inquiry* 12.1 (1985): 59–87.]

————. *Manichean Aesthetics: The Politics of Literature in Colonial Africa.* Amherst: University of Massachusetts Press, 1983.

Lipsitz, George. *The Possessive Investment in Whiteness: How White People Profit from Identity Politics.* Philadelphia: Temple University Press, 1998.

Macksey, Richard, and Eugenio Donato, eds. *The Structuralist Controversy: The Languages of Criticism and the Sciences of Man.* Baltimore, Md.: Johns Hopkins University Press, 1972.

Marable, Manning. *The Great Wells of Democracy: The Meaning of Race in American Life.* New York: BasicCivitas Books, 2002.

———. *How Capitalism Underdeveloped Black America: Problems in Race, Political Economy, and Society.* South End Press Classics Series, vol. 4. Cambridge, Mass.: South End Press, 2000.

Merleau-Ponty, Maurice. *Phenomenology of Perception.* Trans. Colin Smith. Atlantic Highlands, N.J.: Humanities Press, 1961.

———. *"The Primacy of Perception" and Other Essays on Phenomenological Psychology, the Philosophy of Art, History, and Politics.* Ed. James M. Edie. Evanston, Ill.: Northwestern University Press, 1964.

Mills, Charles W. *Blackness Visible: Essays on Philosophy and Race.* Ithaca, N.Y.: Cornell University Press, 1998.

———. *The Racial Contract.* Ithaca, N.Y.: Cornell University Press, 1997.

O'Meally, Robert, and Geneviève Fabre, eds. *History and Memory in African-American Culture.* New York: Oxford University Press, 1994.

———. Introduction to Robert O'Meally and Geneviève Fabre, eds., *History and Memory in African-American Culture.* New York: Oxford University Press, 1994. 3–17.

Sartre, Jean-Paul. Preface to *The Wretched of the Earth,* by Frantz Fanon. Trans. Constance Farrington. New York: Grove Press, 1963. 7–31.

Speke, John Hanning. *Journal of the Discovery of the Source of the Nile.* Mineola, N.Y.: Dover, 1996.

Stanley, Henry M. *Through the Dark Continent . . . .* 2 vols. Mineola, N.Y.: Dover, 1988.

Stoler, Ann Laura. *Race and the Education of Desire: Foucault's "History of Sexuality" and the Colonial Order of Things.* Durham, N.C.: Duke University Press, 1995.

Thiong'o, Ngugi wa. *Decolonising the Mind: The Politics of Language in African Literature.* London: Heinemann, 1986.

Twine, France Winddance, and Jonathan W. Warren, eds. *Racing Research, Researching Race: Methodological Dilemmas in Critical Race Studies.* New York: New York University Press, 2000.

Williams, Patricia J. *The Alchemy of Race and Rights.* Harvard University Press, 1992.

Winant, Howard. "Theoretical Status of the Concept of Race." In Les Back and John Solomos, eds., *Theories of Race and Racism.* New York: Routledge, 2000. 181–93.

Young, Robert J. C. *Postcolonialism: An Historical Introduction.* Malden, Mass.: Blackwell, 2001.

Zack, Naomi, ed. *Race and Mixed Race.* Philadelphia: Temple University Press, 1993.

CHAPTER 1

Putting Materialism Back into Race Theory: Toward a Transformative Theory of Race

Robert Young

This essay advances a materialist theory of race. In my view, race oppression dialectically intersects with the exploitative logic of advanced capitalism, a regime that deploys race in the interest of surplus accumulation. Thus, race operates at the (economic) base and produces cultural and ideological effects at the superstructure; in turn, these effects—in very historically specific ways—interact with and ideologically justify the operations at the economic base.[1] In a sense, then, race encodes the totality of contemporary capitalist social relations, which is why race cuts across a range of seemingly disparate social sites in contemporary U.S. society. For instance, one can mark race difference and its discriminatory effects in such diverse sites as health care, housing/real estate, education, law, the job market, and many other social sites. Unlike many commentators who engage race matters, however, I do not isolate these social sites and view race as a local problem, which would lead to reformist measures along the lines of either legal reform or a cultural-ideological battle to win the hearts and minds of people and thus keep the existing socioeconomic arrangements intact; instead, I foreground the relationality of these sites within the exchange mechanism of multinational capitalism.

Consequently, I believe, the eradication of race oppression also requires a totalizing political project: the transformation of existing capitalism—a system that produces difference (the racial/gender division of labor) and accompanying ideological narratives that justify the resulting social inequality. Hence, my project articulates a transformative theory of race—a theory that reclaims revolutionary class politics in the interests of contributing to a postracist society. In other words, the transformation from actually existing capitalism into socialism constitutes the condition of possibility for a postracist society—a society free from racial and all other forms of oppression. By freedom, I do not simply mean a legal or cultural articulation of individual rights, as proposed by bourgeois race theorists. Instead, I theorize freedom as a material effect of emancipated economic forms.

I foreground my (materialist) understanding of race as a way to contest contemporary accounts of race, which erase any determinate connection to economics. For instance, humanism and poststructuralism represent two dominant views on race in the contemporary academy. Even though they articulate very different theoretical positions, they produce similar ideological effects: the suppression of economics. They collude in redirecting attention away from the logic of capitalist exploitation and point us to the cultural questions of sameness (humanism) or difference (poststructuralism). In developing my project, I critique the ideological assumptions of some exemplary instances of humanist and poststructuralist accounts of race, especially those accounts that also attempt to displace Marxism, and in doing so I foreground the historically determinate link between race and exploitation. It is this link that forms the core of what I am calling a transformative theory of race. The transformation of race from a sign of exploitation to one of democratic multiculturalism ultimately requires the transformation of capitalism.

Within contemporary black humanist discourses, the focus remains on the subject. Hence, diverse intellectual inquiries such as Afrocentrism (Molefi Kete Asante), black feminism (Patricia Hill Collins), and neoconservative culturalism (Shelby Steele) share a philosophical-ideological commitment to the subject. As Asante once put it in a representative formulation, Afrocentrism presents "the African as subject rather than object" ("Multiculturalism" 270). The preoccupation with the subject highlights Asante's rather conservative humanist philosophical position, a position powerfully critiqued by Louis Althusser.[2] In reifying the subject, Asante abstracts the (African) subject from history and posits an "essentialized" identity within an "essentialized" historical period that is unproblematically recuperable through an Afrocentric paradigm. Asante takes the essence of the subject for a universal quality, and as Althusser argues, this means that concrete subjects must exist as an absolute given, which implies an empiricism of the subject (*For Marx* 228). Furthermore, Althusser continues, if the concrete subject is to be a subject, then each must carry the entire essence in himself or herself, and this implies an idealism of the essence (*For Marx* 228). Thus, Asante's philosophical location provides the basis for the transcendental subject: the always already (self) present black subject, from ancient Egypt to the modern black American. What one needs, quite simply, is an Afrocentric methodology, and this Asante grounds in an idealist metaphysic.

As in Eurocentric practices, Asante's project occludes the historical contradictions constitutive of any social formation and, far from advancing a distinctive Afrocentric epistemology, Asante's humanism puts him squarely within the dominant bourgeois philosophical tradition, and his discourse produces similar effects. Under the guise of the transcendental subject, class divisions within the black community are suppressed, and this, in turn, advances the class interests of the elites, whose interests are silently embedded in the project. As in Eurocentric historical narratives, Afrocentrism reclaims the history of the (African) elites. In this way, Afrocentric discourse is knowledge for middle- and upper-class blacks, since it naturalizes their class privilege; for which other class could afford to see "symbol imperialism" (Asante, *Afrocentric Idea*, 56) as the major problem confronting multicultural societies?

Bourgeois philosophical assumptions haunt the Afrocentric project and, in the domain of black feminist theory, Patricia Hill Collins provides an instructive example of this intersection. In *Black Feminist Thought*, Collins posits the "special angle of vision" that black women bring to the knowledge production process (21), and this "unique angle" (22) provides the "standpoint" for Afrocentric feminism, a feminism that she equates with humanism (37). As in the experiential metaphysics of black women's standpoint theory, Collins situates Afrocentric feminist epistemology "in the everyday experiences of African-American women" (207). Consequently, Collins suggests that "concrete experience" constitutes a criterion of meaning (208).

But the experiential, the "real," does not equate to the "truth," as Collins implies. Collins rejects the "Eurocentric Masculinist Knowledge Validation Process" for its positivism but, in turn, she offers empiricism as the grounds for validating experience. Hence, the validity of experiential claims is adjudicated by reference to the experience. Not only is her argument circular, but it also undermines one of her key claims. If race, class, gender, and the accompanying ideological apparatuses are interlocking systems of oppression, as Collins suggests, then the experiential is not the site for the "true" but rather the site for the articulation of dominant ideology. On what basis, then, could the experiential provide grounds for a historical understanding of the structures that make experience itself possible as experience?

Asante and Collins assume that experience is self-intelligible and, in their discourse, it functions as the limit text of the real. I believe, however, that experience is a highly mediated frame of understanding. Though it is true that a person of color experiences oppression, this experience is not self-explanatory and, therefore, it needs to be situated in relation to other social practices. Experience seems local, but it is, like all cultural and political practices, interrelated to other practices and experiences. Thus, its explanation comes from its "outside." Theory, specifically Marxist theory, provides an explanation of this outside. Experience does not bespeak the real, but rather it is the site of contradictions and, hence, in need of conceptual elaboration to break from cultural common sense, which is a conduit for the dominant ideology. It is this outside that has come under attack by black humanist scholars through the invocation of the black transcendental subject.

Indeed, the discourse of the subject operates as an ideological strategy for fetishizing the black experience and, consequently, it positions black subjectivity beyond the reach of Marxism. For example, in *The Afrocentric Idea*, Asante dismisses Marxism because it is Eurocentric (8); but are the core concepts of

Marxism, such as class and mode of production, relevant only for European social formations? Are African and African American social histories/relations unshaped by class structures? Asante assumes that class hierarchies do not structure African or the African American social experiences, and this reveals the class politics of Afrocentricity: It makes class invisible. Asante's assumption, which erases materialism, enables Asante to offer the idealist formulation that the "word creates reality" (*Afrocentric Idea* 70). The political translation of such idealism is, not surprisingly, very conservative. Asante directs us away from critiquing capitalist institutions, in a manner similar to the ideological protocol of the Million Man March, and calls for vigilance against symbolic oppression. As Asante tellingly puts it, "symbol imperialism, rather than institutional racism, is the major social problem facing multicultural societies" (*Afrocentric Idea* 56).

In the realm of African American philosophy, Howard McGary Jr. also deploys the discourse of the (black) subject to mark the limits of Marxism. For instance, in a recent interview, McGary offers this humanist rejection of Marxism: "I don't think that the levels of alienation experienced by Black people are rooted primarily in economic relations" (Interview 90). For McGary, black alienation exceeds the logic of Marxist theory and thus McGary's idealist assertion that "the sense of alienation experienced by Black people in the U.S. is also rooted in the whole idea of what it means to be a human being and how that has been understood" (Interview 90). McGary confuses causes and effects and then misreads Marxism as a descriptive modality. Marxism is not as concerned with descriptive accounts, the effects, as it is with explanatory accounts; that is, it is concerned with the cause of social alienation because such an explanatory account acts as a guide for praxis. Social alienation is a historical effect, and its explanation does not reside in the experience itself; therefore, it needs explanation and such an explanation emerges from the transpersonal space of concepts.

In theorizing the specificity of black alienation, McGary reveals his contradictory ideological coordinates. First, he argues that black alienation results from cultural "beliefs." Then, he suggests that these cultural "norms" and "practices" develop from slavery and Jim Crow, which are fundamentally economic relations for the historically specific exploitation of black people. If these cultural norms endogenously emerge from the economic systems of slavery and Jim Crow, as McGary correctly suggests, then and contrary to McGary's expressed position, black alienation is very much rooted in economic relations.

McGary's desire to place black subjectivity beyond Marxism creates contradictions in his text. McGary asserts that the economic structures of slavery and Jim Crow shape cultural norms. Thus, in a postslavery, post–Jim Crow era, there would still be an economic structure maintaining contemporary oppressive norms—from McGary's logic this must be the case. McGary remains silent, however, on the contemporary economic system structuring black alienation: capitalism. Apparently, it is legitimate to foreground and critique the historical

connection between economics and alienation but any inquiry into the present-day connection between economics and alienation is off limits. This other
economic structure—capitalism—remains the unsaid in McGary's discourse, and
consequently McGary provides ideological support for capitalism—the exploitative infrastructure that produces and maintains alienation for blacks as well as
for all working people. In a very revealing moment, a moment that confirms my
reading of McGary's procapitalist position, McGary asserts that "it is possible for
African-Americans to combat or overcome this form of alienation described by
recent writers without overthrowing capitalism" (*Race* 20). Here, in a most lucid
way, we see the ideological connection between the superstructure (philosophy)
and the base (capitalism). Philosophy provides ideological support for capitalism,
and in this instance, we can also see how philosophy carries out class politics at
the level of theory (Althusser, *Lenin,* 18).

McGary points out "that Black people have been used in ways that white people
have not" (Interview 91). McGary's observation may be true, but it does not mean
that whites have not also been "used"; yes, whites may be "used" differently, but
they are still "used" because that is the logic of exploitative regimes—people
are "used," that is to say, their labor is commodified and exchanged for profit.
McGary's interview signals what I call an isolationist view. This view disconnects
black alienation from other social relations; hence, it ultimately reifies race and,
in doing so, suppresses materialist inquiries into the class logic of race. That is to
say that the meaning of race is not to be found within its own internal dynamics but rather in dialectical relation to and as an ideological justification of the
exploitative wage-labor economy.

This isolationist position finds a fuller, and no less problematic, articulation
in Charles W. Mills's *Racial Contract,* a text that undermines the possibility for a
transracial transformative political project. Mills evinces the ideological assumptions and consequent politics of the isolationist view in a long endnote to chapter
1. Mills privileges race oppression, but, in doing so, he must suppress other forms
of oppression, such as gender and class oppression. Mills acknowledges that there
are gender and class relations within the white population, but he still privileges
race, as if the black community is not similarly divided along gender and class
lines. Hence, the ideological necessity for Mills to execute a double move: He must
marginalize class difference within the white community and suppress it within
the black community. Consequently, Mills removes the possibility of connect-
ing white supremacy, a political-cultural structure, to its underlying economic
base.

Mills's empiricist framework mystifies our understanding of race. If "white
racial solidarity has overridden class and gender solidarity" (138), as Mills proposes, then what is needed is an explanation of this racial formation. If race is
the "identity around which whites have usually closed ranks" (Mills 138), then
why is this the case? Without an explanation, it seems as if white solidarity re-

flects some kind of metaphysical alliance. White racial solidarity is a historical articulation that operates to defuse class antagonism within white society, and it is maintained and reproduced through discourses of ideology. The race contract provides whites with an imaginary resolution of actual social contradictions, which are not caused by blacks but by an exploitative economic structure. The race contract enables whites to scapegoat blacks, and such an ideological operation displaces any understanding of the exploitative machinery. Hence, the race contract provides a political cover that ensures the ideological reproduction of the conditions of exploitation, and this reproduction further deepens the social con- tradictions—the economic position of whites becomes more and more depressed by the very same economic system that they help to ideologically reproduce.

Mills points out that the Racial Contract aims at economic exploitation of black people, and this is certainly the case, but it also exploits all working people—a notion suppressed within Mills's black nationalist problematic. From Mills's logic, it seems that all whites (materially) benefit from the Racial Contract, but if this is true, then how does he account for the class structure within the white com- munity? His argument rests upon glossing over class divisions within American and European communities, and I believe this signals the theoretical and politi- cal limits of his position. The vast majority of white Europeans are workers and therefore subjected to capitalist exploitation through the extraction of surplus value, and this structural relationship operates irrespective of race/ethnicity/ gender/sexuality. In other words, neither whiteness nor the Race Contract places whites outside the logic of exploitation. Indeed, the possibility for transracial collective praxis emerges in the contradiction between the (ideological) promise of whiteness and the actual oppressed material conditions of most whites.

The class blindness in Mills is surprising because he situates his discourse with- in "the best tradition of oppositional materialist critique" (129), but that tradition foregrounds political economy. Mills undermines his materialism through the silent reinscription of idealism. For example, he argues that "The Racial Contract is an exploitation contract that creates global European economic domination and national white privilege" (31). Indeed, for Mills "the globally-coded distribu- tion of wealth and poverty has been produced by the Racial Contract" (37). The "Racial Contract" does not create global European economic domination, this results from control of capital by the international ruling class, but the Racial Contract ideologically legitimates the "color-coded distribution of wealth and poverty." Thus, the race contract effectively naturalizes a racial division of labor, and of course this operation fractures (multiracial) class solidarity.

As Cheryl I. Harris insightfully puts it, "It is through the concept of whiteness that class-consciousness among white workers is subordinated and attention is diverted from class oppression" (286). Therefore, if whites organize around race, as Mills asserts, then this is only because of an always already ideological interpellation (to "whiteness") and not a divine (racial) mandate, even though it has the appearance of obviousness. Indeed, the very aim of ideology is to produce cultural obviousnesses; hence the project of materialist analysis involves a critique of ideology and not the reification of common sense. Contrary to Mills, I believe a more effective materialist class analysis foregrounds exploitative social-economic structures and the consequent class struggle between the international ruling class and the international proletariat.

My project situates race in relation to the international division of labor. Race emerges historically and within specific political-economic coordinates. These coordinates link the logic of race to the logic of capitalist exploitation. In other words, race is implicated in the historic and ongoing (class) struggle to determine the ratio of surplus value. For me, then, race signals a marking for exploitation, and this economic assignment, in turn, generates an accompanying ideological machinery to justify and increase that exploitation. Any understanding of this economic assignment, which represents a historically objective positionality, has been removed from the contemporary intellectual scene. Race represents not just a cultural or political category, as many critics attest, but it represents a historic apparatus for the production, maintenance, and legitimation of the inequalities of wage labor. As in other modes of social difference, like gender and sexuality, race participates in naturalizing asymmetrical social relations.

The materialist view has been systematically erased from contemporary cultural intelligibility. I have already critically engaged some exemplary instances of black humanist discourses and, specifically, their invocation of the transcendental subject to dismiss Marxism. If the humanists deploy the problematics of (black) subjectivity to suppress materialist notions of race, the postmodernists draw upon the problematics of signification to deconstruct materialism. At this point, I shift to probe into the politics of poststructuralist accounts of race.

One can trace the shift in African American cultural theory from the subject to semiotics as early as the 1980s. Houston Baker announces this paradigm shift in *Blues, Ideology, and Afro-American Literature.* In this text, Baker "envision[s] language (the code) 'speaking' the subject" and consequently, "[t]he subject is 'decentered'" (1). Throughout the 1980s and 1990s, Baker and Henry Louis Gates Jr., in particular, have been principal architects in advancing a tropological theory of race. The textualization of race represents one of the hegemonic views of race, and it is evident in the writings of theorists like Lawrence Hogue, Claudia Tate, Anthony Appiah, Barbara Johnson, David Theo Goldberg, Paul Gilroy, Mae Gwendolyn Henderson, Tommy L. Lott, Valerie Smith, Mason Stokes, Siobhan B. Somerville, Cornel West, and Howard Winant, among others.

The linguistic turn in social theory enables the recent antireductionist views on race. Concepts like Winant's "racial formation," Paul Gilroy's "multi-modal" (*There Ain't* 28) and David Theo Goldberg's "grammatical" reading of race ("Racist Discourse" 95) reflect the antireductionist logic that currently dominates contemporary theorizing on race. All three theorists vigorously oppose reducing race to class, but apparently it is acceptable to reduce race to a "hybridity" of factors (Goldberg, "Racist Discourse," 93), which once again establishes liberal pluralism as the limit of politics. Indeed, at the moment, it is fairly commonplace to reduce race to culture, or politics, or desire. Hence, these theorists are not so much opposed to reductionist theories, they simply are opposed to class understandings of race and, in this way, they articulate a conceptual displacement of materialism (in the name of epistemological skepticism) and, consequently, they reclaim the autonomy of race (in the name of liberalism).

The logic of autonomy moves away from the transcendental subject, but it gives way to reification of discourse. For instance, Goldberg theorizes race and class as autonomous "fields of discourse" ("Racist Discourse" 87). After detotalizing the social, Goldberg introduces a very problematic split between racism, which deals with the issue of "exclusion," and class theory, which deals with the issue of "exploitation" ("Racist Discourse" 97). Goldberg's text raises an important question concerning the relationship between exclusion and exploitation. He is unable to provide an effective response, however, because of his commitment to a nonreductive analysis of race, and this leaves him without a historical explanation of the constitution of (racist) discourse. Goldberg examines racist discourse "in [its] own terms," but he has a very difficult time accounting for the "persuasiveness" of racist discourse. In its own terms, racist discourse is very compelling for racists, but this begs the questions Why is racist discourse so persuasive in the first place? Why does the social formation make available such a subject position? These are urgent questions because of the nature of Goldberg's project, which attempts to identify "racists on the basis of the kinds of beliefs they hold" ("Racist Discourse" 87). The identification of racists on the basis of their beliefs does not explain the origin of such beliefs in the first place. Thus, the question remains: Why do racists hold such (racist) beliefs? For Goldberg, it appears that racists hold racist beliefs because of racist discourse! Goldberg cannot offer an explanation of these beliefs because this would take him outside of the formal grammar of racist discourse.

In Goldberg, the obsession with autonomy engenders a reification of discourse and the political implications of this are quite revealing. For Goldberg, discourse—not class struggle—becomes the motor of history: "it is in virtue of racist discourse and not merely rationalized by it that such forced manipulations of individual subjects and whole populations could have been affected" ("Racist Discourse" 95). He continues: "Instruments of exclusion—legal, cultural, political, or economic—are forged by subjects as they mould criteria for establishing racial otherness" ("Racist Discourse" 95). Racial alterity makes sense not on its own terms but in relation to "instruments of exclusion." To move beyond Goldberg, I suggest that these instruments, in turn, must be related to existing property relationships. In short, the logic of alterity justifies and hence assists in the maintenance of class-generated social inequality. The preoccupation with "autonomy" and "racial discourse formation" makes it seem as if social life is a matter of "contingency." This view blocks our understanding of the one constant feature of daily life under capitalism: exploitation. Under capitalism, exploitation is a not a discursive contingency but a structural articulation, and this structure of exploitation underpins (post)modern social life.

At the moment, then, the discourse of autonomy displaces the structure of exploitation and in this regard I believe one can map out the ideological collusion taking place in race theory. As I pointed out earlier, the humanists posit the "uniqueness" of black subjectivity, and now we can see the postmodern corollary that posits the "uniqueness" of racial discourse. I refer to these positions as the "pedagogy of autonomy" because both instruct subjects to value the local. In both instances, the discourse of autonomy provides an ideological framework for protecting the "unique" against its conceptual other—knowledge of the social totality. The pedagogues of autonomy assume that the unique, in its immediacy to the concrete, provides access to the real, and it therefore grounds knowledge. These (antireductionist) pedagogues reduce knowledge to the concrete and consequently mystify our understanding of race because they disconnect it from larger social structures like class and ideology.

By downplaying the determinate structures of class and ideology, it seems as if one could merely dispense with race because of a crisis in raciology, as Gilroy suggests in his recent text, *Against Race*. Gilroy's notion of "post-race" offers a cultural cosmopolitanism to resolve the crisis in racial representation, but he has very little to say about economics. In fact, he is explicitly anti-Marxist (*Against Race* 336), and in this regard, his text continues his longstanding and unrelenting attacks against Marxism. His notion of cosmopolitanism provides the most recent concept for displacing class theory. Cosmopolitanism will take us beyond the positivistic faith of Marxism and usher in a postrace dispensation. His caricature of Marxism runs counter to one of the core concepts of Marxism—class struggle. Recall the opening lines of the *Communist Manifesto*: "The history of all hitherto existing society is the history of class struggles" (9). If Marxism highlights the historicity of class antagonism, then, contrary to Gilroy, there is very little room for transhistorical positivistic pieties. Gilroy is not as interested in engaging Marxism as much as he is in constructing an ideological alibi for dismissing Marxism.

Gilroy's idealist understanding of postrace emerges from his post-Marxism, which he launched in an earlier work. Indeed, it is his earlier work that clearly shows the link between the discourse of (racial) autonomy and the politics of reformism. Specifically, in *There Ain't No Black in the Union Jack*, Gilroy "supplements" class analytics with new urban social movements. With Gilroy, however, the "supplement" operates as a code for recuperating liberal pluralism (what Gilroy calls "multi-modality" (*There Ain't* 28). Consequently, we do not get a sustained theorizing of the dialectical relationship between class and race, but rather we get what ultimately amounts to an abandonment of class theory (*There Ain't* 245). Here is why he must abandon class theory: The trajectory of class theory calls for revolutionary transformation of existing capitalist society. This is not Gilroy's project, however, nor the project of the new urban movements.

Gilroy endorses the new social movements precisely because "the new movements are not primarily oriented towards instrumental objectives, such as the conquest of political power or state apparatuses" (*There Ain't* 226). Instead, the new social movements desire autonomy within the existing system (*There Ain't* 226), and therefore, they foreground the "sphere of autonomous self-realization" (*There Ain't* 233). In other words, they do not want to change an exploitative system, they merely want a little more (discursive) freedom within it, and this (reformist) project signals agency for Gilroy. For Gilroy, the new social movements represent agency, and in this regard, they replace the proletariat—the historic vehicle for social transformation—but their agency, to repeat, is directed toward reforming specific local sites, such as race or gender, within the existing system. In short, they have abandoned the goal of transforming existing capitalism—a totalizing system that connects seemingly disparate elements of the social through the logic of exploitation for a new goal: creating more humane spaces for new movements within capitalism.

So, then, what is so new in the new social movements? It is certainly very old in the way it rehabilitates liberal notions of the autonomous subject. Its newness is a sign of the contemporary crisis-ridden conjuncture in capitalist social relations. This crisis of capital and the ensuing rupture in its ideological narrative provides the historical condition for articulating resistance along the axes of race, class, gender, ecology, and so on. Even though resistance may take place in very specific domains, such as race, gender, ecological responsibility, or sexuality, among others, this does not mean that the crisis is local. It simply indexes how capitalist exploitation brings every social sphere under its totalizing logic. Rather than point up the systematicity of the crisis, however, the theorists of the new social movements turn to the local, as if it is unrelated to questions of globality.

With Gilroy and the new social movements, we are returned once again to the local, and the experiential sets the limits of understanding. Gilroy asserts that people "unable to control the social relations in which they find themselves . . . have shrunk the world to the size of their communities and begun to act politically on that basis" (*There Ain't* 245). If this is true, then Gilroy, at the level of theory, mirrors this as he shrinks his theory to the dictates of crude empiricism. Rather than opening the possibility of collective control over social relations, which points in an emancipatory direction, Gilroy brackets the question of social relation and, consequently, he limits politics to the cultural (re)negotiations of identity.

If Gilroy deploys the postcolonial racialized agent for displacing class, then Homi Bhabha's postcolonial theory detaches race from political economy by reinscribing race within problematics of signification. In *The Location of Culture*,

Bhabha's last chapter, "Race, Time, and the Revision of Modernity," situates the question of race within the "ambivalent temporality of modernity" (239). In this way, Bhabha foregrounds the "time-lag" between "event" and "enunciation" and, for Bhabha, this produces space for postcolonial agency. Political agency revolves around deconstructing signs from totalities and thereby delaying the connection between signifier and signified, and resistance is the effect of this ambivalence. Hence, for Bhabha, "the intervention of postcolonial or black critique is aimed at transforming the conditions of enunciation at the level of the sign" (247). This idealist reading of the social reduces politics to a struggle over the sign rather than the relations of production.

Indeed, Bhabha reunderstands the political not as an ideological practice aimed at social transformation—the project of transformative race theory. Instead, he theorizes "politics as a performativity" (15), but what is the social effect of this understanding of politics? Toward what end might this notion point us? It seems as if the political now calls for (cosmopolitan) witnesses to the always already permanent slippage of signification and this (formal) process of repetition and reinscription outlines a space for "other forms of enunciation" (Bhabha 254). But will these "other forms of enunciation" naturally articulate resistance to the dominant political and ideological interests? For Bhabha, of course, we "need to think beyond narratives of originary and initial subjectivities and to focus on those moments or processes that are produced in the articulation of cultural differences" (1). Cultural differences, in themselves, do not, however, necessarily mean opposition. Indeed, at the moment, cultural difference represents one of the latest zones for commodification and, in this regard, it ideologically legitimates capitalism. Bhabha homogenizes (cultural) difference and consequently he covers over ideological struggles within the space of cultural difference. In short, this other historical site is not the site for pure difference, which naturally resists the hegemonic, for it, too, is the site for political contestation.

Bhabha's formalism makes it seem as if ambivalence essentially inheres in discourse. Ambivalence results from opposed political interests that inflect discourses, and so the ambivalence registers social conflict. In *Marxism and the Philosophy of Language*, Voloshinov offers this materialist understanding of the sign: "Class does not coincide with the sign community, i.e. with the community which is the totality of users of the same set of signs for ideological communication. Thus various different classes will use one and the same language. As a result, differently oriented accents intersect in every ideological sign. Sign becomes an arena of class struggle" (22). The very concept—ideology—that could delineate the political character and therefore class interests involved in structuring the content of discourses, Bhabha excludes from his discourse.

In the end, Bhabha's discourse advocates what amounts to discursive freedom, and he substitutes this for material freedom. Like Gilroy, Bhabha's discursive freedom takes place within the existing system. In contrast to Bhabha, Marx theorizes the material presupposition of freedom. In the *German Ideology,* Marx argues that "people cannot be liberated as long as they are unable to obtain food and drink, housing and clothing in adequate quality and quantity" (61). Thus for Marx "'Liberation' is an historical and not a mental act" (*German Ideology* 61). In suppressing the issue of need, Bhabha's text reveals his own class interests. The studied preoccupation with "ambivalence" reflects a class privilege, and it speaks to the crisis for (postcolonial) subjects torn between national affiliation and their privileged (and objective) class position within the international division of labor. The ambivalence is a symptom of social antagonism, but in Bhabha's hands it becomes a transhistorical code for erasing the trace of class.

Here then is one of the primary effects of the postmodern knowledge practices: Class is deconstructed as a metaphysical dinosaur. In this regard, postmodernists collude with the humanists in legitimating the sanctity of the local. Both participate in narrowing cultural intelligibility to questions of (racial) discourse or the (black) subject and, in doing so, they provide ideological immunity for capitalism. It is now very difficult to even raise the issue of class, particularly if you raise the issue outside the logic of supplementarity—today's ruling intellectual logic, which provides a theoretical analog to contemporary neoliberal political structures.

In one of the few recent texts to explore the centrality of class, bell hooks's *Where We Stand,* we are, once again, still left with a reaffirmation of capitalism. For instance, hooks argues for changes within capitalism: "I identify with democratic socialism, with a vision of participatory economics within capitalism that aims to challenge and change class hierarchy" (156). Capitalism produces class hierarchy; therefore, as long as capitalism remains, class hierarchy and antagonism will remain. Hence, the solution requires a transformation of class society. However, hooks mystifies capitalism as a transhistorical system, and thus she can assert that the "poor may be with us always" (129). Under this view, politics becomes a matter of "bearing witness" to the crimes of capitalism; but, rather than struggle for capitalism's replacement, hooks calls for strategies of "self-actualization" and redistributing resources to the poor. She calls for the very same thing—collectivity—that capitalism cannot provide because social resources are privatized under capitalism. Consequently, hooks's program for "self-esteem" is an attempt to put a human face on capitalism.

Whether one considers the recent work by African American humanists, or discourse theorists, or even left-liberal intellectuals, these various groups—despite their intellectual differences—form a ruling coalition and one thing is clear: Capitalism sets the limit for political change, as there is no alternative to the rule of capital. In contrast to much of contemporary race theory, a transformative theory of race highlights the political economy of race in the interests of an emancipatory political project. Wahneema Lubiano once wrote that "the idea of race and the operation of racism are the best friends that the economic and political elite have in the United States" (vii). Race mystifies the structure of exploitation and masks the severe inequalities within global capitalism. I am afraid that, at this point, many contemporary race theorists, in their systematic erasure of materialism, have become close (ideological) allies with the economic and political elites, who deny even the existence of classes. A transformative race theory pulls back into focus the struggle against exploitation and sets a new social priority "in which the free development of each is the condition for the free development of all" (Marx, *Communist Manifesto*, 31).

Notes

1. For the classic theorization of the base and superstructure problematic, I point the reader to Marx's preface to *A Contribution to the Critique of Political Economy*, and a more specific elaboration of the dialectical relation is found in Friedrich Engels's letter to Joseph Bloch. Both these texts are readily available in Robert Tucker's *Marx-Engels Reader*. A more recent theorization is available in Louis Althusser's *Lenin and Philosophy* and *For Marx*. On the subject of race, an Althusserian account is presented in Stuart Hall's "Race, Articulation, and Societies Structured in Dominance." Hall's essay was originally published in 1980; however, by the 1990s, Hall shifts to a semiotic notion of race and sees race as a "floating signifier." In many ways, Hall's intellectual trajectory on race mirrors the larger shift from the material to the semiotic in social theory.

2. For a sustained Marxist critique of humanism, see Louis Althusser's "Marxism and Humanism" in his *For Marx*.

Works Cited

Althusser, Louis. *For Marx*. New York: Verso, 1990.
———. *Lenin and Philosophy*. New York: Monthly Review Press, 1971.
Asante, Molefi Kete. *The Afrocentric Idea*. Philadelphia: Temple University Press, 1987.
———. "Multiculturalism: An Exchange." *American Scholar* (Spring 1991): 267–72.
Baker, Houston A. *Blues, Ideology, and Afro-American Literature: A Vernacular Theory*. Chicago: University of Chicago Press, 1984.
Bhabha, Homi K. *The Location of Culture*. New York: Routledge, 1994.
Collins, Patricia Hill. *Black Feminist Thought*. New York: Routledge, 1991.
Goldberg, David Theo, ed. *Anatomy of Racism*. Minneapolis: University of Minnesota Press, 1990.
———. "Racist Discourse and the Language of Class." Pp. 84–101 in *Exploitation and Exclusion: Race and Class in Contemporary US Society*, edited by Abebe Zegeye, Leonard Harris, and Julia Maxted. New York: Hans Zell, 1991.
Gilroy, Paul. *Against Race: Imagining Political Culture Beyond the Color Line*. Cambridge, Mass.: Harvard University Press, 2000.
———. *There Ain't No Black in the Union Jack*. Chicago: University of Chicago Press, 1991.
Harris, Cheryl I. "Whiteness As Property." Pp. 276–91 in *Critical Race Theory: The Key Writings That Formed the Movement*, edited by Kimberlé Crenshaw, Neil Gotanda, Gary Peller, and Kendall Thomas. New York: New Press, 1995.

Hogue, W. Lawrence. *Race, Modernity, Postmodernity.* Albany: State University of New York Press, 1996.

hooks, bell. *Where We Stand: Class Matters.* New York: Routledge, 2000.

Lott, Tommy L. *The Invention of Race.* Malden, Mass.: Blackwell, 1999.

Lubiano, Wahneema, ed. *The House That Race Built.* New York: Vintage, 1998.

Marx, Karl, and Friedrich Engels. *Communist Manifesto.* New York: International Publishers, 1986.

———. *The German Ideology.* New York: International Publishers, 1989.

McGary, Howard Jr. Interview. Pp. 73–93 in *African-American Philosophers: 17 Conversations,* edited by George Yancy. New York: Routledge, 1998.

———. *Race and Social Justice.* Boston: Blackwell, 1999.

Mills, Charles W. *The Racial Contract.* Ithaca, N.Y.: Cornell University Press, 1997.

Somerville, Siobhan, B. *Queering the Color Line.* Durham, N.C.: Duke University Press, 2000.

Stokes, Mason. *The Color of Sex.* Durham, N.C.: Duke University Press, 2001.

Voloshinov, V. N. *Marxism and the Philosophy of Language,* translated by L. Matejka and I. R. Titunik. Cambridge, Mass.: Harvard University Press, 1986.

Winant, Howard. "Racial Formation Theory and Contemporary US Politics." Pp. 130–41 in Abebe Zegeye, Leonard Harris, and Julia Maxted, eds. *Exploitation and Exclusion: Race and Class in Contemporary US Society.* New York: Hans Zell, 1991.

Zegeye, Abebe, Leonard Harris, and Julia Maxted, eds. *Exploitation and Exclusion: Race and Class in Contemporary US Society.* New York: Hans Zell, 1991.

CHAPTER 2

Commonsense Racial Formation:
Wahneema Lubiano, Antonio Gramsci, and
the Importance of the Nonpropositional

Alexis Shotwell

> The problem of the future world is the charting, by means of intelligent
> reason, of a path not simply through the resistances of physical
> force, but through the vaster and far more intricate jungle of ideas
> conditioned on unconscious and subconscious reflexes of living things;
> on blind unreason and often irresistible urges of sensitive matter; of
> which the concept of race is today one of the most unyielding and
> threatening.
> —W. E. B. Du Bois, *Dusk of Dawn: An Essay toward an
> Autobiography of a Race Concept*, 1940

Although Du Bois was writing in 1940, much of the intricate tangle of ideas around "race"—the problem of the color line—continue to bear the marks he lays out. Race and ethnicity are ideas and realities that are often articulated in terms of their blind unreason, their conditioning by things unconscious and subconscious, their unyielding nature, and their threat. I am interested in beginning to chart one kind of path, toward why race and ethnicity might stand as "blind" and "irresistible"—as not subject to reason—but still commonsensical. In this chapter, I argue that implicit, nonpropositional frameworks are a crucial aspect of racial formation and that we need an account of the implicit to address the maintenance and transmission of racist norms. Because I think the implicit plays a central role in maintaining "race" as a system of domination, I find it necessary to try to find ways of addressing aspects of racial formation that inhere in the nonpropositional. In the United States, the last fifteen years have seen a decided turn toward a rhetoric of "color blindness," for example, bringing implicit racialized stances of uneasiness together with a liberal discourse of "freedom and equality for all." Such a rhetoric pushes key aspects of racialization into silence. As many theorists have discussed, the claim that not-noticing race is an antiracist act undermines many explicitly antiracist projects; the gutting of affirmative action legislation is a product of such a process. I begin by examining the idea that conceptions of "race" are significantly unarticulated—that they stand as commonsensical. My examination of this idea takes two tacks. First, I argue that theorists of race and ethnicity make use of the notion of common sense because they need a cluster of concepts that will express implicit aspects to racialization. Second, I argue that the category of "common sense" delineates nonpropositional epistemic frameworks, which turn out also to be the grounds for ideology's connection to culture.

The theorists I draw on most centrally in this endeavor are Wahneema Lubiano, for her incisive reading of cultural production, and Antonio Gramsci, for his nuanced account of the terrain of the commonsensical as a political formation. Lubiano offers a model of theorizing engaged in and arising out of struggle; her work on the movement of politics through culture presents the best sort of pessimism and optimism. I attend particularly to the work Lubiano does on cultural artifacts of racist practice and antihegemonic resistance: She renders films, newspaper articles, and songs differently legible. Similarly, Gramsci exemplifies thinking deeply enmeshed in practice. I follow Stuart Hall in reading Gramsci both with an eye toward how he cannot be disentangled from his particular circumstance and with an understanding that this characteristic is central to Gramsci's promise. I value his account for its articulation of the commonsensical as a dense, contradictory, irreducible ground from which liberatory potential arises. Lubiano and Gramsci are presenting compatible but different accounts of the role of ideology as productive of common sense; reading them together gives a nuanced picture of this production and allows me to argue that common sense is the racialized ground on which culture promulgates ideology. My aim here is to create a kind of theoretical palimpsest by an addition that might provide some useful conceptual resources for antiracist struggle.

Many theorists of race and ethnicity working in the humanities have called on political philosopher Antonio Gramsci's formulation of the notion of common sense in their thinking about race and ethnicity. Michael Omi and Howard Winant, write, for example, that "race becomes 'common sense'—a way of comprehending, explaining, and acting in the world" (Omi and Winant 60). They are using Gramsci's understanding of common sense to get at what it is for racialization to be systematically woven through our social structure in such a way that everyone is subject to particular racial formations. This is in part a cultural process. How does a Gramscian understanding of common sense help someone who is theorizing race and racism? It seems that Gramsci's notion of common sense (particularly as it relates to his articulation of ideological hegemony) is appealing in part because it gives a framework for thinking through the way what is spoken hooks into what is not expressed in words but is still known. It opens a way of thinking about how the unspeakable can be mobilized for political ends. Or, in other words, it might be that speaking of "common sense" is calling up, among other things, a way of thinking about how the nonpropositional is involved in race and ethnicity. I am interested in the complex of unarticulated beliefs, feelings, inclinations, attitudes, emotions, first-pass responses, and so on, that underlie and shape racialized understanding.

This chapter addresses a number of interlinked questions: What is nonpropositional, or tacit, knowledge? Is Gramsci's conception of common sense also a conception of nonpropositional knowledge? Why might it be important that there be some component of people's understanding that is not in words? What is the force of that? How have some theorists of race and ethnicity taken up Gramsci's discussion? Beginning to answer these requires an attention to how both common sense and the nonpropositional might figure in racial formation and racism and to think about the connection between culture and ideology. I argue that racialization, racism, and racial formation involve significant taken-for-granted, often implicit, understandings, and that such commonsense knowledges provide the connection through which culture and ideology affect one another. I am exploring the way that cultural formations might change or affect racial formation on the level of commonsense, everyday ideology.

European-derived philosophy, broadly, has for the most part rejected everyday, unconsidered conceptions as grounds for, or counting as, knowledge. Knowledge is often thought to be primarily propositionally expressive; for something to be considered "true and justified belief"—a common test phrase—it must be something that can be, or is, articulated and evaluated. There have been philosophers, even within this tradition, interested in nonpropositional knowing; William James and Bertrand Russell's understanding of knowledge by acquaintance, Gilbert Ryle's discussion of knowing-how and knowing-who, and Michael Polanyi's discussion of tacit knowledge are notable. The field of aesthetics has perhaps the longest history of explicit treatment of something like this concept. Susan Babbitt creates an important theoretical model of how nonpropositional knowledge figures in liberatory personal transformation; my discussion here is deeply indebted to her work on this concept. I use the term to mean, broadly, the understanding you have that is not, and perhaps cannot necessarily be, put into words.

In the "Western analytic" Anglo-American philosophical tradition, there has been relatively little attention to the category of "nonpropositional knowledge." Much epistemological study has been devoted to what it is to know and to questions around knowing—what is an adequate analysis of belief, certainty, justification, grounds for knowledge claims, or truth. The knowledge discussed in many beginning philosophy texts takes the form of discussion about the classic proposition "S knows that p." "S" is often claimed to know "p," if S believes p, if S has good reasons to believe p, and if p is in fact the case. In the Routledge Contemporary Introduction to Philosophy series, for example, Robert Audi frames the notion of knowledge in this way: "it looks as if we have a very substantive threefold necessary condition for (propositional) knowledge. Specifically, it seems that knowledge is at least justified true belief: that one knows something only if one believes it, it is true, and one's belief of it is justified" (Audi 215). This claim has appeal: It is somewhat testable and intuitively plausible, and it offers the possibility of verifiable knowledge. It seems, however, that defining knowledge as "true and justified belief" requires the deployment of an implicit *framework* of practices, understandings, and situated knowledges. Most of this framework is not an explicit part of "true and justified belief"; it is implicit in the judgment of truth and justifiability and enables the exercise of that judgment. What matrices of understanding might position what is known ("p")? "P" exists only in relation to a matrix of assumptions, practices, presuppositions, suppressed propositions, emotions, and potentially other nonpropositional things—the framework that conditions the possibility of knowledge. This framework is especially visible in the functionings and deployment of racial formation.

My philosophical stakes in this discussion lie with an understanding that the implicit is a crucial, yet underinterrogated, element in knowledge. We do not have an adequate epistemology without an account of how the nonpropositional is at play in the construction and verification of knowledge. This philosophical interest, while genuine in itself, is ultimately in the service of my political stakes. I'm interested in an understanding of the nonpropositional as something that might be useful for changing the world and for reducing suffering in the world. There is something missing from an account of political formation that takes propositional possibilities to be the only interesting political field. Oppression is frequently occluded by its inherence in the intangible, and the intangible is invisible to much thinking about systems of domination. We are thus missing tools for addressing such occlusion and, accordingly, for addressing oppressive practices. I agree with Raymond Williams's claim that dominative hegemony happens in the "fibres of the self" (212). We need an explicit account of how to perceive activity at that scale. Williams's analogy indicates a subtle, connective, and hidden aspect of ideology's work.

The term *nonpropositional* sets itself immediately against the term *propositional;* it is what the propositional is not. I am thinking of propositionality as claim-making; to put something propositionally is to put it in a linguistically intelligible form that could be evaluated as true or false. I am thinking of our background, taken-for-granted understanding of being in the world as our nonpropositional knowledge; the nonpropositional is what makes things make sense to us. This is a particular subset of the realm of everything that is not in words; some tacit knowledge is highly politically salient. I am bracketing, here, the discussion of whether these sorts of understanding can count as knowledge, traditionally conceived—while I think there is reason to consider the nonpropositional a form of knowledge, it may not be verifiable in the way propositional knowledge can be.

Frameworks of expectation and assumption, learned patterns, inclinations, intentions, and curiosities can be thought of as implicit elements in our understanding of the world. They can be thought of as epistemic because they function as grounds for, justifications for, explicit "that *F*" claims (like, for example: "I know *that* my name is Alexis"). I am thinking of the nonpropositional as what is implicit in our actions and thinking; I mean the term to encompass two different kinds of nonpropositionality. The first is the sort of knowledge that you can exercise but that cannot, ever, be put completely into words; it is skill based, practical, or know-how. Skills, like being able to knit a sweater, or being able to swim, are "known" only insofar as one has the ability to exercise them. A person can tell me many things about how to swim, but I will not know how to do it unless I actually acquire the understanding of moving in particular ways in water. To lose the ability to swim is in some key way to lose the knowledge of how to swim. Many examples of a practical sort of knowledge relate to things that you could say about them; knowing how to swim, or how to pound a nail effectively, for example, are skills that can be improved by someone who is good at them saying things to us about how to do them better ("Maybe if you turn your head more when you take a breath you won't swallow so much water!" "Hold the hammer further back along the handle!"). This is knowledge that is ontologically unspeakable, though its expression might be explicit.

The second sort of nonpropositional knowledge could be put in words but is not, now, in words. And "now" is always shifting, of course; what stands as implicit moves under the surface of propositional knowledge and can be brought into explicitness in language. There is always a great deal that could be said but is not and perhaps has never been put into words. You can, for example, give some propositional content to how far apart it's appropriate for people to stand, what bothered you about a particular conversation, or how you multiply two by two. Each of these is, of course, a different sort of potentially propositional nonpropositional knowledge. Having a feeling about a conversation might arise out of a propositional interaction (a conversation), but the sense of bother about the conversation may not be articulated; you might just feel fussy, and through that feeling unpack the botheredness. On one level, this knowing is not a capital K sort of knowledge; it seems paradigmatically personal. What I want to pick out about it, though, is the way making a feeling or sense explicit is a movement from something that begins as inchoate and inarticulate to something articulate. Explaining how you multiply two by two, as a knowledgeable and accomplished multiplier, may not fully express how you do multiplication. It will attempt, though, to make explicit an activity that likely has moved into an implicit understanding; at one point in your learning to multiply, probably people explained the process to you propositionally. Mastery of that process is in part a nearly intuitive ability to do the process; explaining it, then, requires a movement back into the explicit.

Socially assumed understanding is a good example of a potentially propositional, generally inexplicit variety of knowledge; it is rarely made explicit. Knowing how far apart people ought to stand, for example, is learned through particular social relations and is dependant on the structures of those relations; such understanding shifts according to who is involved, the relationship between them, and the situation. But there is something that is understood about appropriate distance, and that holds as true in those relations, such that when the "appropriateness constraint" is violated people participating in that particular framework of understanding recognize the faux pas. To people outside the framework of implicitly given constraints the appropriateness may be difficult to discern. Homophobic responses to men in the United States having any physical contact are suspended in some sports contexts, for example—a close football-hug is acceptable on a football field, even between men who might keep a distance from one another in a bar. Such understandings can be put into words—as one does in teaching a friend from another country how to relate to people in this one—but unless we encounter a limit case of that sort, we will tend to simply act—simply stand—in ways we "know" are appropriate.

For something to be unspoken, perhaps unspeakable, is for it to be inaccessible in a significant way—not only to conventional Western philosophy. We evaluate as true or false what can be put in the form of a proposition. Other kinds of experience or knowledge often don't count. It matters whether racism—and race—as an ideological formation is nonpropositional. I think that racialization, racism, and racial formation involve significant nonpropositional understandings; the nonpropositional both creates and undermines the ground of "race." Nonpropositional understanding is a key ingredient in the "hooking together" of knowledge generally, and of liberatory resources in particular. If racist and sexist practices implicitly define a field, being comfortable in that field involves deploying and often benefiting from those practices. The implicit is significant even—perhaps especially—when it remains implicit.

The intersection of inarticulate frameworks of understanding with systems of power is visible in the exercise of dominative privilege. While implicit understanding always moves in relation to power, thinking about the implicit as it manifests in "unconscious" racism, for example, highlights the relevance of having an account of the inarticulate for doing antiracist work. Theorists of race and ethnicity have used the notion of a "racial common sense" to get at the idea that there are substantial inarticulate, and possibly unarticulable, elements of racial formation. Thinking about common sense as an implicit ground of racial formation provides resources for more adequate theorizing of this messy, associative realm[1] and also a potential approach for shifting racialized implicit understanding. Thinking and talking about race and ethnicity is a dense, complex project. For many of us, such thinking and talking evokes fear and discomfort—albeit different kinds of fear and discomfort that depend on how we are positioned on racialized, classed, and gendered scales. This affective response indicates one reason for thinking about race in relation to the implicit: The relation functions as an example of the political and personal significance of the implicit and also as an object of study.

I opened by suggesting that Gramsci takes common sense to inhere in everyday unconsidered conceptions—what I have been referring to as that which is taken for granted, understood, implicit, nonpropositional, and tacit in our ways of understanding the world. Having laid out what I mean by implicit, tacit, or nonpropositional knowledge, I turn to a consideration of whether Gramsci is in fact making such a claim.

For Gramsci, the consciousness implicit in a person's activity—the person's common sense—is a significant part of ideology. I will look at Stuart Hall's discussion of this link, below. Piper's discussion of racialized implicit understanding as the commonsense grounds for her work calls for a consideration of what that "common sense" might be. Gramsci talks about common sense as having three main characteristics: it is "[1] incoherent and [2] inconsequential, [and 3] in conformity with the social and cultural position of those masses whose philosophy it is" (419). Many people have talked about Gramsci's conception of common sense in terms of incoherence (the first characteristic I have picked out) and reduced notions of its inconsequential (or, sometimes the word is translated as "nonconsecutive") and conformative nature to a kind of deep muddledness. Stuart Hall, for example, says, "'Common sense' is not coherent: it is usually 'disjointed and episodic,' fragmentary and contradictory" ("Gramsci's Relevance" 431). David Lionel Smith argues that "For Gramsci [common sense] . . . is an undifferentiated mix of habit, superstition, fact, hearsay, dissent, prejudice, etc.: the ideology of common experience" (181). Notice that though Smith does include "dissent" as part of common sense, he is arguing that there is little liberatory potential inherent in it and that it is primarily something to be struggled against. I think (following Hall) that Gramsci embeds precisely liberatory potential in common sense, in order to get at what might be useful about it. That liberatory potential inheres in the nonpropositional or implicit nature of common sense.

Gramsci argues that "common sense is an ambiguous, contradictory, and multiform concept" (423). For common sense to be nonconsecutive (what I have picked out as a second characteristic of Gramsci's understanding of common sense) is for it to hold, in some sense or aspect, the possibility of contradiction. The commonsensical can hold both P and not-P and not be particularly bothered—perhaps not even notice. One's common sense need not maintain standards of logical consistency. For common sense to be uncritically absorbed is for it to enter our consciousness uninterrogated. Part of the difficulty, then, in any attempt to critically absorb common sense—assuming one wanted to do so—might be that the very nature of common sense resists a critical view, which is, at base, an articulate, propositional understanding. For something to be coherent and voiced is for it to no longer be commonsensical.

A third characteristic of common sense is its adherence to the philosophy of what Gramsci calls "the masses of the people." There is a cycle in which common sense conforms to the conceptions of most everyone and in turn shapes taken-for-granted understanding. We all have a common sense, which we are shaped by and which in turn we collectively shape—commonsense conceptions can change. Gramsci says that the philosophy of common sense "is the 'philosophy of non-philosophers,'" or in other words the conception of the world that is un-critically absorbed by the various social and cultural environments in which the moral individuality of the average person is developed. One might aim to create spaces where either nonracist conceptions are uncritically absorbed or where common sense can be critically interrogated. As I discuss below, Hall argues that that common sense is the "terrain of conceptions and categories on which the practical consciousness of the masses the people is actually formed" ("Gramsci's Relevance" 431). For Gramsci, common sense is not a single unique conception, identical in time and space. It is "the 'folklore' of philosophy, and, like folklore, it takes countless different forms" (419). Common sense conforms to most people's basic understandings of their world—that's what it is for it to be commonsensi-cal—and also causes people's everyday, unconsidered conceptions.

It is important that common sense also includes aspects of what Gramsci calls "good sense"—the elements of our unconsidered assumptions that are "the healthy nucleus" of common sense "which deserves to be made more unitary and coherent" (328). Good sense is, in some way, the grounds from which common sense is changed. Common sense is not, in other words, simply a mass of undif-ferentiated "bad stuff." It contains, in some way, connections to what has come before us in whatever cultures we inhabit; we could use a genealogical method to get at the complexity and contradictoriness of that history. We build on the "fragmentary collection of ideas and opinions" (328) to create a conscious direc-tion in political activity and social change. This is one of the spaces where Gramsci argues we must maintain a link between formal, coherent philosophy—in the somewhat rarified sense he gives that term—and common sense. Where a com-mon sense conception has developed into a philosophy—as with the Catholic Church, in Gramsci's consideration—it always bear the risk of returning to an inchoate common sense. Insofar as good sense is held as common sense, Gramsci argues that it coincides with philosophical thought.

How might Gramsci's conception of common sense—in both its "good sense" formation and its reactionary or counterrevolutionary sense—be thought of as a kind of tacit, nonpropositional knowledge? Recall a first characteristic of common sense—that it is incoherent. For common sense to be incoherent indicates that it has not been formed into any kind of theoretical or propositional articulation. In the context of how common sense might evolve into a critical conception of reality, Gramsci writes, "The active man-in-the-mass has a practical activity, but has no clear theoretical consciousness of his practical activity, which nonetheless is an understanding of the world in so far as it transforms it. . . . One might almost say that he has two theoretical consciousnesses (or one contradictory conscious-ness): one which is implicit in his activity and which in reality unites him with all his fellow workers in the practical transformation of the real world; and one, superficially explicit or verbal, which he has inherited from the past and uncriti-cally absorbed. But this 'verbal' conception is not without consequences" (333). This quote is extremely evocative. It pulls up a number of interlinked strands of thinking around knowledge, understanding, activity, multiple consciousnesses, political action, history and memory, and the consequences of how we understand the world. The contrast Gramsci makes between implicit and explicit consciousness, between practical and theoretical activity, situates common sense as a kind of implicit understanding. The conception is only superficially "verbal"; it influences one in all sorts of wordless ways. Many of those influences are actually harmful; they prevent people from taking action and reduce them to a state of passivity. Contradictory consciousness is both practical activity (implicit) and inherited conception (superficially explicit but actually less than explicit). Both sides of that consciousness seem to be commonsense aspects of a person's being. For Gramsci common sense is both inchoate and inarticulate. It is not, however, *unarticulable*; Gramsci holds that what stands as common sense is at least potentially propositional.

I have talked about the sense in which common sense is taken to be discontinuous. It is important that common sense is not just muddled. Gramsci thinks common sense can become liberatory through being made articulate, continuous, where it had been unenunciated. He links common sense and folklore; his notion of folklore has been characterized as implicit, or nonpropositional. Alberto Maria Cirese writes, "the implicitness of the mode of expression, the unorganic character of combination, the fragmentation of internal organization, the passiveness of the conflict, the simplicity or elementariness of the intellectual category [confirms] the social class to which folklore belongs" (228). Folklore, like common sense (or, perhaps, common sense, like folklore) maintains an implicit mode of expression. It is as-yet inarticulate and nonverbal.

Gramsci argues that we always partake in some common sense, and that to investigate our unspoken conception of the world is to bring some of that conception to the foreground. Looking at common sense, in his words, "means therefore to make it a coherent unity . . . the starting point of critical elaboration is the consciousness of what one really is, and is 'knowing thyself' as a product of the historical process to date which has deposited in you an infinity of traces, without leaving an inventory" (324). "Making an inventory" articulates a process of forming both coherence and expressiveness out of uninterrogated assumptions. That a movement beyond common sense is, for Gramsci, significantly a movement into articulate, word-based, conception indicates that common sense is normally implicitly understood. And that the historical process results in a sedimented collection of an "infinity of traces" without leaving an account of those traces, "without leaving an inventory," indicates the implicit quality of commonsense (un)consciousness. And yet, as Gramsci indicates, what stands as common sense to us is deeply important to our lived experience.

One way the commonsensical is important to our experience is through its relation to ideology. For me, ideology is always situated in the context of relatively early work at the Birmingham Centre for Contemporary Cultural Studies (CCCS).

Arising out of Richard Hoggart's, Raymond Williams's, and E. P. Thompson's thinking about culture and class in the late 1950s and early 1960s, the CCCS developed, under Stuart Hall's directorship, into a institution very much influenced by Gramsci. The writing of this time at the CCCS is clearly related to a working through of Althusser's reading of Marx and Engels's *German Ideology*. In Stuart Hall's thinking, though, Gramsci becomes a fruitful thinker precisely in the places his notion of ideology differs from the later Althusser. Hall wants to retain a polyvalent voicing of ideology, and one that intrinsically holds contradiction and liberatory potential in its makeup.

Hall takes up Gramsci's thinking generally in much of his work and highlights a connection between racialized ideology, hegemony, and common sense. Hall argues that "'racism,' if not exclusively an ideological phenomenon, has critical ideological dimensions" ("Gramsci's Relevance" 439). Hall defines ideology as "the mental frameworks—the languages, the concepts, categories, imagery of thought, and the systems of representation—which different classes and social groups deploy in order to make sense of, define, figure out and render intelligible the way society works" ("Problem of Ideology" 26). Hall depicts the frameworks of ideology as inhering in a kind of practical, rather than simply theoretical, knowledge—a distinction that indicates a leaning, even at the ideological level, away from a primarily word-based understanding of the function of practical consciousness.

The ideological dimensions of race and ethnicity are, like everything ideological, always situated in webs of meaning and understanding; the discourse of race is historically moored in particular ways and takes meaning from the place it attaches and interweaves with broader social connotations and implications. Discourse, for Hall, refers to the way that ideology manifests in material ways; it is not only words, but a concrete realm of knowledges and effects. He is attempting to get at how particular ideas and concepts take hold of actual people and groups of people and produce "material forces" ("Problem of Ideology" 27, 41). Ideology is the field of struggle of an "infinity of subtle variations through which the elements of a discourse appear spontaneously to combine and recombine with each other, without material constraints of any kind other than that provided by the discursive operations themselves" ("Problem of Ideology" 41). This appearance of spontaneity happens in the context of a history that influences the lines along which ideology is likely to develop. The sedimentation of such lines, or fields, in Hall's terms, is the terrain of common sense; common sense, as practical thinking of the "masses of the people," in Gramsci's phrasing, bears on what is possible and likely in ideological and therefore hegemonic formations. Wahneema Lubiano gives a persuasive reading of some of these formations; I discuss her work below.

Hall argues that for Gramsci, common sense expresses the "terrain of conceptions and categories on which the practical consciousness of the masses of the people is actually formed. It is the already formed and 'taken-for-granted' terrain, on which more coherent ideologies and philosophies must contend for mastery" ("Gramsci's Relevance" 431). Common sense relates to ideology in the way that a grouping of children's building blocks—perhaps consisting of partially formed and also completed structures, random blocks, and so on—relates to a briefly reorganized and better-structured grouping. The materials remain the same, whether they are deployed in the current formation or left to the side, and they can be taken out of formation and reused in a kind of bricolage. At the same time, there will be formations that any builders using those particular materials are more comfortable creating—formations that accord with what has been made before, for example—what is understood to be possible. Such comfort will be the effect of particular ideologies.

For Hall, the self can be constructed through ideology's effects; the subjects of ideology are, then, contradictory pluralities. He argues that for Gramsci conscious-ness is multifaceted and collective. It is "a consequence of the relationship between 'the self' and the ideological discourses which compose the cultural terrain of society" ("Gramsci's Relevance" 433). In Gramsci's words, "The personality is strangely composite . . . [it contains] Stone Age elements and principles of a more advanced science, prejudices from all past phases of history . . . and intuitions of a future philosophy" ("Gramsci's Relevance" 440). If Hall is right about the connection between ideological formation and self-formation, the collective and social nature of ideological formation also contributes to a complex and "inter-discursive" manifestation of the self in an ideological field. Such a manifestation would also dialogically effect the interaction between the self and culture.

David Lionel Smith's discussion of common sense in relation to racial for-mation and culture is useful on this count. He writes, "Race is a commonsense notion. It falls apart under rational scrutiny, yet it is exceedingly difficult for us to attack" (182). More, commonsense notions of particular racialized identity, while demonstrably harmful in many ways, provide also a "sense of identity, community, and history" (182). This disjunctive and contradictory quality in part gives rise to the "self-vindicating character of common sense [which] gives notions like race a powerful durability." (182). Smith argues that because racial categories inform our consciousness, we cannot easily dismiss them. "The chal-lenge," he says, "is to understand what race is, how it functions, and ultimately to theorize how we might endeavor within a culture bound by race to subvert the subordinating strictures that race was designed to perpetuate" (181). These strictures are commonsense understandings of race; they twist, constrain, and prevent accounts of social and cultural expressions of race. How might these same implicit frameworks give rise to the potential for heterodox or resistant racial formations? Wahneema Lubiano's discussion of culture as the ground for contradictory, potentially liberatory, common sense is helpful here. Lubiano also helps to situate racialized common sense in terms of cultural production.

"Necessarily," writes Wahneema Lubiano, culture has been black people's "terrain of struggle" ("*Black Nationalism*" 233). Lubiano articulates a powerful conception of the movement of common sense through culture in ideologically inflected formations of race and ethnicity. Her use of the term mirrors a broad manifestation of the concept of common sense—both in the sense Lubiano uses it and in texts on race and ethnicity using Gramsci very explicitly. I want to discuss Lubiano first in order to fill out the relationship between culture and common sense and second in terms of the liberatory potential her work opens in relating to culture. Lubiano's oeuvre consistently and lucidly unpacks the cultural production of ideology; I offer, here, a very partial reading of her theoretical framework, offering my account of nonpropositional knowledge to her articulation of ideology and race, particularly in terms of commonsense formation.

In "Black Nationalism and Black Common Sense" Lubiano offers an example of ideological commonsense formation deployed on always already racialized grounds. She argues that black nationalism is a commonsense formation that describes a wide range of activities and articulations, manifesting a critique of the history and present racism of the U.S. state *and* a method for the state to enact, perpetuate, and extend its racist work. Both these functions, and many more, are predicated on the relation between ideology and common sense, as Gramsci uses those terms.

Lubiano claims that black nationalism functions as a narrative of the past; as an articulation of diverse presents; as an explanation of what is "good and beautiful, as style"; as a "rallying cry"; as "a critical analysis—and as an ongoing ever-renewed critique of black existence against white racial domination" ("*Black Nationalism*" 233). In such a manifestation, black nationalism can be seen to provide crucial grounds for liberatory work. It is, Lubiano argues, of "inestimable ideological—commonsensical—importance given the reality that U.S. blacks" control none of the standard markers of nationhood ("*Black Nationalism*" 233). This is why culture, and the common sense that arises out of culturally informed ideology, is the central terrain of struggle. Black nationalism is an example of contradictory common sense, where common sense is defined as "ideology lived and articulated in everyday understandings of the world and one's place in it" ("*Black Nationalism*" 232).

Lubiano sees liberatory potential in narratives of black nationalism; its "work as counter narrative is aestheticized in popular culture" ("*Black Nationalism*" 237). Narratives deploying tropes of black nationalism can turn against, and thereby shift, racist imaginings in fruitful ways; this kind of deployment can function as a defense. Among other things, black identity, for example, is a "sign for [black American] specificity and aestheticizing [black American] resistance to racist trauma" ("*Black Nationalism*" 238). Lubiano also explores, however, how black nationalism could also function "horribly, in 'new world order' terms" ("*Black Nationalism*" 238)—as a state-led mobilization of blackness for the state's "repressive work and its policing of civil society" ("*Black Nationalism*" 245). She highlights, here, the danger of commonsense conceptions: that they can and often do function as deeply conservative.

In discussing the possible virtues of the framework of "multiculturalism," another potentially heterodox racial formation, Lubiano is more specific about the potential dangers in naturalized narratives that benefit the state "to put it bluntly, Black people who consciously think of themselves as part of a Black group often think of themselves as oppositional at the very same time as they are internalizing precisely the state's most effective narratives, narratives that are the medium by which the state dominates the group in ways the group does not recognize" ("Like Being Mugged" 73). Such narratives manifest on the level of popular culture; they form a common sense that functions in the service of state interest—what Gramsci describes as its uncritical absorption and its resistance to critique.

Lubiano discusses a number of manifestations of common sense in popular culture, where culture stands as the grounds for common sense. She argues that media creations, taking film as an example, are always related to an economy of pleasure, politics, and policing, and centrally provide part of the ground on which common senses form. For Lubiano, what is commonsensical does not have to be articulated as, for example, the ideological assumptions tied to the discourse of "black nationalism" for the person who holds it as commonsensical. The common-sensical merely has to function relatively smoothly for that person. Such function-ing is supported by cultural artifacts that reinforce particular assumptions. This is one of the ways, in Lubiano's view, that ideological things stand as common sense. There is a recursive movement between artifacts, practices, and commonsense stances that stabilizes the illusory reality of race as an ideological formation.

Lubiano's concept of common sense thus relies explicitly on how she thinks about ideology; her understanding of the common sense of ideology contains a great deal of contradiction and possibility. This work is always happening in relation to the state; state power, writes Lubiano, does its work by virtue of its invisibility and because it is embedded in the public's understanding of every-day occurrences and beliefs. Photographs, and other salient narratives, are the means by which sense is made in and of the world; they also provide the means by which those who hold power (or influence the maintenance of power) make or attempt to make sense of the world for others. Such narratives are so natural-ized, so pushed by the momentum of their ubiquity, that they seem to be reality. That dynamic is the work of ideology ("Black Ladies" 329).

That is, we can think of ideology in a more or less constraining way, such that what is "given" to us in ideology is inescapable, dominating, and determining of our subject positions. The cartoon version of this notion of ideology takes us to be puppets of our particular, always ideological, social formation.

We can also, however, think of ideological formation as arising from a contra-dictory, multiply determined, shifting common sense—in Gramsci's terms—such that the "ingredients" for heterodox thinking are as present in the ideological soup as the elements making up orthodox social and subject formations. Lubiano is deploying something like the first sense when she writes "our imaginings are very much influenced by how the mechanisms of our daily lives are suggested, produced, maintained, or enforced by powerful state forces, or by powerful entities able to influence or direct the state" (*"Black Nationalism"* 235). She draws on a layered and contradictory notion of common sense and ideology when she writes "Black nationalism is a constantly reinvented and reinventing discourse that generally opposes the Eurocentricism of the U.S. state, but neither historically nor contemporaneously depends upon a consistent or complete opposition to Eurocentrism" (*"Black Nationalism"* 234). This dual sense of ideology as it manifests in common sense is fruitful for Lubiano; it allows her to acknowledge the power of state deployment and use of racist educational systems, for example, while allowing for those systems not always successfully interpellating their subjects. Lubiano effects a powerful, Gramscian reading of both ideology and common sense.

Lubiano's work gives a useful example of how one might situate lived ideology in the realm of the cultural. Much of the terrain of common sense is given to us in the cultural forms of which we partake; the movies, magazines, and pop music we see, read, and hear inform our understanding of the world on deep levels. The "message" of any given movie is, as Lubiano explicates, part of a larger "message"—an ideological formation that rests on harmful commonsense understandings of black masculinity. Lubiano links such a formation to the U.S. state's interest in retaining particular racial and familial orthodoxies. She frames this in *"Jeopardy* quiz-show style": "Answer: the romanticized black patriarchal family and its disciplinary possibilities. Question: what is one way that the state can mobilize blackness to do its repressive work and its policing of civil society?" (*"Black Nationalism"* 245).

For Lubiano, the significance of racialized, and racist, understanding being commonsensical is that it becomes unassailable. Smith has explored some of the mechanisms of this sort of invincibility in the creation of racist common sense. Entertainment fills in critical inquiry and renders much of the discomfort the viewer should arguably experience as speculative pleasure. When a movie or a song functions in the way Lubiano lays out, it both draws upon and creates a set of unarticulated assumptions required to participate in the viewing or hearing. In such a context, it is fruitful to think of what stands as common sense to us in terms of its tacit, implicit, or unspoken character.

But how might understanding common sense as nonpropositional—as significant to the unarticulated assumptions Lubiano explores—get us anywhere in thinking about "race"? I think it opens at least three avenues. First, it addresses the scare quotes Paul Gilroy, for one, puts around the term "race." There is a distance imposed between the reader or hearer and the term in the act of quotation that relies on particular common senses; the mechanism of quotation functions as a trope to both call up and reject stabilizations of race. That trope needs an understanding to swerve toward and pushes against a network of assumptions and profoundly unacknowledged (and unknown) understandings. Naming race calcifies the terms of common sense, at least momentarily. It is possible to understand "race," within quotation marks, as both materially real—having actual, measurable effects on lives—and as not "there"—as a fiction that exists only in particular social spaces, but through which material effects are realized. How does "that long lived trope" (Gilroy, *Against Race*, 48) maintain coherence in the face of the deep obsolescence of phenotypic typing? In part through the shallow, superficial, great power of unspoken commonsense understandings of what race is. So I would argue that having an articulation of race as implicit knowledge helps to describe the mechanism of "race" in its continued creation and development in this world.

Second, thinking through racial formation, in Omi and Winant's sense, as partially nonpropositional provides an account of how consent to hegemonic reproduction of racism is itself materially but not necessarily discursively reproduced. That is, if such an account can be said to help to descriptively give a narrative of the ingredients of racial formation and racism, it is also useful in unpacking the methods by which those ingredients are promulgated. I have not discussed the transmission of common sense from one person to another, or through culture; I agree with Gramsci (and, to some extent, with Althusser) that much of that transmission happens in the realm of the state-modulated social—in churches and schools, among other places. But the content of that transmission, even in the text-based moments of those spaces, is not limited to a particular text. Rather, it inheres in the structures and in the interstices, in the explicit and in the implicit; the nonpropositional helps me think about "where" some of the most difficult racism "lives," when it is not visible in the world. That inexplicit manifestation is one of the markers of "difficult." A conception that includes the implicit contents of racial formation is a more complete conception than one based on mostly propositional formulations. One need not agree with Gramsci that the only use of common sense is in its resolution into coherence, and a philosophy. In some way, I want to retain the argument he gives for common sense's qualities without reproducing his particular teleology for that conception. His argument for what common sense would have to do in order to be an effective political philosophy clearly elucidates its nature as not primarily propositional. It is important, though, that common sense, as an always socially inflected necessary ingredient in understanding one's world, might usefully retain some of the very incoherence and inconsistency that also causes it to be problematic.

Third, then, it seems to me that understanding racial common sense in terms of nonpropositional understanding provides openings for changing that understanding in liberatory ways. Perhaps the fact that there are different senses of the common—different frameworks of nonpropositional understanding, different situated knowledges, different embodiednesses, and so on—is precisely the potential of common sense. That inchoateness, which can never be whole *even if* that is its aim, shows what it is to be ruptured and what it is to require liberatory rupture. And part of common sense is the kernels of good sense—the useful aspects of one's assumptions that Gramsci argues should be rendered more coherent. Further, if the nonpropositional is what changes in a move from racist understanding of the world to a less, or non-, racist stance, we need to have access to how to actively change that understanding. We need, at least, to be able to address the inarticulate but effective ways that ideology might be structured. Lubiano's work on this front is exemplary. Charles Mills likewise addresses this need: "perhaps even more important than ideologies at the explicit and articulated level (for example, libertarianism, biological determinism) are ideologies in the more primeval sense of underlying patterns and matrices of belief, or ideology as 'common sense' . . . the latter may well be more influential and efficacious than the former simply by virtue of their ability to set the terms of the debate, to limit the options deemed worthy of consideration" (Mills, *Blackness Visible,* 34). It is critical to think of commonsense understandings of race and ethnicity in terms of how tacit, nonpropositional knowledge informs those understandings. If propositionality is the only option deemed worthy of consideration in thinking about race and ethnicity, deeply significant aspects of people's experience, potentially liberatory spaces, and key parts of racial formation are passed over in silence.

Note

1. This phrasing is Wahneema Lubiano's, in conversation.

Works Cited

Althusser, Louis. *For Marx,* translated by Ben Brewster. New York: Pantheon Books, 1969.

Audi, Robert. *Epistemology: A Contemporary Introduction to the Theory of Knowledge.* Routledge Contemporary Introductions to Philosophy. Vol. 2. New York: Routledge, 1998.

Babbitt, Susan. *Impossible Dreams: Rationality, Integrity, and Moral Imagination.* Boulder, Colo.: Westview Press, 1996.

Cirese, Alberto Maria. "Gramsci's Observations on Folklore." Pp. 212–47 in *Approaches to Gramsci,* edited by Anne Showstack. London: Writers and Readers, 1982.

Du Bois, W. E. B. *Dusk of Dawn: An Essay toward an Autobiography of a Race Concept.* 1940. New Brunswick, N.J.: Transaction, 1995.

Gilroy, Paul. *Against Race: Imagining Political Culture beyond the Color Line.* Cambridge, Mass.: Harvard University Press, 2000.

Gordon, Avery, and Christopher Newfield. *Mapping Multiculturalism.* Minneapolis: University of Minnesota Press, 1996.

Gramsci, Antonio. *Prison Notebooks.* European Perspectives Series. New York: Columbia University Press, 1992.

Hall, Stuart. "Gramsci's Relevance for the Study of Race and Ethnicity." Pp. 411–40 in *Stuart Hall: Critical Dialogues in Cultural Studies,* edited by David Morley and Kuan-Hsing Chen. New York: Routledge, 1996.

———. "The Problem of Ideology: Marxism without Guarantees." Pp. 25–46 in *Stuart Hall: Critical Dialogues in Cultural Studies,* edited by David Morley and Kuan-Hsing Chen. New York: Routledge, 1996.

———. "Signification, Representation, Ideology: Althusser and the Post-Structuralist Debates." Pp. 88–113 in *Critical Perspectives on Media and Society,* edited by Robert K. Avery and David Eason. New York: Guilford Press, 1991.

Harris, David. *From Class Struggle to the Politics of Pleasure: The Effects of Gramscianism on Cultural Studies.* New York: Routledge, 1992.

Lubiano, Wahneema. "Black Ladies, Welfare, and State Minstrels: Ideological War by Narrative Means." Pp. 323–61 in *Race-ing Justice, En-Gendering Power: Essays on Anita Hill, Clarence Thomas, and the Construction of Social Reality,* edited by Toni Morrison. New York: Pantheon Books, 1992.

———. "Black Nationalism and Black Common Sense: Policing Ourselves and Others." Pp. 232–52 in *The House That Race Built: Black Americans, U.S. Terrain,* edited by Wahneema Lubiano. New York: Pantheon Books, 1997.

———. "Don't Talk with Your Eyes Closed/Caught in the Hollywood Gun Sights." Pp. 68–77 in *Borders, Boundaries, and Frames: Cultural Criticism and Cultural Studies,* edited by Mae Henderson. Essays from the English Institute. New York: Routledge, 1995.

———. "If I Could Talk about It, This Is Not What I Would Say." *assemblage* 20. Special issue on violence/space (1994): 56–57.

———. "Like Being Mugged by a Metaphor: Multiculturalism and State Narratives." Pp. 64–75 in *Mapping Multiculturalism,* edited by Avery Gordon and Christopher Newfield. Minneapolis: University of Minnesota Press, 1996.

———. "Shuckin' Off the African-American Native Other: What's Po-Mo Got to Do with It?" *Cultural Critique* 18 (1991): 149–86.

———, ed. *The House That Race Built: Black Americans, U.S. Terrain.* New York: Pantheon Books, 1997.

Mills, Charles. *Blackness Visible.* Ithaca, N.Y.: Cornell University Press, 1998.

Morrison, Toni. *Playing in the Dark: Whiteness and the Literary Imagination.* Cambridge, Mass.: Harvard University Press, 1992.

———. "Unspeakable Things Unspoken: The Afro-American Presence in American Literature." *Michigan Quarterly Review* 28, no. 1 (Winter 1989): 1–34.

———, ed. *Race-ing Justice, En-Gendering Power: Essays on Anita Hill, Clarence Thomas, and the Construction of Social Reality.* New York: Pantheon Books, 1992.

Omi, Michael, and Howard Winant. *Racial Formation in the United States.* New York: Routledge, 1994.

Piper, Adrian. *Out of Order, Out of Sight.* Vol. 1. Cambridge, Mass.: MIT Press, 1996.

Ryle, Gilbert. *Aspects of Mind.* Oxford: Blackwell Press, 1993.

Smith, David Lionel. "What Is Black Culture?" Pp. 178–94 in *The House That Race Built: Black Americans, U.S. Terrain,* edited by Wahneema Lubiano. New York: Pantheon Books, 1997.

Williams, Raymond. *Marxism and Literature.* Oxford, Eng.: Oxford University Press, 1977.

CHAPTER 3

Supreme Rhetoric: The Supreme Court, Veiled Majoritarianism, and the Enforcement of the Racial Contract

Matthew Abraham

The statement that "law is politics by other means" takes special prominence in analyzing the function of the U.S. Supreme Court in its adjudicatory role as a supposedly countermajoritarian-acting body. Countermajoritarianism refers to the ability of an institution to countermand or act against the predilections of a majority culture, particularly in an effort to protect minority interests. In his *Democracy and Distrust,* John Ely claims that "no matter how open the process, those with most of the votes are in a position to vote themselves advantages at the expense of the others, or otherwise to refuse to take their interests into account" (135). Ely's observation resonates particularly well with the history of the racially divided electorate in the United States, a history that suggests the necessity of countermajoritarian-acting institutions such as the Supreme Court.

The U.S. Supreme Court has always held a paradoxical relationship with racial minorities. On the one hand, the Supreme Court is charged with protecting vulnerable minorities under the *Marbury v. Madison* decision of 1803, which defined a countermajoritarian function for the Court. Countermajoritarianism gives Supreme Court justices the latitude—through life tenure and salary protection—to rule against majority interests if the advancement of such interests hurts "discrete and insular" minorities. On the other hand, the Court has become utterly incapable of living up to its countermajoritarian mandate because of its structural dimensions, which will be examined in the course of this article.

One cannot ignore the socialization process Supreme Court justices go through prior to hearing their first case. Regardless of who you are, the legal training you must endure to climb the ladder of legal success will normalize you within very strict parameters and condition you ideologically to serve majoritarian interests. Legal education itself, as Duncan Kennedy eloquently states in his "Legal Education As Training for Hierarchy," mirrors the social relationships one finds within society at large, with ethnic minorities being as marginalized within the law school framework as they are within the context of other mainstream cultural institutions. In the end, for Kennedy, "legal education is preparation for the hierarchy of the corporate welfare state" (4). The hierarchy of the corporate welfare state finds no greater defender than in the structure of the U.S. Supreme Court, which positions its justices as "guardians of the state religion." Typically, a Supreme Court justice is a federal judge before being selected as a nominee for the Court. One should not forget that Supreme Court justices are chosen by a majoritarian-elected president and then confirmed by a majoritarian-representing Senate. These two crucial majoritarian interventions in the selection of an agent for service within a countermajoritarian institution should give one pause for concern.

If one factors in the socialization process of the law school experience, with the licensing procedures one must endure to gain entrance to the bar, along with clerkships and tenure as a federal judge, and finally the selection and confirmation process through majoritarian-crafted institutions, Supreme Court justices will undoubtedly be the most majoritarian-serving agents imaginable. As Jesse Jackson once quipped, "A Clarence Thomas on the Supreme Court is no different than a Tom Delay in blackface!" These observations lead me to one crucial question: Is the countermajoritarian capacity of the U.S. Supreme Court highly inflated and perhaps ultimately a fiction in the context of American race relations? Is the U.S. Supreme Court—as a sociological fact—incapable of protecting minority interests against the tyranny of the majority?

The U.S. Supreme Court, despite possessing the potential for exercising countermajoritarian discretion—in the protection of minority interests—actually ensures the continual practice of what legal scholars call veiled majoritarianism. Veiled majoritarianism is a phrase that attempts to capture what legal scholars characterize as the promotion of majority interests through supposedly neutral legal principles, principles that—while ostensibly promoting the goal of protecting vulnerable minorities against the "will of the majority"—give Supreme Court justices the discretion to inscribe their socialized belief systems into the law, all the while passing off such inscriptions as objective adjudication.

In his *Trouble with Principle,* Stanley Fish claims that principles—in the end—are insidious because their underlying content will always be filled and governed through someone's partisan point of view. The possibility of principle—or of principled thinking—presents one with an illusory standpoint, a standpoint that is miraculously outside the political and material constraints that always govern material scarcity in a world of special interests. For Fish, such a standpoint simply does not exist; you believe what you believe because your "beliefs and assumptions" are all you have. Expressing a concern for the impossibility of judges actually escaping their belief systems—through legal principle—which the countermajoritarian function requires, Girardeau Spann writes, "the result produced by legal principle reflects little more than the point at which the Court chooses to end the analytical process—a process that can in theory continue indefinitely, producing first one result then another. Rather than serving a constraining function, legal principles ironically end up increasing the court's dependence on majoritarian-influenced discretion, minimizing only the degree to which the impact of such majoritarian influence is likely to be detected" (Spann 81). The promise of principled adjudication, along with the protections of life tenure and lifetime salaries for its nine justices, allows the Supreme Court to position itself as an institution sheltered from the coercive political forces of majoritarian politics. Undoubtedly, a mythos has been created around the Court, casting it as the great protector of the "unheard and the unseen" because of the supposed principled approach it brings to the assessment of competing group claims for valuable societal resources. In an attempt to illustrate the difficulties that those expressing countermajoritarian sentiments encounter within the American legal structure, I will draw upon a personal account.

In the fall of 1996, I was a first-year law student at the University of Arkansas at Little Rock School of Law, sitting in an introductory torts class where the professor was trying to introduce the concept of the reasonable person to approximately one hundred students. In an attempt to elicit the class's participation, the professor asked his students to give him some examples of individuals who exemplified the reasonable person. Names such as "Tom Brokaw" and "Mike Brady" and "Ward Cleaver" were quickly offered to the professor as clear and undeniable examples of reasonableness. Feeling a little mischievous, I raised my hand and offered up the example of "Bill Cosby" as a reasonable person. After a brief period of silence, I noticed several looks of dismay, as I had apparently transgressed some sacred discursive realm in suggesting that a nonwhite person could somehow be the epitome of reasonableness within the law. I would soon come to learn that there were many such sacred discursive realms. Behind me I heard someone exclaim, "Why didn't he just say Juan Diego," an obvious misreading of my own Asian-Indian ethnicity as Hispanic, signifying a parodic contempt for my class participation on this matter of the reasonable person. I also heard someone say, just above a whisper, "What did that boy learn in school?" After class, I was approached by one of my classmates, who wryly asked, "What socialist undergraduate institution did you attend, anyway?"

In his *Legal Education and the Reproduction of Hierarchy,* Duncan Kennedy writes

> while students quickly understand that there is diversity among their fellow students and that the faculty is not really homogeneous in terms of character, background or opinions, the classroom itself becomes more rather than less uniform as legal education progresses. You'll find Fred Astaire and Howard Cosell, over and over again, but never Richard Pryor and Betty Friedan. It's not that the teacher punishes you if you use slang or wear clothes or give examples or voice opinions that identify you as different, though that *might* happen. You are likely to be sanctioned, mildly or severely, only if you refuse to adopt the highly

cognitive, dominating mode of discourse that everyone identifies as lawyerlike. Nonetheless, the indirect pressure for conformity is intense. (63)

Ethnic minority law students face particular psychological hurdles within the law school setting, often facing the contradictory and tension-ridden dilemma: becoming an actor with a legal system that has played an instrumental role in oppressing people of color in the United States:

> Black students learn without surprise that the bar will have its own peculiar form of racism, and that their very presence means affirmative action, unless it means "he could have made it without affirmative action." They wonder about forms of bias so diabolical even they can't see them, and whether legal reasoning is intrinsically white. Meanwhile, dozens of small changes through which they become more and more like other middle or upper middle class Americans engender rhetoric about how the black community is not divided along class lines. On one level, all of this is about how to make partner. (66)

Legal education does not invite a critical interrogation of the premises under-girding legal rules and structures. Such interrogations, in fact, place a student at some risk because he or she becomes caught up in challenging the very founda-tions through which the legal system has evolved. For example, a student asking whether legal rules have their basis in class and race domination would be deemed illegitimate because students are asked to "work" with the system as it exists and not to challenge the warrants that are a central part of legal syllogisms: "It would take an extraordinary first year student who could, on his or her own, develop a theoretically critical attitude toward this system. Entering students just don't know enough to figure out where the teacher is fudging, misrepresenting and otherwise distorting legal thinking and legal reality" (12).

I draw upon this anecdotal evidence and Kennedy's observations for three compelling reasons. First, they illustrate the inability of many to view nonwhites within the logical economy of the law as anything but subpersons, particularly when nonwhites are placed in the position of conceptual ideal, as my Bill Cosby example shows. Second, they show the difficulty that "unconventional thinking" or "left thinking" encounters in legal arenas. Third, as Kennedy argues, legal edu-cation promotes the unavoidable belief in legal hierarchy because "it supports hierarchy by analogy, provides it a general legitimating ideology by justifying the rules that underlie it, and provides it a particular ideology by mystifying legal reasoning" (71).

The reasonable person, in the logical economy I've outlined, is a normative concept in that it isolates a particular subjective position as ideal, deploying this position as rational, reliable, and most important as possessing the capacity to make a legitimate material inscription within legal discourse. By "legitimate material inscription," I mean a meaningful, discursively recognized utterance that carries the force of law with it. In other words, it's that "which counts." My second reason for using my law school experience as a point of departure for my essay is that it highlights the psychological resistances that assertions of person-hood by nonwhites encounter in institutional settings.

In *Becoming Gentlemen: Women, Law School, and Institutional Change,* Lani Guinier, Michelle Fine, and Jane Balin conducted an empirical study showing that women and minority law students face an often psychologically debilitating law-school experience because they must contend with an environment and a discourse that has historically excluded the representation of their experiences. At this point, I should point out that in the course of my attempt to problematize the notion of the reasonable person in my torts class, I—after offering up Bill Cosby as the possibly prototypical reasonable person—pointed out to my classmates that all the individuals we had named were male. My pointing out of this glaring partiality drew some supportive although hidden smiles from my female col-leagues in the class, who were careful to not let their support of my overall point be too visible. In some sense, I'm sure they felt glad that I was the one "taking the fall" on this point rather than they. At one time, the term "reasonable man" circulated in legal discourse as the operative term before being replaced by the "reasonable person."

The concept of the reasonable person plays a prominent part in American jurisprudence. It is a concept that underpins contract law, tort law, property law, and civil procedure. In contract law, for example, the reasonable person provides a safeguard against the creation of illegitimate contracts. A contract ("a bargain for exchange") is formed between two individuals if an offer is made by *party A (the promissor)* to *party B (the promissee)*, if there is something called consideration (usually money) put forward by the promissee that designates a willingness to contract, and finally if an acceptance of the offer is given by the promissee to the promissor. Under the objective theory of contracts, however, the contract is legitimate if and only if the offer could be construed as a legitimate offer from the standpoint of a reasonable person— that is, the promissee—hearing the offer being made. For example, one could view the Hobbesian social contract through this legal paradigm with citizens subjecting themselves to the dictates of the state in exchange for its protection, with the suspension of a citizen's unbridled freedom acting as consideration. If we submit, however, what Charles Mills has come to call the racial contract ("a moral and epistemological contract") to a similar analysis, we come up against several problems. David Theo Goldberg, in his *Racial State,* highlights some of these problems with the racial contract, suggesting that the social contract *qua* social contract racialized the state's condi-tions of possibility more than Mills admits. Goldberg contends that a distinction between the social contract and the racial contract does not necessarily have to be drawn.

Goldberg argues that state theory—in conjunction with various strains of critical race theory—provides a more accurate assessment of the rise of raciality in the context of political and social thought than either state theory or critical race theory can provide on its own. Goldberg examines the centrality of race and the role that race plays in constituting the state. State theory interrogates the particular technologies and discursive objects states mark as relevant to organizing a population into discrete quantities of knowledge, that is, census figures, demographic data, and so on.

By extending Goldberg's analyses to the concept known as "veiled majoritarianism" as developed in the context of Girardeau Spann's *Race against the Court,* one can ultimately prove Mills correct in his description of the racial contract as a moral and exploitative contract that arises out of the logic of the social contract, requiring the separation that Goldberg contests. Mills's description needs a greater elaboration of the hegemonic operation of legal discourse, particularly as this discourse supports the perpetuation of white interests through veiled majoritarianism as propounded by the U.S. Supreme Court.

Veiled majoritarianism, as mentioned at the beginning of this article, is a phrase that describes the advancement of majority interests through countermajoritarian institutions such as the U.S. Supreme Court, which theoretically possesses the capacity to countermand the predatory tendencies of a majority culture. According to Spann, the U.S. Supreme Court has set in place three key assumptions about itself, about the fundamental right of due process, and about racial minorities' access to this fundamental right of due process. These assumptions are (1) the Supreme Court has established a set of fundamental rights upon which the government cannot encroach; (2) the Supreme Court is the expositor and final arbiter of the scope of these rights; (3) racial minorities can appeal only to the Supreme Court for the protection of these rights (Spann 31).

Because the Supreme Court is a veiled majoritarian institution—with the theoretical potential to protect minority interests but in actuality completely lacking such power to do so—racial minorities frequently are sacrificed at the intersection of what Derrick Bell calls the convergence interest. Briefly put, the convergence interest thesis states that the interests of racial minorities will be advanced if and only if such advancement guarantees the parallel advancement of white majority interests. For example, Bell has been a fierce critic of the *Brown* decision of 1954, claiming that—because of the ideological battle the United States was fighting against Communism in the Third World; because of the economic toll segregation was taking upon the South with the necessity of "separate but equal facilities"; and because of the return of disillusioned black World War II veterans to a segregated nation, a nation they had defended—the *Brown* decision should be viewed as advancing state (white) interests and not as a reflection of some commitment to the principle of racial equality.

Goldberg's fusion of state theory and critical race theory allows one to highlight the particularly entrenched and pervasive aspects of racial thinking in the advancement of a state's discursive scope. Girardeau Spann's understanding of veiled majoritarianism demonstrates the continued prominence such conceptualizations occupy in the context of judicial adjudication, which often is able to disguise the advancement of majority interests under the highly principled language of liberalism and the supposedly rule-governed structures of legal interpretation. If we bring together the very important observations of these two theorists, attempting to facilitate greater reflection on the dependency of the state on racialized thinking for the creation of its own governing conditions of possibility, Mills's description and development of the racial contract becomes a crucial component in understanding the discursive operations of contemporary social and political institutions such as the U.S. Supreme Court.

Veiled majoritarianism performs a clear instrumental role in the enforcement of the racial contract insofar as veiled majoritarianism allows for the maintenance of white supremacy within the supposed objective structural dimensions of American law, particularly when the Supreme Court—as the putative upholder of minority interests—postures as a countermajoritarian institution. In some sense, the legal structure mystifies the operation of veiled majoritarianism through the use of rule-governed or principled decision making. In *The Racial Contract*, Mills writes that "the Racial Contract continues to manifest itself, of course, in unofficial local agreements of various kinds (restrictive covenants, employment discrimination contracts, political decisions about resource allocation, etc.)" (73). Veiled majoritarianism can be read as one such manifestation or symptom of such unofficial agreements; however, it is more insidious in its scope and character because it is practiced by a purportedly countermajoritarian institution. More important, Mills writes that "even apart from these, a crucial manifestation is simply the failure to ask certain questions, taking for granted as a status quo and baseline the existing color-coded configurations of wealth, poverty, property, and opportunities, the pretence that formal, juridical equality is sufficient to remedy inequities created on a foundation of several hundred years of racial privilege, and that challenging that foundation is a transgression of the terms of the social contract" (74).

Just as the racial restrictive covenant and the job discrimination contract—as continuing manifestations of the racial contract are harder to prove than more overt forms of discrimination—veiled majoritarianism arises from complex socialization processes that ideologically condition legal actors in quite specific ways and from the structural dimensions of legal thought, which is a superstructural reflection of the economic base. Veiled majoritarianism is a complex effect of this socialization process and reifies structural dimensions and commitments of capitalism in and through legal thought. How can we make veiled majoritarianism "speak" more plainly? I suggest that a first step should be a return to Mills's racial contract and to an alternate characterization of its operation.

In the racial contract, we can imagine a circulating economy of persons ("white signatories") and subpersons ("nonwhite, nonsignatories") being brought together in a quasi contract (an implied contract) of immense and unrecognized dimensions. If we draw upon Laclau and Mouffe's definition of hegemony—as elaborated in their *Hegemony and Socialist Strategy*—"as a metonymic relation," with a part standing for the whole, we can view the structural pervasiveness of the racial contract within the context of our contemporary legal institutions. Although often unrecognized, our political relationships are defined through synecdoche—a kind of metonymy—where phrases such as "all men are created equal" or "all citizens of the United States will be granted equal protection under the law and due process" depend upon very specific historically defined legal descriptions transcending the constraints of an era and assuming the shape of a larger ideal that applies to everyone.

For example, the phrase "all men are created equal" was originally crafted to refer to white, landowning men in the United States, whereas the equal protection and due process clauses of the Fourteenth Amendment were specifically meant to protect the rights of black citizens, particularly after belligerent southern whites refused to acknowledge the Fourteenth Amendment's purported aim: making former black slaves U.S. citizens after the abolition of slavery. Now, however, these often-invoked phrases refer to all American citizens; stripped of their historical context, these phrases define our contemporary political and legal debates.

Whites now regularly invoke the equal protection and due process clauses of the Fourteenth Amendment—attempting to protest a perceived "deprivation" of medical and law school positions that are supposedly "given" to racial minorities because of affirmative action—as protection for one of liberalism's most cherished principles: color-blind evaluation. In addition, those seeking these Fourteenth Amendment protections against racial minority transgressions upon previously all-white "ground" demand the highest level of review: strict scrutiny.

The strict scrutiny doctrine was developed in the context of *Korematsu v. the United States* (1944) which legalized the internment of Japanese Americans during World War II. This doctrine requires the Supreme Court to subject suspect racial classifications that are defined by the state to the highest level of judicial review. Now, whites—as whites—are asking for this level of judicial review to protect what Cheryl Harris has called their "property interest in whiteness" (1713). The legal decisions rationalizing facile invocations of the Fourteenth Amendment by whites as whites—particularly the 1996 *Hopwood* case—represent attempts to contest the legitimacy of affirmative action and can be read as allegories of anxiety.

In describing legal texts as possibly being allegories of anxiety, I am relying upon definitions of allegory that suggest that texts assume meanings far different from their literal suggestiveness and assume a perverse figural capacity, spinning out meanings far beyond the control of writers and readers and assuming an unexpected significance, ultimately parodying themselves. For example, legal decisions that delineated—through statutes—prohibitions against marriage between blacks and whites in the United States are allegories of cultural anxiety about miscegenation in general and an expression of psychosexual fear, in particular on the part of white males, that white women would be attracted to and would procreate with black males. The widely prevalent "one-drop rule" of the first half of the twentieth century can also be read as an allegory of anxiety.

In his *Allegories of Reading,* drawing upon Rousseau's *Discourse on Inequality,* Paul de Man claims that conceptual language—the basis of civil society—is a lie founded upon an error. Indeed, legal discourse depends upon conceptual language to legitimate social relationships that have no real existence outside a state organizing principle. In his *Essence of Christianity,* Ludwig Feuerbach writes that "every limitation of the reason, or in general of the nature of man, rests on a delusion, an error" (7). We can extend these insights to legal mystification. In the same way that religious faith allows for a mystification of the "mental wilderness beyond reason," shibboleths such as principle and rule-governed decision making prevent an interrogation of the interstice of the rules themselves wherein judges exercise a wide degree of subjective discretion that plays a crucial role in promoting majoritarian preferences, particularly when these majoritarian preferences deal with issues of race. Drawing upon the insights of Émile Durkheim, Mary Douglas claims that "the elementary social bond is only formed when individuals entrench in their minds a model of the social order" and that "for a convention to turn into a legitimate social institution it needs a parallel cognitive convention to sustain it" (45). Mills's description of the racial contract can be used as a heuristic to more fully understand the pernicious operation of veiled majoritarianism as a structural convention and as a socialized preference of the U.S. legal system.

Mills's racial contract captures the hegemonic logic of the social contract by identifying the way in which the moral operator ("citizen" or "person") is simply extended to a former subperson population without recognizing that the extension itself acts only symbolically. If we accept Laclau and Mouffe's suggestion that every hegemonic relation ("the transformation of difference into conceptual sameness") is a metonymic relation ("part for the whole") (7), then we should easily be able to identify the hegemonic operation of the social contract as it applies to nonwhites because of their exclusion—as initial signatories—of this contract. The extension of the moral operator supposedly makes up for and hides this initial exclusion. Douglas claims that "there needs to be an analogy by which the formal structure of a crucial set of social relations is found in the physical world, or in the supernatural world, or in eternity, anywhere, so long as it is not seen as a socially contrived arrangement" (48). By drawing an analogy between the "freedom to contract" and the coerced acceptance of social demands placed upon citizens of a state—while making this coerced acceptance appear as a choice—the terms of the social contract become the key aspects of a hegemonic relation. In his "Politics of Rhetoric," Laclau writes: "What is constitutive of a hegemonic relation is that its component elements and dimensions are articulated by contingent links" (237). The logic of the social contract, along with the logic of capital, permeates the interstices of the social fabric. Douglas points out that "when [an] analogy is applied back and forth from one set of social relations to another and from these back to nature, its recurring formal structure becomes easily recognized and endowed with self-validating truth" (48). What does the apparent self-validating truth of the social contract mean for the covert racial contract?

I would like to suggest that legal mystification—as it is disseminated through legal texts—succeeds in masking the terms of the racial contract so successfully that the unveiling of these terms is tantamount to the Nietzschean declaration of the death of God. Although I don't want to draw the neat parallel between Mills and Nietzsche as "transvaluators of all values," I do want to quibble with Goldberg's claim that Mills is not the first to make connections between state formation and racial subjugation and that Bracken, Popkin, West, and Goldberg made such claims long before.

The brilliance of Mills's descriptions of the racial contract resides precisely in its identification of the mystified aspects of the racial contract and the very direct role that morality, epistemology, and legality play in generating the mystificatory terms of that contract. If Nietzsche confronted us with cognition (knowing) as the real problem of man, then Mills seems to confront us with the fact that the concept of contract itself is racialized through and through. If we rely upon Nietzsche's descriptions of morality and immorality arising within the context of the creditor-debtor relationship, would it be all that far-fetched to understand Mills's racial contract as a rationalization of black exploitation—in conjunction with the development of capitalism—through the concept of contract itself?

We seem to beg the question when we seek to understand the rise of the state through racialization. Instead, we should view the rise of race as that upon which the state explicitly relied to make moral, epistemological, and legal claims about the natural inevitability of the freedom to contract. By working backward (from raciality to the state and then through to contract rather than from contract to raciality and then through to the state), we can more accurately assess the position that a legal concept such as countermajoritarianism—as a superstructural myth—occupies in the mystification of veiled majoritarianism.

Legal mystification proceeds through the promotion of ideology, which can be viewed as a "universalization of group interests" and through the work of ideologists who are better known as judges. Duncan Kennedy, in his *Critique of Adjudication,* writes, "One is an ideologist because one has made a commitment to working within a complex body of texts, a discourse, and accepted the blinders and limitations that inevitably go along with the advantages of such a commitment, and because the commitment to the texts goes along with, and sometimes conflicts with, a commitment to a group or groups in conflict with others" (42). Although no judge conceptualizes himself or herself as an apologist for bourgeois domination, the infrastructural gaps within legal rules allow for the exertion and expression of individual wills, desires, and experiences. The projection of the illusion of legal objectivity cloaks these insertions of individual "wills to power," subjecting the supposedly objective legal rule—bound by supposedly rule-governed constraints—to the interpretative whims of a judge:

> In all the Western systems, the discourse that judges, legal authorities, and political theorists use to legitimate the application of state power denies (suppresses, mystifies, distorts, conceals, evades) two key phenomena: (a) the degree to which the settled rules (whether contained in a Code or in common law) structure public and private life so as to empower some groups at the expense of others, and in general function to reproduce the systems of hierarchy that characterize the society in question; (b) the degree to which the system of legal rules contains gaps, conflicts, and ambiguities that get resolved by judges pursuing conscious, half-conscious, or unconscious ideological projects with respect to these issues of hierarchy. (*Critique of Adjudication* 14)

The enforcement of the racial contract requires the constant ideological conditioning of its signatories, its nonsignatories, and the legal actors who enforce its terms. Veiled majoritarianism, as a mystified rationalization of the perpetuation of white privilege that is advanced through the preferences of judges—in and through legal rules that contain gaps, conflicts, and ambiguities—emerges as the very background conditions of racial contractibility itself. It's just this sort of radical reappropriation of legal concepts that must occur (which will certainly turn the legal profession on its head) if we are to come to grips with the deep structural and sociological problems of contemporary legal structures, many of which are attributable to unconscious racial animus, perverse expressions of agnate love, and manifestations of a dysfunctional surrender to a single group's will-to-power. For that reason, racial minorities should stop turning to the Supreme Court for the protection of their interests and should instead focus upon what Girardeau Spann calls "pure politics."

The Supreme Court sends a clear message to racial minorities in the United States: Play pure politics! Pure politics can be played only in clearly majoritarian institutions such as the U.S. Congress and at the level of the state legislature. The Supreme Court is more dependent on racial minorities for its *raison d'être*—from the standpoint of judicial review—than racial minorities are on it.

Works Cited

Bell, Derrick. "*Brown v. Board of Education* and the Interest Convergence Dilemma." In *Critical Race Theory: The Key Writings That Formed the Movement,* edited by Kimberlé Crenshaw, Neil Gotanda, Gary Peller, and Kendall Thomas. New York: New Press, 1995.

DeMan, Paul. *Allegories of Reading: Figural Language in Rousseau, Nietzsche, Rilke, and Proust.* New Haven, Conn.: Yale University Press, 1979.

Douglas, Mary. *How Institutions Think.* Syracuse, N.Y.: Syracuse University Press, 1986.

Ely, John Hart. *Democracy and Distrust: A Theory of Judicial Review.* Cambridge, Mass.: Harvard University Press, 1980.

Feuerbach, Ludwig. *The Essence of Christianity,* translated by George Eliot. New York: Prometheus Books, 1989.

Fish, Stanley. *The Trouble with Principle.* Cambridge, Mass.: Harvard University Press, 1999.

Goldberg, David Theo. *The Racial State.* Oxford, Eng.: Blackwell, 2002.

Guinier, Lani, Michelle Fine, and Jane Balin. *Becoming Gentlemen: Women, Law School, and Institutional Change.* Boston: Beacon Press, 1997.

Harris, Cheryl. "Whiteness as Property." *Harvard Law Review* 106, no. 8 (June 1993): 1707–91.

Kennedy, Duncan. *A Critique of Adjudication (fin de siècle).* Cambridge, Mass.: Harvard University Press, 1997.

———. *Legal Education and the Reproduction of Hierarchy: A Polemic against the System.* New York: New York University Press, 2004.

———. "Legal Education as Training for Hierarchy." In *Politics of Law: A Progressive Critique,* edited by David Kairys. New York: Perseus, 1998.

Laclau, Ernesto. "The Politics of Rhetoric." In *Material Events: Paul de Man and the Afterlife of Theory,* edited by Tom Cohen, J. Hillis Miller, and Barbara Cohen. Minneapolis: University of Minnesota Press, 2001.

Laclau, Ernesto, and Chantal Mouffe. *Hegemony and Socialist Strategy: Towards a Radical Democratic Politics.* New York: Verso, 2001.

Mills, Charles W. *The Racial Contract.* Ithaca, N.Y.: Cornell University Press, 1997.

Nietzsche, Friedrich. *On the Genealogy of Morals and Ecce Homo.* Edited by Walter Kaufman. New York: Vintage, 1989.

Spann, Girardeau A. *Race against the Court: The Supreme Court and Minorities in Contemporary America.* New York: New York University Press, 1993.

CHAPTER 4

Legal Lines: Defining Racism
in a Flexibility Matrix

Tony Zaragoza

The body of U.S. law[1] is a profound example of white supremacy working in conjunction with capitalism. One should not be surprised that laws have routinely functioned to uphold and enable racism and exploitation. Power, derived from historical political-economic accumulation, dominates the writing of law and the wielding of law. But law is not solely dictated by the ruling class.[2] People struggle to have justice encoded into law, but often the imperatives of capitalism and racism find new ways to maintain old relationships. Ongoing changes in U.S. law provide an excellent example of the flexibility of both racism and capitalism as the dialectical interaction between unequal systems and the struggles for justice and equality that such systems spur and spurn.

White racial supremacy is part of the codification of the founding document of the nation. A close look at the Constitution of the United States of America reveals that it has little to do with promoting "the general welfare," as it claims. The Constitution essentially revolves around the very specific welfare of property rights and property owners, including slave owners. The Constitution contrasts sharply with the Declaration of Independence, which advances abstract principles of justice to rally various segments of the population to support a rebellion spearheaded by an emerging capitalist elite who needed the independence of a sovereign state to further build their own advancing enterprises. The Constitution then serves the new U.S. ruling class by consolidating and codifying class power and relationships. It gives power to the wealthiest Americans with the creation of a binding document that is changeable but not easily changed, thus conserving power for property owners, who have now vanquished the major obstacle to advanced independent accumulation as represented by the British Crown, which drained necessary capital via colonial taxes. Dressed in populist guises, the Constitution was a technological breakthrough for capital. Though it does guarantee many basic rights for white citizens, there are property qualifications for officeholders and voters, legal definitions of Africans as property equal to 3/5 of a human being, an electoral college composed of the propertied or their servitors that blocks the will of the people. John Jay's famous dictum—those who own the country should govern it—describes the workings of the Constitution perfectly.

Preceding and following the Constitution were a series of legal agreements with indigenous peoples—many broken treaties—which set legal precedents for dominant white relationships with those on the land they sought to dominate and exploit and whose land they sought to expand into. Most treaties were either unfair and manipulative or ignored entirely while the ongoing violence of "Manifest Destiny" continued the march west. Alongside these treaties and the accompanying cavalry were militia laws that supported armed forces whose primary purpose, according to Mary Frances Berry, was to "control" slaves and protect and promote white property.[3] Brooke Heagerty and Nelson Peery point out that "laws were passed which protected white artisans and skilled workers from competition from African Americans" and "laws against intermarriage and even socializing between African Americans and whites were also passed" (16). Such segregating laws and the legal institution of slavery divided the working classes along race lines and created the space for minor rewards for poor and working-class whites. The legal apparatus of the Jim Crow South (and the equivalent economic and cultural apparatus in the North) enabled legal fascist terror, air-tight political control, and economic servitude (for white and black sharecroppers) that maintained the inferior status of blacks after the Civil War while also encouraging and rewarding poor whites to become active participants, thus nurturing white supremacy and nationalism and safeguarding profit through wage depression and labor control (Heagerty and Peery 18–30).

From the beginning, the legal foundations of the nation are driven by white supremacy in the service of profit and accumulation. Today many claim that this history and its legacy have passed and no longer merit discussion. In an installment of his syndicated column "Along the Color Line" from April 2000 titled "Structural Racism: No Harm, No Foul?" Manning Marable provides a good description of the *disunderstanding* that currently prevails: "Everything's different today. People from divergent racial backgrounds now can compete fairly for jobs, education, housing, and other resources. And if African Americans consistently fall short of their goals, it's nobody's fault but their own. They need to stop complaining about how the 'game' is played, and start working harder to get ahead." Such claims are ubiquitous on campus. I hear it not only from white undergraduate students (90 percent of my classroom), but also from white graduate students, tenured white faculty, and even a few students of color. Once, in an effort to control and contain an after-class discussion on racism, a liberal white history professor explained how much better things are: "You have to admit that we have progressed." I answered back, "You come home with me to Gary, Indiana; Hammond, Indiana; East Chicago, Indiana—areas devastated by racism and capitalism. Let's go visit Northwest Indiana and you show me how much better things are."[4]

Homelessness is increasing. The ghettoes are growing. Barrios are becoming more impoverished. Elsewhere reservations are becoming bigger dumping grounds for nuclear waste. Nationwide more and more youth of color are being targeted, monitored, and incarcerated by the criminal justice system. Meanwhile, upper- and middle-class whites (and people of color who can) are moving farther and farther out and surrounding their communities with fences, gates, and guards. But the "evidence" I offer—people's material conditions and the effects of white supremacy in the service of capitalism—doesn't hold up in "court." It is not provable within the framework of contemporary "civil society."[5] Because the evidence cannot be "seen"; it is attributed to some other factor. For, we are told, it certainly cannot be racism—"that's better."

Why can't the evidence be seen? Philosopher Charles Mills offers an answer. Mills identifies an unnamed political system in operation; a system he calls the Racial Contract.[6] Mills alludes to the (in)famous "Social Contract" described by philosophers like Thomas Hobbes, John Locke, Jean-Jacques Rousseau, and Immanuel Kant. For these philosophers, the Social Contract is the very basis of "civil society," but parallelly the Racial Contract adds to it an "inner logic of racial domination." Mills's concept of a social pact based on differential relations to power helps to examine the historical and contemporary, often unconscious, "naturalness" of white supremacy, a "naturalness" that blurs material relationships, mystifies oppression, and explains away inequality. According to Mills, the Racial Contract requires its own "peculiar moral and empirical epistemology" that involves "an idealized consensus about cognitive norms," what "counts as correct," and what is understood as "rational" within civil society (17). This consensus proclaims an official version of reality that diverges from actual lived experience. In other words, there is a sort of "agreement to misinterpret the world" supported by the "assurance that this set of mistaken perceptions will be validated by white epistemic authority." This epistemology supports and is supported by "an invented delusional world, a racial fantasyland" that is built into the daily life of dominant institutions, dominant stories about the world, and social relationships themselves (18–19).

The role of white epistemic authority cannot be exaggerated with regard to law. Accordingly, in such an epistemic tradition, it is reasonable and believable for John Ashcroft, the highest legal authority in government, to declare, "There is no evidence of racial bias in the administration of the federal death penalty." How do we account for the fact that African Americans were 40.7 percent of those on death row as of 1997 but only 12.3 percent of the population, while whites are 48.0 percent of those on death row as of 1997 and 62.6 percent of the population? Ashcroft's statement directly contradicts reams of documented evidence and the findings of the General Accounting Office, which noted in 1990 a "pattern of evidence indicating racial disparities in the charging, sentencing, and imposition of the death penalty" (U.S. GAO 5). The ideological framework of civil society under such a Racial Contract does not allow for seeing systemic, legal, and enforced white domination in the present. This has been historically true as well. Slaves "were not allowed to give evidence against their masters," and whites understood this not as a system of domination that required the complete silencing of the oppressed, but as the simple "fact" that slaves and nonwhites generally were less than human, were not to be trusted, were not smart enough, and should not be believed (Mills 57). In other words, they were relegated to what Mills would call "subpersonhood" (60). The 1857 Dred Scott Supreme Court case is a perfect example of the legalization/codification of already existent attitudes forming the foundation of postemancipation legal racism. In that landmark precedent, eight of the nine judges in one of the most revered institutions in the nation agreed that Africans were "so far inferior . . . that they had no rights which the white man was bound to respect." Today the framing is different, but the effect is the same. Mistrust is not justified in terms of people of color being less than human. Rather, it is put in terms of people of color not being able to be objective or wanting special privileges[7] or being "oversensitive" and "paranoid"[8] about racism. According to Mills, a "governing epistemic principle" filters information, so that nonwhite cognition "has to be verified by white cognition to be accepted as valid" (60). Racism only exists if whites can see it. If the ideological framework admits oppression, it must cover the objective reality of exploitation with various excuses and justifications using well-financed and widely broadcast toxic constructions: savage, sambo, mammy, wetback, Indian giver, welfare queen, gangsta, and on and on. Each caricature provides excuses for domination and exploitation: excuses for expropriation, for slavery, for colonialism, for exclusion, for disproportionate imprisonment and execution, and so on.

In the past the overtness of the Racial Contract was socially acceptable among whites, an unquestioned part of dominant ideology. But as resistance to the contract grows, those who maintain the contract are forced to modify its workings to keep it intact. Accordingly laws change and language changes, and "the Racial Contract has written itself out of formal existence" (73). What is left, according to Mills, is "*de facto* white privilege and [a] *formal* extension of rights" (emphasis in original) based on "the pretense that formal, juridical equality is sufficient to remedy inequalities created on a foundation of several hundred years of racial privilege" (73). *Brown v. Board of Education* outlaws the legal apartheid formalized by *Plessy v. Fergusson,* but does not end segregation, or white privilege, or the location of stratified unskilled jobs in segregated communities of color. Here's the flexibility: legally and linguistically things have changed. So, in part what my white professor said about things changing was true. But the changes are predominantly superficial. As Mills notes, civil society has "rewritten the Racial Contract in transforming the terms of public discourse so that white domination is now conceptually invisible" (117). The core values and the end result, however, are the same as ever.

The contract is sustained in various ways—militarily, economically, politically—which are all knit together ideologically. For whites (and folks of color attempting to climb the social ladder of white racial domination) there are rewards for "signing" the contract: careers, opportunities, advancement all extended by not rocking the boat of the Racial Contract. Cheryl I. Harris has argued that whiteness acts as a kind of property with a value that must be protected. Thus whites sense a stake in the Racial Contract; it pays to be white. Harris suggests that "white identity conferred tangible and economically valuable benefits, and it was jealously guarded as a valued possession, allowed only to those who met a strict standard of proof" (1731). Individuals regardless of race are also "paid" not to see racism. But the benefits, especially for the masses of poor whites, aren't as great as we are led to believe. All of us, regardless of our histories, are taught not to see it, and *how* not to see it. The "defense" of white supremacy is well funded and pervasive throughout a vast range of dominant cultural forms, ideological frameworks, social institutions, political processes, economic structures, and legal formulations. Most recently in the post-9/11 United States this has been enacted in the Patriot Act, the special registration of people with visas from Muslim countries, the physical harassment and intimidation of Arabs and those who even remotely look Arab, and the detentions of hundreds of "people of interest."

The work of James Blaut complements Mills's explorations of racism in the United States. Blaut starts with a paradox: nowadays there is still a lot of racism, but supposedly very few racists. How can that be? To address the paradox Blaut (along with many others) posits what I would like to call "flexible racism." To maintain the Racial Contract, the outward signs of racism change, but the core values (white supremacy for exploitation) remain the same, as do the goals (white racial domination for accumulation). This flexibility acts by means of defensive formulations and justifications for white supremacy like those used by my history professor. According to Blaut, the dominant theory behind the racism of the early part of European conquest and enslavements was based on Christian ideology and interpretations of the Bible. What the ideological "attorneys" argued was, "They lack souls. They're descendants of cursèd Ham. They aren't using the land right. We can do with it what God intended, for it is our manifest destiny. We can enslave these people, for we are God's chosen ones. We can exclude these people because we were here first." As the religious paradigm shifted and science ascended, dominant understandings of race also looked to scientific justifications for white domination: classification, phrenology, social Darwinism, eugenics, and so forth. This too becomes outdated when race as a scientific category is dismantled by newer genetic understandings of variation and difference within the phenotypic "color" classification system. As biological/genetic-based racial definitions become disproved, the paradigm shifts again toward the cultural.

The groundwork for cultural racism is principally laid by Max Weber and his theories on modernization. Outlining Weber's theory, Blaut says "most of what he wrote about European superiority was axiomatic argumentation about the uniqueness of the European mind—its rationality, its spiritual capacity—and historical argumentation about the unique rise within Europe, and Europe alone, of institutions and structures which alone were the source of modernity" (294). This theory of modernization is used to show European superiority without direct reference to race, but instead to cultural characteristics that enabled Europe to develop more quickly than non-Europeans. As the scientific basis for race faded into the background, racism is grafted onto such theories of modernization, helps justify European colonialism, and morphs into cultural racism. According to Blaut "cultural racism tells us that non-Europeans, long ago, acquired cultural qualities which blocked development, or . . . such qualities are 'traditional,' and therefore have always been present in non-European cultures" (298). Scholars go on the offensive by pointing either to "specific old traits in specific cultures as causes of non-change, or else depict a world-wide zone of 'traditional cultures'—including almost all non-European cultures—which 'traditionally' lacked rationality, or achievement motivation, or sexual continence, or some other quality necessary to forward historical motion" (298). Though cultural justifications for racism supplanted biological justifications,[9] eugenic insistence of white supremacy didn't disappear; in fact such arguments are still making for bestselling books. Look at the immense popularity of Richard J. Herrnstein and Charles Murray's *Bell Curve*. Indeed, many conservative foundations and think tanks grant money to those who can help "prove" white genetic supremacy.[10] The varieties of racist theories add further to racism's flexibility.

Cultural racism can be seen clearly in the models offered by David Duke[11] and Dinesh D'Souza.[12] Academics and sociologists such as Weber[13] and Talcott Parsons[14] snuggle right up between the cultural and biological. And it gets "sophisticated" as a defense for European superiority. Blaut states that "the Weberian argument could be, and was, detached from race and presented as a theory of modernization grounded in the uniqueness of European mentality and culture, permanent qualities which throughout history gave Europeans a continuously more rapid course toward modernity than non-Europeans." Various scholars go to great lengths to defend European cultural superiority from scholarship that questions that supremacy. Take, for example, attacks leveled at Martin Bernal's *Black Athena*, in which Bernal elaborates the indebtedness of Greece to Egypt for philosophy, art, science, and so on, by such scholars as Mary Lefkowitz and John Baines. *Not Out of Africa* and *Black Athena Revisited* exemplify defenses of white cultural supremacy that try to refute any challenges to dominant notions of European cultural superiority and uniqueness (Asante 50, 62).

It would be hard to convince many scholars that Lefkowitz's ongoing project is racist. Blaut explains that this inability to identify the sources of racism is partly due to the fact that civil society is defining "racism" in notions of biological superiority, which most no longer consciously subscribe to, though these notions still permeate and uphold the Racial Contract. Most people have learned to see biological racism as reprehensible but still don't see cultural racism as racism. Outright bigotry seems (to some) less evident: signs above drinking fountains are gone, offensive language is less tolerated in civil society, and outright white-supremacist violence is no longer in fashion with whites. But this is because civil society prioritizes the older forms of racism and obvious and superficial kinds of evidence. Racism has been reduced to outward shows of biologically based racist hostility. As the signs were curtailed, it seemed in the dominant view that racism was curtailed as well.

Not only are U.S. legal understandings of racism based in the earlier biological paradigm, which requires very limited kinds of blatant evidence, but these legal understandings often look at racism merely in terms of individuals and individual incidents, leading Cheryl Harris to the conclusion that legal liberalism leads to a denial of group identity. In other words, the incidents are legally kept isolated so that no connections can be made or patterns established. It is very difficult to address systemic and institutional forms and forces of racism by using those very institutions; the law, for example. And forms of violence like hunger, unemployment, poor schools, poor health care, a racialized criminal justice system, bombings, and invasions, all of which support and are supported by white supremacy and capitalist accumulation, cannot be challenged because the group they affect are not legally seen as a group that shares common experiences. Simultaneously poor whites are distracted from seeing the commonalities they inhabit with poor people of color while also experiencing many of the effects listed above.

Eduardo Bonilla-Silva and Tyrone Forman, seeking answers to the paradox addressed by Blaut, identify the mutability of racist practices. In an article "I Am Not a Racist but . . .," Bonilla-Silva and Forman examine data from surveys that would seem to suggest a general decline in racism. In addition to the survey, Bonilla-Silva and Forman interview each participant for a more in-depth understanding behind and beyond the multiple-choice answers of the surveys. Through these interviews, Bonilla-Silva and Forman find that whites know racism is "bad," "unlike during the Jim Crow period, when Whites openly expressed their racial views" (76). Whites interviewed, however, employed a "discursive flexibility" and avoid using language that would seem racist, while supporting policies that negatively impact people of color and showing an aversion to interracial dating and policies that address current and historical discrimination (77).

Discursive strategies and methods for hiding or disguising what is unallowable can be seen as a "technological" advance that provides flexibility for racism. We see such methods in the classroom and in conversation often. Anecdotes circulate that begin with patented precursors "I'm all for minorities doing well, but not at my expense." Such stories have become "part of the ideological racial repertoire" that attempts to make racist arguments seem reasonable (65). In response to the 1950s and 1960s civil-rights struggles, white supremacy "learned" how to better hide racism, creating subtle racism, or how to make it appear socially acceptable, creating "reasonable" racism. D'Souza calls it "rational" racism. The "legal team" for white supremacy attributes both discrimination and the material conditions of most folks of color to "cultural deficiency" instead of structural forms of oppression.

In "The New Racism," Bonilla-Silva further elaborates Blaut by describing the latest morphing of the flexible-racist ideological repertoire of individual social interaction. He describes the (1) "covert nature of racism," (2) claims of "reverse racism," (3) a political racial agenda that does not mention race, (4) invisibility of the reproduction of racism, and (5) a rearticulation of Jim Crow practices. An example of the "increasingly covert nature of racial discourse and practices" (56) can be seen in the coded language of get-tough-on crime campaigns or George H. W. Bush's Willie Horton ads that used racial scare tactics. While there is a clear "avoidance of racial terminology," there are also "rampant claims of reverse racism" (56). These two form a convenient pair of mutually advancing phenomena: a convenient advocacy of color blindness on the one hand and an equally convenient reminder of race on the other. We see this often when white deviants are afforded the privilege of individualization, while criminal folks of color are seen to represent the race. "Color blindness" and "reverse racism" are also cornerstones of anti–affirmative action arguments.[15] According to such views, selection of applicants should be formally color-blind. But what gets left unsaid is that in the real world the factors leading to candidacy and hiring are not color-blind. Bonilla-Silva and Forman emphasize that "color-blind racism allows Whites to appear 'not racist' ('I believe in equality'), preserve their privileged status ('Discrimination ended in the sixties!'), blame Blacks for their lower status ('If you guys just work hard!'), and criticize any institutional approach—such as affirmative action—that attempts to ameliorate racial inequality ('Reverse discrimination!')" (78). In an attempt to codify "color blindness," Ward Connerly has recently put a color-blind voter proposition known as the "Racial Privacy Initiative" on the ballot in California; Prop 54 would prohibit the state from collecting any data on race except for rare exceptions.[16]

Bonilla-Silva identifies the third feature of the "new racism" in civil society as an "elaboration of a racial agenda over political matters that eschews direct racial reference" (56). For example, get-tough-on-crime initiatives, anti-immigrant discourses, cultural aggression and cultural genocide in the form of forced assimilation never mention race, but whites are the primary beneficiaries, though poor and working-class whites are also affected by many of these laws.[17] The fourth feature, according to Bonilla-Silva, is "the invisibility of most mechanisms to reproduce racial inequality" (56).[18] This invisibility reinforces racism in all facets of society. Tim Wise points to "white denials of racism leading to the dismantling of the few laws that are designed to help make up for continuing injustice and the dismantling of welfare while corporate welfare, the biggest dollars, go to private firms" ("Color Conscious"). Wise also points out the subordination of workers of color: "From 1790 to 1860 alone, whites and the overall economy reaped the benefits of as much as $40 billion in unpaid black labor" and "Each year, according to estimates from the Urban Institute, African Americans lose $120 billion in wages due to labor discrimination" ("Breaking the Cycle"). Imagine what the figure would be if we did a similar global analysis of the historical and ongoing theft of land and resources and the extraction of surplus value from people of color globally that is and has been part of white domination, imperialism, and capitalism.

Finally, the denials of racism and its accompanying indirectness allow and encourage the fifth feature of the new racism, a "rearticulation of a number of racial practices characteristic of Jim Crow period" (56). A great example is the 2000 presidential election. Catherine Danielson has pointed out the pervasiveness of vote fraud. Twenty states have suits now pending. One suit involves widespread cases of polling place irregularities, a fraction of the voting machines needed in districts with high populations of nonwhites, intimidation, faulty and erroneous felon lists, police harassment—and that's just in the state of Tennessee. Common practices include *de facto* segregation, racial profiling, and law enforcement posted in and targeted at communities of color, all of which work to reinscribe Jim Crow practices in new ways.

These five characteristics of the "new racism" variously act as mechanisms of the flexibility of white racial domination. This flexibility has facilitated the domestic reformulation of the repressive apparatus of the Racial Contract using so called "cultural deviance" as a pretext for control and containment of bodies of color. We see this concretely in the War on Drugs. Besides the devastating racist assault on peasants, union organizers, and socialist/liberation movements in Colombia, the War on Drugs has provided an opportunity to target people of color in the United States. Arguments abound that the drug war has not achieved its goals, but according to Noam Chomsky, it is "only reasonable to conclude that the 'drug war,' cast in the harshly punitive form implemented in the past 20 years, is *achieving* its goals, not failing. What are these goals? . . . By adopting these measures, [Daniel Patrick Moynihan] observed, 'we are choosing to have an intense crime problem concentrated among minorities'" (81). But it is concentrated among "minorities" not because people of color constitute the majority of drug users, but because people of color are targeted by law enforcement as the profile of a drug user, when in fact 75 percent of drug users are white (Sklar).

Law enforcement that targets communities of color are partially "necessitated" and partially excused by the war on drugs. Paul Street asks, "What are the widespread results of targeting of people of color by the legal system, in other words how does this exacerbate inequality: disenfranchisement of felons and ex-felons, obstacles in unemployment, deskilling, further criminalizing people of color, take away family etc.?" He answers: "There is a vast literature showing that structural, institutional, and cultural racism and severe segregation by race and class are leading causes of inner-city crime. Another considerable body of literature shows that blacks are victims of racial bias at every level of the criminal justice system—from stop, frisk, and arrest to prosecution, sentencing, release, and execution." A semi-self-replicating cycle is set in motion. The Racial Contract continues repression with a new face and the cultural racism excuse reinforces the ideology of the Racial Contract by showing people of color as criminals on news broadcasts, cop shows, and political campaigns. This leads to and fuels calls for tough-on-crime legislation, while crime becomes equated with nonwhites, leading to more police in communities of color. This in turn leads to police "sweeps" that gut communities of color, and black and brown bodies pile up in prison. This is also profitable industry. Bruce Western and Katherine Beckett stress the politico-economic aspects of law enforcement: "Each prisoner represents as much as $25,000 in income for the community in which the prison is located, not to mention the value of constructing the prison facility in the first place. This can be a massive transfer of value: A young male worth a few thousand dollars of support to children and local purchases is transformed into a $25,000 financial asset to a rural prison community." Prisons become one of the biggest growth industries and private prison firms export their control scheme abroad. Law institutionalizes racism and such institutionalized racism is often itself directly profitable—prison construction, arms manufacturing, employment for whites, and so on. And prison construction is sold to white communities as job opportunities, so that economically faltering rural communities compete for the honor of housing inmates.[19] Prisons become modern plantations that rival sweatshop wages. The new expressions of racism can be seen as a backlash to the gains of the 1960s and 1970s, but also as continuation of past practices: from slavery to sharecropping to proletarianization to prison labor. The gains of the civil-rights movements were followed by an exponential growth in police departments and prisons and the deployment of an increasingly militarized police force along with the federally enabled influx of addictive drugs such as heroin and cocaine. Police departments are increasingly becoming internal armies, while U.S. military bases are situated all over the world.[20]

I don't want to suggest that some things haven't changed. African Americans, Native Americans, Asian Americans, Arab Americans, Latinos, and white allies have fought, struggled, and died to make changes, and change has occurred. The abolitionist movement, the antilynching movement, the civil-rights movement have had important impacts on the extent, form, and content of white supremacy in the United States. As a result, law has been used in attempts to combat racist practices. By no means has law simply and totally been the tool of racism. What I am arguing, though, is that fundamentally the deep structures of white supremacy have remained unchanged and are perhaps stronger through reforms that allow the appearance of equality while acting out a "strategy of containment" (San Juan 32). Each struggle has been met with *reform* but has been followed by backlashes (Steinberg, "Liberal Retreat," 38). The current state of racism, both flexible and blatant, resulted from the retreats and the backlashes that culminated in the Ronald Reagan and George H. W. Bush administrations' total hostility to civil-rights legislation and the gutting of welfare (Steinberg, "Liberal Retreat," 52). More recently, strategies of containment under Bill Clinton have produced reforms[21] centering on conversations,[22] multicultural initiatives, diversity programs[23] and pledges[24]—what Adolph Reed has termed the "elaborately choreographed pageantry of essentializing yackety-yak" (62). Paramount among our current reforms have been hate-crime legislation. Hate-crime laws were the result of hard-fought efforts to make racist and antigay crimes receive harsher punishments in hopes of greater deterrence. Unfortunately, they are rarely used and act more symbolically than substantively. According to Mark Fritz, "States generally use hate crime laws to enhance existing penalties, either by adding years to a sentence, limiting parole, or elevating a misdemeanor to a felony. Yet while hate laws look good on paper after they've been passed by outraged lawmakers, experts in the field say it's not easy to find a cop when you want to enforce one." As examples, Fritz points to Alabama, Arkansas, and Mississippi, where in 1997 hate crimes totaled an unbelievable zero.

The problem is that hate crimes are difficult to prove in court: "Hate crimes have a low conviction rate—about 15%" and "many police departments are put off by the extra FBI paperwork and the difficulty of determining a motive" (Fritz). This was evident here in a fraternity incident on the Washington State University campus during which, in the fall 2000 semester, a black student was involved in an altercation, allegedly with several white men. The altercation ended with the student in the hospital suffering from a broken leg, knocked out teeth, and no suspects. When the incident was finally reported in the student daily, there was outrage at both the incident itself and the lack of coverage.[25] A rally followed, and then a series of administrative steps to begin showing university involvement. One step was a forum for administration, police, and the presidents of the two fraternities involved. There were various ways in which the "fight" was cast as a fraternity quarrel and not a "racial incident." Race, the administration determined, was not a factor. At the forum it was asked, "Officer, legally how do you determine if an incident is racially motivated?" The officer responded that there are generally two criteria. One, the perpetrator(s) used racial slurs during the incident and, two, the perpetrator(s) had a history of racially motivated hate as determined by participation in other racially motivated incidents, by ownership of racist paraphernalia, or by membership in a hate group. None of these could be proved, and therefore it could not be dubbed racially motivated. The legal definition of a racially motivated incident is symptomatic of the larger issues raised by Bonilla-Silva's and Blaut's descriptions of flexible racism. Racism is addressed superficially and individually, defined solely empirically, and thus allowed to hide deeper institutionally, as only the most blatant racist and homophobic attacks can be prosecuted, while bigotry is dismissed in the rest.

Since the passage of hate-crime legislation, there has been another development in the law regarding our ability to legally combat racism: the *Sandoval* decision in April 2001. According to the Mexican American Legal Defense and Education Fund (MALDEF), the Supreme Court, by a 5–4 vote, substantially limited the effectiveness of Title VI of the Civil Rights Act of 1964, an antidiscrimination law that is "widely considered one of the principal gains of the Civil Rights movement." Title VI has been very important for activists, civil-rights workers, and community organizations, for it "prohibits any agency or program that receives federal funding from discriminating on the basis of race, color, or national origin. Its reach is broad, and covers everything from a city's decision to place toxic waste facilities in minority neighborhoods to public college admissions requirements that screen out large numbers of Latino and African American applicants" (MALDEF). The importance of Title VI rests on the fact that it can target discriminatory effects even if discriminatory intent cannot be proven. The *Sandoval* decision rescinds this power, forcing activists and organizations to show discriminatory intent. This requires the same kind of evidence used to prove hate crimes, making it virtually impossible to show deliberate discrimination in the dominant schema of provability.

Again we have the highest legal body in the land codifying the new flexible racist regime, making it far easier both to perform racist acts and far harder to show its existence and many manifestations. This is the face of the "new racism," which further blurs and strengthens the Racial Contract. Such a decision really leads us to question our notions of balance between the branches of U.S. government. The Supreme Court is supposed to protect minorities from the tyranny of the majority. It has the potential to be countermajoritarian and "objective" because, much like tenured faculty, the Supreme Court is supposedly shielded from external pressures through—overt though ineffectual—mechanisms of life appointment and salary protection. But as Matthew Abraham has argued, this is nothing more than a "veiled majoritarianism." The process by which a Supreme Court justice reaches the highest court guarantees an inherently conservative majoritarian subjectivity. This occurs in the socialization process, in the long majoritarian screening process (college performance, law school admittance, law school performance, and the selection and confirmation by majoritarian bodies), and the very processes of the court itself. In the end both the court personnel and its decision-making protocol enable the maintenance of dominant power relations.

As we have seen, the political and legal apparatus of the United States from the very beginning of the nation has served the interests of capital, which has employed white supremacy in a flexible manner as means to strengthen capital.

The law provides a good example of the flexibility of racism. But where does this leave us? There is a range of immediate and long-term solutions such as defense of affirmative action, reparations movements, diversity training, consciousness raising, revolutions of cultural and consciousness, and the reordering of social organization. I would never argue that fighting for a just law, for reparations, or even for liberal tolerance is a waste of time. But I would argue that the fight against racism must be done in conjunction with a broader conceptualization of the problem that includes an understanding of the historical and political economic underpinnings of racial injustice and the dialectical nature of its changes. For such a broad context to make sense, we must understand the role of capitalism in conditioning the terrain upon which racism is nurtured, functions, and thrives. In a paper we presented recently on the need to use the conceptual framework and tools of historical and dialectical materialism to develop a complex and nuanced understanding of racism in capitalism, Marta Maldonado and I argue that we must understand racialization as part of the historically and geographically specific process of class formation of segments of the working class that enable and facilitate exploitation.

Berch Berberoglu offers a succinct definition of capitalism as "driven by the logic of profit for the private accumulation of capital based on the exploitation of labor throughout the world" (3). The very nature of capitalism requires that a few do well at the expense of most others. Epifanio San Juan Jr. explains that the "the necessary element is racial stratification, the sociopolitical construction of racial hierarchy" (32). Capitalism has found racism useful, taken it up and used it, an already existent form of domination, as a means to enable new forms of exploitation. Racism certainly precedes capitalism, but it does not precede class struggle and has existed perhaps simultaneously in some form as the division of labor developed and classes formed. Under other modes of production racism had different forms, purposes, and manifestations and perhaps these various forms deserve different names. "Modern racism," according to Ellen Meiksins Wood, "is something different, a more viciously systemic conception of inherent and natural inferiority, which emerged in the late seventeenth or early eighteenth century and culminated in the nineteenth century when it acquired pseudoscientific reinforcement of biological theories of race" (208). It is under capitalism that the most barbaric forms of racism emerged. But it is also under capitalism that vast resistance movements developed.

In the face of resistance as seen in the post–WWII civil-rights movements, national liberation movements, and feminist movements capitalism necessarily became flexible. This is an ongoing dialectical process. David Harvey has elaborated the concept of "flexible accumulation" as a method for capital to actively seek out and find the most effective ways to create profit and maximize accumulation: Capital moves to decentralization, deregulation, rampant privatization, dispersal of production leading to a "race to the bottom." Racism, as it is employed by capitalism, also "finds" ways to survive and thrive as it encounters obstacles through the employment of flexibility. Similarly in response to decolonizing movements colonization and imperialism had to change superficially as long as the fundamental goals were met; it had to employ a more flexible strategy for achieving its goals. Nkrumah calls this new strategy and its resulting relationships "neocolonialism" (8). The neocolonial strategy was to employ reforms that built a "protective armour around the inner workings of its system" (8). These reforms strengthened fundamental contradictions and blurred them by allowing and encouraging what he calls a "sham independence."

The outcome of the dialectic between capitalism and resistance is that the core values and ultimate goals remain fundamentally the same (profits, expansion, accumulation, white domination, etc.), but the face of domination changes. As Lenin explained, capital will explore and exploit whatever forms and means it finds available at any historical moment. This flexibility has been dialectically produced and can be understood in terms of Antonio Gramsci's notion of hegemony. Hegemony employs the flexibility of dominant constructions of ideology in order to maintain domination. Flexibility allows both for the further belief in and evidence for egalitarian progress (while it continues to exacerbate inequality) and for a kind of legitimation of the capitalist/imperialist system on a superficial level. This leads many to believe that capitalism is just fine and that reform is all that is needed. But reform will never limit the imperatives of capitalism to stratify and exploit.

Racism and sexism and their accompanying exploitation must hide behind the kinds of mystifications we have seen with regard to the law. This hiding might be the suppression or evasion of information. It might be dominant constructions of knowledge. It might be in institutional structures. As we have seen in the *Sandoval* decision, for something to be legally apparent it must be "provable" in terms of dominant constructions of evidence. If it cannot be pinpointed with available legal means, it is much harder to combat and much easier to deny. So as laws are fought for and realized to fight racism, racism slithers away, evades lawful or provable acknowledgment and remains stronger than before, being further maintained through various layers of mystification and a resultant flexibility. The flexibility of racism and capitalism is made necessary by the many struggles that have challenged them and led to seemingly progressive reforms of various kinds. We must come to acknowledge that though they may alleviate some aspects of racism, legal reforms will not end racism. Racism will be made to fully cease only when the relationship of exploitation based on racial hierarchy is broken and reformed along materially egalitarian principles. Perhaps a starting point can be found in uniting to fight against the most blatant and basic forms of inequality that cut across racial lines as found in homelessness, hunger, lack of health care, and so on. Such united political action through concrete struggle can serve to both alleviate the worst kinds of inequality disproportionately experienced by people of color and begin the process of forming political equality by working together for a common cause.

Notes

For their comments and feedback on earlier versions of this essay, I would like to thank Shelli Fowler, Epifanio San Juan Jr., Victor Villanueva, and Jeannette Garceau. Thanks also go to William Takamatsu Thompson whose thoughtful conversation has greatly informed my understanding of racism and to Azfar and Melissa Hussain, with whom I attended the Race in the Humanities conference. All errors in this essay are of course my own.

1. I focus here primarily on a U.S. context, recognizing that contemporary U.S./white domination operates within an international political economy and an international legal framework, though often in history the United States operates rather conveniently above international law.
2. See especially E. P. Thompson's work, *Whigs and Hunters: The Origin of the Black Act.*
3. These situations resemble the "pioneering" Boer trekkers in South Africa and the Zionists in Palestine and their strictly enforced, highly elaborate systems of racial domination and segregation of Apartheid Bantustans and present-day Palestinian occupied territories.
4. I failed to mention the global racism most of the world is subjected to in the form of imperialism, colonialism, and neocolonialism.
5. Following cues from Delia Aguilar, I take "civil society" as the notion of a liberal transcultural consensus that is both white supremacist and thoroughly capitalist.
6. Mills finds the starting point for his book in the *Sexual Contract* by Carole Pateman.
7. This same rhetoric has also been used against fights for equal rights for gay men and lesbians.
8. David Horowitz is (in)famous for this characterization. See particularly a debate between Horowitz and Tim Wise at <http://www.zmag.org/RaceWatch/wisehoro.htm>.
9. Nazism in Germany and fascism in Italy differed in their understanding of racism. Each reflected two different paradigms of racism: Hitler favored a more biological understanding of race and nation, while Mussolini held a more cultural understanding of race and nation.
10. For an in-depth look at such funding, see *No Mercy: How Conservative Think Tanks and Foundations Changed America's Social Agenda* by Jean Stefancic and Richard Delgado.
11. Duke unites both biological and cultural racism. In his book *My Awakening* he writes, "Culture is simply a veneer reflecting the deeper genetic makeup of people."
12. D'Souza writes perhaps the how-to book on cultural racism with his *End of Racism.*
13. See, for example, Weber's *Protestant Ethic and the Spirit of Capitalism.*
14. Talcott Parson, a structural-functional sociologist, translated and popularized Weber's work while bringing it into more of a mid-twentieth-century American context. See for example *The Evolution of Societies* and *The Negro American.*
15. The website <http://www.adversity.net/>, for example, claims to be a "Civil Rights Organization for Color Blind Justice" that seeks to "provide a resource and support system

for victims of reverse discrimination" and "stop the divisive emphasis on race," for "race has no place in America." The site has sections that include "Legal Help" and "Horror Stories," in which readers are informed that Kodak is "extremely hostile to non-minorities" and that in the Benton Harbor "Race Riots" "Black residents of poverty-stricken Michigan town destroy their own homes!"

16. The appeal on the Prop 54 website says, "We acknowledge our diversity, but we celebrate our unity. Instead of a nation of hyphenated Americans, let us be one nation indivisible." You can see it at <http://www.racialprivacy.org/>.

17. Similar was the case in the nineteenth century. As Jacqueline Jones points out, "The lien laws that reduced sharecroppers to wage laborers applied equally to workers of both races, as did fence laws, vagrancy and contract enforcement legislation, and high personal property taxes" (78).

18. We might call this pair "racism-once-removed" or "plausible denial."

19. What doesn't get mentioned, though, is the fact that prisons are then used as what Hilbourne Watson calls "fenced in factories" that in turn superexploit inmates, driving down wages and taking jobs away from those outside in the community, leading to further layoffs, leading to further unrest that then gets used to strengthen and spread racist ideologies.

20. According to John Bellamy Foster, "The U.S. currently occupies foreign territory in the form of military bases in sixty-nine countries—a number that is continuing to increase" (5). The number is seventy-one now with new bases being established in Afghanistan and Iraq.

21. The neoconservative agenda of George W. Bush has swung policy away from liberal lip service on issues of race and racism back to the onslaught on civil rights that began under Reagan. The hostility of the George W. Bush administration contributed greatly to U.S. maneuvering and eventual retreat from the World Conference against Racism. Take for example how the issue of reparations was handled by U.S. delegates and officials. According to Samir Amin, "U.S. and European diplomats labored strenuously to undermine the issue, reducing it, with condescension and a touch of contempt, to a question of the 'amount' that these 'professional beggars' were claiming in damages" (21). Condoleezza Rice blasted calls for reparations as "wasted" time dwelling on history and "pointing fingers backward."

22. The electronic journal of Clinton's "Toward One America: A National Conversation on Race" can be found at <http://usinfo.state.gov/journals/itsv/0897/ijse/ijse0897 .htm>.

23. One coordinator here at WSU actually referred to his vision for a program as "diversity lite."

24. As a result of the protests surrounding a campus assault, a "Diversity Kickoff" was offered in which students, faculty, and staff (many required to attend) signed a diversity pledge while having pictures taken. A group of about thirty students of color and white allies attended the "kickoff" wearing shirts with the word "token" on the front and back.

25. The incident went unreported in the student daily, the *Daily Evergreen,* until a group of black men went to the student's residence to offer assistance to him. It now merited attention and the men were presented in the paper with the headline "Group Slams Assault." The accompanying photograph had four stern black faces approaching a seemingly retreating white man. Both the headline and the photo serve to reinscribe white fear through the use of stereotypes of seemingly inexplicable black anger, aggression, and violence coupled with innocent white victims.

Works Cited

Abraham, Matthew. "Supreme Rhetoric: The Supreme Court, 'Veiled Majoritarianism,' and the Enforcement of the Racial Contract." Paper presented at the Race in the Humanities Conference, University of Wisconsin–La Crosse, 15–17 November 2001.

Aguilar, Delia. "'Transculture' Civil Society, or Capitalism: An Interview with Delia Aguilar." *dis/content* 3.3 (2000): 5–9.

Amin, Samir. "World Conference against Racism: A People's Victory." *Monthly Review* 53.7 (2001): 20–23.

Asante, Molefi Kete. *The Painful Demise of Eurocentrism: An Afrocentric Response to Critics.* Trenton, N.J.: Africa World Press, 1999.

Baines, John. "The Aims and Methods of Black Athena." In Mary R. Lefkowitz and Guy Maclean Rogers, eds., *Black Athena Revisited.* Chapel Hill: University of North Carolina Press, 1996. 27–48.

Berberoglu, Berch. *Globalization of Capital and the Nation-State: Imperialism, Class Struggle, and the State in the Age of Global Capitalism.* Lantham, Md.: Rowman and Littlefield, 2003.

Bernal, Martin. *Black Athena: The Afroasiatic Roots of Classical Civilization.* London: Free Association Books, 1987.

Berry, Mary Frances. *Black Resistance, White Law: A History of Constitutional Racism in America.* New York: A. Lane, Penguin Press, 1994.

Blaut, James. "The Theory of Cultural Racism." *Antipode* 23 (1992): 289–99.

Bonilla-Silva, Eduardo. "The New Racism: Racial Structure in the United States, 1960s–1990s." In Paul Wong, ed., *Race, Ethnicity, and Nationality in the United States.* Boulder, Colo.: Westview Press, 1999. 55–101.

Bonilla-Silva, Eduardo, and Tyrone A. Forman. "'I Am Not a Racist but . . .': Mapping White College Students' Racial Ideology in the USA." *Discourse and Society* 11.1 (2000): 50–85.

Chomsky, Noam. *Rogue States: The Rule of Force in World Affairs.* Cambridge, Mass.: South End Press, 2000.

Danielson, Catherine. "Vote Fraud in Tennessee: Worse Than Florida?" *AlterNet.* Date posted: 3 March 2001. Date accessed: 4 April 2001. <http://www.alternet.org/story.html?StoryID=10589>.

D'Souza, Dinesh. *The End of Racism: Principles for a Multiracial Society.* New York: Free Press, 1995.

Duke, David. *My Awakening: A Path to Racial Understanding.* Mandeville, La: Free Speech Press, 2000.

Foster, John Bellamy. "Imperialism and 'Empire.'" *Monthly Review* 53.7 (2001): 1–9.

Fritz, Mark. "Hate Crimes Hard to Track as Some Areas Report None." *Los Angeles Times,* 23 August 1999.

Harris, Cheryl I. "Whiteness as Property." *Harvard Law Review* 106 (1993): 1709–91.

Harvey, David. *The Condition of Postmodernity: An Enquiry into the Origins of Cultural Change.* Cambridge, Mass.: Blackwell, 1989.

Heagerty, Brooke, and Nelson Peery. *Moving Onward: From Racial Division to Class Unity.* Chicago: People's Tribune/Tribuno del Pueblo Press, 2000.

Herrnstein, Richard J., and Charles Murray. *The Bell Curve: Intelligence and Class Structure in American Life.* New York: Free Press, 1994.

Horowitz, David. "Tim Wise/David Horowitz Exchange on Racism." *Znet.* <http://www
.zmag.org/RaceWatch/wisehoro.htm>. Date posted: August 2000. Date accessed: September 2000.

Jones, Jacqueline. *The Dispossessed: America's Underclasses from the Civil War to the Present.* New York: Basic Books, 1992.

Lefkowitz, Mary R. *Not out of Africa.* New York: Basic Books, 1996.

Lefkowitz, Mary R., and Guy MacLean Rogers, eds. *Black Athena Revisited.* Chapel Hill:
University of North Carolina Press, 1996.

Maldonado, Marta Maria, and Tony Zaragoza. "A Historical-Materialist Analysis of Environmental Injustice in the Workplace: Towards an Agenda for Praxis." Paper presented
at the annual meeting of the Society for the Study of Social Problems, Atlanta, August
2003.

Mexican American Legal Defense and Education Fund and the Applied Research Center.
"Supreme Court Blunts Civil Rights Sword with *Sandoval* Decision." *ColorLines.* <www
.colorlines.com>. Date accessed: 30 May 2001.

Mills, Charles. *The Racial Contract.* Ithaca, N.Y.: Cornell University Press, 1997.

Nkrumah, Kwame. *Handbook of Revolutionary Warfare: A Guide to the Armed Phase of
the African Revolution.* New York: International Publishers, 1968.

Parsons, Talcott. *The Evolution of Societies.* Edited by Jackson Toby. Englewood Cliffs,
N.J.: Prentice Hall, 1977.

Reed, Adolph Jr. "Yackety-Yak about Race." In Stephen Steinberg, ed., *Race and Ethnicity
in the United States.* Malden, Mass.: Blackwell, 2000. 60–63.

San Juan, Epifanio, Jr. "The Question of Race in the 21st Century." *Dialogue and Initiative*
18 (Spring 1999): 31–34.

Sklar, Holly. "Reinforcing Racism with the War on Drugs." *Z Magazine,* December 1995,
19–24.

Stefancic, Jean, and Richard Delgado. *No Mercy: How Conservative Think Tanks and
Foundations Changed America's Social Agenda.* Philadelphia: Temple University Press,
1996.

Steinberg, Stephen. "The Liberal Retreat from Race." In Stephen Steinberg, ed., *Race and
Ethnicity in the United States.* Malden, Mass.: Blackwell, 2000. 37–54.

———. *Race and Ethnicity in the United States.* Malden, Mass.: Blackwell, 2000.

Street, Paul. "Color Bind: Prisons and the New American Racism." *Dissent* 48.3 (2000):
49–54.

Thompson, E. P. *Whigs and Hunters: The Origin of the Black Act.* New York: Pantheon
Books, 1975.

U.S. General Accounting Office. *Death Penalty Sentencing: Research Indicates Pattern of
Racial Disparities.* Report to Senate and House Committees on the Judiciary. GAO/
GGD-90–57, February 1990.

Watson, Hilbourne A. *Globalization, Liberalism, and the Caribbean: Deciphering the Limits
of Nation, Nation-State, and Sovereignty under Global Capitalism.* Rio Piedras, P.R.:
Universidad de Puerto Rico, Instituto de Estudios del Caribe, 1995.

Weber, Max. *The Protestant Ethic and the Spirit of Capitalism.* Gloucester, Mass.: P. Smith,
1988.

Western, Bruce, and Katherine Beckett. "How Unregulated Is the U.S. Labor Market?
The Penal System as a Labor Market Institution." *American Journal of Sociology* 104
(1999): 1030–60.

Wise, Tim. "Breaking the Cycle of White Dependence: A Call for Majority Self-Sufficiency." *Znet.* <http://www.zmag.org/ZSustainers/ZDaily/2001–05/19wise.htm>. Date accessed: 19 May 2001.

———. "Color-Conscious, White-Blind: Race, Crime and Pathology in America." *Znet.* <http://www.zmag.org/RaceWatch/colcons.htm>.

Wood, Ellen Meiksins. *Democracy against Capitalism: Renewing Historical Materialism.* Cambridge, Eng.: Cambridge University Press, 1995.

CHAPTER 5

A Reversal of the Racialization of History in Hegel's Master/Slave Dialectic (Douglass's "Heroic Slave" and Melville's "Benito Cereno")

Joseph Young

Madison Washington, the protagonist of "The Heroic Slave" (1853), is a figure designed to subvert radical deformations of the humanity of African Americans in theory, argument, and fictionalization that defend proslavery ideas. To dislodge the enforced displacement of the literal, appropriate meaning of the African American as human being, Frederick Douglass constructs a protagonist who attacks semantic bulwarks of proslavery thought with the power and eloquence of language, a distinction embraced by cultural ideologues as the highest expression of humanity. Douglass also gives his protagonist a courageous willingness to confront the master in violent rebellion, signifying a human being with transcendent nobility. Complementing Douglass's efforts, Melville's "Benito Cereno" (1854) offers the figure Babo, who subverts and dethrones postulations about the slave's lack of intelligence and courage presented in proslavery rationalizations such as Hegel's *Phenomenology of Spirit* (1807), in which the slave, figuratively inscribed within the ontology of "the Other," is the cowardly paradigmatic opposite of the audacious master. Madison and Babo articulate elements of the antislavery faction and a phenomenology of self-consciousness as protagonists who achieve agency and who exemplify a conception of the slave that departs from racist constructions. Using a hierarchy of form based on Manichean aesthetics, such constructions attempt to deform blacks' ontological status as human by equating race with species and hence rationalizing their acceptance as chattel. The narratives of Douglass and Melville, informed by a liberated vision of the slave's humanity and quickened by an ever-increasing number of slave revolts, responded to the necessity for a new dialectic of master and slave, a dialectic that depended on the African American composing his own discourse and becoming a force in his own fate.

Although legislation had universally outlawed slavery as a legal institution in the North by 1830, David Walker's *Appeal* (1829) and Nat Turner's Revolt (1831), as forces antithetical to slavery, both literalized and actualized the process that

dispossessed blacks of their humanity so much that they, along with other abolitionist activities, intensified northern-inspired antislavery sentiment to militant
levels (Franklin and Moss 159). Even William Lloyd Garrison, the premier voice
in militant abolitionism who initially was abhorrent to the idea of violence and
who followed a program of nonviolent resistance, by 1850 had acknowledged the
philosophy of force as a fundamental part of abolitionist dogma and had accepted
the inevitability of slave revolts and perhaps even civil war. Other humanitarian
socialist movements such as the Great Revival, which included among its concerns
the improvement of the general conditions of the poor and powerless, joined the
rising tide of the abolitionist movement, ensuring both greater momentum and
maturation. For the glory of God and man, the Great Revival's followers led a
jihad against a host of petty sins, including drink, debauchery, squalid conditions
of schools and jails, infringement of women's rights, and monopolists. "But no
grosser sins could they find in Christendom than pride of pigment, property in
men, the enslavement of one Christian brother by another" (Miller 185).

African Americans, extending back to the pre–Revolutionary War period,
participated in and gave ardent support to the abolition of slavery, employing
all manner of public and private expediencies ranging from activities associated
with the Underground Railroad to the formation of civil institutions to achieve
their ends. Before the nineteenth century, Benjamin Banneker and Prince Hall,
among others, strongly denounced slavery and formed for its elimination organizations like the Free African Society of Philadelphia. By 1830 African Americans
had formed fifty antislavery organizations. Blacks were essential in organizing
the American Anti-Slavery Society and the American and Foreign Anti-Slavery
Society. The New England Anti-Slavery Society, founded by Garrison in 1831,
elected Frederick Douglass as its president in 1847. Established to raise funds and
to help escaping slaves secure freedom, vigilance committees were frequently
dominated by African Americans. Black abolitionists also contributed to the cause
of emancipation as journalists. Most of the black newspapers before the Civil War
were abolitionist-inspired, including the first black newspaper, *Freedom's Journal*,
founded in 1827 by John B. Russwurm and the inexhaustible Samuel Cornish. The
paper was short-lived, but Cornish followed it with the *Rights of All* (1829), the
Weekly Advocate (1836) and, the most effectual, the *Colored American* (1837–41).
William Whipper edited the *National Reformer* (1838–39) in Philadelphia, and
David Ruggles issued the *Mirror of Liberty* (1838–40). Martin R. Delany published
the *Mystery* (1843–47) and then helped Frederick Douglass with the *North Star*
(1847–49). Black abolitionists not only could write but also had a gift for oratory.
Douglass became one of the best-known orators in the country, lecturing in the
East and West of the United States and in England abroad. Nevertheless, it was
the Underground Railroad before the Civil War that commanded a frontal assault
on the citadel of slavery and became a most useful weapon in the abolitionist's
arsenal to end slavery. Governor John A. Quitman of Mississippi declared that

100,000 slaves valued at more than $30 million were lost to the South between 1810 and 1850. Although the number of slaves does not tally with the number the census gives for blacks residing in the North who were natives to slaveholding states, it does approximate estimates made by Wilbur H. Siebert, who believed that 40,000 slaves passed through Ohio alone (Franklin and Moss 172). Blacks participated in the Underground Railroad not merely as its most precious cargo but also among its most valuable engineers and conductors along with southern and northern whites. Harriet Tubman, an African American and one of the greatest of all conductors on the Underground Railroad, was able by her own account to have gone south nineteen times and liberated more than 300 slaves. Other black officials on the Underground Railroad were also prolific in liberating slaves: Elijah Anderson had by 1855 led more than 1,000 slaves to freedom and John Mason delivered 1,300 to freedom. Levi Coffin, a Quaker, helped more than 3,000 slaves escape because of his zeal and strategic location in southern Indiana (Franklin and Moss 170–71).

Unable or unwilling to view the urgency that it was experiencing as originating at some level from the slave, the former slave, the fugitive slave, or the free northern black in concert with other whites, the South became decidedly militant and tunnel-visioned. The South dismissed the gains in personal freedom presumed to have been a result of the early-1800s Enlightenment as part of a temporary phenomenon or heresy, essentially threatening to the southern way of life and given to the vulgar radicalism of those misguided enough to want a sordid Industrial Age. Apologists for slavery gloried in juxtaposing "the affectionate paternalism of the master toward his 'hands'—the word 'slave' gradually fell into disuse among respectable planters of the Cotton Kingdom—with the harsh insecurity, the depression breadlines and seasonal unemployment of 'free' factory workers" (Miller 187). This made the vision of the "Old South" as the final majestic kingdom of civility not only palatable to some of her detractors but also a pleasurable reverie, a sweeter contemplation for her kindred. Nevertheless, as late as 1860 only 1 percent of southern families owned one-fourth of all slaves. Black infant mortality rates claimed every second child. Most leading southwestern planters lived in log cabins even up to 1840. With a staple crop that essentially destroyed the land (like tobacco, cotton consumed the land), the South was forced into an unrelenting and desperate need for constant expansion that could conceivably include not only Texas, New Mexico, and California, but also Cuba and Central and South America and beyond. Moreover, the South was a land where clerk, artisan, slave trader, landless shopkeeper, poor white, and shackled black were all without consideration; yet in the face of all of this, it took, presumably, a total war to reveal to the beloved of the South the irrationality, the fragility, and the iniquity of this planter autocracy (Miller 187).

From the beginning and as part of the strategy of dispossessing African Americans of their humanity, there were oblique and subtle defenders of slavery in the emerging American polity. After Thomas Jefferson's *Notes on the State of Virginia* was published (first general editions in 1787), apologists for slavery were quick to use it as evidence of the inferiority and thus suitability of African Americans for slavery, though some scholars have touted Jefferson's *Notes* as essentially an antislavery work. Conscious sublimation of Jefferson's duplicity and hypocrisy arose in racists' ideological reasoning that embraced an effete disgust with slavery (Jefferson clearly was no abolitionist and he did own slaves) as ineffectual in removing the supposed rationale for the institution, the slave's assumed need for supervision. To understand Jefferson, a man of culture, one must, it was argued, savor the complexity of his central dilemma: he hated slavery but thought blacks inferior to whites (Jordan 429, 436–39). "I advance it therefore as a suspicion only, that the blacks, whether originally a distinct race, or made distinct by time and circumstances, are inferior to the whites in the endowments both of body and mind" (qtd. in Jordan 439). There is no empirical demonstration or verification that blacks are a race separate from whites, but Jefferson concludes so anyway based simply on the cultural advantages experienced by whites. Still as surprising, Winthrop Jordan notes, is Jefferson's profound interest in promoting American education and yet he is profoundly uninterested in educating blacks (355). "It is not their condition then," Jefferson remarks, "but nature, which has produced the distinction" (Jordan 438). Reverberating Shakespeare's figure of the half brute, wholly savage Caliban of *The Tempest*, who is interchangeable with any of the supposed uncivilized European "others," Jefferson's comments about blacks could have been enunciated by Prospero as he delineates the effects of education on such a character: "A devil, a born devil, on whose nature/ Nurture can never stick" (IV. I. 192–93). Under the assumed warrant of biology (of conflating race with species) and the authority of the emerging racial stereotype (an emotional fetish and displacement with the exoticism of color), Jefferson attempts to explicitly separate the black from the white by conjuring up and literalizing racial hierarchies. Jefferson's apocryphal image of the African American would serve as a milestone for the mythological Negro, coming after Caliban and Man Friday, but before Sambo. It would, in the least, influence the portrayal of black characters in much of American literature, and it would shape the national psyche and contaminate interactions between blacks and whites perhaps for centuries to come.

By 1826 southerners had become determined and ferocious advocates of slavery. They understood their duty to naturalize or revive what appeared to be a besieged ideology; to evoke (as would that great romantic racist historian, Barthold Niebuhr) the rhetoric of conquest and progress; and, moreover, to evoke the seemingly crumbling paradigms of "victors as demonstratively better than the vanquished," "history as triumphs of the strong and vital over the weak and feeble," "race as the primary principle of historical explanation," "races with intrinsic essences," and "the European as the apotheosis of all races" (Bernal

31–32, 297–98). And indeed, Edward Brown's *Notes on the Origins and Necessity of Slavery,* which utilized Whitemarsh B. Seabrook's earlier pamphlet and which in turn relied heavily on Aristotle's *Politics,* proclaimed that slavery has always been the means by which a people move from barbarism to civilization (Franklin and Moss; Jenkins). Southern advocates of the proslavery position were attempting to construct a narrative of Western history that would vindicate their appropriation of humans as a means of facilitating their own advancement. By inscribing them as "others" and by assigning them a figurative position below whites in order to rationalize such acts, African Americans were maintained as slaves. To defend this racial hierarchy, the South employed dialogues of monocultural flogging and ruthless racist diatribes; both were argumentative subspecies of a rhetoric of savage resistance to any notion of the slave's humanity.

George Fitzhugh was among the South's most eminent champions, defending its ideals by insisting that slavery had not been harmful to the South; on the contrary, slavery had solved all its problems by allowing it to develop a high degree of culture, since slaves were available to do the work (Franklin and Moss 175). Fitzhugh even criticized the Enlightenment ideas of liberty and equality in a 1850 pamphlet entitled *Slavery Justified,* maintaining that what the poor and weak needed was the protection best provided by a communistic system like the southern plantation. In *Sociology for the South; or, The Failure of a Free Society* (1854), Fitzhugh assails other Enlightenment ideas such as "self-evident truths" and "inalienable rights," and he argues that the problem between the North and the South stems from the eighteenth-century movement in question and John Locke. In this age, the human mind became arrogant in its attempt to reify ideas, endeavoring to conflate the moral with the physical world by experimenting with establishing governments based on philosophical axioms. Under the influence of Jefferson and a few misguided patriots, the musings of the Declaration of Independence contaminated a pure colonial rebellion of independence. It is a document composed of postulates that are at war with slavery, indeed, with all subordination, all government, and all order. Clearly, Fitzhugh not only provides an unconventional defense of slavery, but he also overstates his case, claiming that individuals like Jefferson truly wanted to extend the rights of a republic to slaves. Yet European and American whites in large part, even if against slavery, were not necessarily abandoning their imperial dream. The growing number of slave revolts in the Western Hemisphere—in particular, those in the United States—were making it painfully obvious that chattel slavery had outlived its usefulness in its ability to transport whites from a tributary (Western feudalism) mode of production to a capitalistic (free-market) mode. The master's emotional dependency on the slave (a result of a culture that made it perhaps excessively pleasurable for the planter autocrats) was proving for him too much to bear as he contemplated ending such a relationship. Hence, the proslavery advocates insisted on slavery's legitimacy as they attempted to naturalize or literalize their ideology. Yet the most militant abolitionists, with the possible exception of John Brown and company, were receptive to the titular character of Harriet Beecher Stowe's *Uncle Tom's Cabin* (1852), which is a figurative formulation of slave behavior almost completely devoid of the indignation that would motivate a slave to rise up and overthrow his master.

All the above is but a prologue to an analysis of Frederick Douglass's "Heroic Slave," itself a contribution to the antislavery movement. Not only is Douglass's work a polemical critique of the South's assumptions about the slave's assumed inferiority, however, but it also takes issue with the abolitionist's formulation of African American character as it became manifest in Stowe's *Uncle Tom's Cabin.* The Christian virtues of sacrifice and redemptive love martyr Uncle Tom as he displays them on two occasions: first, in his refusal to betray his escaped fellow slaves, Cassy and Emmeline, knowing all along that Simon Legree (his third master, a brutal, drunken, degenerate planter) will flog him to death for not doing so; and second, in his boundless capacity to forgive his master when Tom, while being slowly beaten to death, responds to Legree's declaration that "I'll conquer ye, or kill ye! . . . I'll count every drop of blood there is in you" by telling him that he would give his heart's blood to save him [Legree] if his life or his soul needed it (Stowe 508). The phenomenology of Tom's self-consciousness is such that he instinctively defers to his master's needs, and he retains only minimal dimensions of an assertive self-consciousness for himself. Tom's reaction represents the last stage in the Hegelian dialectic for a slave. Hegel's reading of slavery is that the slave lacks the courage and therefore the will to resist tyranny in an open struggle and can achieve freedom only through the discipline of a work ethic, Christian stoicism, and forgiveness. Although Tom does not betray his fellow fleeing slaves, his essential victory is only in death; his deliverance from slavery comes from the white master, based on the master's volition. Douglass rejects this fancifully figurative image of the black slave and this form of spiritual resistance; he responds instead with a heroic slave who is enthusiastically willing to engage in a contest of wills with the master unto death, if necessary. Douglass's heroic slave displays the phenomenology of self-consciousness somewhat like Hegel's warrior-master, who becomes a full-blown person by negating an alien will.

Hegel's master-slave dialectic, with the deference of the slave, assumes the superiority of the master. Hegel builds on what Aristotle had enunciated already about slavery in his first book of *The Politics,* that freedom is a relational notion, that freedom of self is a social construct. Such a notion conforms to an alleged natural pattern that produces mind/body, male/female, human/nature dualities, for example. The relation between master and slave is the most primitive expression of this construct or intersubjectivity; it emerges out of a complicated set of transcendental formulations, the first and most important of which is what Hegel in the *Phenomenology of Spirit* characterized as a "battle for recognition" (104–38). Such a battle features the domination of "appetite" or desire (the point

at which a human first becomes conscious of oneself) by an emerging self that
asserts itself as the center of all things (to Hegel, the "person" is that for which
life exists as this unity), independent of the "genus of life," or rather, not attached
to that unity called life. This movement toward absolute abstraction, of rooting
out all immediate being in a dialectic negation of nature, is accomplished by
risking one's life in combat with another of independent will. By doing so, one
proves superiority over animals and animal-like selves and achieves what Hegel
calls "recognition." The victor in such a contest of wills, the more courageous
combatant, becomes the master; the loser proves less of a person, becoming a
thing, a slave.

Although the normative Hegelian interpretation of slavery presupposes that
the slave is cowardly and is without the mettle to stand against oppression openly,
Douglass provides an example of such a contest. It is a narrative of freedom and
self-affirmation that underscores a decisive moment in his autobiography, *My
Bondage and My Freedom* (1855): his struggle with Covey, the slave breaker. The
battle revived in Douglass both the notion of freedom and a sense of his own
manhood (140). Having escaped slavery himself, Douglass gives credence to his
fictionalized tale of an insurrection on board the *Creole* in 1841, one of the scores
of documented slave revolts both domestic and foreign at sea. Freedom to Hegel
is the highest level of consciousness, and the slave achieves it only by a stoic
withdrawal from and an acceptance of the humiliation of physical existence. Yet
Douglass introduces his hero, Madison Washington, not in a cowering, passive,
or stoic acceptance of his condition, but in a "galling consciousness," gripped
by an exasperating soliloquy in a pine forest, asking himself in effect, What is
life to a slave? What is freedom? Am I a coward? A man? Why do not I run away?
Douglass's protagonist is committing himself to a kind of self-interrogation that
is linked to an interrogation of culture and the reasoning that would condone
his enslavement. Predating projects by Theodor Adorno and Jean-Paul Sartre,
Douglass posits a form of negative Hegelian dialectic, analyzing the relation of
individual consciousness to society. Madison comes to realize that he is comprehended or figuratively held within a totalizing schema (Hegel's master/slave
dialectic) that incorporates him as a subhuman other. Because this schema is
enforced by the whip, the gun, and brutal ontologies (even before I was born,
"the scourge was platted for my back; the fetters were forged for my limbs"), to
break free of this schema requires violence. What the protagonist concludes is
also anti-Cartesian, for to be aware of self is not enough. He is compelled to act.
His queries and reflections result in his resolve to accept the upshot of a Hegelian gambit: to gain his liberty or die in the attempt (Douglass "Heroic Slave"
176–78).

In occupying the privileged site of the master/slave dialectic, Madison ex-
udes not the crude outlines of a figurative subperson but features that embrace
a European totality by highlighting elements of the heroic age of Homer and

Virgil, not to aspire to be the white other, but to crash that supposed ontology. Tall, symmetrical, round, and strong, Madison is of honorable form; his arms are like polished iron. His movements combine both the strength and agility of a lion. Though his face is black, it is also comely. His entire appearance projects Herculean strength; and while intelligent and brave, he is neither savage nor forbidding. Instead of appearing as the Hegelian reverse of the warrior-master, the slave looms more like Achilles, the central figure of Homer's *Iliad*. Achilles is a young man of almost limitless beauty and strength, extremely courageous and skilled in combat. He is also an excellent orator who typically uses his skill for the common good. Madison is not afflicted by any of the tragic flaws of Achilles as a type, but he does possess most of his heroic qualities. Madison is neither victimized by the violence of his emotions nor blinded by arrogance and the desire for vengeance. Nevertheless, Madison does carry a heavy burden like Aeneas of Virgil's *Aeneid*. On his shoulders, Aeneas bears the weight of the future Roman Empire. He must perform his duty to his people, to his family, and to the gods.[1] So does Madison. He must be free, as his soliloquy reveals, to be true to his acute sense of consciousness, brought on from his experiences as a slave that forced the emergence of a personal code that he is no coward. Still, he cannot leave his poor Susan (his wife) and two children behind. This is the central dilemma in the life of a heroic slave. Madison is also decisive, concluding that he can best help his family if he is free.

Although Madison has determined adversaries, he also has Arcadian allies of the sort that can both nurture and recognize the heart of a hero. Nature, or the wildering woods, as a countermercantile medium, gives Madison a spiritual realm of sorts to which he can retreat to think and reflect and cultivate his sense of self. For five years the dismal swamps also give him refuge and a means to stay within the vicinity of his wife while he is a fugitive slave in the South. Nature also gives Madison another ally: a northern traveler through Virginia. After drawing his horse up to drink, Mr. Listwell accidentally overhears Madison's soliloquy. From Madison's articulated reflections, he gleans the true nature of this slave's heart and, becoming a figure that both foresees and recovers from the Heideggerian mass forgetfulness of being, decides to become an abolitionist to atone for his past indifference to this ill-starred race. This was in the spring of 1835. Five years later and emblematic of his name, Mr. Listwell proves to be more than a fair-weather friend by sheltering Madison and giving him a bountiful meal when he coincidentally shows up at Listwell's home in Ohio on the run. Madison recounts for his hospitable and charitable hosts (Listwell and his wife) what has happened during the past five years. He tells how he broke for his freedom two weeks after that morning in the woods, how he became lost, how he had to return to the plantation for provisions, how his wife gave him provisions, how they decided that Madison would escape through the swamps, and that the swamps caught fire. He fled both fire and slavery, which forced him north. Listwell commits himself to helping Madison get to a land of liberty, in spite of the fugitive slave laws of Ohio. Madison makes it to the safety of Canada with Listwell's help.

Madison's adversaries are human agents who own the system of slavery outright (like the plantation autocrats) or who support it in some way (the slave keepers and traders, proslavery defenders or advocates, slaves in league with the plantation system, and whites indifferent to slavery). Douglass uses tropes of subversion and irony in his treatment of adversaries to reveal their antipathy and sarcasm and to underscore their incongruous and ignoble human behavior, their skillful deceit of others and of themselves. In this way, Douglass subverts and corrupts the normative status of the privileged totalizing schema of the proslavery position. The beginning of this narrative opens with a masterful stroke of subversion and a declaration of irony: one of the sons of Virginia, who is just as heroic and worthy of freedom as a Thomas Jefferson or a Patrick Henry, "and who fought for it with a valor as high, an arm as strong, and against odds as great, as he who led all the armies of the American colonies through the great war for freedom and independence, lives now only in the chattel records of his native state" (Douglass "Heroic Slave," 175). After Madison's first dash for freedom, he loses his way and then returns to the plantation for provisions, but he avoids some of his fellow slaves who are passing the time merrily. He despises their acquiescence in their own degradation that their seeming contentment infers. Madison decides that he dare not enter the slave quarters, "for where there is seeming contentment with slavery, there is certain treachery to freedom" (Douglass 190). A year after Madison has fled to Canada, Listwell is passing the night in a famous public tavern, an old rookery about fifteen miles outside Richmond, Virginia. Many slave traders are present because the largest ever sale of slaves is scheduled to be held in Richmond the following day. It is not clear why Listwell is in the vicinity; what is clear, however, is that he is undercover (possibly as an informant for the Underground Railroad). None of the irony in this situation is lost on Listwell; he must assume deportment suitable to the context, which forces him to hold his tongue on the subject of slavery. It is a disposition that he loathes, hating slavery so much that he feels it the immediate duty of every man, without compromise and without concealment, to cry out against it. Nevertheless, like Erasmus, he is not a martyr, concluding "that it was wiser to trust the mercy of God for his soul, than the humanity of slave-traders for his body" (Douglass 214). On an early morning walk, Listwell sees for the first time in his life the hideous sight of a slave gang comprising all sizes, ages, and both sexes, presided over by a horrid trio of slave keepers, all to fill the pockets of men too lazy to work for an honest living. Just before Listwell is about to doubt the existence of a God of justice, as his eyes are running up and down the fettered ranks, he catches the eye of Madison Washington.

Without being noticed, Listwell greets his friend and returns to hear Madison's story after the slave keepers go to breakfast: Madison had returned to his old master's place to recover his wife. After Madison took her in his arms, the dogs were on them almost immediately; in the ensuing flight, his wife was killed and he was wounded and captured. He was sold to a slave trader and placed in this gang of 130 human beings bound for the New Orleans market. The only assistance that Listwell can provide Madison at this point is to slip into Madison's pocket the three files that he had purchased; he darts back into the crowd as the slave gang passes en route to the *American Slaver.*

Coincidence and characterization are interesting features of the narrative structure of Douglass's text. The two significant coincidences in the narrative, both extraordinary circumstances—when Madison fortuitously stumbles onto Listwell's home after he becomes a fugitive slave, and when Listwell by happenstance discovers Madison on the slave gang—serve the purpose of advancing the plot development and of fostering the thematic element that a supernatural power or a wakeful providence had linked their destiny (Douglass 221–22). Noteworthy also is the polemic that in the face of such a cosmic atrocity as slavery, there is a God of justice assisting individuals who have the integrity to recognize the evil of the institution. Just as coincidence foregrounds specific thematic elements, so does characterization. The hero Madison Washington has already been characterized as the meeting place of heroic virtue.[2] What is left is the actual contest that will confirm his stature. Listwell, the previously indifferent northern white, converts into a fanatical abolitionist who is truly a foul-weather friend to Madison. Listwell is one of two whites whom Madison converts; the second will be forthcoming. The slave keepers are the seat of villainy; and their allies, the proslavery advocates, we will see, are citadels of deceit and self-deception. The contented slave is noteworthy only as a bed of treachery for other slaves.

Douglass uses a completive anachronism (a retrospective story) and an embedded narrative (a story within a story) to fill the narrative gap about what happens onboard the *American Slaver.* The episode turns on the slave's willingness to fight for liberty. Even Douglass has argued that "the very submission of the slave to his chains is held as an evidence of his fitness to be a slave; it is regarded as one of the strongest proofs of the divinity of slavery, that the negro tamely submits to his fetters. His very nonresistance . . . is quoted as proof of his cowardice, and his unwillingness to suffer and to sacrifice for his liberty" (qtd. in Boxill 42–43). Two months after the Virginia slave brig sailed, Jack Williams has a conversation with the first mate of that brig in the Marine Coffeehouse at Richmond. Douglass composes the episode as an argumentative conversation that is inherently dramatic and dialectic in nature, pitting proslavery arguments against the heroic behavior of the slaves. Williams believes that the insurrection onboard the *American Slaver* "was the result of ignorance of the real character of *darkies* in general" (Douglass 226). He implies that all he would need to quell a "nigger insurrection" is a half-dozen resolute white men and a good stout whip or a stiff rope's end. To use a gun is to show respect, and to respect slaves is to encourage their attacks. Tom Grant, the first mate, does not believe that Williams's theory about black inferiority can stand the test of saltwater. Grant suggests that such a theory may be asserted on land where Williams has the support of the community and the physical force of the state and national governments at his command; but he denies that blacks are naturally cowards, and he adds that it may be merely expedient for blacks to act cowardly on shore. At this point, Williams appears frustrated and ashamed, and he is concerned about redeeming the Virginia sailor's character. He cannot fathom how slaves, who are so depraved that one drop of their blood can make cowards of hundreds, could subdue their betters. Grant, on the other hand, is comfortable presently with deferring to the slave when contemplating the contest between master and slave. On the high seas, the slave has proven himself capable of obtaining freedom by answering a higher call, and Grant no longer feels he can tolerate slavery: "I'm resolved never to endanger my life again in a cause which my conscience does not approve" (Douglass 230).

Grant's respect for the slaves is an emphatic illustration of Douglass's belief, fully articulated in *My Bondage and My Freedom,* that the slave becomes a man not when he becomes a solvent entrepreneur and acquires the comforts of property and position, but when he can assert himself in confrontation with the "other," thereby transcending social bigotry. Douglass, as does Hegel, views the acquisition of freedom as inherent in the recognition that is won in struggle. "A man without force," argues Douglass, "is without the essential dignity of humanity. Human nature is so constituted, that it cannot honor a helpless man" (Douglass, *My Bondage* 140). Madison Washington anticipates this articulation; he discards the submissive notion of passage from slavery to liberty that moves the slave along a path of Christian humility, abstract reason, and Hegel's contrivance for freedom through the discipline of the work ethic. He also departs from the pacifism of the Garrisonian Christian abolitionists and fully embraces what Cynthia Willett characterizes as "the courageous will of Hegel's sovereign master" (165). The details of Madison's passage from slavery to liberty also avoid the ubiquitous sentimentality of Stowe's *Uncle Tom's Cabin*; they establish the black formation of self in realms other than strict white supervision or paternalism.

Those details provide no relief for Williams, who has difficulty understanding, as he puts it, how a dozen or two closely ironed ignorant Negroes can get their fetters off and kill a white captain and their master and then sail the ship into a British port where every "darky" of them is set free (Douglass 232). Grant explains the importance of their shrewd and competent leader, Madison Washington, a powerful African American with the impeccable diction and pronunciation of a schoolmaster. The attack begins about twilight just before a squall, all hands having been ordered on deck to lie aloft, when Grant hears a pistol discharge from the starboard. Turning around, Grant observes the deck covered with blacks with broken fetters in their hands; they knock him senseless to the deck. When Grant regains his consciousness, he sees Captain Clark and Mr. Jameson, owner of most of the slaves, lying dying on the quarterdeck; Madison is at the helm. Grant is horrified that a "black murderer" commands the brig but is reassured when Madison says, "God is my witness that Liberty, not malice, is the motive for this night's work. . . . We have done that which you applaud your fathers for doing, and if we are murders, *so were they*" (Douglass 234–35, emphasis not mine). Madison enunciates his ideal of freedom in a poignant irony designed to underline his new self-formation, fully aware of the need for a liberating consciousness (of "broken fetters") and of the need for moving this new consciousness toward action, toward physical resistance. Madison offers not to kill Grant if he lands them in Nassau, adding that if the brig touches a slave-cursed shore, he will put a match to the magazine himself and blow the brig into a thousand pieces. By this time a squall had burst upon them; and Madison, taking the helm, meets the storm with the equanimity of a seasoned sailor. After the squall breaks, as if invoking the universal given to all people, Madison states the following: "Mr. mate, you cannot write the bloody laws of slavery on those restless billows. The ocean, if not the land, is free" (Douglass 237).

By reversing the dialectic, Madison displaces the master and occupies the position of sovereign self. Such a conception of self, though dethroning the master, does embrace Hegel's battle for recognition and it does generate the dualities of subject and other; for that reason, it does not defeat the Hegelian dualities nor the dialectic structure. Douglass's hero does not breach the totality of the Hegelian schema. For the moment, however, simply overthrowing the master's claim of metaphysical and ontological superiority is enough. Even if Madison were to proclaim that his ability to subvert the master is a function of his intrinsic nature, his humanity, such a proclamation of ahistorical transcendental human essence would be the fissure that would allow the ontological imperialism of self and other in the first place. Yet Douglass was not concerned with any desire to bring to fruition any late twentieth century antihumanist projects. Even if it were possible to defeat the Hegelian dualities (perhaps more a function of language and perception than a politically motivated agenda), Douglass was more concerned with overthrowing the Western notion that a black slave was ontologically antithetical to the hero.

Just as "The Heroic Slave" is about a revolt at sea, so also is Herman Melville's "Benito Cereno" (1855). The Hegelian duality as well is present in the story, along with Captain Delano, a major character possessing a profound naiveté or sublimated racism that makes him responsible for the titular character's mental suffering and anguish. Benito Cereno's position as both an insider and an outsider to the Hegelian schema allows him to defeat the dualities, or at least to observe how their representations of reality are flawed. The Hegelian dialectic operates in reverse in this narrative, too; the rebel slave leader, Babo, dominates the will of his so-called white superior, Don Benito, the Spanish captain. Moreover, the warrior-master as displayed by the American captain Delano can achieve only liminal levels of a self-consciousness that should allow him to dominate or re-ject the blind credulity of his racist belief in the inferiority of blacks. Such a schema is thwarted somewhat by the American captain's nascent realization, which contradicts his racist beliefs, producing conflictual emotional structures. Melville's narrative is a cautionary tale detailing the folly implicit in such a belief system; it is, therefore, an antislavery document. Based on an actual slave revolt at sea, "Benito Cereno" uses much of Amasa Delano's autobiography, *Narrative of Voyages and Travels* (1817), which recounts how Captain Delano encountered a Spanish slave ship in distress off the coast of Chile, boarded her to offer assistance, and eventually learned that slave rebels commanded the Spanish ship secretly. As the premier officer of a large sealer and general trader, Captain Delano represents American expansionism, the regime of commerce, wealth, power, and repression. Most of the encounters with the Spanish ship are filtered through the prism of Delano's consciousness, providing the reader an opportunity to share a kind of intimacy with his character. Misreading Delano cleverly and superficially, one could conclude that he has a benevolent heart and, "being a person of a singular undistrustful and good nature, not liable, except on extraordinary and repeated excitement, and hardly then, to indulge in personal alarms, any way involving the imputation of malign evil in man" (Melville 96). The "evil" in this case, of course, would be the slave who rejects his role as slave, as subhuman other, and the rebel. Nevertheless, when given the option of two possible impressions of reality, Delano is unable to cast off a false image of the world, despite repeated prompting from his environment to the contrary, if in doing so he must release his impassioned embrace of the romantic fantasy of white superiority. Most of the narrative is a catalogue of such a delusion.

Captain Delano's initial impression from his whaleboat of the Spanish ship *San Dominick,* after it had sailed into the harbor of St. Maria and drew near land, is that it "appeared [which was no purely fanciful resemblance] like a white-washed monastery after a thunder-storm, seen perched upon some dun cliff among the Pyrenees" (Melville 97). The context of the image suggests that the ship seems out of place. It is like a whale beached in the mountains instead of on the shore, a kind of Noah's ark after the waters have subsided. At first, the image of the ship triggers in the captain sublimated guilt-laden emotions, alluding to the failure of a Western institution like the church that, after running its course, had become beached on something other than its principles. As Chapman Cohen has pointed out, countries most ostentatious in their parade of Christianity have witnessed slavery's worst features (52–53; Stirling 367–80, 528–45). A nearer view of the ship reveals to Delano that it is a Spanish merchantman, first class, carrying slaves and other valuable freight from one colonial port to another. Delano accepts this as a truer character of the vessel that has seen better times owing to the slovenly neglect that pervades her. True to the interests of his class, Delano chooses as more noteworthy not the atrocity of slavery, which the ship surely represents, but the condition of the ship, especially the principal relic of faded grandeur: the ample oval of the shieldlike sternpiece. The medallion is decorated with sets of mythological figures, the centerpiece being "a dark satyr in a mask, holding his foot on the prostrate neck of a writhing figure, likewise masked" (Melville 98). The symbolism is not too oblique here. The stern's centerpiece is clearly a figuration of the hegemonic structure, the power relationships currently onboard the Spanish ship. When the dark satyr is finally unmasked, Delano will discover this also. Until then, however, Delano finds it absurd to treat seriously the black slave who is by Western mores analogous to the quasi-human goatmen of Greek legend who spend most of their time in amorous pursuit of wood nymphs and who are associated with the ecstatic, orgiastic, and irrational Dionysus.

After boarding the Spanish ship, Captain Delano is inundated with indications that something is amiss, but he rationalizes those disturbing impressions with interpretations that are more comfortable and compliant with his assumptions about the world. Delano attributes, for example, the strangeness of the ship (it looks as if it has just emerged from the deep) and its occupants (especially the conspicuously chanting four elderly grizzled blacks who are crouching sphinx-like, picking oakum in strategic positions on the ship; and six other blacks on the quarterdeck, each scouring a rusty hatchet in his hand, occasionally clashing it like a cymbal against another's hatchet in a show of bravado) to suffering, and he convinces himself that nothing more relaxes the desirability of good order than misery. Delano interprets the cautious reserve of Don Benito as the retiring indifference of a recluse; and he compares the noisy indocility of the blacks and the sullen inefficiency of the whites to the steady, excellent conduct of Babo, who performs his duties to the Spanish captain with affectionate zeal, which has earned for "the negro the repute of the most pleasing body-servant in the world; . . . less a servant than a devoted companion" (Melville 102–3). Delano even offers at one point to purchase Babo for fifty doubloons (roughly seventy pounds sterling). One of the more glaring instances of Delano's credulousness is his acceptance of Don Benito's narrative that explains how the ship and company came to be in its present condition. For the untutored in seamanship or maritime affairs, Benito's tale is a competent attempt at masking the obvious. For the skilled professional sea captain that Delano is assumed to be, however, the explanation should have been as inadequate as beggar's rags for sails. It should seem incredulous that so much ill fate could befall a single ship on one voyage. Here are just a few examples: about 190 days out, heavy gales beset the ship off Cape Horn; three of Benito's best officers and fifteen sailors are lost with the main yard in a moment; sacks of Mata and water pipes have been thrown into the sea to lighten the hull, which proves to be fatal when the breeze suddenly deserts the ship in sultry calms; scurvy breaks out; and disabled mariners cannot manage the ship.

Just astonishing as his credulousness is Delano's acquiescence in the face of violence against whites by blacks. In one instance of insubordination against whites,

Captain Delano observes a black boy who, enraged at a word dropped by one of his white companions, seizes a knife and strikes the lad over the head, inflicting a gash from which blood flows. When Benito returns one of his half-lunatic looks in response to the American captain's remark that had such a thing happened on board the *Bachelor's Delight,* instant punishment would have ensued, Delano concludes that Don Benito is a paper captain. In another instance, Benito and his crew are eagerly awaiting coming supplies. Delano notices among the crowd two blacks accidentally incommoded by a white sailor. The two blacks dash the sailor to the deck and jump on him. The American captain is then distracted by one of Benito's coughing fits and, most important, by Babo's Johnny-on-the-spot quickness in coming to his master's aide. Apparently Delano is infatuated more with Babo's subservience than with the insolence of the other blacks.

The American captain's reaction to Spanish sailors onboard who try to warn him increasingly poses burdens on his system of ethical reflexes. Although these warnings challenge his assumption about the nature of things and induce a kind of emotional crisis, they do not really change him. Spanish sailors repeatedly try to nonverbally communicate to Delano via meaningful glances and expressive gestures that profoundly perplex him while he waits for his whaleboat to arrive. What seems to console the captain, apart from the sight of his whaleboat (*Rover* by name, eliciting a thousand comforting associations), are his solitary musings about primitive peoples. Delano's attention turns to, in the diction of that day, "a slumbering negress": "There's naked nature, now; pure tenderness and love, thought Captain Delano, well pleased" (Melville 129). He is gratified with the manner of black women; in his understanding, like most uncivilized women, they are at once tender of heart and resilient of constitution, ready equally to fight or die for their infants. Delano convinces himself that perhaps these are the very women whom the Scottish physician-explorer Mungo Park (1771–1806) observed while in Africa, and of whom he provided an account. Delano seems comforted for the moment, and Melville manages an effective symbol that captures the anxiety tightening in the captain's head. As he regains the deck from the quarter gallery, Delano observes an aged sailor working a handful of ropes into a large knot. The aged sailor seems like an Egyptian priest of Ammon, weaving Gordian knots for the temple. Delano studies the knot, "his mind, by a not uncongenial transition, passing from its own entanglements to those of the hemp" (Melville 132). Not having experienced such an intricately constructed knot before, "for a moment, knot in hand, and knot in head, Captain Delano stood mute" (Melville 132). Obviously, the knot is a metaphor for the entanglements that have become part of Delano's understanding since first sighting the Spanish ship: entanglements arising from impressions that have challenged his assumptions, his preconceptions about the world and in particular about blacks, revealing that the bigotry in his head is woven with the intricacy of a Gordian knot.

Yet the centerpiece of the first part of "Benito Cereno" is the shaving scene. It is reminiscent of the central mythological figure on the sternpiece. Here multiple levels converge concerning the three principal characters of the narrative, but Delano's impressions in the scene are most telling. Sometime after the whaleboat has arrived to bring the provisions, a white messenger boy announces that it is shaving time and asks the master to go into the cuddy, a deck cabin formed by the poop. Benito is seated in a misshapen armchair that seems to Delano at first like some rudely extravagant Middle Age device of torture. After Babo begins to shave Don Benito, however, Delano's visions of torment evaporate into thoughts concerning the suitability of Negroes for avocations involving one's person, their "docility arising from the unaspiring contentment of a limited mind, and that susceptibility of blind attachment sometimes inhering in indisputable inferiors" (Melville 141–42). Although Delano's experiences onboard the *San Dominick* have induced feelings of frustration and apprehension in him, being in the sociably inclined cuddy and observing the servant Babo so debonairly going about the work of shaving his master, towel on the arm, having chosen a multicolored apron for his master's chin (actually the Spanish flag), returns to Delano's memory all the affections he has for the Negro. Yet Delano cannot resist the vagaries, those antic conceits, that come and go in a flash; as he beholds the servant elevating the razor momentarily in one hand, the other hand dabbling the lather on the Spaniard's lean neck, he sees in Babo a headsman and in Benito a man at the block. When Delano refers to the tale of the Spanish ship's trials, in particular the gales and the calm after them, he says that if Benito had not told him this, he would find such an account incredible. At this point, Benito gives a start and Babo draws blood. After a small delay, at Babo's urging, Benito resumes explaining the contradictions in his story.

The importance of this scene at one level is that it affirms what the reader has learned about the good captain's character thus far. Delano is comfortable only with a conceptualization of the black that is mostly like Stowe's Uncle Tom: passive, docile, content in his place because he is inferior and not given to a greater ambition. Delano scrupulously embraces this characterization of the black, despite the contrary flashes of insight he gets from Babo's person and personality. Delano remains committed to his misguided preconceptions to the end, and Benito pays the price for the American captain's lack of discrimination, as when he tells Benito that he finds the calm after the gales almost incredible. This tattered part of the tale is meant to clue the American captain in on discovering that the story is indeed a falsehood. Nevertheless, apparently Babo is quicker in wit than Delano, and Benito pays for it in his own blood. Delano gets another glimpse of Babo's true nature after he has returned to his whaleboat, when Benito leaps over the bulwarks and lands at his feet, and Babo leaps after him in hot pursuit. Even then, Delano is more certain that the black is probably performing his duty as a faithful servant rather than acting as a rebel carrying out a desperate act of revenge.

The profundity of Captain Amasa Delano's naiveté, or more correctly his bigotry, is displayed in just how far afield his impressions are. Showing great intellect, tremendous leadership skills, a knowledge of psychological warfare, and a decisive ability to act, Babo, the great maestro, composes and orchestrates first a servile insurrection at sea and then an elaborate masquerade in which the whites are forced to act as if in control of a slave ship while the blacks, appearing to be in a kind of relaxed captivity, covertly are in command. Before a royal tribunal convened to investigate the incidents onboard the *San Dominick,* Don Benito testifies that from beginning to end Babo was the plotter, the helm and keel of the revolt. He further testifies that it was Babo who devised all the expedients, mixing deceit and defense. The six Ashantees were his bravadoes; and Atufal (actually his lieutenant), though presented as chained, could in a moment drop the chains. Four aged black caulkers were appointed to keep whatever order they could muster on deck. Babo had also advised Don Benito that if he did not conduct himself in accordance with his instructions, he would be killed. He identifies Babo as the one who decided to have Don Alexandro killed (the owner of most of the slaves and Don Benito's close friend) and to use his skeleton to terrorize the whites into complying with his orders. Babo's ultimate goal is to reach Senegal; if he fails that, he will settle for vengeance. Babo therefore is a study in the kind of counterdominance necessary to break clear of the ontology of the "other."

Part of that dominance involves asserting the creative prerogative of a sovereign self. Melville constructs a most profound Hegelian reversal; he depicts Don Benito as actually a creation of Babo so that, in effect, the slave creates his master. A second level of convergence in the shaving scene is Babo's agency. At the conclusion of his shave, Benito "sat so pale and rigid now, that the negro seemed a Nubian sculptor finishing off a white statue-head" (Melville 146). As opposed to the European construction of the African as a Hegelian mirror reversal of himself, the African makes the white into his own spitting image, a homunculus, a manikin: "the servant for a moment surveyed his master, as, in toilet at least, the creature of his own tasteful hands" (Melville 146). Melville rounds out his study of dominance with the symbolism implicit in Benito's silver-mounted sword. That indubitable symbol of despotic rule is not a sword at all, but only the ghost of one; having been made rigid, the scabbard is empty. The machinations of the slave have replaced the pretensions to superiority.

To emphasize the theme of dominance, Melville makes use of certain symbols. Upon studying the Spanish ship from his whaleboat for the first time, Captain Delano notes that canvas is covering what could be the ship's figurehead. "Seguid vuestro jefe" (follow your leader, in Spanish) is painted below the canvas. It is not until the blacks are revealed in full revolt, after Benito had leaped into Delano's boat, that the canvas shroud is ripped away, revealing the skeletal remains of Alexandro Aranda's body in substitution for the image of Christopher Colon as the figurehead. "Follow your leader" is the creed of the enthusiastic disciple who is compelled, perhaps by choice, to obey the command of a ruler. Babo had painted this sentence, and it carries a warning for onboard proslavery loyalists: follow your leader and die. Or follow your leader by relinquishing the status of sovereign self (that is, master) and by accepting the status of an appropriated other (in this case, a justifiably subdued captive); become mute and compliant and live. Though it must have felt like slavery to the whites, Babo offers them imprisonment or death.[3] This is the method that Babo uses to intimidate the defiant whites onboard. Before the royal tribunal, Don Benito shows in testimony that four days after Babo had decided to have Aranda killed, Babo showed him a skeleton that had been substituted for the figurehead and said to Benito, as he did to all the Spaniards onboard, "Keep faith with the blacks from here to Senegal, or you shall in spirit, as now in body, follow your leader" (Melville 172). Babo's intimidation of proslavery whites also overthrows the old regime of Christopher Colon, the so-called "discoverer of the new world," but more accurately the bringer of slavery to the Western Hemisphere. Near the painted expression "follow your leader" is the ship's name in stately capitals: "San Dominick." Haiti (the western French segment of Hispaniola) was the first land discovered by Christopher Columbus in the new world. Slavery was first introduced in the Western Hemisphere on this island in 1493. It was also the scene of raging and dreadful slave rebellions from the late 1790s until the mid-1800s.

"The Heroic Slave" and "Benito Cereno" present narratives of self-formation and the counterstereotype of a more thoughtful, suffusive figure of black subjects, having both the mettle and the complexity to confront a brutal Hegelian master. Faced by racist theories like those enunciated in Jefferson's *Notes on Virginia* and by the martyrdom of characters like Stowe's Uncle Tom that impose a moral and ideological control over slave rebels and their supporters, Douglass and Melville each construct an alternative eloquence arising out of an alternative epistemology that substitutes the phantasmal theatrics of a white racist's imaginary of cowardly slaves with the real threat of violent rebellion. Madison Washington is committed to a rite of manhood like Hegel's "struggle for recognition," and Babo's ability to orchestrate a complex and masterful revolt is unique for its intricacy but equal to the metonymy "a hive of subtlety" (Melville 184) attributed to his mind. Both possess intellectual acuity as rebel leaders, underscoring the folly of those who believe that the slave is unable and unwilling to confront a white master who embraces a tradition that locates the abode of the gods and the house of being in war. Melville and Douglass each present a phenomenology of the insurrectional spirit of slaves willing to compose their own discourse. Both are cautionary tales for the proslavery and the sympathetic liberal whites who are blissfully ignorant or who experience a blessed serenity (as in "Bonito Sereno") in their delusion of the permanently pacified compliant slave.

Notes

1. See Homer, *The Iliad,* especially 18.22–27 (pages 375–76), 20.97–102 (pages 406–7), and 20.259–66 (page 411). Also see Virgil, *The Aeneid,* especially 1.1–19 (page 3), 1.510–31 (page 17), and 1.739–57 (page 23).

2. And I believe if we examine a synthetic feature of his characterization—the hero's name "Madison Washington," for example—we will agree that Douglass is concerned less with portraying a hero that is so because of the blue blood flowing through his veins and is concerned more with illustrating features of virtue that require freedom as its life's blood. The name does appear in Henry Highland Garnet's 1843 paper entitled "An Address to the Slaves of the United States of America," in which the rebel leader is described. See also "Functions of Character," an excerpt from Phelan, *Reading People, Reading Plots* 1–14, for a discussion of the components of character based on narrative theory.

3. See Patterson, *Slavery and Social Death: A Comparative Study,* 2–14 in particular, for a discussion of slavery as social death. Patterson shows how all forms of slavery are characterized by the slave's sense of powerlessness and dishonor, though I believe his notion needs refinement. He should distinguish an innocent person enslaved who experiences a sense of dishonor from a convicted criminal (a prisoner of war from a defeated invading army, a mass murderer, or the like) justifiably imprisoned who experiences a sense of humiliation. Both persons may claim to have been or felt dishonored, but only one actually has been dishonored.

Works Cited

Bernal, Martin. *Black Athena: The Afroasiatic Roots of Classical Civilization.* Vol. 1. New Brunswick, N.J.: Rutgers University Press, 1987.

Boxill, Bernard R. "Radical Implications of Locke's Moral Theory: The Views of Frederick Douglass." Pp. 29–48 in *Subjugation and Bondage: Critical Essays on Slavery and Social Philosophy,* edited by Tommy L. Lott. Lanham, Md.: Rowman and Littlefield, 1998.

Brown, Edward. *Notes on the Origin and Necessity of Slavery.* Charleston, S.C.: A. E. Miller, 1826.

Cohen, Chapman. *Christianity, Slavery, and Labour.* London, Eng.: Pioneer, 1936.

Douglass, Frederick. "The Heroic Slave" [1853]. Pp. 174–239 in *Autographs for Freedom,* edited by Julia Griffiths. Vol. 1. Miami: Mnemosyne, 1969.

———. *My Bondage and My Freedom.* Edited by John Stauffer. New York: Modern Library, 2003.

Fitzhugh, George. *Slavery Justified, by a Southerner.* Fredericksburg, Md.: Recorder printing office, 1850.

———. *Sociology for the South; or, The Failure of a Free Society.* Richmond, Va.: A. Morris, 1854.

Franklin, John Hope, and Alfred A. Moss Jr. *From Slavery to Freedom: A History of Negro Americans.* 6th ed. New York: Knopf, 1988.

Hegel, G. W. F. *Phenomenology of Spirit* [1807], translated by A. V. Miller. New York: Clarendon, 1978.

Homer. *The Iliad,* translated by Richmond Lattimore. Chicago: University of Chicago Press, 1970.

Jenkins, William Sumner. *Pro-Slavery Thought in the Old South.* [1935]. Repr., Gloucester, Mass.: Peter Smith, 1960.

Jordan, Winthrop D. *White over Black: American Attitudes toward the Negro, 1550–1812.* Chapel Hill: University of North Carolina Press, 1968.

Lott, Tommy L., ed. *Subjugation and Bondage: Critical Essays on Slavery and Social Philosophy.* Lanham, Md.: Rowman and Littlefield, 1998.

Melville, Herman. *Billy Budd, Benito Cereno, and The Enchanted Isles.* New York: Readers Club, 1942.

Miller, William. *A New History of the United States.* Rev. ed. New York: Dell, 1971.

Patterson, Orlando. *Slavery and Social Death: A Comparative Study.* Cambridge, Mass.: Harvard University Press, 1982.

Phelan, James. *Reading People, Reading Plots: Character, Progression, and the Interpretation of Narrative.* Chicago: University of Chicago Press, 1989.

Stirling, William. "The Cloister-Life of Emperor Charles V." *Fraser's Magazine* Apr.–May 1851: 367–80, 528–45.

Stowe, Harriet Beecher. *Uncle Tom's Cabin; or, Life among the Lowly.* New York: Modern, 1938.

Virgil. *The Aeneid,* translated by Robert Fitzgerald. New York: Vintage Books, 1990.

Willett, Cynthia. "The Master-Slave Dialectic: Hegel vs. Douglass." Pp. 151–70 in *Subjugation and Bondage: Critical Essays on Slavery and Social Philosophy,* edited by Tommy L. Lott. Lanham, Md.: Rowman and Littlefield, 1998.

CHAPTER 6

"Dark-Faced Europeans": The Nineteenth-Century Colonial Travelogue and the Invention of the Hima Race

Gatsinzi Basaninyenzi

> The Hamites—who are "Europeans," i.e. belong to the same great branch of mankind as the whites—are commonly divided into two great branches, Eastern and Northern.
> —C. G. Seligman in *Races of Africa*

> There are some isolated Caucasoid groups, such as the cattle Fulani in West Africa and the Hima and Tutsi in the interlacustrine area of East Africa, who have adopted the language of their Negroid neighbors.
> —Robin Hallett in *Africa to 1875: A Modern History*

> I argue that the Rwandan genocide needs to be thought through within the logic of colonialism.
> —Mahmood Mamdani in *When Victims Become Killers*

In 1994 when the Tutsi genocide was taking place, many people who watched the carnage on television wondered how the killers could tell the Tutsi and the Hutu apart. After all, the two groups are black, they share the same territory, and they speak the same language. Indeed, it is doubtful that a *Time* magazine article describing the Tutsi as having a "lighter skin and aquiline, almost European features" and the Hutu as being "darker skinned and stockier" (Gibbs 61) could have given a convincing explanation to those who read it looking for answers. Yet it is specifically this kind of "racial" differentiation found in the *Time* magazine article that informed the ideology of the Tutsi genocide. In his seminal book on the subject—*When Victims Become Killers*—Mahmood Mamdani distinguishes two types of genocide: "the genocide of the native by the settler" and "the native impulse to eliminate the settler" (9–10). The Tutsi genocide, he says, "needs to be understood as a natives' genocide"—a genocide perpetrated by people who saw their mission "as one of clearing the soil of a threatening alien presence. This was not an 'ethnic' cleansing but a 'racial' cleansing" (14). The Hutu intelligentsia who conceived the ideology of the Tutsi genocide had "scientific" references to show that the Tutsi were an alien race. Several anthropologists, including Charles G. Seligman, whom I have quoted above, had theorized that the Hamites, an ethnic group in which they included the Hima of Uganda and the Tutsi of Rwanda and Burundi, were Caucasians who had centuries ago migrated to the region from Ethiopia and had intermarried with the native populations of the so-called Negroid race. This theory, which has been dubbed the "Hamitic hypothesis," was by no means original. I want to propose that Richard F. Burton's travelogue, *The Lake Regions of Central Africa,* which was originally published in 1860, was the first text to racialize the Hima, and by extension the Tutsi. John Hanning Speke's and Henry M. Stanley's racialization of the same in their travelogues, I argue, was a rehashing of Burton's racial categorization of the Hima.

It all begins in 1857, three years before the publication of *The Lake Regions of Central Africa.* Burton is in eastern Africa to, among other things, "determine the exportable produce of the interior and the ethnology of its tribes" (23). While traveling through the Karagwa region, he notices that its inhabitants, the Hima (whom he calls Wahuma), have physical features similar to those that nineteenth-century race theorists used to identify groups that constitute the Caucasian race. Burton's racial characterization of the Hima comes as a surprise, for before encountering them, he has been traveling through regions populated by "pure Negroes," whom he calls barbarians—a common appellation of blacks in nineteenth-century racial discourse. The "barbarian," Burton says, "appears an embryo of the two superior races. He is inferior to the active-minded and objective, the analytic and perceptive European, and to the ideal and subjective, the synthetic and reflective Asiatic" but has in common with "the lower Oriental types stagnation of mind, indolence of body, moral deficiency, superstition, and the childish passion" (490). As an adherent of nineteenth-century scientific racism, Burton was well versed in the jargon of the racial discourse on the Other. In *First Footsteps in East Africa; or, An Exploration of Harar,* published four years before *The Lake Regions,* he describes eastern Africa's populations as being "composed of three distinct races," among them "the Aborigines, such as the Negroes, the Bushmen, Hottentots, and other races, having such physiological peculiarities as the steatopyge, the tablier, and other developments described, in 1815, by the great Cuvier" (70).

In 1815 Georges Cuvier, dubbed the father of paleontology, had been one of the three French naturalists who studied the genitalia of Saartjie Baartman, a Hottentot woman who had been brought from South Africa and exhibited in London and Paris as a specimen of African aborigines. After her death, Cuvier dissected her to determine the place of the Negro race in nature, which he concluded was just a little above that of animals. In his *Animal Kingdom* he wrote that "the projection of the lower parts of the face, and the thick lips, evidently approximate [the Negro race] to the monkey tribe" (105).

Clearly, "the great Cuvier," about whom more will be said later, had a significant influence upon Burton's idea of the Negro race. In *The Lake Regions,* Burton wrote that "the barbarian" of eastern Africa is "intellectually unfit to discriminate between a cent and a dollar" (31), and he looks at a stranger "with a wild and childish stare" (32). Further in the travelogue he describes the Wamrima as being "debauched, apathetic, dilatory, and inert" and adds that they "appear to be unfitted by nature for intellectual labor" (43).

Still, he says that the Hima have "reflective faculties," have a nose that is "more of the Caucasian type," and are "not deficient in intelligence" (391). Not only does Burton find the Himas' physical features markedly different from those of the neighboring "barbarians," they are also "superior in civilization and social constitution to the other tribes of Eastern and Central Africa" (391). Among the Hima Burton includes the "Watosi" (Watutsi), "a pastoral people who are scattered throughout these lake regions" and who "refuse to carry loads, to cultivate the ground, or to sell one another" (398).

The racialization of the Hima in travelogues by Burton, and later by John Hanning Speke and Henry Morton Stanley, I suggest, is not only inscribed in nineteenth-century racial discourse, it also exposes its incoherence.

Although Burton's list of publications is impressive (forty-three volumes of exploration and travel, more than one hundred articles, and several volumes of translation), he could hardly be considered an intellectual in the academic sense of the word: He never held an academic post. He seems to have sought acceptance in intellectual circles in England, but without success. In *The Lake Regions,* he takes pride in having published a paper in the *Journal of the Royal Geographic Society of Britain,* but he also complains that his theoretical formulations have not been taken seriously by scientists who required travelers and missionaries "to eschew theory and opinion . . . to see and not to think; in fact, to confine ourselves to transmitting the rough material collected by us, that it may be worked into shape by the professionally learned at home. But why may not the observer be allowed a voice concerning his own observations, if at least his mind be sane and his stock of collateral knowledge be respectable?" (*Lake Regions* vii). Without a doubt, Burton wished his travelogues to contribute to prevailing racial theories, such as those by Cuvier, new empirical data and knowledge about the Negro race in its "natural" habitat.

Cuvier argued that fossils were a result of major catastrophes, the last of which was the flood that is recorded in the Bible. He did not, however, subscribe to the popular Christian myth according to which all races are descended from the three sons of Noah—Japheth, Ham, and Shem. In fact, in his taxonomy of races (Caucasoid, Mongoloid, and Negroid), Jews, who in the Christian racial mythology are Semites (descendants of Shem), are classified among Caucasians. His theory was that the morphological differences among races were due to their having escaped the flood from different shores. The three races, he wrote, are not only distinct morphologically, but their abilities or lack of them are innate—genetically determined. The "white race," for example, with its "oval face, straight hair and nose, to which the civilized people of Europe belong and which appear to us the most beautiful of all, is also superior to others by its genius, courage and activity." The Mongoloids, on the other hand, "have institutions and practices [that] differ from ours as much as their appearance and temperament. They speak in monosyllables; they write in arbitrary hieroglyphs; they have a moral politics only, without religion. . . . Their yellow color, prominent cheeks, narrow slanting eyes, and thin beard make them so different from us that it is tempting to believe that their ancestors and ours escaped from the great catastrophe on two different shores" (qtd. in Martin Rudwick 244). At the bottom of the scale is "the most degraded of human races, that of the negroes, whose form approaches most closely to that of the beast, and whose intelligence has nowhere risen to the point of reaching a regular form of government or the least appearance of sustained knowledge, has nowhere preserved either annals or traditions . . . all its characters show clearly that it escaped from the great catastrophe at another point than the Caucasian and Altaic [Mongoloid] races, from which it had per-haps been separated long before that catastrophe took place" (qtd. in Rudwick 246).

Needless to say, Cuvier's theory of races was consistent with that prevailing in eighteenth- and nineteenth-century European intellectual and academic circles. The example of Georg W. F. Hegel, one of the most influential intellectuals of the time, is sufficient here. In his *Lectures on the History of Philosophy*, what dis-tinguishes the "Teutonic race" from other races is the "freedom of Thought" (or conscious knowledge). "The only distinction between the Africans and the Asiatics on the one hand, and Greeks, Romans, and the moderns on the other hand," he says, "is that the latter know and it is explicit to them, that they are free, but the others are so without knowing that they are, and thus without existence as being free. This constitutes the enormous difference in their condition" (22). Using the criteria of rational thought and evolution of thought for his hierarchization of races, Hegel says that the Chinese are superior to Africans, for they were once, two thousand years ago, capable of rational thinking (3).

Like Cuvier, Hegel places Africans at the bottom of the racial hierarchy. In *Philosophy of History*, he says that "the Negro . . . exhibits the natural man in his completely wild and untamed state" (93). He adds that the Negro has no con-scious or rational knowledge of God and, without a moral sense, "cannibalism is looked upon as quite customary and proper. . . . The devouring of human flesh is altogether consonant with the general principles of the African race" (95). And as far as "political constitution" is concerned, "the entire nature of this race is such as to preclude the existence of any such arrangement" (96). Hegel's conclu-sion is that "want of self control distinguishes the character of the Negroes. This condition is capable of no development or culture, and as we see them at this day, such have they always been" (98).

Although Burton does not seem to have been familiar with Hegel, the latter's assertions on "the African proper" (as Hegel referred to the African south of the Sahara) were current in nineteenth-century racial discourse on the Other. When Burton says that "as a rule, the civilized or the highest type of man owns the sway of intellect, of reason," that "the semi-civilized—as are still the great nations of the East—are guided by sentiment and propensity," and that "the barbarian [African] is the slave of impulse, passion, and instinct" (490), he may as well cite Hegel.

Franz Joseph Gall, dubbed the father of phrenology, is another figure to have contributed to nineteenth-century scientific racism in general and to Burton's racial theories in particular. For Gall, the shape of an individual's head was an index of his or her moral and intellectual dispositions. In other words, for him an individual's moral and intellectual dispositions were physiologically determined. He wrote, "As the organs and their localities can be determined by observation only, it is also necessary that the form of the head or cranium should represent, in most cases, the form of the brain, and should suggest various means to ascertain the fundamental qualities and faculties, and the seat of their organs" (qtd. in Young 12). In his study of skulls and crania of animals and humans that he had collected, Gall found that "twenty seven fundamental faculties were shared between men and animals," and this sharing could be explained only in terms of the concept of the "chain of being" (Young 34).

Although Burton does not explicitly use the concept of the "chain of being" in his travelogues, it is obvious that for him the Negro race constitutes the link between animals and humans, while the Hima constitute the link between the Negro race and the other races in the hierarchy. Borrowing from Gall, to whom he makes reference in *Zanzibar* (415), Burton uses the concepts of phrenology to show the relationship between the "barbarian's" facial features and his "animality," on the one hand, and the Hima's facial features and their "humanity," on the other hand. "Between [the Hima] and the southern races," he says, "there is a marked physical difference" (*Lake Regions* 392). For example, the Wazaramo's "face is usually lozenge-shaped, the eyes are somewhat oblique, the nose is flat and patulated, the lips tumid and everted, the jaw prognathous . . . the expression of countenance is wild and staring, the features are coarse and harsh, the gait is loose and lounging" (*Lake Regions* 89). In contrast, the Hima's "heads are of a superior cast; the regions where the reflective faculties and the moral sentiments, especially benevolence, are placed, rise high; the nose is more of the Caucasian type; the moderate masticating apparatus, which gives to the negro and the lower negroid his peculiar aspect of animality, is greatly modified, and the expression of the countenance is soft, kindly, and not deficient in intelligence" (*Lake Regions* 392).

In sum, for Burton, the Hima are the Wamrima's racial Other. Not only does he find them to be intelligent, benevolent, and socially well organized, he also finds them to have a high moral sense. "Adulterers are punished by heavy fines in cattle, murderers are speared and beheaded . . . and thieves are blinded by gouging out the eyes with the finger-joints of the right hand and severing the muscles" (396). The Wamrima, on the other hand, are "systematic liars" (45).

Clearly, Burton should be credited with, or rather faulted for, having invented the Hima race. Nevertheless, it is John Hanning Speke's only travelogue, *Journal of the Discovery of the Source of the Nile,* that many scholars cite when they discuss the origin of the Hutu–Tutsi conflict in Rwanda and Burundi. Gerard Prunier, for example, writing in 1995, does not mention Burton when he discusses the "racial" context of the genocide of the Tutsi, whom Burton says are of the same racial stock as the Hima. For Prunier, "the man who started it all was John Hanning Speke, the famous Nile explorer" (7). Admittedly, Burton's *Lake Regions* devotes only ten pages to the Hima, while Speke's *Journal* devotes to them about eighty pages. It is Burton's racial theory of the Hima, however, as pointed out above, that informs Speke's.

Before writing his *Journal,* Speke had been Burton's protégé and traveling companion during their exploration of Harar in 1856, and of the source of the Nile in 1857 and 1858—the two expeditions that provided Burton with material for *First Footsteps in East Africa* (first published in 1856) and *The Lake Regions of Central Africa.* The two had a falling out, however, during their second expedition when Speke struck out on his own and claimed to have discovered the source of the Nile—a lake that he named for Queen Victoria. In 1859, now on his own, Speke left London to head an expedition whose purpose was to establish "the truth of my assertion that the Victoria Nyanza, which I discovered on the 30th of July, 1858, would eventually prove to be the source of the Nile" (31). Four years later, he published *Journal of the Discovery of the Source of the Nile,* a travelogue about the expedition. Although this was the second time that he was traveling through the same territory, having been with Burton the first time, not once is Burton mentioned in Speke's travelogue. Indeed, it could be argued that Speke's publication of the *Journal* was, symbolically and to some extent epistemologically, a break with Burton.

In the Introduction section of the travelogue, Speke implicitly denounces Burton's racial bigotry. "If my account should not entirely harmonize with pre-conceived notions as to primitive races," he warns his European audience, "I can not help it" (xvii). His purpose, it is clear, was to represent Africans as human beings whose backwardness resulted from not having been introduced to Christianity. Unlike Burton, whose representation of Africans was in the theoretical framework of the Great Chain of Being, Speke's representation of them was in the context of the equally racist Christian myth of the origin of blacks. According to the myth, blacks are descended from Ham, who was cursed by his father Noah. In the Old Testament story upon which the myth is based, the flood has destroyed all mankind save Noah, his sons, and their wives. One day, Ham goes into his father's tent and finds him drunk and naked. Instead of covering his nakedness, he goes outside and tells his brothers about what he has just seen. Shem and Japheth, walking backward to avoid seeing their father in that state, clothe him. When he becomes sober, he blesses them and curses Ham's son, Canaan, and his progeny: "Cursed be Canaan; a servant of servants shall he be unto his brethren. And he said, Blessed be the Lord God of Shem; and Canaan shall be his servant. God shall enlarge Japheth, and he shall dwell in the tents of Shem, and Canaan shall be his servant" (Gen. 9.25–26; KJV). It is this biblical text that Speke has in mind when he says, "We should, when contemplating these sons of Noah, try and carry our mind back to that time when our poor older brother Ham was cursed by his father, and condemned to be the slave of both Shem and Japheth" (xvii). Also unlike Burton, whose real objective had been to contribute to England's mercantile projects and "science" of race, Speke's objective was to further the cause of what Rudyard Kipling was later to call "the white man's burden"—the regeneration of Africans through the spread of Christianity and Western civilization. Speaking to this project of regeneration, Speke wrote, "Whatever, then, may be said against [Africans] for being too avaricious or too destitute of fellow-feeling, should rather reflect on ourselves, who have been so much favored, yet have neglected to teach them. . . . To say a Negro is incapable of instruction is a mere absurdity" (xvii).

Notwithstanding Speke's apparent epistemological break with Burton, his "racial" characterization of the Hima is not quite different from Burton's. Like Burton, Speke describes the Hima as being superior to the neighboring tribes not only in physical appearance but also in morality and intelligence. Also, his description of the Hima king, Rumanika, is intended to make him distinct from the "pure" African: His "politeness took us [Speke and Grant, his traveling companion] aback"; he was "of noble appearance and size"; he shook hands "in true English style, which is the peculiar custom of the men in this country"; he was "as gentle as ever"; his children were "all models of the Abyssinian type of beauty, and as polite in their manners as thorough-bred gentlemen"; and the insights of his "intellectual conversations" were remarkable (199–224). His conclusion: "we both felt and saw we were in the company of men who were as unlike as they could be to the common order of the natives of the surrounding districts. They had fine oval faces, large eyes and high noses" (203). To account for these so-called Caucasian features, Speke theorizes that the Galla of Ethiopia had migrated to and settled in this region.

Speke's racial theory of the Hima, as observed above, is far from being original. In *First Footsteps,* Burton calls the Galla of Ethiopia "half-castes" who are descended "from Menelek, son of Solomon by the Queen of Sheba," and concludes, judging by "their features and figures . . . that they are descended from Semitic as well as Negrotic (Nigro-Hamitic) progenitors" (70). In a footnote, he adds that "the Gallas . . . are not a black people" (71). Although in *The Lake Regions* Burton does not explicitly say that the Hima had emigrated from Ethiopia, he implies it when he speculates that they are of "a foreign and superior origin" (398). It is then quite evident that Speke, who had traveled with Burton through Ethiopia, borrows from him when he says "I propose to state my theory of the ethnology of that part of Africa inhabited by the people collectively styled Wahuma [Hima], otherwise Gallas or Abyssinians. My theory is founded on the traditions of the several nations, as checked by my own observation of what I saw when passing through them. It appears impossible to believe, judging from the physical appearance of the Wahuma, that they can be of any other race than the semi-Shem-Hamitic of Ethiopia" (241). The Hima, Speke adds, are not confined to the Karagwa region, for the Tutsi "are of the same stock" (244).

Speke's link of the Hima to Abyssinians, and ultimately to King Solomon, is not without an ideological purpose. The Hima, he says, were a Christian "race" whose long separation from their ancestors had wiped out any traces of Christianity. With some education, he says, the Hima could easily regain their lost Christianity. He tells Rumanika that "if he would give me one or two of his children, I would have them instructed in England; for I admired his race, and believed them to have sprung from our old friends the Abyssinians, whose king, Sahela Selassie, had received rich presents from our queen. They were Christians like ourselves, and had the Wahuma not lost their knowledge of God they would be so also" (207).

Clearly, Speke, like Burton, makes of the Hima an exotic people—a hybrid race with markedly Caucasian features. When Henry Morton Stanley, another nineteenth-century traveler, later wrote about them, all he had to do was to reproduce their "exoticism." In other words, Stanley's representation of the Hima was a rewriting of his two predecessors.

Before embarking on his expedition to eastern and central Africa, he collected "over one hundred and thirty books upon Africa, which I studied with the zeal of one who had a living interest in the subject" (1:2). These books must have included Burton's and Speke's travelogues, for one of the aims of the expedition, as he put it, was "to clear up . . . all that remained still problematic and incomplete of the discoveries of Burton and Speke, and Speke and Grant" (1:2). Ideologically, however, Stanley shared Speke's project of the African's regeneration, as evidenced in his use of metaphors in the title of his two-volume travelogue, *Through the Dark Continent* (first published in 1878) and in his discourse on Africa. If for Stanley Africa south of the Sahara was "a dark continent," it was because it did not have "the light"—Christianity. He wrote, "It is, therefore, a duty imposed upon us by the religion we profess, and by the sacred command of the Son of God, to help them out of the deplorable state they are now in" (1:38). In the preface to the 1899 edition of the travelogue, he considers the year 1875 to be of remarkable importance, for it was the year that Uganda would have "the first glimmerings of the dawn"(xi). As a result of Stanley's appeal to the Church Missionary Society in England, two missionaries would be sent to the region to dispel the "darkness" with their "light," inaugurating the process of incorporating the region into the modern enlightened world of Europe.

As the scientist and the Christian that Stanley professed to be, he wished to be "free from prejudices of cast [sic], colour, race, or nationality" (2:38). Early in the travelogue, without mentioning names, he, as Speke had done before him, decries the bigotry of some European travelers: "One of them lately said that the negro knows neither love nor affection; another that he is simply the 'link' between the simian and the European. . . . The traveller should not forget the origin of his own race, the condition of the Briton before St. Augustine visited his country, but should rather recall to mind the first state of the 'wild Caledonia' and the original circumstances and surroundings of Primitive Man" (1:36–38). Stanley's posture as a scientist "free from prejudices of cast [sic], colour, race, or nationality," however, is not maintained for long, especially when he compares the Hima to the Waganda in terms of race and aesthetics.

While at King Mtesa's court, he observes the king's five hundred "wives" and "concubines" in order to "become acquainted with pure African beauty." Of those five hundred women, he says, not more than twenty were "worthy of a glance of admiration from a white man with any eye for style and beauty, and certainly not more than three deserving of many glances." These three, he says, "were of the Wahuma race, no doubt from Ankori. They had the complexion of quadroons, were straight nosed and thin-lipped, with large lustrous eyes" (241–42). Further in the travelogue, Stanley describes the Hima of Gambaragara as having

> a remarkably light complexion, approaching to that of dark-faced Europeans, [and] differed altogether in habits and manners from the Waganda. . . . The people are a peculiarly formed race. At one time they are said to have been all white, and to have emigrated from Northern Unyoro, but at the present time the black and light-complexioned are about equal in number. The blacks are the result of successive wars during ancient times and intermarriages between the captors and captives, the result being a singularly long-limbed and slender-bodied people. . . . The women are said to be singularly beautiful; I have seen several of them, and though I will not call them beautiful, as we understand the term in Europe and America, they are superior to any women I have seen in Africa, and have nothing in common with negroes except the hair. (336)

Later when Stanley meets Rumanika, the Hima king whom Speke had written much about, he finds him superior to King Mtesa in every aspect: "Nature, which had endowed Mtesa with a nervous intense temperament, had given Rumanika the placid temper, the soft voice, the mild benignity, and pleasing character of a gentle father." Rumanika's refinement, Stanley suggests, must be due to his racial difference: "His face was long, and his nose somewhat Roman in shape; the profile showed a decidedly refined type" (1:359–60).

During his travels Stanley does not get to see any Tutsi, whom both Burton and Speke had said to be of the same racial stock as the Hima, but his Arab informant tells him of the beauty of the Tutsi queen in Rwanda. According to the informant's account, she is "a tall woman of middle age, of an almost light Arab complexion, with very large brilliant eyes." Rumanika, the informant adds, "is a man of [the Tutsi's] own blood" (1:357).

Although Stanley's racialization of the Hima merely reproduced Burton's and Speke's theories, his travelogue, which was perhaps more widely read than his predecessors', played a major role in reinforcing the myth of the Hima race. And like other myths of race that masqueraded as science, the myth of the Hima race contradicts itself on two levels: racial essentialism and environmental determinism.

According to nineteenth-century racial essentialism, each race has innate characteristics, which Burton, Speke, and Stanley reproduced in their travelogues. For Burton, it is a rule that "the civilized or highest type of man owns the sway of intellect, of reason; the semi-civilized—as are still the great nations of the East—are guided by sentiment and propensity; and the barbarian is a slave of impulse, passion, and instinct" (*Great Lakes* 490). For Speke, laziness is "inherent" among "the true curly-head, flab-nosed, pouch-mouthed negro—not the Wahuma" (xx). For Stanley, Arabs "have the vices of their education, blood, and race" (1:36). By the logic of racial essentialism, there is no such a thing as a hybrid race. In a chapter in *Types of Mankind* titled "Hybridity of Animals, Viewed in Connection with the Natural History of Mankind," nineteenth-century American phrenologist J. C. Nott distinguishes distinct races (for example whites and blacks) and varieties within a race—what he calls "proximate races" (for example "Teutons, Celts, Pelasgians, Iberians, and Jews"). When "proximate races" breed, he says, "they produce offspring perfectly prolific: although even here, their peculiarities cannot become so entirely fused into a homogeneous mass as to obliterate the original type of either." On the other hand, when distinct races, "such as the Anglo-Saxon with the Negro, are crossed, a different result has course. Their mulatto offspring . . . acquire an inherent tendency to run out, and become eventually extinct" (397–98).

The theme of miscegenation and the character of the tragic mulatto in American literature are good examples of Nott's theory of racial hybridity, to which Burton also subscribed. In *Zanzibar; City, Island, and Coast*, Burton describes the deficiencies among the Waswahili of Zanzibar, who are of mixed blood. "Veritable half-castes," he says, the "Wasawahili [*sic*] have inherited the characters of both parents," making them look incongruous: They "appear physically inferior to those of the seaboard: as in the days of Marco Polo, they are an emphatically ugly race. . . . The national peculiarity is the division of the face into two distinct types, and the contrast appears not a little singular. The upper, or intellectual part, though capped by woolly hair, is distinctly Semitic—with the suspicion of a caricature—as far as the nose-bridge, and the more ancient the more evident is the mixture. The lower, or animal half, especially the nostrils, lip, jaw, and chin is unmistakably African" (415). Ironically, the Hima, whom Burton, Speke, and Stanley make to be a hybrid race, are described as having a nobility of character, a physical beauty far surpassing that of other Africans, and well-organized social institutions.

The invention of the Hima race also contradicts the then widely held notion that Africans were savages because of their tropical environment. In fact, Burton suggests that Arabs who had lived long in sub-Saharan Africa had deteriorated not only physically but also morally and intellectually: "The grandsons of purest Arabs who have settled in Africa, though there has been no mixture of blood, already show important physical modifications worked by the 'mixture of air,' as the Portuguese phrase is. The skin is fair, but yellow-tinted by over-development of gall; whilst the nose is high, the lips are loose, everted, or otherwise ill-formed; and the beard, rarely of the amplest, shrinks under the hot-house air, to four straggling tufts upon the rami of the jaws and the dondyles of the chin. Whilst the extremities preserve the fineness of Arab blood, the body is weak and effeminate; and the degenerate aspect is accompanied by the no less degraded mind, morals, and manners of the coast people" (*Zanzibar* 375).

Paradoxically, the Hima, who supposedly migrated to the region so many centuries ago that they have lost not only their "original" language but also their Christianity, do not show the slightest sign of physical, moral, or intellectual deterioration. If they have a dark skin, the travelogues suggest, it is not because of the "hot-house air" but because of their intermarriage with the other ethnic groups.

The racialization of the Hima by Burton, Speke, and Stanley was not an innocent exercise. They were laying down an ideological structure for the colonial enterprise, which in Rwanda and Burundi made the Tutsi agents of civilization because of their supposed racial superiority. In 1894, when the first European, the German count Gustav Adolf von Goetzen, arrived in Rwanda, leading a scientific and military expedition, he made the same racial characterization of the Tutsi that Burton, Speke, and Stanley had made in their travelogues. Shortly after von Goetzen's expedition, German colonization of Rwanda began, lasting until 1916, when Belgium took the country over. Needless to say, both regimes set up colonial institutions that reflected the prevailing racial notions of the three ethnic groups in Rwanda—the Tutsi, the Hutu, and the Twa—in that order. The Tutsi, whom a 1925 document of the "Ministère des Colonies" described as being "gifted with a vivacious intelligence," having "a refinement of feelings which is rare among primitive people," and being "natural-born leaders, capable of extreme self-control and of calculated good will," held positions of power next to those held by whites. "The Batutsi," Pierre Ryckmans wrote, "were meant to reign. Their fine presence is in itself enough to give them a great prestige vis-à-vis the inferior races which surround [them]" (qtd. in Prunier 11). The Hutu, who were described as being "short and thick-set with a big head, a jovial expression, a wide nose and enormous lips" and were "less intelligent, more simple, more spontaneous," were made to do all the manual labor under the supervision of Tutsi chiefs and subchiefs. And the Twa, who were described as having "a monkey-like face and a huge nose" and being "quite similar to the apes whom he chases in forest" (qtd. in Prunier 6), were relegated to the margins of Rwandese society. Basically, the Hutu and the Twa were living under a colonialism within a colonialism—the two justified and legitimated by a racial ideology that was reproduced in textbooks and in all social practices. As would be expected, the three groups internalized the colonial ideology of their "racial" inequality. As Prunier puts it, "a very dangerous social bomb was almost absent-mindedly manufactured" through the years of colonialism and its "racial" differentiation of the Rwandese population (9).

The "racial" bomb, to use Prunier's metaphor, started exploding in 1957, when a group of Hutu intellectuals drafted a document titled "Notes on the Social Aspect of the Racial Native Problem in Rwanda," which, among other things, denounced "the political monopoly of one race, the Mututsi" (qtd. in Prunier 45). Two years later, in 1959, killings of the Tutsi by the Hutu began, causing thousands of Tutsi to flee to neighboring countries and ushering in a Hutu government. Ironically, one of the political programs of the new Hutu government was to produce a different racial ideology by placing the Hutu at the top of a new racial hierarchy. When the Tutsi in exile tried to force their way back into Rwanda, the Hutu "racial" hegemony became threatened, and preparations for the genocide of the Tutsi inside the country began. Given the legacy of the "racial" politics of the country since Count von Goetzen's "scientific" expedition, it is not surprising that the rhetoric of the genocide used colonial racial categories. A few months prior to the genocide, a newspaper article told the Hutu: "You are an important ethnic group of the Bantu. . . . The nation is artificial, but the ethnic group is natural." Also in a speech, Leon Mugesera, a Hutu ideologue, warned the Tutsi: "I am telling you that your home is in Ethiopia, that we are going to send you back there quickly, by the Nyabarongo [River]" (Human Rights Watch). A few months later during the genocide, the Nyabarongo river was littered with thousands of Tutsi bodies. The racial theories in the colonial travelogues of Burton, Speke, and Stanley had not only been reproduced in textbooks that Mugesera had read and used to justify the Tutsi genocide, they had also become knowledge that respected journalists could dispense. As Ashley Montagu reminds us, "the idea of 'race' represents one of the most dangerous myths of our time, and one of the most tragic" (23).

Works Cited

Burton, Richard F. *First Footsteps in East Africa, or, An Exploration of Harar.* [1856]. New York: Dover Publications, 1987.

————. *The Lake Regions of Central Africa.* [1860]. New York: Dover Publications, 1995.

———. *Zanzibar; City, Island, and Coast.* 2 vols. London: Tinsley Brothers, 1872.

Cuvier, Georges Leopold. *The Animal Kingdom Arranged in Conformity with Its Organiza-tion . . . .* London: G. B. Whittaker, 1827–32.

———. "Varieties of the Human Species." In Emmanuel Chukwudi Eze, ed., *Race and the Enlightenment,* 104–8.

Eze, Emmanuel Chukwudi, ed. *Race and the Enlightenment: A Reader.* Malden, Mass.: Blackwell, 2001.

Gall, Franz Joseph. *On the Functions of the Brain and of Each of Its Parts . . . .* 6 vols. Trans-lated by Winslow Lewis Jr. Boston: Marsh, Capen & Lyon, 1835.

Gibbs, Nancy. "Why? The Killing Fields of Rwanda." *Time,* 16 May 1995. 57–63.

Hallett, Robin. *Africa to 1875: A Modern History.* Ann Arbor: University of Michigan Press, 1970.

Hegel, Georg Wilhelm Friedrich. *Lectures on the History of Philosophy.* 3 vols. Trans. E. S. Haldane. New York: Humanities Press, 1963.

———. *The Philosophy of History.* Trans. J. Sibree. New York: Dover Publications, 1956.

Human Rights Watch. *Leave None to Tell the Story: Genocide in Rwanda.* March 1999. <http://www.hrw.org/reports/1999/rwanda>.

Mamdani, Mahmood. *When Victims Become Killers.* Princeton, N.J.: Princeton University Press, 2001.

Montagu, Ashley. *Man's Most Dangerous Myth: The Fallacy of Race.* 4th ed. New York: World Publishing, 1964.

Nott, J. C., and George R. Gliddon. *Types of Mankind.* Philadelphia: Lippincott, Grambo, 1854.

Prunier, Gerard. *The Rwanda Crisis: History of a Genocide.* New York: Columbia Univer-sity Press, 1995.

Rudwick, Martin J. S. *Georges Cuvier, Fossil Bones, and Geological Catastrophes: New Trans-lations and Interpretations of the Primary Texts.* Chicago: University of Chicago Press, 1997.

Seligman, Charles Gabriel. *Races of Africa.* New York: Oxford University Press, 1966.

Speke, John Hanning. *Journal of the Discovery of the Source of the Nile.* [1863]. Mineola, N.Y.: Dover Publications, 1996.

Stanley, Henry M. *Through the Dark Continent.* 2 vols. [1878]. New York: Dover Publica-tions, 1988.

Young, Robert M. *Mind, Brain, and Adaptation in the Nineteenth Century.* Oxford, Eng.: Clarendon Press, 1970.

CHAPTER 7

Toward a Political Economy of Racism and Colonialism: A Rereading of Frantz Fanon's *Wretched of the Earth*

Azfar Hussain

The Haunting Specters of Political Economy

In this essay I propose to undertake a rereading of Frantz Fanon's last major work, *The Wretched of the Earth,* in order to articulate a political economy of racism and colonialism in contemporary contexts. Although a host of theorists and activists have discussed this work since the time of its publication,[1] my rereading of Fanon—which I characterize as an interventionist and recuperative one—is prompted by several distinct yet interrelated concerns as well as my reactions against certain discursive practices in the metropolis. Let me then quickly tabulate such practices to make and mark my point of departure for the reading proposed.

Fanon is well received in certain areas of the metropolitan humanities today. For instance, in contemporary ethnic studies and *culturalist* postcolonial hermeneutics, Fanon is repeatedly invoked, deployed, and mobilized in the service of framing and fashioning what postcolonial critics—in their alliances with French poststructuralists—call the archaeology, genealogy, semiology, and even the tropology of the colonial and postcolonial conditions.[2] While such appropriations of Fanon have proved provocative and even provided certain useful tools and protocols of "reading," thus nourishing the dominant textualist culture of the metropolitan academy, the very Fanon of the discourse of political economy—political economy as a historical and dialectical science of praxis—has remained virtually ignored.

In fact, the practices of the humanities in general—despite (or because of) their ongoing discursive transactions with the trinity of such post-marked theories as poststructuralism-postcolonialism-postmarxism and despite their transdisciplinary content and character—tend to remain indifferent to the conceptual and analytical resources of political economy. One consequence of this indifference is that certain crucial contexts, contours, and coordinates of *global racism* remain relatively unexplored in the humanities. Even when certain practices of the metropolitan social sciences encompass and enunciate a global political economy of capitalism—theoretically and hermeneutically useful as it is—they still remain more or less blind to the kind of political economy of racism and colonialism in which Fanon, as I would argue, remains interested. In other words, in such a context, while the specters of Marx and Marxism at least occasionally haunt the spaces of the social sciences, "race"—and racism as a deeply *localized* yet profoundly *world-systemic* material-discursive phenomenon—turns out to be a blank. One particularly dramatic example of race-as-a-blank in the social sciences is the very domain of contemporary mathematical economics and econometrics in which the mathematical—rather, mathematical mysticism—continues to perpetrate epistemic violences on "race" as a category of understanding the world-economic as a force field of tensions and transactions between production relations and power relations.[3]

My reading, then, is a reaction against those disciplinary or discursive practices in the metropolitan humanities and in certain areas (if not all) of the social sciences that I have hitherto quickly contoured. Also, prompted by contemporary historical-material conditions in which the axiomatics of racism differentially yet decisively operate in the five new capitalist monopolies that the Egyptian political economist Samir Amin categorically identifies as "[1] the control of technology; [2] global financial flows (through the banks, insurance cartels, and pension funds of the center); [3] access to the planet's natural resources; [4] media and communications; and [5] weapons of mass destruction" (12), I cannot but mark my proposed rereading of Fanon by certain questions: Can we *really* read Marx today without reading him together with Fanon—or together with W. E. B. DuBois, Aimé Césaire, and C. L. R. James, for example? In other words, can we even remotely conceptualize—let alone mobilize—Marx's labor theory of value in today's contexts without simultaneously positing what I wish to call—and later formulate as—a race theory of value?[4] I intend to ask, if not decisively address, such questions increasingly by way of retracing and reconstellating certain relatively uncharted tracks and trajectories in Fanon's *Wretched of the Earth*. Such an intervention, I hope, would not only enable me to enunciate at least a few general contours of a political economy of racism and colonialism as such, but would also prompt me to develop and deploy the analytics of such a political economy in the service of antiracist, anticolonial, anticapitalist, and antipatriarchal struggles in the domain of the humanities itself.

But why *The Wretched of the Earth*? While selecting this text, I take cues from the South African literary critic Dennis Walder, who notes, "Fanon's *The Wretched of the Earth* remains more important for postcolonial thinking. Why? In the first place Fanon wrote from the perspective of a colonial subject in the thick of an independence struggle [the Algerian Liberation Movement of 1954–62], addressing other colonial subjects. . . . *The Wretched of the Earth* has spoken more directly, profoundly and lastingly than any other single anti-colonial work on behalf of and to the colonized" (57). Although Walder's account seems a little exaggerated, others, from Renate Zahar and Peter Geismar through Irene Gendzier and Emmanuel Hansen down to Cedric Robinson and Edward Said[5]—their different approaches to Fanon notwithstanding—suggest that *The Wretched of the Earth* is Fanon's most explicitly political work. By no means, however, do I imply that *The Wretched of the Earth* inaugurates a complete *coupure épistémologique* with Fanon's earlier works or even with his first work, *Black Skin, White Masks.* Stuart Hall describes this work as "Fanon's first and most explicitly psychoanalytical text" (15) and Anne McClintock similarly characterizes it as "the most psychological of Fanon's texts" (94). But I do not see—nor do both Hall and McClintock—an absolute rupture between the "political" and the "psychological" in Fanon's entire *oeuvre.* I agree with McClintock when she maintains that even the explicitly psychoanalytical discourse of *Black Skin, White Masks* remains politically and socially engaged (94). But I turn to *The Wretched of the Earth* mainly for the reason that more than any of Fanon's works *The Wretched* not only provides theories and strategies of the *politics* of colonial domination and decolonization in a sustained manner but also offers insights into a political economy of racism and colonialism—insights that attest to Fanon's own kind of Marxism, a Marxism organically tempered by the specific historical-material and colonial-racial conditions that produced and influenced him, while also informing and inflecting his work.

In fact, following Fanon's own imperative, as he spells it out toward the beginning of *The Wretched of the Earth,* that "Marxist analysis should always be slightly stretched every time we have to do with the colonial problem" (40), I argue that Fanon does not abandon his "Marxism" as such, but only *stretches* it in an attempt to provide insights into the logic of capital in the colonial context and into the logics of colonialism and racism—potentially interconnected as they remain—in the capitalist context itself. And Fanon does so—I further argue—in ways in which those very logics bring together both the categories of class and race into a dialectically charged and active interaction, even clearing and forging the space for fashioning what might be called a race theory of class. Briefly put: a race theory of class—as Fanon's own work tends to envisage—posits that production relations under modern capitalism have historically remained race relations in such a way that race itself comes to constitute class, and that, thus, one cannot sufficiently account for class formations without considering race as a determining factor. I use a tentative diagram here to visualize at a preliminary level certain interrelationships between class and race and for that matter between capitalism and racism/colonialism. And I will argue later that those interrelationships—variously vectoring and valencing the sites of both production relations and power relations—characterize the kind of political economy of racism and colonialism Fanon seems interested in (see figure 1).

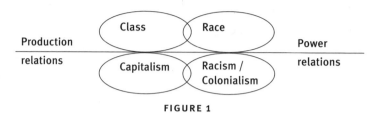

FIGURE 1

But Fanon does not articulate his *political-economic* insights and ideas in a sustained and systematic manner. He is not a political economist in the sense that Karl Marx or Ernest Mandel is. And I agree with Peter Geismar when he points out that "*The Wretched of the Earth* was never intended as a *detailed* [emphasis mine] analysis of economic change; it was more clearly an *outil de combat,* part of the war against colonialism" (*Fanon* 200). As I hope to show, however, Fanon makes revealing and instructive—and sometimes tangential yet suggestive—remarks on political economy in *The Wretched of the Earth* while pursuing many other trajectories of the colonial condition and possible decolonization.

I shall then argue that if we can bring together—and also *slightly stretch*—Fanon's remarks, however sporadic and scattered, on the dialectical logic of colonialism/racism and capitalism, we can "critically elaborate" (417), to use Gramsci's phrase, a particular brand of political economy of colonialism and racism in contemporary contexts. Such an elaboration is likely to constitute what Fanon himself calls "knowledge of the practice of action" (*Wretched* 147) or what Gramsci calls the "epistemological value" (401) of praxis. Thus, in the service of anticapitalist, antiracist, and anticolonial struggles, I underscore the need for knowledge of Fanon's political economy as a political epistemology. Later in this essay, I will describe that very economy as Fanon's "Marxist" political economy of *labor, land, language,* and *the body*—the four crucial material-discursive sites on which Fanon consistently focuses in *The Wretched of the Earth*—to suggest that the logics of capitalism, racism, and colonialism—in their dialectical transactions and tensions—manifest themselves in those very sites, and that any anticapitalist, antiracist, or anticolonial struggle, therefore, must have to heed those sites as the potentially strategic areas of resistance and movement. In fact, Marxist critics—let alone "non-Marxist" and postcolonial ones—have *not* so far made any systematic effort to explore the contours of such a political economy in Fanon's work—particularly a political economy that embraces all at once those four crucial material-discursive sites of both *oppression* and *opposition.*

Thus my proposed reading of Fanon is a *double* departure—a departure not only from the postcolonial Fanon but also from the traditional Marxist and anti-Marxist protocols of reading. Despite my certain disagreement with Stuart Hall about his endorsement of Bhabha's reading of Fanon, my position is partly inspired by Hall's own plea: "Rather than trying to recapture the 'true' Fanon, we must try to engage the after-life of Frantz Fanon" (14). Indeed, given the facts that colonialism is far from experiencing "the end of history;" that "late capitalism" has kept "neocolonialism" alive more strategically and dangerously than ever before; that capitalism, neocolonialism, and racism as production relations and power relations remain potentially interconnected and interlocked in the contemporary world system in ways in which one can, for instance, no longer fully demystify the logic of global capital without simultaneously demystifying the macrologic of racism, and that, as Fanon himself suggests almost *à la* Lenin and Gramsci, "the struggle continues" (*Wretched* 140), the very political-economic strands of Fanon's work deserve and demand increasing critical interventions today. Insofar as the question of political economy is concerned, one may then begin with an exploration of Fanon's understanding of the logic of capital itself.

Reading Fanon's Political Economy of Racism and Colonialism: Whither "M-C-M'"?

Fanon's enunciation of the logic of capital in the context of what he calls "the colonial problem" (*Wretched* 40) has crucial Marxist resonances and registers. I argue that part of Fanon's engagement with a political economy of racism and colonialism seems informed by his understanding of what might be called "the colonial logic of capital." And Fanon's own mode of articulating this logic seems to be stretching Marx's "general formula of capital" (*Capital* 1:53). It is useful, then, to pursue certain ramifications of Marx's "formula"—which underlies the entire theoretical operation of *Capital* in that we can subsequently engage Fanon's brand of political economy itself. Marx represents his formula as "M-C-M'" (*Capital* 1:53). Here M stands for money, C for commodity, and M' for more money or capital. He notes: "M-C-M' is in reality the general formula of capital as it appears prima facie within the sphere of circulation" (*Capital* 1:153).

Deceptively simple, this M-C-M' circuit, encoding the message that money begets money, yokes together a number of divergent yet interrelated conceptual issues. First, on deconstructing the logic of the M-C-M' movement, one sees that the Euclidean straight line ostensibly emulating the Aristotelian *megathos* of a beginning, a middle, and an end from M to M' through C is an illusion. For capital here circles back to money in order to transform it into capital again. Thus capital always enacts what Marx calls *Kreislaufsprozess* (movement in circuits). In other words, capital is cyclically and even infinitely transformative, self-expanding, and therefore characteristically movement-prone. Indeed, capital ceases to be capital as such when it is "thrown out of circulation" (*Capital* 1:153). Marx renders this point even more explicit thus: "The circulation of money as capital is, on the contrary, an end in itself, for the expansion of value takes place only within this constantly renewed movement. The circulation of capital has therefore no limits" (*Capital* 1:150).

Second, the circuit M-C-M′ both conceals and reveals the borderlines between money and capital. According to Marx, while money *per se* can be spent once and for all for buying commodities, capital on the other hand is initially spent in money form for buying commodities so as to sell them in exchange of more money. Thus both commodities and capital involve the notion of exchange value (*Capital* 1:148). Marx writes, "The circuit M-C-M′, on the contrary, commences with money and ends with [more] money. Its leading motive, and the goal that attracts it, is therefore mere exchange-value" (*Capital* 1:148). In other words, mathematically speaking, certainly M–M′, while M′ = M + ΔM (ΔM standing for added money) and P = M′ − M (P standing for profit). Thus, if $100 (M) initially advanced ends up yielding $150 (M′) through buying and selling a given commodity (C), the capitalist's profit (P) can be calculated as: $150 − $100 = $50.

Third, I argue that the circuit M-C-M′ is at once *semiological, phenomenological, genealogical,* and certainly *political-economic.* It is semiological in the sense that the circuit does not merely deploy symbols but also stresses the possibility of representation through signs, forging and enacting a circuit of signifier-signified. Although commodities are material objects, they also appear and circulate as signs that constitute and represent—and are represented by—the market in which the law of exchange dictates the motion of signs. Money—a "concrete abstraction" as it is like a commodity—is also a sign. It designates a powerful mode of signification in the semiotic-social space of exchange called the market. Now the phenomenology of M-C-M′ resides in the very process of capital's continuous becoming. Indeed, capital cannot always neatly be characterized by a *state of being,* for capital tends to remain in a *process of becoming.* In this particular sense, capital is hostile to ontology but hospitable to phenomenology. M-C-M′ is also genealogical in a certain sense because it does not point up production relations in neutral terms but in terms of multiple power relations, particularly in terms of the relations between the dominant (capital) and the subaltern (labor), suggesting that *production relations* are also *power relations* and vice versa. And certainly the political economy of M-C-M′ encompasses the entire material life of production and exchange and their historical, social, and political consequences, accommodating the semiological, the phenomenological, and the genealogical all at once.

Fourth, the two fundamental components of political economy that Engels underlines in his classic definition of political economy, such as *production* and *exchange,*[6] in their relational dynamic bring up the basic point that the production of commodities leads to the production of capital and thus to the production of profit through realizing the exchange value of commodities. This is precisely the general framework of political economy within which Fanon deals with "the colonial problem" in terms of what he calls "the spectacular flight of capital" (*Wretched* 103) and "the relentless dialectic of the [capitalist] system" (*Wretched* 103). And this is a system that keeps its *Kreislaufsprozess* of M-C-M′ alive on the basis of commodities or raw materials produced by the colonized in the service of the expansion of capital in the "mother country." Fanon uses the term "colonial mercantilism" (*Wretched* 51) to describe this system. I argue that he thus begins to offer insights into a *political economy of colonialism* in ways in which one can now readily think of terms like "(neo)colonial commodity," "(neo)colonial capital," "(neo)colonial profit," "(neo)colonial exchange value," among others—terms that Fanon himself does not use but can be usefully deployed to describe Fanon's brand of political economy.

But, as both Fanon and Marx would argue, commodities or capital—be they colonial or not—do not simply fall from the sky. In order to orchestrate the full import and resonance of Marx's M-C-M′ and thus to demystify the processes of producing commodities and capital, it is also important to invoke Marx's labor theory of value. Despite its complexity that has hitherto invited converging and conflicting interpretations, the theory of value can be understood in terms of at least one basic premise of it that may be quickly stated thus: The production of values—exchange value and surplus value—is but a function of labor power *variously realized* in a given social space.[7] In other words, the realization of labor power makes the production of commodities possible, and as the production of commodities leads to the production of capital through the usual market mechanism of exchange under capitalism; the realization and for that matter the exploitation of labor power also makes the production of capital itself possible, suggesting thereby that both commodities and capital conceal and reveal labor power in the process of producing value. Surplus value, then, is simply produced by nothing but "surplus labor" itself. Thus, given this very calculus of production, it is possible to formulate Marx's M-C-M′ in terms of a big L (or Labor) accounting for the entire circuit of production thus: M-C-M′ = f (L)," thereby also pointing up the site in which labor comes into conflict with capital itself—the site of class struggle, that is.

Indeed, *The Wretched of the Earth* attests in certain ways to the political-economic formulation enunciated above, a formulation in which the big L, standing for labor, can be read as colonial labor in general—and for that matter as decisively *racialized labor*—and certainly as the labor of the colonial peasant in particular. And, indeed, Fanon does not homogenize class differences and construe colonialism as a monolithic category in order to fashion and circulate a generalized metanarrative of oppression. As is evident in *The Wretched of the Earth*, Fanon pits—hyphenatedly speaking—colonial-racialized-indigenous-agrarian labor against metropolitan capital on the one hand, and against "the national bourgeoisie"—or even against the urban working class in the colonized territory—on the other, thus suggesting that a political economy of colonialism must take into account both the categories of race and class—rather different classes—in their dialectical opposition and transaction.

In the beginning chapter of *The Wretched of the Earth*, Fanon immediately foregrounds a race/class dialectic characterizing the colonial condition. Fanon, for instance, writes, "In the colonies the economic substructure is also a superstructure. The cause is the consequence; you are rich because you are white, you are white because you are rich. This is why Marxist analysis should always be slightly stretched every time we have to do with the colonial problem" (40). In this passage Fanon for the first time provides a quick but a crucial outline of what I have repeatedly called a political economy of colonialism and racism—an economy that, to begin with, is predicated on a dialectical interplay between Marx's spatial-architectural tropes such as superstructure and substructure (base). Like Antonio Gramsci, Fanon here complicates the narrowly economistic "Marxist" model of base (the economy) and superstructure (culture, ideology, politics, etc.). The model in question delimits the material and analytical horizons of both base and superstructure through positing a causally determined, linear, and binary relationship between those two categories—base and superstructure—while thus postulating that the base always already determines the superstructure. Fanon moves beyond this determinist and binarist model of cause and effect. Rather, he suggests the possibility of enacting a more dialectically engaged political-economic approach to the colonial problematic of production relations whereby the substructure or base itself can rightly be viewed as superstructure and vice versa. In the passage cited above, Fanon also speaks of an economy in which capitalism and colonialism support and strengthen one another—an economy in whose historically specific configuration of production relations and power relations Marx's privileged category of class is never abandoned but is only "slightly stretched" so as to accommodate the category of race itself. Fanon, for instance, repeatedly observes that "whites" exist as the "rich classes" and the rich "classes" exist as "whites."

Fanon's "stretching" of Marxism, however, does not necessarily amount to any fundamental antagonism to Marxism, as some Marxist and non-Marxist critics would have us believe. Such a stretching, I argue, rather bespeaks Fanon's insistence on *rethinking* Marxism in the colonial context so as to expand the analytical horizon of Marxism itself. Of course, Marx does not entirely evade the questions of racism and colonialism, although it is true that he does not rigorously engage them in the way that Fanon does. Marx, however, provides certain significant clues to Fanon's "stretched" political economy by sowing the seeds of—if not by fully developing—what I have earlier called a race theory of value, when Marx writes "Direct slavery is just as much the pivot of bourgeois industry as machinery, credits, etc. It is slavery that gives the colonies their *value* [emphasis added]; it is the colonies that created world trade [or global capital]" ("Poverty of Philosophy" 364).

Also, in *Capital*, Marx particularly stresses the production relations between what might be called colonial labor or colonial resources and colonialist capital.

He observes, "The discovery of gold and silver in America, the extirpation, enslavement and entombment in mines of the aboriginal population, the beginning of the conquest and looting of India, the turning of Africa into a warren for the commercial hunting of black-skins signalized the rosy dawn of the era of capitalist production" (1:751). Marx does not stop here but further focuses on the motion of colonialist capital in the following passage: "The colonial system ripened, like a hothouse, trade and navigation. . . . The colonies secured a market for the building manufactures, and through the monopoly of the market, an increased accumulation. The treasures captured outside Europe by undisguised looting, enslavement, and murder, floated back to the mother country and were there turned into capital" (*Capital* 1:753–54).

The Marx of the above passage seems to be prompting Fanon's own metaphor of "the spectacular flight of capital" introduced earlier. Marx suggests that the expansion and primitive accumulation of capital are based on plundering and exploiting resources, goods, or commodities—captured in Marx's word "treasures"; that such resources are produced by labor power outside Europe (colonial/racialized labor power, that is); and that capital itself enacts a movement that is both transformative and transnational. It is to this very Marx—and also to Lenin—that Fanon decisively returns in *The Wretched of the Earth*, in at least its one crucial passage that needs to be quoted at some length:

> Capitalism, in its early days, saw in the colonies a source of raw materials which, once turned into manufactured goods, could be distributed on the European market. After a phase of accumulation of capital, capitalism has today come to modify its conception of the profit-earning capacity of a commercial enterprise. The colonies have become a market. The colonial population is a customer who is ready to buy commodities; consequently, if the garrison has to be perpetually reinforced, if buying and selling slackens off, that is to say if manufactured and finished goods can no longer be exported, there is clear proof that the solution of military force must be set aside. A blind domination founded on slavery is not economically speaking worthwhile for the bourgeoisie of the mother country. The monopolistic group within this bourgeoisie does not support a government whose policy is solely that of the sword. What the factory owners and finance magnates of the mother country expect from the government is not that it should decimate the colonial peoples, but that it should safeguard with the help of economic conventions their own "legitimate interests." (*Wretched* 65)

Fanon's return to the very center of M-C-M' is unmistakable in the passage cited above. Fanon is not abandoning a Marxist analysis at all. Rather he is both applying and stretching it. Also, given Fanon's familiarity with Lenin—a case recently argued by Dennis Walder, who maintains that Fanon's position in *The Wretched* is actually a "development of Lenin's classic account of the endless need of industrial capitalism" (56)—it is possible to argue that Fanon's Marx is at least occasionally mediated through Lenin. This point is particularly confirmed by Fanon's own understanding of "the monopolistic group" (65), a group that he emphatically mentions in his passage. In fact, the Lenin of *Imperialism* offers a useful background to Fanon's understanding of colonial capital, a historical form of capital that is monopolistic: "The principle feature of modern capitalism is the domination of monopolist combines of the big capitalists. These monopolies are most firmly established when all the sources of raw materials are controlled by the one group. . . . Colonial possession alone gives complete guarantee of success to the monopolies against all the risks of the struggle with competitors. . . . The more capitalism is developed, the more the need for raw materials is felt, the more bitter the competition becomes, and the more feverishly the hunt for raw materials proceeds throughout the whole world, the more desperate becomes the struggle for the acquisition of colonies" (82). This Lenin of "monopolistic colonial capitalism" Fanon partly echoes in his passage quoted at some length earlier.

But what seems remarkable about Fanon's attempt to understand the logic of monopolistic capital in the colonial context is that he traces the circular and multiple movements of commodities and labor, pointing out the irony of the very process of creating value. Here a step-by-step analysis of the entire circuit of production and exchange—the two fundamental components of political economy as identified by Engels—is likely to illustrate the point I am trying to make vis-à-vis a political economy of racism and colonialism.

First, raw materials that the colonizer plunders from the colonized territory are produced by indigenous agrarian labor power. Thus this labor power, realized and embodied as it is in raw materials, is also looted and exploited by the colonizer, as Fanon seems to be suggesting. Second, as Fanon further indicates, the transformation of those raw materials into "manufactured goods" is impossible without the exploitation of labor power or industrial labor power—this time, of course, in the metropolitan territory. So far, thus, one can trace a double movement of labor power through the circuit of the production of manufactured goods. Third, those raw-materials-turned-manufactured-commodities return to their source—to the colonized country, which in Fanon's observation now turns out to be a market. And it is in this site of exchange that the original producers, that is, the colonized—ironically enough—buy their own products, albeit in different forms. In other words, the colonized turn out to be the victims of the very use value and exchange value they themselves are able to create and generate! For that matter, the colonized become the worst victims of their own labor power under colonialist monopoly capitalism. Indeed, colonial labor power is a form of labor power that is out and out *unpaid*. Marx's observation on labor power, although not specifically made in the colonial context, seems relevant. He says, "Capital, therefore, is not only, as Adam Smith says, the command over labor. It is essentially the command over *unpaid labor*" (*Capital* 1:500). This unpaid colonial-racialized-agrarian-indigenous labor then becomes the most profitable source of the expansion and accumulation of metropolitan capital.

One would do well here to look at the distinction—a crucial distinction that brings up the issue of "class-differential-within-class" in which Fanon is consistently interested—between the exploitation of "metropolitan labor" and the plundering of "colonial labor." While metropolitan industrial labor is paid in certain form and the rate of payment is directly proportional to the degree of capitalist exploitation, colonial-racialized-agrarian labor remains unpaid from the very outset. What accompanies the logic of such unpaid colonial labor is the very racist assumption that such labor is not only available but also "cheap" and "inferior" to the degree that it does not deserve payment in cash or kind and is, therefore, infinitely exploitable. Also, this highly exploited colonial-racialized-agrarian labor is different, as Fanon further argues, from colonial industrial labor—the labor of the urban working class in the colonial territories. This class, according to Fanon, is "in a comparatively privileged position" (109). This is why—stretching the Marx and the Engels of *The Communist Manifesto*—Fanon says later in *The Wretched of the Earth*: "In capitalist countries, the working class has nothing to lose; it is they who in the long run have everything to gain. In the colonial countries the working class has everything to lose" (109).

Acutely class-conscious as he is, Fanon does not merely end up dwelling on the logic of colonialist-metropolitan capital as such. His political economy also focuses on the *differentia specifica* of what Fanon calls "the bourgeois faction of the colonized people" (*Wretched* 109). While Marx and Engels argue in *The Communist Manifesto* that "the bourgeoisie, historically, has played a most revolutionary part" (9), Fanon argues that in the colonized countries the bourgeoisie has not played this role at all. For instance, he writes in *The Wretched of the Earth*, "The national middle class which takes over power at the end of the colonial regime is an underdeveloped middle class. It has practically no economic power, and in any case, it is in no way commensurate with the bourgeoisie of the mother country which it hopes to replace" (119–20).

A critical elaboration of Fanon's political economy needs to accentuate the point that Fanon underlines several levels and layers of class alliances and class antagonisms within a totality of colonial production relations. First, Fanon identifies possible class alliances—and also antagonisms—between the metropolitan bourgeoisie and the national bourgeoisie; second, he also indicates the possibility of both alliances and antagonisms between the metropolitan proletariat and the "comparatively privileged" (109) working class in the colonized territory; third, he suggests the possibility of alliance and the existence of antagonisms and differences between that "privileged" urban working class and the peasants in the colonized country; fourth, he stresses the possibility of a "nationalist" alliance as well as class antagonisms between the national bourgeoisie and peasants, including even the *lumpenproletariat*. Thus, Fanon renders the sites of national-colonial

struggles and class/race struggles much more complex, conflictual, and overdetermined than a traditional Western Marxist political economy could envisage.

While both Marx and Lenin pay only marginal attention to peasants and virtually no attention to the *lumpenproletariat,* Fanon—like Antonio Gramsci, Mao
Tse-tung, and Che Guevara—does pay serious attention to those classes in ways
in which peasants as well as the *lumpenproletariat* can be seen as the crucial
agents of change in history. Again, Fanon stretches his Marxism by way of "third-
worlding" it, so to speak. On the possible revolutionary role of peasants in an
anticolonial struggle, Fanon, for instance, writes in *The Wretched of the Earth,*
"The peasantry is systematically disregarded for the most part by the propaganda
put out by the nationalist parties. And it is clear that in the colonial countries
the peasants alone are revolutionary, for they have nothing to lose and everything to gain" (48). Here, in his emphasis on the revolutionary role of peasants,
Fanon edges close to another "third-world" version of Marxism called Maoism.
Mao Tse-tung maintains, for instance, "It was [the peasants] who fought, who
organized, and who did the revolutionary work. They alone are the deadliest
enemies of the local bullies and evil gentry . . . they alone are able to carry out
the work of destruction" ("Peasantry" 254). But Fanon's "Maoist" underwriting
of the revolutionary role of peasants is not merely confined to the level of their
"violent" insurrectionary participation. Not only does Fanon stress the point that
the "peasantry precisely constitutes the only spontaneously revolutionary force
of the country" (*Wretched* 99), but he goes on to maintain that in the course of
the inevitable armed struggle, "the peasants, who are all the time adding to their
knowledge in the light of experience, will come to show themselves capable of
directing the people's struggle" (*Wretched* 114). Thus Fanon also attributes to the
peasantry the role of a revolutionary leadership—even the kind of leadership that
can only come from "organic intellectuals," to use Gramsci's famous term.

Fanon's "Gramscian-Maoist" insistence on the revolutionary agency of peasants in terms of both insurrectionary participation and organic leadership is
consistent with what I would like to call Fanon's colonial-agrarian labor theory
of value. That is, for Fanon, peasants—or agrarian laborers in the colonized territory—constitute the greatest source of conflict with capital. It is possible to argue
that in Fanon's engagement with the colonial problem, the paradigmatic Marxist model of the labor/capital conflict in the colonial context achieves a double
dimension on the ground that colonial agrarian labor is *not merely exploited but
is doubly exploited*—certainly by the metropolitan bourgeoisie in the first place
and then also by the national bourgeoisie, despite their "undeveloped" formation,
which is, as Fanon argues, different from that of the metropolitan bourgeoisie.
Indeed, in this instance, Fanon envisages a *double dialectic.* And this very dialectic
of the contradiction of colonial agrarian labor with metropolitan capital on the
one hand, and with "national" capital on the other, is further nuanced by the
factor of race that Fanon brings into play vis-à-vis the exploitation of colonial
agrarian labor. In other words, as Fanon seems to suggest, the metropolitan

bourgeoisie *alone* doubly exploits—in terms of *both* class and race—colonial agrarian labor, racialized as it remains.

This polyvalence of the dialectic makes Fanon's political economy of racism and colonialism different from—if not *discontinuous* with—traditional Marxist political economy. While Fanon certainly retains Marx's labor theory of value at a crucially fundamental level, Fanon nevertheless nuances the notion of value in terms of the colonial agrarian question—a question that points to several levels and layers of exploitation, rendering the categories of *both* class and race *equally important*. Also, specific historical forces and factors—relevant as they are to the African/Algerian context itself—contribute to and account for the *differentia specifica* of Fanon's political economy of racism and colonialism. History itself rendered it clear to Fanon that both industrial labor—and therefore industrial capital—did not amply develop in Africa, and that its mode of production was generally agrarian—a mode of production that is *doubly* affected by the forces of *both* feudal exploitation and colonial-capitalist exploitation. Historically, therefore, for Fanon, the question of the revolutionary agency of the peasantry becomes more important than the question of the proletariat. It is precisely in this context that Fanon and Mao meet, yet they part company in that Mao's reason for regarding the peasantry as the most revolutionary is entirely economic, while Fanon's reasons are both economic and racial.

Moreover, Fanon's stretching of Marxism—and for that matter, his third-worlding of Marxism—goes a step further than Mao's in the sense that Fanon stresses the revolutionary role of the *lumpenproletariat* as well. For instance, he writes, "The *lumpenproletariat*, that horde of starving men, uprooted from their tribe and from their clan, constitutes one of the most spontaneous and the most radically revolutionary forces of a colonized people" (*Wretched* 129). But Marx treats the *lumpenproletariat* with suspicion. In *The Communist Manifesto* Marx and Engels consider the *lumpenproletariat* as "the dangerous class, the social scum, that passively rotting mass thrown off by the lowest layers of old society" (18). Following this argument in particular, a score of Marxists tend to dismiss *tout court* the possible revolutionary agency of the *lumpenproletariat* in mass movements and therefore also tend to dismiss Fanon's view of the *lumpenproletariat*. It should be noted, however, that Marx himself *does not summarily dismiss* the *lumpenproletariat*. For instance, in *The Class Struggles in France*, Marx writes that the *lumpenproletariat* is "thoroughly malleable but capable of the most heroic deeds and the most exalted sacrifices" (219–20). In other words, Marx suggests that the *lumpenproletariat* can play a positive role only if advantage can be taken of their "malleability." Lenin endorses Marx's position, suggesting that the *lumpenproletariat* can play a positive role only when they are led by the proletariat. Although Mao sounds more positive than Marx and Lenin about the role of the *lumpenproletariat*, Mao is not without suspicion, as he writes, "Able to fight very bravely but *apt to be destructive*, they can become a revolutionary force when properly guided" (*Analysis of Classes in the Chinese Society* 11).

Fanon in some ways certainly takes cues and clues from Marx, Lenin, and Mao. Like them, for instance, Fanon is aware of the "malleability" of the *lumpenproletariat*. He even uses the word *maneuvering* to echo Marx's "malleability." Fanon, for example, notes, "Colonialism will also find in the *lumpenproletariat* a considerable space for maneuvering. For this reason any movement for freedom ought to give its fullest attention to this *lumpenproletariat*" (*Wretched* 109). Fanon's Marxist-Leninist-Maoist suspicion about the "malleability" of the *lumpenproletariat*, however, does not lead him to make them subservient to either the proletariat or the peasantry. In fact, Fanon accentuates the need for engineering a praxis of a nonhierarchical alliance among workers, peasants, and the *lumpenproletariat* against capitalism, racism, and colonialism.

The question of the revolutionary agency of both the peasantry and the *lumpenproletariat* also brings up the politically charged issues of both land and the body. Fanon maintains that the land remains the fundamental target of colonial-racial violence; so does the body. On the very issue of land, Fanon writes, "For a colonized people the most essential value, because the most concrete, is first and foremost the land: the land which will bring them bread, and above all, dignity" (*Wretched* 44). Colonialism, as Fanon time and again suggests, violently alienates both the peasantry and the *lumpenproletariat* from their own land—the fundamental site of agricultural labor as well as the fundamental source of livelihood ("bread"). In fact, both labor and land in the colonial context remain inextricably intertwined, given the fact that the colonial mode of production is fundamentally an agricultural mode of production, which, however, remains variously implicated in the capitalist mode of production of the "mother-country." Given this complex and overdetermined relationship, then, the exploitation of colonial agrarian labor by metropolitan capital amounts to the exploitation of the land itself. Thus, in the context of Fanon's brand of political economy, one can even think of a *land theory of value,* meaning that land is not only directly conquered and snatched away by the colonizer but that land, being the site of labor, also turns out to be a predominantly productive source of value and surplus value—profit for the colonizer, in a word. Thus, the politics of decolonization inevitably turns out to be the politics of land—the struggle over land for both the peasantry and the *lumpenproletariat.*

Tied to the land—as well as to labor—remains the body, a charged microsite of contestation in *The Wretched of the Earth.* In fact, Fanon's political economy of the body tends to track many itineraries of struggle, given the fact that Fanon speaks of the body in numerous contexts in his entire *oeuvre.* One might say that Fanon has a Foucault-like persistence in theorizing bodies of different kinds. Thus, to begin with, one can, for instance, point to the *body biologic* or the physical body, which, according to Fanon, is not only objectified, fetishized, or treated as a microsite of *difference,* but is also mutilated by the technology of the white gaze. Fanon suggests time and again in his works from *Black Skin, White Mask* to *The Wretched of the Earth* that the body of color gets fixed and even split under the gaze of the white man. One can also speak of the *body politic,* which, as Fanon suggests, remains subject to colonial violence in the sense that colonialism disrupts and even destroys the entire indigenous mode of self-governance and autonomy, and for that matter the native's right to self-determination. Then there is the *body discursive*—the body of indigenous knowledges, literatures, folklores, myths, languages, and other discursive practices of the colonized—which is also violently disrupted, dismantled, and even destroyed by colonialism. Fanon's accent falling again and again on language as a site of struggle is indeed another way of emphasizing the very body of the colonized as a charged space of oppression and opposition.

I am now interested in pursuing yet another trajectory of Fanon's body discourses that directly relates to the *body economic*—that is, the racialized body as a site of colonial-agrarian labor. To exploit this labor is then to exploit the body itself, and by implication, to exploit the racialized-body-as-land and land-as-the-racialized-body. Following Fanon's own suggestions, one can even say at this point that the colonized body of an agricultural laborer produces value: use value, exchange value, and ultimately surplus value, and for that matter, profit for the colonizer. Thus it is possible to advance a *body theory of value.* This, of course, also indicates that the politics of decolonization turns out to be the politics of the body—the struggle over the body, which, in the colonial context, does not belong to the peasantry and the *lumpenproletariat.* Decolonization is therefore the Other's violent recovery of the othered body—the body as a means of production—always-already owned by the colonial exploiter.

Conclusion: Fanon and Us

Fanon's brand of the political economy of racism and colonialism can, then, profitably combine Marx's labor theory of value with a body theory of value and a land theory of value, which together can be subsumed under—if not simply reduced to—what I have earlier posited as a race theory of value. Such a political economy, thus, suggests that strategies for a decolonization movement—and, by extension, strategies for anticapitalist, antiracist, antipatriarchal, and anticolonial struggles—all must aim at *fully* recovering and *totally* liberating the body, labor, land, and the language of the oppressed all at once from the exploitative world system of colonial/racist capitalism and capitalist colonialism/racism. In other words, Fanon's political economy of racism and colonialism—as I have hitherto enunciated and elaborated it by means of rereading *The Wretched of the Earth* together with Marx—also turns out to be a political economy of labor, land, language, and the body—sites and categories whereby the logic of racism and colonialism can be explained even in their totality at this historical conjuncture.

This conjuncture is obviously characterized by an unprecedented globalization of capital and, for that matter, an unprecedented globalization of racism.

Immanuel Wallerstein is right in pointing out in his most recent piece "A Left Politics for an Age of Transition": "Racism is pervasive throughout the existing world-system. No corner of the globe is without it as a central feature of local, national, and world-politics" (22). Thus the ongoing stubborn U.S. recolonization of the "third world"—the *world of color,* if you will—can be reckoned not only as a military project but also as a capitalist-imperialist-racist intervention in the land, labor, language, and the body of the third-world peasants and working-class masses. And, indeed, today's capitalism-racism-(neo)colonialism-imperialism can be seen as the macrostructures and networks of production and power that thrive on the exploitation, domination, appropriation, violation, and even destruction of the land, labor, language, and the body of the global subaltern from Puerto Rico to Palestine to the Philippines, or from Afghanistan to Iraq, for instance.

Finally, in the light of my rereading of Fanon together with Marx, let me advance a couple of categorical propositions in the service of a political-economic analysis of contemporary production relations and power relations at both local and global levels:

1. To the extent that racism is colonialist, that colonialism is racist, that capitalism is colonialist, that colonialism is capitalist, that capitalism is racist, and that racism is capitalist, today one cannot fully comprehend the logic of capitalism without simultaneously articulating a political economy of racism and (neo)colonialism (in other words, today, Marx and Fanon need to complement one another), and thus one cannot make sense of the conflict between labor and capital without understanding that such a conflict—and for that matter the law of value itself—historically has never remained race-neutral. In fact, the contemporary international division of labor—or call it the labor line—is decisively the color line and gender line.

2. The sites of labor, land, language, and the body are not merely the sites of oppression but also the sites of opposition. Thus, a political economy of labor, land, language, and the body envisages, endorses, and even enacts a dialectic of hegemony/counterhegemony. Such a political economy also suggests that to look for interrelationships among those sites is to see how one form of exploitation and oppression remains linked or even leads to another and thus how one kind of opposition can be linked to another in the service of anticapitalist, antiracist, anticolonial, and antipatriarchal struggles at both local and global levels.

Notes

1. For a thorough review of such discussions of Fanon's work, see Sekyi-Otu.

2. For a historical-materialist critique of the contemporary postcolonial appropriation and dematerialization of Fanon's otherwise praxis-oriented work, see San Juan, 27–28.

3. See, for instance, Amin, *Specters of Capitalism,* 115–16. Also see my essay "Reviewing Amin," 14–18.

4. Elsewhere I propose and posit what I call a race theory of value. See, for instance, my editorial essay "The Color Line," 1–4.

5. See Geismar, *Fanon* 189–201; Gendzier 197; Hansen 115–69; Robinson 79–91; Zahar xiii. While all such writers reckon *The Wretched* as Fanon's single most important political work, Said celebrates its liberationist politics from an explicitly culturalist perspective (268–74).

6. Engels defines political economy thus: "Political economy, in the widest sense, is the science of laws governing the production and exchange of the material means of subsistence in human society. Production and exchange are two different functions" ("Political Economy" 163).

7. For a lucid interpretation of the theory of value, see Amin, *The Law of Value and Historical Materialism,* 9–14.

Works Cited

Amin, Samir. *The Law of Value and Historical Materialism.* New York: Monthly Review Press, 1978.

——. "The Political Economy of the Twentieth Century." *Monthly Review* 52.2 (2000): 1–17.

——. *Specters of Capitalism: A Critique of Current Intellectual Fashions.* Trans. Shane Henry Mage. New York: Monthly Review Press, 1998.

Bhabha, Homi K. "Remembering Fanon: Self, Psyche, and the Colonial Condition." In *Colonial Discourse and Post-colonial Theory.* Ed. Patrick Williams and Laura Chrisman. New York: Columbia University Press, 1994. 112–23.

Engels, Friedrich. "Political Economy." *Anti-Duhring.* Trans. Emile Burns. New York: International Publishers, 1939. 163–251.

Fanon, Frantz. *Black Skin, White Masks.* Trans. Charles Lam Markman. New York: Grove Press, 1967.

——. *The Wretched of the Earth.* Preface by Jean-Paul Sartre. Trans. Constance Farrington. New York: Grove Press, 1963.

Geismar, Peter. *Fanon.* New York: Dial Press, 1971.

——. "Frantz Fanon: Evolution of a Revolutionary. A Biographical Sketch." *Monthly Review* 21 (1969): 19–30.

Gendzier, Irene. *Frantz Fanon: A Critical Study.* New York: Pantheon Books, 1973.

Gramsci, Antonio. *Selections from the Prison Notebooks.* Ed. and trans. Quintin Hoare and Geoffrey Nowell Smith. London: Lawrence and Wishart, 1971.

Hall, Stuart. "The After-life of Frantz Fanon." In *The Fact of Blackness: Frantz Fanon and Visual Representation.* Ed. Alan Reed. Seattle: Bay Press, 1996. 13–37.

Hansen, Emmanuel. *Frantz Fanon: Social and Political Thought.* Columbus: Ohio State University Press, 1977.

Hussain, Azfar. "The Color Line: The Problem of the Twenty-first Century." *dis/content* 3.2 (2000): 1–4.

——. "Reviewing Amin: Metaphors, Mathematics, Markets, and the Political Economy of the Frivolous." *dis/content* 4.1 (2001): 15–18.

Lenin, Vladimir I. *Imperialism: The Highest Stage of Capitalism.* New York: International Publishers, 1977.

Mandel, Ernest. *Late Capitalism.* Rev. ed. Trans. Joris De Bres. Atlantic Highlands, N.J.: Humanities Press, 1975.

Mao Tse-tung. *Analysis of Classes in Chinese Society.* Peking: Foreign Languages Press, 1956.

———. "The Peasantry and Working-Class Leadership." In *The Political Thought of Mao Tse-tung.* Rev. ed. Ed. Stuart R. Schram. New York: Praeger, 1969. 236–64.

Marx, Karl. *Capital.* Vol. 1. Trans. Samuel Moore and Edward Aveling. Ed. Friedrich Engels. New York: International Publishers, 1987.

———. *Capital.* Vol. 3. Trans. David Fernbach. New York: Vintage, 1981.

———. *The Class Struggles in France.* In Karl Marx and Friedrich Engels, *Selected Works.* Moscow: Progress Publishers, 1969.

———. "The Poverty of Philosophy: The Metaphysics of Political Economy." In *A Handbook of Marxism.* Vol. 1. Comp. Emile Burns. New York: Haskell House, 1970. 378–70.

Marx, Karl, and Friedrich Engels. *The Communist Manifesto: A Handbook of Marxism.* Selected by Emile Burns. New York: Haskell House, 1970. 1–59.

McClintock, Anne. "'No Longer in a Future Heaven': Gender, Race, and Nationalism." In *Dangerous Liaisons: Gender, Nation, and Postcolonial Perspectives.* Ed. Anne McClintock, Aamir Mufti, and Ella Shohat. Minneapolis: University of Minnesota Press, 1997. 89–112.

Robinson, Cedric. "The Appropriation of Frantz Fanon." *Race and Class* 35.1 (1993): 79–91.

Said, Edward W. *Culture and Imperialism.* New York: Alfred A. Knopf, 1993.

San Juan, Epifanio, Jr. *Beyond Postcolonial Theory.* New York: St. Martin's Press, 1998.

Sekyi-Otu, Ato. *Fanon's Dialectic of Experience.* Cambridge, Mass.: Harvard University Press, 1996.

Walder, Dennis. *Postcolonial Literatures in English: History Language Theory.* Oxford, Eng.: Blackwell, 1998.

Wallerstein, Immanuel. "A Left Politics for an Age of Transition." *Monthly Review* 54.1 (2002): 17–23.

Zahar, Renate. *Frantz Fanon: Colonialism and Alienation.* Trans. Willfried F. Feuser. New York: Monthly Review Press, 1974.

CHAPTER 8

Afrocentricity and the Eurocentric Hegemony of Knowledge: Contradictions of Place

Molefi Kete Asante

Afrocentricity creates, *inter alia,* a critique of social history in the West (Asante 1998). Such an action is at once a liberalizing and a liberating event, marking both the expansion of consciousness and the freeing of the mind. One cannot gain such expansion and freedom without setting off a transformation in the way knowledge is acquired, legitimized, and projected (Mazama 2001). Even the manner in which the acquisition of knowledge is legitimized and knowledge is then disseminated will be affected by an agency analysis that strips from oppressors the right to establish norms of human relations. Exploration into the social knowledge necessary to free the minds of the oppressed involves a critique. Too often the contemporary social scientists, and indeed too many African social scientists among them, reframe and reshape the Eurocentric model and project it as universal. I have always believed that Eurocentricity was possible as a normal expression of culture but could be abnormal if it imposed its cultural particularity as universal while denying and degrading other cultural, political, or economic views.

To put it bluntly, the suppressing of anyone's personality or economic or cultural expression creates a state of oppression. The operators of such systems or the enforcers of such individual or collective suppression are oppressors. What the oppressed must do to regain a sense of freedom is to throw off the layers of oppression that result from all forms of human degradation (Kebede 2001). The Afrocentrist sees these forms as class and biological discriminations and oppressions that must be dealt with on a cultural and psychological level, both at the oppressor end and the oppressed end of the spectrum. Indeed, both experience freedom when this is done. This is why I always seek a critique of hegemony and other forms of domination.

This essay seeks to establish the grounds upon which we can build a useful social discourse without abandoning African agency. I shall do this by offering some general statements regarding the Afrocentric idea and then show, through a critique, how a contemporary social scientist uses the particular vantage point of Europe to write Africans out of centrality, even within our own historical context. What I mean by this notion of critique is the observation and commentary on the historiography of sociology and the sociology of history by Afrocentrists committed to the freeing of the minds of the oppressed. All science becomes by virtue of such an agency analysis antioppressive and antiracist in its critical nature.

Using Maulana Karenga's (1993) twin towers of tradition and reason, the Afrocentrist establishes the subject analysis for culture on contemporary racist and sexist interpretations of human phenomena. Thus, the grand sociological narrative, and narratives of other disciplines, imposed by Western scholars to enshrine Europe and European individuals as the norms of human culture, human relations, human interactions, social theory, and social institutions must be called to task for their universalizing actions (Reviere 2001). In fact, some social scientists are already rewriting the script with a more human and sensitive—yes, sensitive—approach to humanity. I have avoided the term *inclusive* because I see that term as giving the impression that "minorities" are to be included in Europe, and this is certainly not my intention. In the notion of *inclusive* is the idea that Europe is classified above other cultural spheres, not alongside them. My idea is that communication between cultures is a cocultural affair, not an affair of superior and inferior cultures.

What the Afrocentric critique has shown is that one cannot write an authentic sociology of the world based simply on the structure of northern European thought. To assume, as the Western academy often does, that history starts with Europe or could be written by assembling only European facts is the grandest arrogance in human scholarship. Inevitably we are at the contradiction of place when the particular is transformed into the absolute. Nothing could create such a false sense of human purpose and place as the doctrine of racial superiority, which has unfortunately affected everything in the Western academy.

Such a construction of human knowledge means that to the Eurocentrist a totalizing rhetoric of science is desirable and possible. Because Afrocentricity has demonstrated that openness to human agency is its operative principle, the Afrocentric critique of this position is particularly severe. There can be no coherent totalizing rhetoric of science based merely on the European example. Yet it is this position that has been pushed incessantly by many Western scholars. To a nauseating degree it appears that the lessons of progressive sociologists and historians of European origin are ignored by the Eurocentric mainstream. I have rarely seen the evidence of Andrew Hacker, Joe Feagin, or Sidney Willhelm, for examples, in the policies of the U.S. government. The reason for the emergence of Stephan Thernstrom, Mary Lefkowitz, Marvin Harris, and Diane Ravitch, among others, as leading scholars has a lot to do with the lack of sound standards and criteria for human ethics. You can still be considered a good historian or a good sociologist and yet be a sexist or racist in traditional terms. Problematizing becomes a science of covering for the worst types of outrages against humanity. There is a reason advanced for the vilest and most venal forms of discrimination and racism. Thomas Jefferson's enslavement of Africans is problematized as part of the general attitude of the day and thus Jefferson must be understood within the context of his times. The Afrocentrist rejects such scurrilous arguments on the ground that human dignity is itself the most abiding standard by which we should judge our treatment of other humans. The fact that Eurocentrists can make arguments to excuse the racism of white philosophers, politicians, and historians demonstrate the degree to which cultural chauvinism has influenced the historiography.

However, no good Afrocentrist can also be a racist or sexist. What is the reason for this difference between the Eurocentric and Afrocentric conceptualizations? The answer lies in the fact that Afrocentricity actually celebrates agency on the part of any individual or group of individuals who identify as a collective creating history or making human social relations. Furthermore, Afrocentrists are cognizant of the fact that culture and economics are twin pillars in the eradication of oppression. One without the other leads to continuing disenfranchisement of African people in the American society. Positive social relations, by which I mean economic, political, and cultural relations, are predicated upon freedom. Without freedom the African person in America is merely a pawn in the hands of the globalizing ethos of white corporate capital, which leads ultimately, it seems to me, to another form of enslavement and domination. To speak of globalization is to speak of some form of cultural and social equality in which all parties arrive at an agreement for mutual acceptance of interchanges and exchanges, not for the domination of one particular cultural style on the rest of the world. I realize at the moment that I am writing that a Weberian analysis where class and status are different might yield other responses to globalization, but in the end whether a person who participates in the Western hegemony is of one class or any other class, one status group or any other status group, the controlling dynamic seems to be the obliteration of other, particularly competing, views of the world. This is the principal violation of the nature of social relations that must be laid at the feet of the West.

We know as Afrocentrists, long under the dominance of Western science, that there are no universal values and characteristics that are derived from one cultural group alone but yet applicable to all groups. All human beings create their contributions to the world on the basis of their cultural foundations. They may add to the archive on the basis of class or biology, that is, as a proletarian or a female, but they may contribute simply as a member of a community where people share similar interests in any number of things.

I do not want to give the impression that Afrocentrists find nothing useful in the Western construction of sociology, because that would be taking my argument to the extreme. What most worries me is the continuation of the Western notion that all human history can be placed on a time chart and plotted from ancient Greece forward as the heritage of the world. Granted, it is one of the human heritages, but it is woefully lacking in its scope and depth. There is no one giant time chart of the world and belief in this universal chronology leads to the idea of discovery. The way Eurocentrists construct this argument for a Greek-derived hegemony is to argue that there must be a starting point in time for everything and if it cannot be found in Europe then it is unknown. If it is unknown, that is, if its origin cannot be determined, then it is of little interest to human civilization. Nevertheless, Afrocentrists have made it quite clear that no one can simply assume a position as arrogant as that and we now fully understand why we cannot say that Sophocles or Aeschylus discovered drama or Plato discovered political science. We know that since we are unaware of all of the possibilities of written documents in Africa, Asia, or South America, we must say we do not know. Discoverers in the European construction of reality are always Europeans. This should normally give one pause, but if you assume a European superiority then an inauthentic and unlikely event becomes normal, expected, and even predictable. Who else could have discovered dynamics or the printing press, paper, medicine, or architecture?

Afrocentricity has reopened methodological categories of Eurocentric scholarship. In recent years we were drawn to the debate over naming when we challenged terms such as "minority," "disadvantaged," "underdeveloped," "marginal," "the Other," "ethnomusicology," "mainstream," "prelogical," and "prehistorical." But it soon became clear that the reactionary rear guard would take the rising chorus of criticism against such terms as an attack on the freedom of speech or academic freedom. The right wing would recast the issue as political correctness and the press would take up each case as an example of someone trying to impose a thought police on the free will of the thinker. In a reactionary environment it becomes easy for reactive forces to undermine the possibilities of human interaction based on equality and dignity. They are emboldened by the political rhetoric to seek isolation, narrowness, and petty clan conservatism.

But any critique of hegemony will see this grab for anti-African space as part and parcel of the socializing process by which the reactionary elements attempt to define reality for others. Rather than accept the definitions offered by the subjects themselves, the reactionary forces are fond of maintaining their right to call people by any name and to assign to them any attribute they care to because it is their legitimate right to do so.

There is no lonely rage in the construction of agency among African people in America; we are profoundly engaged in a collective experience for self-determination and self-definition. This is not an antiwhite position; it simply ignores the definitions and constructions set up by white (and some blacks can be white) sociologists and historians. What matters to us is the ability to write our own story and to cooperatively set the terms of our engagement with the larger white and often domination-seeking world. But what disturbs me is the fact that he-gemonists rarely give in to the human sensibility of mutuality when they think they have the political and economic power to set the terms of engagement. Inevitably those who see themselves as oppressed will break free from such one-sided engagement and bring an end to the interaction. Periodic eruptions in the U.S. society that are falsely labeled riots or civil unrest are directly related to this breaking away from engagements that are dehumanizing and suffocating. When the sociologists and other social scientists rush to determine the cause of the latest urban expression of this breaking away, they often ask the wrong questions and seek culprits in the wrong places. All conflagrations are merely symptomatic of the search for agency and subject place. I would ask, what are the oppressive forces seeking to hold a lid on the achievements, aspirations, and expressions of cultural and economic development of the African people in this place? Answering this question will greatly enhance the sharpness of the social analysis in any urban community from Cincinnati to Los Angeles to Boston. Western social scientists are ensnared in a conceptual net that allows only a few to escape and consequently there is a hardy similarity to their analyses. The overanalyzed discourse on racism becomes in such a context nothing more than an elaboration on race relation and race formation themes; racism itself remains safely ensconced in the brains of the social scientist, away from real detection.

Now the real problem for oppressed African people is the fact that many African sociologists have succumbed to the same constructions as the white sociologists. They are victims of the hegemonic influences of their teachers and are therefore caught in a uniquely stifling bind. While I am the first to admit that I have some elements in my own thinking that need purging, I believe that there are many African scholars in the United States and the United Kingdom who write as if they are not just conceptually European but also anti-African agency.

Periodically there appears a book that runs counter to the wisdom of experi-ence in the African American community. *Against Race* by the sociologist Paul Gilroy is just such a book. Gilroy, a British scholar who teaches at Yale University, created a stir with the postmodern work *The Black Atlantic.* I see this *Against Race* as a continuation of that work's attempt to deconstruct the notion of African identity in the United States and elsewhere. It is precisely the kind of sociology that I have been explaining. The fundamental argument of the book runs squarely against the lived experiences of African Americans. The history of discrimination against us in the West, whether the United States or the United Kingdom or other parts of the Western world, is a history of assaulting our dignity because we are Africans or the descendants of Africans. This has little to do with whether we are on one side of the ocean or the other. Such false separations, particularly in the context of white racial hierarchy, hegemony, and domination, is nothing more than an acceptance of a white definition of blackness. I reject such a notion as an attempt to isolate Africans in the Americas from their brothers and sisters on the continent. It is as serious an assault and as misguided as the 1817 Philadelphia conference that argued that the blacks in the United States were not Africans but "colored Americans" and therefore should not be returned to Africa. To argue as Gilroy does that Africans in Britain and the United States are part of a "black Atlantic" is to argue the "colored American" thesis all over again. It took us one hundred and fifty years to defeat the notion of the "colored American" in the United States, and I will not stand idly by and see such a misguided notion accepted as fact at this late date in our struggle to liberate our minds. We are victimized in the West by systems of thinking, structures of knowledge, ways of being, that take our Africanity as an indication of inferiority. I see this position as questioning the humanity and the dignity of African people.

It should be clear that Gilroy's new book, *Against Race,* is not a book against *racism,* as perhaps it ought to be, but a book against the *idea of race* as an organizing theme in human relations. It is somewhat like the idea offered a decade or more ago by the conservative critic Anne Wortham in her reactionary work, *The Other Side of Racism.* Like Wortham, Gilroy argues that the African American spends too much time on collective events that constitute "race" consciousness and therefore participates in "militaristic" marches typified by the Million Man March and the Million Woman March, both of which were useless. The only person who could make such a statement had to be one who did not attend. Unable to see the awesome power of the collective construction of *umoja* within the context of a degenerate racist society, Gilroy prefers to stand on the sidelines and cast stones at the authentic players in the arena. This is a reactionary posture. So *Against Race* cannot be called an antiracism book although it is antirace, especially against the idea of black cultural identity whether constructed as race or as a collective national identity.

Let us be clear here, *Against Race* is not a book against all collective identities. There is no assault on Jewish identity, as a religious or cultural identity, nor is there an attack on French identity or Chinese identity as collective historical realities. There is no assault on the historically constructed identity of the Hindu Indian, or on the white British. Nor should there be any such assault. But Gilroy, like others of this school, sees the principal culprits as African Americans who retain a complex love of African culture. In Gilroy's construction or lack of construction, there must be something wrong with African Americans because Africa remains in their minds as a place, a continent, a symbol, a reality of origin and source of the first step across the ocean when they are really not African. But Gilroy does not know what he is talking about here. This leads him to the wrong conclusions about the African American community. The relationship Africans in the Americas have with Africa is not of some mythical or a mystical place. We do not worship unabashedly at the doorsteps of the continent although we have an active engagement with all that it means. Are we always conscious of it? Of course not! You will not find all African Americans walking around the streets of Philadelphia or Chicago or Los Angeles thinking about engaging Africa, yet we know almost instantly that when we are assaulted by police, denied venture capital or criticized for insisting on keeping Europe out of our consciousness without permission, that Africa is at the center of our existential reality. We are most definitely African, though modern, contemporary Africans domiciled in the West.

Actually Gilroy spends a considerable amount of time in this book explaining how race, a false concept, "is understood." He writes, "Awareness of the indissoluble unity of all life at the level of genetic materials leads to a stronger sense of the particularity of our species as a whole, as well as to new anxieties that the character is being fundamentally and irrevocably altered" (Gilroy 2000: 20). I do not know how Gilroy can move from this position to indict the African people as the carriers of this anxiety about "race," clearly a concept that was never promoted by African people in this country or on the continent. It is essentially an Anglo-Germanic notion, manufactured and disseminated to promote the distinctions between peoples and to establish a European hierarchy over Africans and Asians, as well as to define a hierarchy among Europeans themselves.

This blaming-the-victim type of discourse denies the agency of the oppressed at the same time. It is reminiscent of Gates and West's tropes that "black agony and anguish" or "black heartache and heartbreak" or "black hopelessness" are at the core of America's racial crisis (Gates and West 1996: 82–112). Somehow, as they understand, we are denied space or place because we are black. This is a different idea than that of the Afrocentrist, who argues that your place and space must be a part of your own definition and determination. But neither Gilroy nor Gates and West want to take this up, because it leads them to an acceptance of the black nationalist position. In other words, the intellectual position of Afrocentricity, that is, its theorizing elements, can only lead to a form of self-actualization on the part of African people. What Africans seek is not a handout, a dole, or a gift from America, but the legitimate rights and privileges that come with humanity. This is not a cry, a plea, or a petition, but a fundamental necessity for a correct perspective on identity, race, and the future of the American people. Gilroy has lost sight of the central problem of white racial hierarchy and therefore can concentrate on the inadequacies of the oppressed. But all oppressed people are burdened with political, psychological, economic, and cultural problems that unfortunately come with the nature of oppression. It is only a reorientation, however, to centrality, subject place, and agency that will deal with the problems concomitant to such a state.

I am of the opinion that Gilroy has little understanding of what Randall Robinson means in *The Debt: What America Owes to Blacks*. In fact, Gilroy would proclaim Robinson's work to be of the genre that does not extend "beyond the color line." But it is not color that creates problems in the Western world between African-descended people and whites, particularly Anglo-Germans. It is rather a strange belief on the parts of whites that they are superior to Africans, that they have a right to establish and maintain a hierarchy over blacks by force of arms or customs or laws or habits.

Gilroy's notion that antiracism has lost credibility and authority and therefore there has to be a new language "beyond the color line" seeks to get us to renounce race thinking as a dramatic strategic gesture. The problem with this line of thinking, however, is that those who practice racism, those who support it in their workplaces and in their daily lives, the institutions that discriminate against people on the basis of their "race" understand what they are doing. What is absurd is our belief that they are ignorant of the false divisions that are maintained by white racial domination. The terror is that those who perpetrate racism are often callous in their work.

It may be true that fascism is a major political orientation of national wills in the last century, as Gilroy contends, but fascism' s most daring and dangerous manifestation has always been in white racial domination and white supremacist notions. This is true whether they have been expressed in Germany, Britain, Australia, or the United States. To deplore or lambaste African fraternal gatherings without an appreciation of the successful historical reactions to racism and white supremacy in the American public by black nationalism is to miss the point of this century. The most exacting antidote to white racism is African American nationalism, where African agency, self-determination, and self-actualization allow Africans to live their lives regardless of white racial insanity. Racism is a form of madness; sociologists must stop considering it merely a distortion of the social situation. Thus, the African person in the United States and the United Kingdom has been able to exist through the resilience of spirit necessary for survival. Otherwise, in violent reactions or in acquiescence the African person becomes lost in the same madness of race as the white racist. Avoidance of madness is the great achievement of Africans in America under oppression.

One of the advantages of having an organic relationship with the ordinary people of the African American community is that one does not forget what the issues are in the struggle against racial domination. Ordinary Africans in the United States are not wrestling with the identity issues of the elite classes who are seeking ways to express an abstract cosmopolitanism devoid of actual contact with African people. I believe that Gilroy's issues are those of Africans who are trying to de-Africanize Africans in order to make us more acceptable to whites. This was the old canard when the issue was our hair, our skin color, or our speech. But we knew even then that these were false issues and that nothing could please the racist but the annihilation of the African. Unfortunately, instead of the racist having to perform the task of making Africans invisible, now scholars like Gilroy rush to demonstrate that there is something wrong with being an African.

The reality is that any new language about race or identity ought to be straightforward, blunt, and uncompromising. It should say that one does not have to give up his or her heritage, ancestry, or color in order to exist in the world. Why should African-descended scholars be promoted for advancing ethnic abstractness? I prefer the language of my late father who said, "if you cannot accept me as I am and for who I am then that is your problem, not mine." I do not believe that this is arrogant or militant; I believe it is the only authentic voice that is necessary to bring about a new language of race in this century.

There is much to applaud in Gilroy's visionary statement about an intercultural society, but it is not the "raceless future" aspect of his argument. First, I do not look forward to such a colorless, heritageless, abstract future and do not see why anyone should look for it. Only those who have a need to escape from their own histories have a need for such a raceless future. On the contrary, it is much more hopeful that we defeat the notion of racial superiority and establish a broad new moral vision based on mutual respect for all human beings. I cannot believe that racelessness in and of itself, whether that means racial amalgamation or the obliteration of the African phenotype, would amount to anything except the diminishing of the world. Perhaps we should insist that *race* be replaced with the more accurate term, *culture,* when we mean the legacy of a collective people. Where Gilroy has a point is his intense desire to counter the rise of European fascism, but I think that he has the wrong idea about how to counter that resurgence. To me, it is not in the elimination of race or races, but in the elimination of *racism,* the defeat of white racial domination, that we will discover the way to a new humanism.

There is a constant barrage of discordant voices urging discourse on multiculturalism and people-of-colorism. None of these voices appears to understand the principles I have tried to articulate in this discussion of Afrocentricity. Our critique of social history is meant to liberate us from having to depend upon whites to give us freedom. Never in human history has freedom ever been given to an oppressed people without a struggle, and the most intense struggle is always the struggle for the minds of the oppressed. To the degree that the traditional social scientists have refused to deal with white racial domination or white racial supremacy as doctrines that are pervasive in the literature of the West, they have created a false structure that serves to block or eliminate the authentic voices of liberation. Once we have overcome these categories and concepts and landed in a place where the expression of Africanity is not viewed as a threat and the presence of an Afrocentric consciousness is not seen as antiwhiteness, we will be centered in a new world.

Works Cited

Asante, Molefi Kete. 1998. *The Afrocentric Idea.* Philadelphia: Temple University.

Gates, Henry Louis, Jr., and Cornel West. 1996. *The Future of the Race.* New York: Knopf.

Gilroy, Paul. 2000. *Against Race: Imagining Political Culture beyond the Color Line.* Cambridge, Mass.: Harvard University Press.

————. 1993. *The Black Atlantic: Modernity and Double Consciousness.* Cambridge, Mass.: Harvard University Press.

Karenga, Maulana. 1993. *The Introduction to Black Studies.* Los Angeles: University of Sankore Press.

Kebede, Messay. 2001. "The Rehabilitation of Violence and the Violence of Rehabilitation: Fanon and Colonialism." *Journal of Black Studies* 31.5: 539–62.

Mazama, Ama. 2001. "The Afrocentric Paradigm: Contours and Definitions." *Journal of Black Studies* 31.4: 387–405.

Reviere, Ruth. 2001. "Toward an Afrocentric Research Methodology." *Journal of Black Studies* 31.6: 709–28.

Robinson, Randall. *The Debt: What America Owes to Blacks.* New York: Dutton, 2000.

Wortham, Anne. 1981. *The Other Side of Racism: A Philosophical Study of Black Race Consciousness.* Columbus: Ohio State University Press.

CHAPTER 9

New Frameworks in Philippine Postcolonial Historiography: Decolonizing a Discipline

S. Lily Mendoza

Within the last three decades, a conscious and carefully theorized move to adopt a closed circuit of communication in the practice of scholarship (the context of "we-speaking among ourselves" versus "we-speaking with Others") has been radically revising the way knowledge is being produced in the Philippine post-colonial academy. This new framework, termed *Pantayong Pananaw* (roughly, awkwardly, a "for-us" perspective) appears to present the first-ever serious challenge to the heretofore well-entrenched hegemony of racialized theorizing in the nation's western-oriented academic disciplines. Racist discourse having been systematically installed in the Philippine academy as part of America's social engineering strategy to subjugate the country's populace during its occupation of the islands (1898–1941), the academy continues to remain the logical site of contestation for would-be "organic" intellectuals wishing to create a more "in-digenously conceived" knowledge base as a platform for pushing the agenda of national self-determination. This paper critically examines the historical impera-tive and theoretical premises of this newly emergent discourse on civilization within the problematic demands of nationhood and nation building in a post-colonial context. Among other things, it evaluates its political potential, promise, and cross-contextual relevance as a model not only for deconstructing colonial legacies in formerly colonized academies but, more important, for generating new cultural energies and initiatives for constructive self-reinvention and col-lective empowerment.

Colonial Discourse: The Politics of Knowledge Production

Historically, colonial domination in the Philippines—as elsewhere—does not come merely as a material force in the form of military occupation and control. Rather, its greater violence comes in the form of a totalizing discourse meant not only to capture bodies to bring them to subjection, but to encourage the internalization by the subject people of their own colonial/racialized subjectivity. Through such discursively inscribed mechanisms of control and ideological surveillance, colonialism secures its subjects' willing submission, thereby making further external coercion superfluous. Gramsci sees this "voluntary" giving of consent to the ruling power as the "hegemonic" function of ideology in a given society. Ideas become hegemonic when accepted as "common sense," defined as the "'philosophy of the multitude' . . . the conception of the world which is uncritically absorbed by the various social and cultural environments in which the moral individuality of the average man and woman are developed" (Augelli and Murphy, citing Gramsci 17). Within this framework, subject peoples are made to believe in the normativity and naturalness of their subject positions. This is accomplished through their systematic portrayal in racialized colonial narratives as the degraded "other"—"barbaric," "uncivilized," "unfit for self-rule," vis-à-vis the "inherent superiority," "benevolence," and "God-ordained authority" of their colonial "benefactors" (compare Parekh).

In postcolonial theory, the "processes of subjectification" are secured mainly through discursive practices (Bhabha 67). Colonial discourse, according to Bhabha, is an "apparatus of power" whose "predominant strategic function is the creation of space for 'subject peoples' through the production of knowledges in terms of which surveillance is exercised" (70). This notion of dominant power exercised through knowledge production finds its echo in Foucault's conception of the inextricable link between power and knowledge as evidenced in the various institutional practices that constrain and regulate various forms of discourses, that is, who gets to say what to whom and what counts for truth and knowledge in any given period. The relevant question asked in this regard is, "What are the constitutive conditions that make possible this particular conception of truth at this historical moment?"

Common to these critical conceptions of the link between discourse/knowledge and the construction of subjectivity when applied to the colonial condition is their potential for exposing (and unraveling) the artificial suturing in colonial narratives—a suturing accomplished through the articulation of otherwise unnecessary relations of ideological elements in the ensuing discursive formation. Thus, what is purported to be merely "given" or "natural" may, through such interrogation of the process of ideological construction, be deconstructed, that is, shown up to have been ideologically assembled to produce the appearance of naturalness. In this way, the natural condition may then be resisted, and the meanings keeping it in place unfixed and disarticulated and other narratives put in their place. In other words, if ideology as a discursive formation has served as a powerful weapon of domination in the hands of colonial rulers presenting as unmediated and universal truths their self-legitimating narrative versions of history, then a deconstructive rereading of the same can challenge and smash the fixity of those ideologically sutured meanings by exposing their political and historical contingency and by unpacking their various mechanisms of repression and control.

In the Philippine case, what has remained a formidable obstacle to such a deconstructive project is the deep embeddedness of a racialized ideology naturalized and institutionalized within the country's educational system begun at the time of Spanish colonization (1565–1898) and further systematized during the U.S. colonial occupation of the islands at the beginning of the twentieth century.[1] This is an ideological discourse conceived as having basis in an "inherent" human nature, a universal conception of the social good, a positivist view of knowledge, and an individualist value orientation. Premised on enlightenment rationality and white racial superiority, this modernist discourse is responsible for the perpetuation of a state of neocolonialism in the country long after the formal ending of U.S. occupation of the islands in 1946. Specifically, academic disciplines such as economics, political science, sociology, psychology, anthropology, and philosophy, when used as tools for social analysis of Philippine problems, offered no alternative solutions to those already in place and complicit with a neocolonialist framework, thereby perpetuating dependency, underdevelopment, and further cultural degradation (Enriquez, *From Colonial, Pagbabangong-Dangal;* Constantino, "Mis-education," *Neocolonial Identity,* "Westernizing Factors"). Faced with that state of affairs, nationalist scholars within the Philippine academy found it crucial not only to critique systematically the sedimented legacy of western theorizing practices within the disciplines, but more important, to displace them with an entirely different brand of knowledge production. The concern is to ensure that the knowledge thus produced is articulated, not to foreign/neocolonial interests, but to the interests of the "nation"—here problematized as signifying the "cultural" nation grounded in the discourses of the ethnolinguistic communities versus the elite-controlled official "nation-state."

Epistemic Violence through Colonial Theorizing

According to Deetz, theory has a threefold function. One is that it serves as a way of "directing attention" (71–74), that is, it helps in determining what questions can be asked, what counts as knowledge, what are "useful" areas of study, and so forth. Second, it is a way of "organizing experience" (74–75). Depending on the particular value orientation that informs theory, it influences its consumers to make certain categorizations, sensitizes them to adopt and follow certain lines of relation and not others, and inclines them to cast their experiences in the distinctions and patterns made thereby. Third, theory, according to Deetz, is a way of "enabling useful responses" (75–77). The assumption is that the use of theories in everyday life presupposes a pragmatic motive, that is, "constructs are developed and elaborated in directions that help people accomplish life goals" (76).

In all these roles, theory is seen as determining what sort of knowledge is produced and whose interests are pursued when employed as a viewing lens. Such conception of theory differs radically from the representational (reflective) view of the same in modern science. Instead of the presumed givenness and transparency of the world revealing itself unproblematically to individual knowers with the use of the "proper" scientific tools, Deetz's constructionist perspective allows for a multiple conception and interpretation of the world based on the viewers' differing theoretical biases. Within the context of colonial education, the imported western theoretical lenses grounded in Cartesian and Newtonian logic tend to disappear in a host of mystifying discursive assumptions. Foremost of these is the claim that poses western "scientific" findings as totally "objective," "value-free," and uncontaminated by cultural assumptions or by any kind of mediation by human interpretation. Findings, then, are simply "statements of fact," neutral descriptions presented as such—without challenge—in classrooms. Research issues are imported via imported textbooks as well as via the export of scholars abroad, all the more to perfect the mimicry upon their return, that is, should they even come back at all. Kurien (in Atal), speaking of the state of social science in Asia, indicts thus: "We are neither Asian nor scientists. Our knowledge about the problems of our own societies is largely bookish, and the books that we read are mainly from the West. . . . We are beggars, all of us—we sneak under many an academic table to gather the crumbs under them. And we mix these bits and make a hash which we pretend to relish, but which we can hardly digest. We have hardly made a contribution to academic cuisine, and have thought it impossible to prepare a dish of our own, with a recipe we have made, using ingredients we have" (37). Such marginalization, if not total discreditation, of native intelligence and indigenous capacities in the production of authoritative knowledge, along with their systematic displacement with a colonialist ideology effectively posing as an innocent, "value-free," and "universal" epistemology, has not been without far-reaching consequences. As Shor (in Shor and Freire) contends, "Domination is . . . the very structure of knowing; concepts are presented irrelevant to reality; descriptions of reality achieve no critical integration; critical thought is separated from living. This dichotomy is the interior dynamic of a pedagogy that disempowers students politically and psychologically" (137). The acute alienation resulting from such irrelevant education results inevitably in disinterest, poor performance, withdrawing behavior, rote learning, and, not seldom, in acute psychological problems. Freire notes that the reality reflected back to students through classroom discourse and narratives serves either an affirming or disconfirming function. When knowledge representations in the classroom consistently reflect back a reality far removed from the learners' own, "learning" invariably becomes an exercise in self-alienation and self-marginalization. This is insofar as such knowledge serves to consistently invalidate, deny, and disparage the learners' reality in their own eyes and presents little by way of more affirming interpretations of the learners' experience of the world. Little wonder then that findings had been documented showing that "as [Filipino] students progress through the grades, their preference for their own nationality decreases" (Canieso-Doronila 72).

Theorizing, then, far from being an innocent exercise, inevitably traffics in issues of power. Possessed with constitutive power to bring about the materiality of their vision, theories are productive of consequences in the concrete world of social relations, especially when forged into a hegemonic mold. Institutionalized, they take on a "disciplinary" character (Foucault), making possible the privileging of certain forms of knowledge, the negation of difference, and the suppression of dissenting voices. And yet, because hegemony, in Gramsci's terms, is also a dynamic process exercised through the struggle over meaning and signification, there is yet hope of the possibility of resistance through the production of a counterideology that can be used as an instrument of liberation.[2] Constantino intimates a similar hope when he notes the dialectics operative in any oppressive condition: "It is true that the poverty of the masses is a major cause of their poverty of culture. But this poverty itself breeds its own dynamic as it transforms the feeling of deprivation into a desire to negate the condition itself. This process in turn develops its own forms of expression and action which if crystallized and systematized become the matrix of a people's culture. A real people's culture will constitute the negation of a culture that is merely an appendage or an emanation from a foreign culture which obliterated our pre-colonial and revolutionary cultures" ("Westernizing Factors" 12).

Colonial Domination in the Philippine Educational System: A Historical Overview[3]

The Philippine experience of colonial domination speaks of more than 350 years of Spanish rule (1521–1898) and half a century of American occupation (1898–1946) with a brief three-year interlude of Japanese occupation (1941–1944). Constantino sums up the colonial narrative as the Filipinos' misfortune of having been "liberated" four times in their history: "First came the Spaniards who 'liberated' them from the 'enslavement of the devil,' next came the Americans who 'liberated' them from Spanish oppression, then the Japanese who 'liberated' them from American imperialism, then the Americans again who 'liberated' them from the Japanese fascists. After every 'liberation' they found their country occupied by foreign 'benefactors'" (*History* 10). This "liberatory" narrative effectively formed the warp and woof of the fabric of colonial education in the Philippines. Historically, a system of national education was first set in place by the Spaniards in 1863. Scholars note, however, that education under the Spaniards was more of a "haphazard affair" whose main concern under the management of the Spanish friars was to provide reinforcement for the colonial edifice by using "religion as the core of Spanish cultural control" (Constantino, *Neocolonial*, 32–33). The first schools and institutions of higher learning were founded mostly by the various religious orders. Instead of teaching the natives Spanish, the friars learned the local dialects and systematically kept the former from gaining access to liberal ideas through the teaching of Spanish, fearing that such access to liberal ideas might lead to rebellion. Not until the 1860s did the Spanish civil government make an attempt to secularize the country's educational system and enact an educational reform decree to improve the state of education and require the teaching of the Spanish language (Agoncillo and Guerrero 109–11).

Colonial education under the Americans, on the other hand, proved far more systematic. Consistent with the broad purposes of American occupation, the purported goal was to train Filipinos to become "citizens of an American colony" (Constantino, "Mis-education," 129). Constantino, however, in part quoting Judge James H. Blount (whom President William H. Taft had appointed to the Court of First Instance, and who had earlier fought against the Filipinos as a captain of U.S. Volunteers), underscores American equivocation in educating Filipinos, noting subjugation—not parity—in U.S. intent: "Clearly, from the Filipino point of view, the United States was now determined 'to spare them from the dangers of premature independence,' using such force as might be necessary for the accomplishment of that pious purpose" ("Mis-education" 129). Toward this agenda of conquest and the preclusion of independence, Constantino regards the decision to adopt English as the medium of instruction as "the master stroke" in the plan to use education as an instrument of colonial policy ("Mis-education" 130). He notes that this linguistic move, even more than the alien content of American colonial education, secured the capture of the Filipino mind, binding it to a colonial way of thinking. Constantino puts it simply:

> Language is a tool of the thinking process. Through language, thought develops, and the development of thought lead[s] to the further development of language. But when a language becomes a barrier to thought, the thinking process is impeded or retarded and we have the resultant cultural stagnation. Creative thinking, analytic thinking, abstract thinking are not fostered because the foreign language makes the student prone to memorization. Because of the mechanical process of learning, he is able to get only a general idea but not a deeper understanding. So, the tendency of students is to study in order to be able to answer correctly and to pass the examinations and thereby earn the required credits. Independent thinking is smothered because the language of learning ceases to be the language of communication outside the classroom. A student is mainly concerned with the acquisition of information. He is seldom able to utilize this information for deepening his understanding of his society's problems. ("Mis-education" 142)

A move to address this language issue then became part of a larger effort to revamp and restructure the Philippine education system immediately after the forced "grant" of independence[4] by the United States. Although progress was slow and efforts seemed feeble at the start, the movement to adopt a national language based on one of the existing regional languages, Tagalog,[5] instead of English soon gained momentum and today forms the centerpiece of nationalization efforts in the country. A tradition that would arise out of this endeavor to gain control of the country's educational apparatus is the movement for indigenization in the Philippine academy.

The Indigenization Movement in the Philippine Academy[6]

The indigenization movement in the Philippine academy appears to have developed from various sectors of the intelligentsia enthusiastic about a nationalist (anticolonial) imperative. Although traceable to a long tradition dating back to the resistance movements against Spain and continuing into the American colonial period in Philippine history, the nationalist movement in the academy began rapidly building momentum only with the commencement of the project of rewriting Philippine history and systematically debunking the colonial narratives written mostly from the perspectives of American scholars and missionaries who came in the early 1900s (compare Agoncillo and Guerrero, *History*; Constantino, *History, Philippines*; Ileto, *Pasyon*). The impetus continued into the 1960s and 1970s, by the end of which time a distinct "Filipino" versus the "colonial" version had begun to crystallize into a common framework for analyzing Philippine social, political, and cultural realities cutting across the various social science disciplines.

By the late 1970s, such an impetus taking place in the discipline of history found a similar echo in the discipline of psychology, with the significant pioneering work of Enriquez (*From Colonial*), who developed the concept of liberation psychology or *Sikolohiyang Pilipino* (Filipino psychology). It was a potent formulation that called into question the whole framework of western experimental psychology that, until then, had reigned supreme in the Philippine academy as the only legitimate psychology. As well, such revisioned psychology effectively exposed much of the negative framing and (mis)representation of Filipino culture(s) as only so much racialized, ethnocentric cultural (mis)readings by those unable to gain access to the internal codes of the culture.

In anthropology, a rethinking of disciplinary perspectives began with the works of Jocano (*Philippine*; "Rethinking") reacting to studies done by American anthropologists Beyer and Fox (in Bennagen) and those of Covar (*Kaalamang Bayan*; "Pilipinolohiya"). Jocano (*Philippine*), along with anthropologists Salazar ("Ang Kasaysayan") and Bennagen, among others, challenged what they deemed to be the unimaginative explanations of Filipino origins based on "wave migration" and "diffusionist" theories. These theories tended to trace anything and everything found in the Philippines, including the early inhabitants and their material and symbolic culture, as deriving, or as having been adapted, from the outside (neighboring continents). From this unidirectional tracing of influence came the implicit assumption that everything Filipino is, hence, "borrowed," "unoriginal," and always coming from elsewhere. This calls to mind the historic racialized belief that no work of technical or artistic sophistication could have possibly been produced in Africa and that any evidence to the contrary must either be considered an "aberration" or "anomaly" or otherwise coming from other, better-known, "more developed" civilizations (compare Coombes). Such portrayal of Philippine prehistoric culture and civilization was seen as one more baseless interpretation that needed countering, all the more because it was presented in old textbooks as fact, with the slide from theory to fact obscured by the lack of alternative interpretations up to that point (compare Jocano, "Questions"; Salazar, "Matter").

An early contribution to a more contextualized rethinking of the social sciences is an article from communication scholar Feliciano titled "The Limits of Western Social Research Methods in Rural Philippines: The Need for Innovation." A further important contribution in this regard is the firsthand research work of humanities scholar De Leon ("Roots"; "Towards a People's Art"). In both essays, De Leon explores the surviving indigenous art forms of the various ethnic communities nationwide. Belying allegations of "cultural lack" and "deficiency" among precolonial Filipinos before contact with the purportedly "superior" cultures of the West, he documented a vast array of rich, diverse, and unique Philippine precolonial art forms. These, he argued, persisted through time against the onslaught of colonization and westernization. Using art as a projective tool, he combined rigorous cultural analysis of Philippine traditional arts with insights from *Sikolohiyang Pilipino* to establish an alternative "image of the Filipino in the arts." This alternative portrayal of Filipinos through their indigenous cultural productions challenged the colonial stereotypes of Filipino natives as "barbaric," "uncivilized," and "culturally deficient" before the coming of the West. On the basis of his studies, De Leon would argue for the need to ground the national vision of a future on Filipino indigenous cultures instead of slavishly copying foreign models of development.

Meanwhile, in political science, Constantino's nationalist writings (e.g., *History*, "Mis-education," and *Philippines*) delivered the most scathing denunciation of the systematic process by which the colonial stereotypes and representations of Filipinos, their culture, and their history were naturalized in the popular imagination through the instrumentality of a colonial educational system. His groundbreaking essay, "The Mis-education of the Filipino," in particular, criticized the persistence of neocolonial conditions in the Philippines long after the formal ending of American rule in the country. In unmasking the vested interests that have fueled the maintenance of a dependent Philippine economy through educational policies that catered more to foreign than to local interests, he helped end, once and for all, the innocent view of knowledge production as a neutral enterprise. In doing so, he further underscored the need to recapture agency in determining the kind of education needed for Filipinos to win the struggle for self-determination, particularly in the ideological arena.

In all these efforts, the challenge had to do not only with the need to change the subject content of the disciplines from "foreign" to "Philippine" material but, more important, to change the conceptual tools of analysis. Autonomously conducted at first, the search for new concepts, categories, instruments, and theoretical frameworks better suited to Philippine cultural and social realities eventually progressed into an intensely interdisciplinary endeavor. Scholars from the various disciplines realized the need to do "science" and scholarship differently from their western counterparts, part of which was eschewing the latter's penchant for overspecialization and zealous disciplinary turf guarding and boundary control.

Pantayong Pananaw as "Indigenous" Theorizing: Forging a New Discourse on Civilization

One formidable challenge to the undoing of epistemic colonization is how to seize a space of initiative not always already implicated in the very ideology it seeks to overturn. As Pratt describes the colonized condition in this regard, "Under conquest social and cultural formations enter long-term, often permanent states of crisis that cannot be resolved by either conqueror or conquered" (26). In the Philippine case, one effect of the thoroughgoing displacement of the people's precolonial history, culture, and identity and their supplantation with a colonialist epistemology has been to disallow the possibility of a language for speaking or talking meaningfully about Philippine realities outside the colonizer's gaze. With categories of thought themselves deriving from an alien (and alienating) perspective, the challenge was how to resist getting trapped into mere maneuvers of discursive reversal undertaken in exclusive reaction to the dominating ideology. Instead, the goal was to begin again, this time, from an entirely new initiative using as resource precisely the discarded, delegitimated knowledges and perspectives of the indigenous population without needing to constantly reference the default canons of western thought even just as a point of contrast or departure. While early efforts by proponents of indigenization countering such canons of western thought were considered a necessary starting point in the struggle against racialized knowledge in the academic disciplines, the resulting discourse from such attempts was inadequate. Those who would eventually push for a more thoroughgoing critique of the disciplines hold the view that such discourse remains trapped in a purely reactive mode and, as such, is incapable of forging a discourse that can serve as a platform for reconstituting Filipino subjectivity and help the push toward national self-determination (compare Mendoza, *Between the Homeland;* Santa Maria).

A framework that emerged out of this imperative to move away from a merely reactive to a reconstructive stance in the retheorization of knowledge in the Philippine academy is that of *Pantayong Pananaw* (roughly, awkwardly, a "For-Us" Perspective) coming out of the discipline of historiography and conceived by University of the Philippines professor Zeus Salazar in collaboration with colleagues at the history department. Based on Salazar's account ("Ang Pantayong Pananaw"), the crystallization of his attempt to develop a Filipino discourse on civilization began in the early 1970s as he was laying the foundation for a course in historiography that included topics in methodology, philosophy, and approaches to the writing of history. Coincidentally, in 1974, he was called upon to critique and comment on an encyclopedia project commissioned by Malacanang, the Philippine presidential palace then under former president Ferdinand E. Marcos. It is here where he first had the chance to articulate the beginning outlines of what he terms a *Pantayong Pananaw* (a "for-us" perspective grounded in a context of "we-speaking among ourselves") in contrast with a *pangkaming pananaw"* (also a "for-us" perspective but grounded in a context of "we-speaking to others"). The encyclopedia series was titled *Filipino Heritage* but was written exclusively in English. For that reason, Salazar objected to the project on the grounds that it appears to have been written not from a Filipino perspective but from the perspective of elite intellectuals whose primary aim was to speak to outsiders about "us" (i.e., *kami* or we-speaking to others) instead of *to* or *with* fellow Filipinos in the context of *tayo* (we-speaking among ourselves). The latter imperative would have meant, among other things, writing the series in a language understood by the majority of Filipinos. Therefore, Salazar deemed the project as having the effect of once more constituting the nation as an "object" of study from the outside, by an outsider perspective, for the consumption and benefit of outsiders. Such a framework, notes Salazar, ensures that the discursive base will not be founded on the concepts, sentiments, and understandings of Filipinos but on terms still mainly controlled by foreign categories of thought inherent in the choice of English as its medium. The will of the Palace prevailed, however; Salazar's comments were disregarded, and the encyclopedic volume was published.

By 1988 Salazar had managed to further refine his thinking on what has now come to be known as the *Pantayo* perspective. He was given the chance to expound on the constitutive elements of this communication-based framework in a professorial chair lecture titled "Ang Pantayong Pananaw sa Kasayayan, Lipunan at sa Agham Panlipunang Pilipino" (roughly, "A 'For-Us' Perspective in History, Society, and Philippine Social Science"). In summary, Salazar's framework rests on the distinction among the various taken-for-granted speaking contexts implied in the use of the various personal pronouns found in all the Filipino regional languages, namely, *kayo* (you-plural), *kami* (we-exclusive), *sila* (they), and *tayo* (we-inclusive). Salazar explains his choice of the last pronoun referent as symbolic of the ideal context in which he wants to ground a national discourse on civilization. The two contending possibilities among the four pronoun referents are *kami* (we-speaking to others) and *tayo* (we-speaking among ourselves). Salazar chooses the latter because for him, *kami* implies a context where the speaker is discoursing with an "other." When such is the case, in order to communicate, she must constantly take the other's context and perspective into consideration and explain herself to the outsider-participant in terms that the latter can understand. The constraint put on the speaker by such a normative context is likened to all the years in Philippine history when Filipinos as colonial subjects had been constantly forced to define, justify, and explain themselves to a dominant "other" (e.g., the Americans) as a matter of survival. Within a context of domination, the "other" in this situation becomes the constant reference point for the speaker's self-definition, thereby precluding the possibility of constituting the self from within. As Fanon notes, under colonial rule, the self is constantly being constituted as "other" and thereby disallowed from assuming its necessary role as self. Within Salazar's framework, the struggle to resist self-annihilation under colonial domination constitutes the "reactive phase" in the indigenization movement. Here, the normative discourse goes, "This is who you say we are, but this is not who we are. *This* is who we say we are." Hence, the self within a *Pangkami* discourse is compelled constantly to assume a reactive (and necessarily essentializing) stance in that it is constrained to devote most of its energies to countering degraded and degrading colonial narratives told about it and to define itself only in relation to such.

What Salazar ("Ang Pantayong Pananaw") proposes as an alternative response is to close off that circuit of interaction so that the discourse is to be carried on, this time, only by and among Filipinos without the inclusion (constant intrusion/meddling) of outside participants. That way, he says, Filipinos can discourse and communicate freely in their own terms, in their own language, in their own thought patterns and manner of relating and with their own interest in view.

Historically, Salazar argues, there was not one unified *Pantayong Pananaw* among the ethnolinguistic groups in the Philippine archipelago prior to the coming of Spain. Maggay speculates in this regard, "It is a matter of conjecture whether the Philippines, without the outside static of prolonged colonization, could have developed the sort of cultural homogeneity that characterizes nations like Japan, for instance. What is clear seems to be the decisive arrest of what could have been a natural movement towards consolidation, a process that other, more integrated cultures had time to grow into from being themselves strife-torn in the days of warring shogunates and medieval fiefdoms" ("Philippine Country Paper" 11). Although not totally discounting such a possibility even while doubting any "naturalness" in the movement toward consolidation, Salazar ("Ang Pantayong Pananaw") would rather trace the constitution of the Philippines into a national political entity to the efforts of the elites in the Christianized areas to attain reforms and eventual independence toward the end of the Spanish colonial regime.[7] Salazar refers to these elites as "the acculturated group" or the "ladino"[8] class, whose transactions and acculturative collaborations with the Spaniards he describes as being very "convoluted" (51). On the one hand, he sees these ladinos as being responsible for helping the Spaniards insert their culture into the lives of Filipinos mainly by indigenizing it and translating works in Spanish into Tagalog (one of the Philippine regional languages). On the other hand, the same elites also proved instrumental in the hispanization of Filipino culture by promoting the learning of Spanish. Because of their privileged status as culture brokers knowing both Spanish and Tagalog, these elites are noted to have prospered during the Spanish regime, going on to become the elite during the American occupation. Included in the ranks of such, in Salazar's estimation, are the Filipino propagandists who, during the latter part of the Spanish period, became exposed to liberal and progressive ideas in Europe and launched a movement for reform against Spanish abuses and oppression. Although coming from an anticolonial resistance position, the Propaganda Movement is regarded by Salazar as still having primarily a *pangkami* (we-speaking to others) form of discourse. This is because the Filipino propagandists wrote mostly in Spanish, directed their writings to the Spaniards, and used concepts and ideas they learned from the liberal traditions of Europe, which the Spaniards understood only too well.

During the American period and up until today, these elites continue to derive from the ranks of the ladino-descended and the European-educated propagandists, with the addition today of Fulbright scholars and other intellectuals sponsored by American foundations, and by Japan and other "First World" countries. That such scholars and intellectuals continue to discourse in English and use alien constructs in their study of Philippine society adopted mostly from their graduate studies abroad, in Salazar's view, only serves to marginalize Filipino culture in their own eyes even when desiring to work for national liberation. Whether from the ideological left or right, Salazar finds that the discourse of such individuals remains unrelated to the larger discourses of the greater majority of the Filipino masses, whose primary mode of communication is in their indigenous languages governed by totally different modes of thinking, conceptualizing, categorizing, and speaking about their reality. But being also the economic elite, such educated Filipinos, notes Salazar, have also managed to forge a discourse of their own among themselves and, by their sheer dominance and economic power in society, have succeeded in hegemonizing their perspective and constituting it as the normative "national culture" for all Filipinos.

Indigenization scholars, however, are one in rejecting what they consider a "bogus" representation of Filipino culture insofar as such elite version of "national culture" is still just a "xerox" copy of western discourse, "schizophrenic" at best in its attempt to represent the nation (ironically) within the discourse of foreign civilizations (Salazar, "Ang Pantayong Pananaw," 61). Because of the contradictions between their borrowed consciousness and their own traces of Filipino subjectivity rooted in accidents of birth and the indigenous influence of maids and household helpers who are likely to have reared them, it is these elites, in Salazar's view, who suffer from an identity crisis, who are "split" in their consciousness, who have a "damaged American culture," and who are responsible for the widespread poverty and alienation of the larger community from the centers of power through their insistence on the use of an alienating language and exclusionary discourse. Maggay ("Philippine Country Paper"), concurring with Salazar, similarly inveighs:

> Perhaps the greatest single source of anomie in this country, there exists in the Philippines an invisible yet impermeable dividing line between those who are able to function within the borrowed ethos of power structures transplanted from without and those who have remained within the functional and meaning system of the indigenous culture. Termed by academics as the "great cultural divide," this sharp disjunction in sensibility has on top a thin layer of culture brokers known as the "ladino" class, often co-identical with the economic and political elite but also including middle class intellectuals and technocrats sufficiently educated and domesticated into the formal systems of power introduced into the country by its colonial past. The vast bottom half consists of that supposedly silent and inert mass whose universe of discourse is limited to the indigenous languages and whose subterranean consciousness has remained impervious to colonial influence. Thus is a situation where the grammar of power is conducted within the terms and the structures of a language alien to the people's ways of thinking and feeling, rendering centers of power not only inaccessible but profoundly uninteresting, a political sideshow that interfaces only tangentially with what to the poor is the more serious business of survival. (3)

Salazar admits that, at the moment, even while the Filipino ethnic communities may be said to have their own respective *Pantayong Pananaw,* there is still no one *Pantayong Pananaw* discourse to serve as a unifying discourse for all Filipinos. But because he believes in the strength, vibrancy, and close interrelatedness of the cultures of indigenous Filipino communities, his vision is for indigenously grounded Filipino intellectuals to help move the nation toward this direction, that is, toward the possibility of "calibrating ethnicity progressively into nationhood" (Azurin 12).

Re-visioning Knowledge Production in the Philippine Academy: Promise and Prospects of *Pantayong Pananaw*

Over the course of three decades since its first systematic articulation in the Philippine academy, *Pantayong Pananaw* as a framework for theory revision appears to have gained no mean achievement in a number of areas. First, it appears to hold the promise of being able to constitute a "genuinely" Filipino intellectual tradition that is not merely derivative from, nor reactive to, colonialist ideology, but positively reconstructive, that is, productive of new kinds of knowledge and subjectivity. This is evident in its noted effectiveness in reversing the tide of theorizing practice from the normative "outside-in" trajectory (i.e., from mere adaptation of foreign-originated models of knowing) to the initiating of new problematics and new approaches to theorizing grounded in the intellectual resources and thought categories of Filipinos. Much of this reversal takes place within what I have called a normative "closed circuit of interaction" in *Pantayong Pananaw*. I offer an analysis of the importance of this discursive move elsewhere (Mendoza, *Between the Homeland*) thus:

> What is often not understood . . . is that such a closed circuit of interaction is really merely a *given*, a default position of every other *ethne* or a group of people in a shared community of belonging—a position otherwise known as "ethnocentricism." What is anomalous in the Philippine case is that owing to the historic displacements of colonialism, what has prevailed so far is a form of reverse ethnocentrism, that is, the adoption of the view from the outside as the normative Filipino worldview. Discourse (particularly of the state) is one carried on in a wide-open circuit of communication penetrated freely by dominant discourses emanating from the outside (the national community) without any clear controlling reference point from within. Here, it is often the case that others are allowed to monopolize the initiative, determine the agenda, and dictate the terms and trajectory of the engagement. Whether in actuality or psychically via the internalized gaze of the other/s, what is seen to prevail in this order of things is an alien platform dictating the national agenda and making mockery of the term "national interest" of which, historically, there had not been a clearly articulated one (if at all). (182)

Appearing to be merely a methodological concern, closing the circuit of inter-action to involve only community participants (i.e., "Filipinos," however prob-lematically defined) in the task of national discourse formation within *Pantayong Pananaw* attains far-reaching implications when understood as posing such questions as the following: What would our discourse look like when we no longer feel the need to justify ourselves to others but instead begin talking among ourselves? What other kinds of issues, subjects of discussion, and interests will begin to occupy our discourse on knowledge as a nation? How will we differently carry on such engagement? What/whose norms, whose rules of engagement will we choose to follow? Who might begin to want to participate in our conversations that might not have felt included in the past? Who are likely to feel excluded? What new perspectives might arise when formerly marginalized members of society begin to claim their voices and take their places in the discursive arena? Applied to the various disciplines, such questions have been known to incite other kinds of theoretical problematics than those currently prevailing. For example, Filipino "culture" and "identity" (in the singular) begin assuming a plurality formerly (strategically) suppressed in the forced binary construction of the debates within the context of decolonization (the necessary "us" versus "them" framing of the anticolonial discourse). Removed from that open circuit of communication, plural Filipino cultures and identities begin to emerge as the homogenizing imperative of the anticolonial stance gives way to a closed context of interaction in which Filipino community members are compelled to focus on problems arising from within the national community itself.

Second, *Pantayong Pananaw's* mandated use of the Filipino language[9] as the normative medium of communication serves a democratizing function that promises to abolish what is deemed by indigenization scholars as the longstanding scourge of Philippine society, that is, "the Great Cultural Divide" between the country's English-speaking elite and the masses of Filipino poor whose linguistic ethos remains that of Filipino along with the other indigenous languages. Language itself being a powerful system of representation, the shift from English to Filipino is here viewed to be more than a mere formalistic gesture avowing (guaranteeing) nationalist sentiment. Rather, it is seen as facilitating transformation of the very structures of knowing. As Goldberg notes in this regard, "To control the conceptual scheme is ... to command one's world" (9). Linguistic recuperation within the practice of *Pantayong Pananaw,* then, yields a view of history as "necessarily consisting of a narration that 'makes sense' and that has relevance or meaning to a particular constituent group of people as audience" (Mendoza, *Between the Homeland,* 45).

Currently, there is available a whole new set of writings in Filipino coming from this renewed perspective, not only in history but in other disciplines as well.[10] With the adoption of Filipino as the normative language of the discourse on civilization, *Pantayong Pananaw* proponents also hope to do away with the heretofore anomalous exclusionary (elitist/racist) requirement of English as a prerequisite to becoming an "educated" Filipino citizen.

Finally, *Pantayong Pananaw* models a nonessentializing approach to the problem of identity and national consensus formation that has potential for going beyond a mere discursive reversal or inversion of binary oppositions in contexts of de/colonization (e.g., us/them, indigenous/colonial, inside/outside, native/foreigner) and allows for more complex articulations of subject relations without in any way forcing discursive closure. This is accomplished by the emphasis on *process* rather than on substantive *outcomes* in the discourse construction. Responding to charges of "linguistic essentialism" leveled by detractors who find problematic the unconditional valuing of work done in Filipino regardless of ideological content, *Pantayong Pananaw* proponents note that "language as a controlling element in the *Pantayong Pananaw* discourse is ... its own corrective mechanism, that is, one might enter the *talastasan* [discourse] bringing what might be considered a 'reactionary' agenda, but that is quite alright for as long as the people are given a chance to consider it on their own terms. And such is possible only when the medium of expression is in their language" (Navarro, qtd. in Mendoza, *Between the Homeland*, 80).

Taking away the need for brokerage by the educated elite by removing what has been the historic barrier to mass participation in the national discourse, notably, the normative requirement of English, then, opens up the discursive space to the energies and contributions of as many potential participants in the national community as possible. A collective *project* and a work in progress rather than an already constituted discursive product, *Pantayong Pananaw* eschews "expert authority" as determinative of any discourse's legitimacy. Instead, it relies on the freed-up creative energies and participation of an entire people in the production of knowledge toward collectively defined interests and aspirations. It is here, in the impossible task of seizing a space of initiative in a postcolonial academy struggling to break free from the legacy of centuries of epistemic colonization, that the discursive strategy of *Pantayong Pananaw* is posited as yet offering an alternative framework for reconstituting an empowered native subjectivity out of the wreckage of historical trauma.

Notes

1. In its bid to join the superpower race to acquire territories during the age of European expansionism at the beginning of the twentieth century, the United States decided to invade the Philippines in 1898 and acquire it for its territorial possession. Heretofore admitting only to a diplomatic, not imperialist, history, more recent U.S. historiography is only now beginning to acknowledge the Philippines as America's "first Vietnam" (Francisco).

2. Compare Gramsci's conception of the dual role of ideology, reframed as hegemony, as a potential instrument of both repression and liberation.

3. Some portions of this historical overview appear in Mendoza, *Nuancing* and *Between the Homeland*.

4. Contrary to U.S. claim of benevolence, the "grant" of independence is noted to have been compelled more by the opposition to the keeping of the Philippines as a territorial possession from domestic U.S. agricultural producers, who "protested against competition from cheap Philippine agrarian products entering the United States under 'free trade'" (Pomeroy 9).

5. Tagalog is noted to have figured as the "language of the [Philippine] revolution" in the 1896 nationwide uprising against Spanish rule (Salazar, *Wika*).

6. Versions of this section appear in Mendoza (*Nuancing* and *Between the Homeland*).

7. Versions of this section showing the application of *Pantayong Pananaw* to historical analysis also appear in Mendoza (*Nuancing* and *Between the Homeland*).

8. Referring to Filipino-Spanish mestizos.

9. More recently, the successful hegemonization of Tagalog-based Filipino has had the salutary effect of inciting the other regional groups likewise to celebrate and work to ensure the survival, as well as promotion, of their respective languages and cultures. This

development is welcomed by most proponents of *Pantayong Pananaw* who find English domination—and not the existence of multiple vernacular languages—problematic.

10. See Navarro, Rodriguez, and Villan (187–92) for a comprehensive listing of representative publications, including master's theses and dissertations covering the last three decades of *Pantayong Pananaw* scholarship. Some of the more recent publications are Veneracion; Santillan and Conde; and Salazar (1999, 2000).

Works Cited

Agoncillo, Teodoro A., and Milagros C. Guerrero. *History of the Filipino People.* 5th ed. Quezon City, Philippines: R. P. Garcia, 1977.

Atal, Yogesh. "Call for Indigenization." In *Indigenous Psychology: A Book of Readings,* edited by Virgilio G. Enriquez. Quezon City, Philippines: Akademya n g Sikolohiyang Pilipino, 1992. 31–50.

Augelli, Enrico, and Craig Murphy. *America's Quest for Supremacy and the Third World: A Gramscian Analysis.* London: Printer Publishers, 1988.

Azurin, Arnold Molina. *Reinventing the Filipino Sense of Being and Becoming.* Quezon City, Philippines: University of the Philippines Press, 1993.

Bennagen, Ponciano L. "The Indigenization and Asianization of Anthropology." In *Indigenous Psychology: A Book of Readings,* edited by Virgilio G. Enriquez. Quezon City, Philippines: Akademya n g Sikolohiyang Pilipino, 1992. 1–30.

Bhabha, Homi K. *The Location of Culture.* London: Routledge, 1994.

Canieso-Doronila, Maria Lourdes. *The Limits of Educational Change: National Identity Formation in a Philippine Public Elementary School.* Quezon City, Philippines: University of the Philippines Press, 1989.

Constantino, Renato. *A History of the Philippines: From the Spanish Colonization to the Second World War.* New York: Monthly Review Press, 1975.

———. "The Mis-education of the Filipino." In *Rediscovery: Essays in Philippine Life and Culture,* edited by Cynthia Nograles Lumbera and Teresita Gimenez-Maceda. Quezon City, Philippines: National Book Store, 1977. 125–45.

———. *Neocolonial Identity and Counter-Consciousness: Essays on Cultural Decolonization,* edited by Itzvan Meszaros. White Plains, N.Y.: M.E. Sharpe, 1978.

———. *The Philippines: A Past Revisited.* Quezon City, Philippines: Tala, 1975.

———. "Westernizing Factors in the Philippines." Self-published monograph, 1977.

Coombes, Annie E. *Reinventing Africa: Museums, Material Culture, and Popular Imagination in Late Victorian and Edwardian England.* London: Yale University Press, 1994.

Covar, Prospero R. *Kaalamang Bayang Dalumat n g Pagkataong Pilipino.* Lunsod Quezon, Philippines: College of Social Sciences and Philosophy, University of the Philippines, 1993.

———. "Pilipinolohiya." In *Pilipinolohiya: Kasaysayan, Pilosopiya at Pananaliksik,* edited by Violeta Villaroman Bautista and Rogelia Pe-Pua. Manila, Philippines: Kalikasan Press, 1991. 37–45.

Deetz, Stanley T. *Democracy in an Age of Corporate Colonization: Developments in Communication and the Politics of Everyday Life.* Albany: State University of New York Press, 1992.

De Leon, Felipe M., Jr. "The Roots of a People's Art in Indigenous Psychology." In *Indigenous Psychology: A Book of Readings,* edited by Virgilio G. Enriquez. Quezon City, Philippines: Akademya n g Sikolohiyang Pilipino, 1992. 311–27.

———. "Towards a People's Art." *Lipunan* 3 (1981): 1–15.

Enriquez, Virgilio G. *From Colonial to Liberation Psychology.* Quezon City, Philippines: University of the Philippines Press, 1992.

———. *Indigenous Psychology: A Book of Readings.* Quezon City, Philippines: Akademya n g Sikolohiyang Pilipino, 1992.

———. *Pagbabangong-Dangal: Indigenous Psychology and Cultural Empowerment.* Diliman, Quezon City, Philippines: Akademya n g Sikolohiyang Pilipino, 1994.

Fanon, Frantz. *The Wretched of the Earth.* Trans. Constance Farrington. New York: Grove Press, 1968.

Feliciano, Gloria D. "The Limits of Western Social Research Methods in Rural Philippines: The Need for Innovation." *Lipunan* 1 (1965): 114–28.

Foucault, Michel. *Power/Knowledge: Selected Interviews and Other Writings, 1972–1977.* Ed. C. Gordon. Trans. C. Gordon et al. Brighton, U.K.: Harvester, 1980.

Francisco, Luzviminda. "The First Vietnam: The Philippine-American War of 1899–1902." In *Letters in Exile: An Introductory Reader on the History of Filipinos in America.* Resource Development and Publications, UCLA Asian American Studies Center: The Regents of the University of California, 1976. 1–22.

Freire, Paolo. *The Politics of Education: Culture, Power, and Liberation.* New York: Bergin and Garvey, 1985.

Goldberg, David Theo. *Racist Culture: Philosophy and the Politics of Meaning.* Oxford, U.K.: Blackwell, 1993.

Goldberg, David Theo, Lisa C. Bower, and Michael Musheno, eds. *Between Law and Culture: Relocating Legal Studies.* Minneapolis: University of Minnesota Press, 2001.

Gramsci, Antonio. *Selections from the Prison Notebooks.* Ed. and trans. Quintin Hoare and Geoffrey Nowell Smith. New York: International Publishers, 1971.

Ileto, Reynaldo C. *Pasyon and Revolution: Popular Movements in the Philippines, 1840–1910.* Quezon City, Philippines: Ateneo de Manila University Press, 1979.

Jameson, Fredric. "Notes on Globalization As a Philosophical Issue." In *The Cultures of Globalization,* edited by Fredric Jameson and Masao Miyoshi. Durham, N.C.: Duke University Press, 1999. 54–77.

Jocano, Felipe Landa. *Philippine Pre-history.* Quezon City, Philippines: Philippine Center for Advanced Studies, 1975.

———. "Questions and Challenges in Philippine Prehistory." In *Kasaysayan at Kamalayan: Mga Piling Akda Ukol sa Diskursong Pangkasaysayan,* edited by N. M. R. Santillan and M. B. P. Conde. Lunsod Quezon, Philippines: Limbagang Pangkasaysayan (LIKAS), 1998. 37–56.

———. "Rethinking Filipino Cultural Heritage." *Lipunan* 1.1 (1965): 53–72.

Maggay, Melba Padilla. *Pagbabalik-loob: A Second Look at the Moral Recovery Program.* Quezon City, Philippines: Akademya n g Sikolohiyang Pilipino, 1993.

———. "Philippine Country Paper: Issue Paper on Social Integration. World Summit on Social Development." Unpublished manuscript, 1994.

Mendoza, S. Lily L. *Between the Homeland and the Diaspora: The Politics of Theorizing Filipino and Filipino American Identities.* New York: Routledge, 2002.

———. "Nuancing Anti-essentialism: A Critical Genealogy of Philippine Experiments in National Identity Formation." In *Between Law and Culture: Relocating Legal Studies,* edited by David Theo Goldberg, Lisa C. Bower, and Michael Musheno. Minneapolis: University of Minnesota Press, 2001. 224–45.

Mulder, Niels. *Inside Southeast Asia.* Amsterdam, Neth.: Pepin Press, 1996.

Navarro, Atoy, Mary Jane Rodriguez, and Vicente Villan, eds. *Pantayong Pananaw: Ugat at Kabuluhan: Pambungad sa Pag-aaral n g Bagong Kasaysayan.* Lunsod Mandaluyong, Philippines: Palimbagang Kalawakan, 1997.

Parekh, Bhikhu. "Liberalism and Colonialism: A Critique of Locke and Mill." *The Decolonization of Imagination: Culture, Knowledge and Power,* edited by Jan Nederveen Pieterse and Bhikhu Parekh. London: Zed Books, 1995. 81–98.

Pomeroy, William J. *An American Made Tragedy: Neo-colonialism and Dictatorship in the Philippines.* New York: International Publishers, 1974.

Pratt, Mary Louise. "Transculturation and Autoethnography: Peru 1615/1980." In *Colonial Discourse/Postcolonial Theory,* edited by Francis Barker, Peter Hulme, and Margaret Iversen. Manchester, U.K.: Manchester University Press, 1994. 24–46.

Salazar, Zeus. "Ang Kasaysayan: Diwa at Lawak." *Dyornal n g Malawakang Edukasyon* 27–28 (1974–1975): 163–69.

———. "Ang Pantayong Pananaw bilang Diskursong Pangkabihasnan." In *Pilipinolohiya: Kasaysayan, Pilosopiya at Pananaliksik,* edited by Violeta Villaroman Bautista and Rogelia Pe-Pua. Manila, Philippines: Kalikasan Press, 1991. 37–45.

———. "The Exile in Philippine History." *Asian and Pacific Migration Journal* 8.1–2 (1999): 19–64.

———, ed. "A Legacy of the Propaganda: The Tripartite View of Philippine History." In *The Ethnic Dimension: Papers on Philippine Culture, History and Psychology,* edited by Z. A. Salazar. Cologne, Ger.: Counselling Center for Filipinos, Caritas Association for the City of Cologne, 1983. 106–26.

———. "The Matter with Influence: Our Asian Linguistic Ties." In *The Malayan Connection,* edited by Zeus A. Salazar. Lunsod Quezon, Philippines: Palimbagan n g Lahi, 1998. 59–80.

———. "The Pantayo Perspective As a Discourse towards Kabihasnan." *Southeast Asian Journal of Social Science* 28.1 (2000): 123–52.

———. *Wika n g Himagsikan: Lengguwahe n g Rebolusyon: Mga Suliranin n g Pakahulugan sa Pagbubuo n g Bansa.* Bagong Kasaysayan, Lathalain Blg. 8. Lunson Quezon, Philippines: Palimbagan n g Lahi, 1999.

Shor, Ira, and Paulo Freire. *A Pedagogy for Liberation: Dialogues on Transforming Education.* South Hadley, Mass.: Bergin and Garvey, 1987.

Sta. Maria, Madelene A. "Is the Indigenization Crisis in Philippine Social Sciences Resolved in Sikolohiyang Pilipino?" *Layag* 1.1 (December 1996): 101–20.

Veneracion, Jaime. *Agos n g Dugong Kayumanggi: Isang Kasaysayan n g Sambayanang Pilipino. Binagong Edisyon.* Quezon City, Philippines: Abiva, 1998.

CHAPTER 10

Between Unconsciously White and Mythically Black: European Race Discourse as Modern Witchcraft Practice

James W. Perkinson

This essay seeks to probe the historical emergence of white supremacist practice as a kind of modernist embodiment of "witchcraft discourse" that discovers its "witch-enemy" precisely in the moment of attempting to eliminate discourse about such from social intercourse. Race, racialization, and racism will be comprehended as integral to the constitution of the humanities in the European academy, which established itself, in part, as a repudiation not only of religious superstition at home but magic and sorcery in the colonies (Eze; Gilroy, *Black Atlantic*). The analysis will invoke the historical metaphor of the "great chain of being," by which European colonialism and imperialism organized its others into a manageable taxonomy to argue that something like that ontological grammar remains at work in contemporary social organization, has as its intention the stealing and consumption of the substance of others in a now-global enterprise of capitalist appropriation and accumulation, and masks its own avaricious and rapacious potency under the naturalizing function of a cultural "common sense" that until recently could claim authoritative backing by way of philosophy and the social sciences (Eze; Gramsci; Haymes; Mills). In such an enterprise, witchcraft, I am arguing, can be "good to think with" as a mode of communicative critique, signifying with a kind of "boomerang effect" in the intercultural space of rupture between the west and the rest.

More generally, the essay is part of a larger project seeking to take seriously the challenge of (African American) historian of religions Charles Long to understand the entire postcolonial situation as an international encounter demanding not so much scientific elucidation as "serious human conversation" (Long, "Chicago Tradition," 102). While Long's own specific focus is obviously the comparative study of religious practices around the globe, he is also unapologetic in insisting that colonial contact itself was a mode of intercultural communication that, for the colonized, was irremediably "religious" (Long, "Chicago Tradition"). What he means by this is that aboriginal cultures the world over were made to "undergo the west" in such an intensity and extent of "metabolic violence" that the result was terror at the level of metaphysics (Long, *Significations*). The overwhelming and irresistible epiphany of western commercial and cultural interests on indigenous practices did not only shatter native bodies in the wars and rapine of conquest, but ruptured the entire cosmogram of native forms of intelligence in the drive to civilize (Long, *Significations*). Where the western Christian "myth of origins" was maintained intact and even hyperfetishistically "confirmed" in the experience of contact, in virtue of the ruthlessness of western domination, indigenous myths of origin were utterly shattered (Long, *Significations*).

For Long, that experience of overwhelming violence, of a depth of dismemberment that cuts not only into bone but brain, exploding not only the body but the birth memory, which cannot even be "sited" in the mode of meaning making of local culture, is experienced in those cultures as the kind of rupture that initially founds a "myth of origin" in the first place (*Significations*). That is to say, indigenous culture was pushed, by contact, all the way back into its *primordium,* had its full universe exploded, had to renegotiate its entire existence—and did so in the only mode capable of comprehending a cosmos: myth. In contrast to the west, for the rest, the experience was irreducibly "religious" (Long, *Significations*). It required dealing with contingency and terror on a cosmic scale. The result was the Native American "Ghost Dance," African millenarian prophetism, Caribbean *vodun,* Jamaican Rastafari, the black church in the United States, and cargo cults in the South Pacific (Long, *Significations*).

Long's project is to try to take seriously the conditions of the postcolony in a manner that does not elide the depths and delirium of the rupture that modernity has meant across the globe. Simply to advert to western scientific/humanitarian discourse to attempt even to perceive these depths and delirium—much less explain them—is already to miss the meaning of presuming the superiority. Long will not have it. He insists on a conversation that entertains the possibility that cargo cult idiom or Rasta ritual may well be more accurate for the real "human" meanings of contact than the dispassions of objectified "othering" that constitute western academic disciplines beholden to the Enlightenment. At the very least, he insists on reciprocal *hermeneusis* (Long, "Chicago Tradition").

The project here, then, is an attempt, in light of that demand, to think "race" in terms of "indigenous ritual." At the very least it is an effort to relativize the western scientific paradigm and the universalizing humanities discourses that have nestled close to that paradigm. It is not an attempt to repudiate such an *episteme,* but rather—to borrow a jazz term—to "swing" it, to put it in antiphonal and improvisational circulation (West, "Black Culture"; West and hooks). The project constitutes a thought experiment, not pretending to pull capitalist practice and its humanist *apologia* fully into indigenous forms of discourse (as V. Y. Mudimbe has well argued, there is no such thing as pure precontact "tradition" left), but rather attempting to "out" it as the "mythology of origins" (of white notions of supremacy) and "practicality of rapacity" (concentrating and consuming resources globally) it actually has been historically (Mudimbe x-xi, 4–5). Undoing such a supremacy, I argue, requires exposing and enervating its first and constituting gesture.

African Witchcraft and European Statecraft

I choose to formalize the first part of the argument under the double delineation of "craft work" to highlight the active prosecution of "world construction" engaged in both by *indigenous village cultures* in Africa and the *globalizing nation-states* of modern Europe. Fundamental to my understanding is the perception of modernity as having, in some sense, begun with the commercial enterprise of 1492, quickly finding its peculiarities of "production for exchange" ramified in the colonial competitions emerging between nation-states following the breakup of religious Europe in the Reformation and gradually organizing its class priorities in monopolistic enterprises pursuing their economic hegemony in successive regimes of political imperialism and slave trading (Dussel).

Within the archives of these emergent European nationalisms are records of the attempts of various colonial administrations to manage their respective encounters with certain indigenous practices collectively delineated, by way of supposed homology with European experience, as "witchcraft." That such a homology organizes non-gender-specific native practices into a gendered European category is not accidental to its power. But these "official" struggles disclose a fundamental paradox: a domain of indigenous practice is comprehended in post-Enlightenment European discourses as largely superstitious and fictional but simultaneously occasions legislative sanction and punitive surveillance (Bongmba; Fields). "Witchcraft" reproduces its wiliness in the very moment of its suppression.

"Witchcraft" emerges in colonial perspective and practice as a structuring device that mediates meanings of "European order" and "indigenous disorder." This sleight-of-hand potency as an accusation that creates the very thing it projects is not dissimilar to its power at the level of local village life. In indigenous practice, the charge that someone is a witch, or has acted as such, often serves as a retroactive explanation for disease, death, or a reversal of fortune (Bongmba). It functions both to open and to delineate a field of conflict inside extended family relations, which then witnesses accusation and counteraccusation in a context of crisis (Bongmba). Ironically, colonial policies seeking to suppress native practices demarcated as "witchcraft," in effect, accomplish the same kind of differentiation and explanation. The very charge of witchcraft practice can itself be understood as a form of witchcraft. In this colonial permutation, however, the crisis it marks and mediates is one of political administration, not interpersonal fortune.

But the slipperiness gets very slick indeed in thinking this way. Academic study of indigenous practice pursued under the rubric of witchcraft is far too broad and much too debated a subject to do justice to in a single essay. For the purposes of the assay proposed here, I will root reflection among considerations of only one study of local practices and discourses delineated as witchcraft. Elias Kifon Bongmba's *African Witchcraft and Otherness: A Philosophical and Theological Critique of Intersubjective Relations* offers a self-reflective probe of such practices among the Wimbum people of contemporary Cameroon under the indigenous rubric of *tfu*. Bongmba is careful in his study, and that care will have to suffice, for now, for the particular spin I want to introduce into the academic discussion. Far from universalizing his examinations of witchcraft, Bongmba tracks *tfu* in its specifically local spatial context (the Northwest Province) across a recognized time of historical change (the intensified local effects of globalization and urbanization in the latter half of the twentieth century) and in relationship to his own personal predilection for postmodern perspectives on ethnographic initiatives. My own use of Bongmba's insights obviously will take him out of context.

Like Long, Bongmba is committed to hearing, not dismissing, the call of "the other"—even if its craft is "occult." His project, nonetheless, is avowedly critical: a reading of practices native to his own place, under the impress of the ethics of Emmanuel Levinas. My own is obviously the inverse, witchcraft "read back" toward ethics. Both of us, however, take seriously the prospect of meaning making in multiple modalities and the circumscription of the mode in local code.

Indeed, part of the charge to be leveled at Enlightenment-based academics and their contemporary offspring is a profoundly interested occultation of their own local benefits and effects—the metabolism of "exotic" cultures and "other" myths not only for the sake of western "new age" solace but also for academic profit in selling "knowledges" and imperialist advantage in the struggle for "intelligence." The adventitious western claim of universalism for its own regimes of truth is simply one more gesture of domination. But this is not a new criticism.

Bongmba seeks to take seriously—rather than dismiss offhandedly or totalize morally—the idiom of witchcraft practice while still evaluating critically its negative manifestations and pursuits. I seek rather to site western discourse inside such a craft and ask which is really "witch"? But first we need a bit more (Geertzian) "thickness."

The Practice

Bongmba's project seeks to challenge the overshadowing power of *tfu* discourse to account for experiences of violation within the moral space of interpersonal relations. What he aims for is "not fantastic tales of witchcraft per se, nor the drama of hunting down witches and cleansing the community of them," but rather display of the way "specific problems [are] perceived among Wimbum when charges and accusations are made by one person against another" (20). It is a question of indigenous articulations of "who is causing another to be ill," and "how that 'other' perceives it" (20, quoting Crick 344). In the process, Bongmba distinguishes three local terms for practices that could be comprehended as witch-craftlike interventions into the social or natural orders in clarifying his choice to focus on *tfu*. *Tfu* is the most comprehensive historical term that invokes local meanings of practices pursued "under cover of night," partaking of intimations of "darkness" and "secrecy," which usually carry a tonality of malevolence and demand healing remedies or protective medicines.

In further delineating the practice, though, the terrain gets tricky. For Bongmba *tfu*, on the ground, seems to designate a form of both knowledge and ability that is secret, nonhereditary, and capable of being "intentionally deployed for the benefit of the practitioner, possibly at the expense of the victim" (25–26). It is not involuntary, although a person who has *tfu* can reputedly "open the eyes" of those who heretofore have not had it by giving the latter the human flesh (of a sacrificed relative of the former) to eat disguised as some other kind of meat. The result is a chain of indebtedness that requires a payback in kind of sacrificed human flesh, which is then believed to be consumed by a gathering of *tfu* prac-titioners. The degree to which the belief in such a "*tfu* cannibalism" represents a metaphorical account of illness and social stress "eating people alive" (rather than actual physical consumption) is an open question, but Bongmba refuses to entirely dismiss the phenomenon as metaphor. He simply confesses that—like anyone else uninitiated into the destructive domain of *tfu yibi*—he cannot know of a knowledge that, by definition, he does not have.

More recently, the advent of capitalist relations in the local Wimbum economy has rendered *tfu* talk potent in deciphering a new horizon of aggression. The metabolizing of the village in a metropolitan aggrandizement that is finally global in scope is grasped in local knowledge as a new modality of "eating and being eaten." Wimbum have negotiated their own interpolation in world markets and metropolitan politics in a logical extension of *tfu* metaphorics. The traditional notions of "local family" *tfu* practice have been supplemented by terms that designate a nationalizing of witchcraft patterns. *Nyongo* and *kupe* witchcraft imply activities to create zombies who, rather than being killed and eaten, are supposedly "entranced" into a form of ongoing slave labor. The emphasis here is on explaining acquisitions of wealth. These new terms push *tfu* out of its consanguineous orbit, adumbrating uses of the power to gain riches that can preempt blood relationship in favor of a money nexus. In the process, the space of *tfu* is expanded beyond the family, and at the same time the practice is nar-rowed to a single transaction between otherwise unrelated individuals. Either a gift or a loan, it is believed, is sufficient to render one unwittingly vulnerable to "sacrifice." Structurally, this expansion of *tfu* suspicion is intimately linked to the emergence of urban elites who "have inserted themselves into the exploitative capitalist relations by pursuing an extravagant lifestyle" (39).

And even the academic enterprise becomes fodder for the mill of accusation. Bongmba himself sets the stage for our own deliberations to come when he has the good grace to recount a playful challenge to his construction of *tfu* by fellow African scholar Emmanuel Eze. Eze acknowledges the maze of perplexity entertained in the scholarly attempt to "read" *tfu* and then asks whether Bongmba does not himself "have *tfu*," since Bongmba has argued that only those who have the power know the power and he (Bongmba) has, in fact, been able to make that form of knowledge convincingly clear (i.e., "known") in his writing. Either that, Eze agues, or Bongmba should perhaps dispel the mystery once and for all and assert that no such knowledge really exists, that it is all a ruse of power, holding generations in thrall to various configurations of domination and dissembling. A third possibility—that *tfu* practitioners may perhaps be the promulgators of powers and knowledge that they do not know they have—is also laid on the table (Bongmba). Bongmba is uncompromising in asserting that he does not have *tfu*, but equally that he cannot just "write it off" as ruse. He is also adamant about the fact that such powers are intentionally prosecuted in practice and are not just lying there "dormant . . . waiting for the researcher to awaken" them (53). But the great unaddressed possibility in Bongmba's response is the degree to which "academic study" itself may not be comprehended, from the side of indigenous practice, as effectively a form of *tfu* practice, operating through a researcher like him, even though it remains for him to acknowledge its arousing by the indigenous community.

Maybe Bongmba—and scholars in general—do unwittingly practice *tfu* in a form that is prodigiously effective precisely in its relative imperceptibility. Whether such a construction would be at all useful in a general sense, my own project here does seek to specify that, at least in the case of explicitly "racializing" knowledges, as well as in the more implicitly "normalizing" social practices of whiteness, *tfu*-like effects have taken place in the ongoing histories of western contacts and exchanges with indigenous cultures, as I shall outline below.

The Imagination

To recapitulate, the "*tfu* effects," mentioned at the end of the last section, characterizing the history of contact, are primarily those of finding one's self and substance "being consumed" by an invisible "project" that resists analysis. The diminishment is brought to the forefront of consciousness and query by a discourse field that identifies occult powers serving an asymmetrical economy. In a mystery, advantaged power players, perceived as using insider information, are brought under local suspicion as the "secret agents" of intractable illnesses and early demises. While public charges may succeed in mobilizing local communal sanctions against such suspects, the charges can also backfire and occasion a continuous round of charge and countercharge, intensifying suspicion and investing the entire economy of interaction with misgiving and accusatory ire.

The ambiguity of such a field of knowledge/power shows up when one asks how *tfu* practitioners might understand their own *tfu* actions. Apparently, the power is at times actively prosecuted to bring about deleterious effects, and confessions of them are offered by the practitioners. But what exactly is the motive force of such action? In village culture, presumably the prize is power/knowledge itself: having recourse—or at least being perceived as having recourse—to an occult domain of force that rewards with a certain pleasure in consuming (figuratively, if not in reality) "flesh-of-the-other." What is "accumulated" is perhaps both social status and interior confidence—a kind of self-awareness of potency and mobility in a context of ceaseless calculations of power and consequences. The "capital" accumulated would be a certain "fear" that protects against incursions in kind. While this line of reflection does not purport to decide the issue of the reality of *tfu*, it does at least position its potency in the realm of perception. In a culture of *tfu* suspicion and belief the possibility is open to ongoing manipulation and brokerage.

And, of course, once the village is metabolized in the metropolitan circuits of globalizing capital, it is not surprising in the least that *tfu* is imagined behind a new kind of accumulation. Not only bad fortune is comprehended in the explanatory scheme, but good "fortune." Wealth accumulation is probatively imagined as the outcome of a similar mobilization of unseen powers, leveraged, in one way or another, by "sacrifice" of human flesh somewhere along the line (only now in a "zombified" form of living death). Whether expressing misfortune or metafortune, the condition to be explained is a perceived break in the texture of mundane mutuality and reciprocity.

Tfu is thus simultaneously the perception and predication of a particular kind of *difference making,* its coding and questioning as the knowledge of a threat and the threat of a knowledge, which works at the depth where cultural symbolics and psychic investments intertwine and define a world. It bifurcates the world into an in-group of *tfu* practitioners, who are understood to sacrifice the "flesh" of outsiders to the group members and *tfu* discoursers, who, not having access to the power/knowledge of the practitioners, talk about its possible employment and presumed effects. The former are understood more in terms of covert use of a power than overt discourse about a morality; the latter have as their only protection (unless they secure patronage of, or themselves employ, a practitioner), the mobilization of talk about that power as a moral question.

At core, *tfu* discourse would then seem to designate a domain of secretive and differentiating power that is fundamentally preoccupied with consumption, with "eating and being eaten." To what degree "physical consumption of actual human flesh" is in view, as compared with a more metaphorical figuration for different kinds of material deterioration like illness, stress, mental incapacity, and finally death, on the one hand, or material aggrandizement at the expense of others elsewhere, on the other, remains an open question that is beyond my concern here. I am concerned with the "imagination of consumption" in the social field of *tfu* practice as a metaphorical perception of a real metabolism of the material conditions and psychic vitalities of life, which has power to teach beyond itself.

Enter into the discussion Frantz Fanon, Martiniquean colonial subject seeking education in the French state capital, writing of his experience on the streets of midcentury Paris, where he is accosted by the cry of a mere boy, shivering in fear of this sudden apparition of darkness, puncturing his bright safe world with untold epiphany, throwing himself into his mother's arms with the shout "Look Mama . . . a Negro. . . . Look . . . a Negro. . . . Mama, the [Negro]'s going to eat me up" (Fanon 114).

Mythic Blackness and Unconscious Whiteness

When Europe began its conquest and colonization of the rest of the globe in 1492, the colonial theater ultimately became the site of struggles for economic hegemony on the part of emerging European powers. Resource flows from the colonies were critical in underwriting intra-European conflict and increasingly became the focus of the ongoing competition in the international slave trade and the control of colonial lands that solidified into separate European identities (Dussel). To what degree, however, the practical "crafting" of the modern state can also be understood as dialectically "colored" by the craft work of the colonized remains an open question (Herskovitz; Murphy). The historical process was inevitably complex, and the way of describing it just ventured only a gross caricature. But it does set the stage for the question of import here.

European power, in effect, "ate" African substance in the slave trade (as well as "native" substance in the colonial structures set up throughout the Americas, Asia, and the Pacific). Whatever the discourse, the fact of the effect is clear. A "witchery" of heretofore unimaginable potency ravaged African and aboriginal cultures. The necessary reflexive consideration that must be probed in turn is the degree to which a fear of "being eaten in kind" is then constitutive of the modern identities that emerge out of that process.

Fanon's account centuries later is revealing. The great truism of modern white supremacy in America is the white male fear that black males will attract and intermarry with white females and produce, in the words of the Grand Wizards of KKK infamy, "a bastardized mongrel race!" (Spencer 165–71). Of course, who really produced illegitimate mixed-blood offspring is the telling question of the history of misogyny. But that is still a white male fear that remains "outside" the white male body. It is a fear about status and competition in connection with sexuality that arguably has structured gender relationships and erotics in the white community—not to mention almost everything else in our social order—at quite profound psychosocial levels in this country. The little boy in Fanon's account, however, fears "being eaten."

It is not my purpose to offer psychoanalytic speculations on the origins of such a fantasy but to read it metaphorically and politically. In *The Isis Papers,* for instance, Frances Cress Welsing homes in on what she calls "the white supremacy system" as the organizing construct necessary to fathom the deep purpose underneath much of the machinations and mesmerizations of the global order in both its local and translocal sweep. That purpose, according to her, is finally the forestalling of "white genetic annihilation" (ii). Combating the global system of oppression, and the exploitation of people of color that is that system's necessary condition of possibility, entails, she says, unlocking the "secret of the colors" (viii). It is a secret largely inaccessible to our more usual "high frequency" order of everyday awareness, as being too profoundly encoded into our subconscious. It must be engaged on the lower frequency level of the symbol.

Grafting my own take onto her approach, I would similarly intersplice genetics and symbolics. Genetically, white disappearance would obviously be disappearance *back into* the registers of melanin that "whiteness" mutated from in the first place (given our best understanding, to date, of the evolutionary trajectory of *homo sapiens* as having originated in Africa). That is to say, it would be disappearance back into "color." Symbolically, I would suggest, the deep fear is then that of "being eaten" by perceived difference. But the attempt to forestall such by mobilizing a *practice* of white supremacy masked in a *discourse* of black racialization is indeed a riddle and a secret—an attempt to combat fear that constructs the very "difference" it fears in the first place. I would suggest that one productive way of reading such a tactic is to consider it as a kind of preemptive "first strike"—on the part of a profoundly prodigal witchcraft—aiming the accusation of "blackness" at people of color in order to lock them up inside a discourse of charge and countercharge that fractures unity and bleeds energy in endless calculations of which "which" is the real witch. All the while, of course, the ultimate witch stands devouring and invisible, shrouded in the enigma of an invisible white light. But here again, in tracking the development and power of such a tactic, history is helpful.

A Genealogy of Supremacy

The last five hundred years of modern geopolitical aggression and transnational economic domination by which Europe transplanted itself around the globe and took over, is more clearly organized in its basic life-world patterns and power privileges by the racial category of white/nonwhite than by any other observable category of demarcation (Mills). Modernity *is* the advent of white supremacy as a global system of hegemony. My contention is simply that "whiteness" is also the great category of bewitchment that both masks and mobilizes the basic circuits of consumption that are that system's *raison d'être.*

In developing a "genealogy" of this claim regarding whiteness, we can imagine the construct as a linkage of Foucauldian erudite and naïve knowledges. The erudite knowledge will be supplied by Hegel, subject to criticism. The naïve knowledge is this indigenous African reading of trauma and early death as "unnatural," caused by an enemy. The two combined form my overall attempt to "know" racialization as a form of witchcraft.

The claim runs something like this: White supremacy is the basic structuring practice of the modern world system in terms of which extraction, appropriation, production, and consumption of resources are differentially organized. The race discourse mobilized by that practice has gone through continuous "development" that can be periodized historically (Pagden). It was first worked out as a theological discourse effecting a sharp divide of spiritual discernment between presumed "Christianity" and perceived infidelity and sorcery in the early period of conquest and colonization (Omi and Winant). It was reworked into a metaphysical discourse on geography and biology in the Enlightenment and further shifted into anthropological discourse regarding cultural difference in the twentieth century (Mills; Omi and Winant; Pagden; West, *Prophesy Deliverance*). In the United States in particular, in the 1960s, that discourse was contested in the identity politics of black power activism, challenging the "assimilation designs" of the Chicago School "ethnicity paradigm" with a demand for pluralism and autonomy, and despite its subsequent dismemberment in the "reform and co-opt" tactics of the state, was emulated by other groups concerned about preserving other forms of identity from being "metabolized" by whiteness (Omi and Winant). I understand my own effort here as also contestatory in attempting to mobilize indigenous categories to unmask race discourse as perhaps most suggestively "known," if not accurately analyzed, not as theology, ontology, or anthropology, but as itself the quintessential witchery of modernity.

The Metaphysical Moment

Hegel's work on Africa in his *Lectures on the Philosophy of World History* provides the "classically" modern perception of the so-called "Dark Continent" as through-and-through the land of the cannibal (in what follows, as excerpted by Eze). Review of the "principal moments within the African spirit" (Eze 129) for Hegel, as with any other review of spirit, requires grasping the religion. It is through and through a religion of sorcery, he says, of arrogating to oneself a "power over nature" (129) that leads directly into the belief that death is never simply a matter of natural causes but of the will of an enemy using such sorcery to kill. It occasions a resort to sorcery in kind, a battle of magics. Its mode is "frenzy" and "delirium," convulsive efforts of a "dreadful enthusiasm" (130–31), which, should they fail in successfully manipulating nature itself or the natural object set up as empowered fetish, will then occasion wholesale sacrifice of onlookers by the sorcerers, whose bodies are then devoured and their blood drunk "by their fellows" (131). Dead ancestors are likewise conjured for assistance in power mongering and indeed, in the "most fearful" moment of abomination, says Hegel, will possess their priestly *serviteurs* and command human sacrifice. The sum of such, for him, is "the superstition of witchcraft, whose terrible rule once prevailed in Europe too" (132). It issues in a political order of tyranny—the fetishizing of a power of contempt for all that is human, the licensing of cannibalism, the normalizing of the devouring of the human body as simply flesh "like all other [animal] flesh" (134). But then Hegel waxes unwittingly revealing in his argument, saying more than he undoubtedly intended.

Such cannibalistic offerings of human flesh are not primarily for the sake of food, says Hegel, but "for festivals" (Eze 134). After being tortured and beheaded, for instance, the body parts of many hundreds of sacrificed prisoners "are returned to those who took them prisoner so that they may distribute the parts" (134). Hegel does not tell us why. He only says, "In some places, it is true, human flesh has even been seen on sale in the markets" (134). But in any case, "at the death of a rich man, hundreds [of such prisoners] may well be slaughtered and devoured" and "as a rule the victor consumes the heart of his enemy" and "at magical ceremonies . . . the sorcerer will [kill] . . . and divide [a] body among the crowd" (134).

And then, without any pause, Hegel immediately links *this practice* with a *rationale for slavery.* "Since human beings are valued so cheaply," he says, "it is easily explained why *slavery* is the basic relationship in Africa" (Eze 134; emphasis Hegel's). Basic for whom? He continues: "The only significant relationship between the Negroes and the Europeans has been—and still is—that of slavery" (134). But Hegel is underscoring African, not European, motivation: "The Negroes see nothing improper about it, and the English, although they have done most to abolish slavery and the slave trade, are treated as enemies by the Negroes themselves" (134). Or rather, we might have to say, he is working toward a simultaneous apology for European involvement: "For one of the main ambitions of the kings is to sell their captured enemies or even their own subjects, and, to this extent at least, slavery has awakened *more humanity* among the Negroes" (134; emphasis mine). "More humanity" as compared with what? Presumably with the aforementioned sacrifice and ritual devouring, or marketing, of prisoners' flesh.

Hegel will continue with a justification for the project of a slavery that, although "unjust in and of itself," nevertheless is a necessary part of the process of human movement from the "state of nature" to the "higher ethical existence" in the rational cultures exemplified by European states (Eze 135). Slavery, in this compass, is "a moment of transition" in the development of the Idea toward the historical achievement of a "substantial ethical life of a rational state" in which slavery then ceases to exist (135). Africa as a whole, for Hegel, remains enmeshed in the "natural spirit" on the far side of the threshold of history: The necessary dialectical move of the African spirit is from "witchcraft" through "slavery" toward ethical rationality.

For my purposes in this essay, there are two important reflections that offer themselves in such thinking. Africa is, in the Enlightenment imagination embodied by Hegel, the land of the open mouth, the cavernous orifice of darkness. For this quintessential modern, who stands at the apex of modernity, African cannibalism is not a peripheral manifestation but a central characteristic. According to Hegel, before captured African prisoners began to be traded to European slavers, they faced the prospect of being eaten. Compared to the local Cameroonian practice we examined above, in which *tfu* practice was originally limited to family conflicts, Hegel's account presents a somewhat more encompassing practice. He appears to be talking about "enemies" captured from beyond the clan or village. Yet the *dénouement* is the same. Flesh is ritualistically consumed.

For Hegel, the advent of the slave trade in such a situation constituted an improvement of conditions on the ground. And what's more, witchcraft practice becomes the rationale for enslavement. "Since human beings are valued so cheaply," he says, slavery is "easily explained" (Eze 134). But *mutatis mutandis* then, I would argue that the linkage between witchcraft and slavery might just as readily be understood in inverse relationship. Slavery itself might just as easily be explained as "witchcraft in a more rigorous mode." It does not at all escape the "fest of flesh" it supposedly remedies. It is perhaps more accurately conceived as a cult in kind, actively acceding to the communion in carrion, now traded in living form, for an appetite exponentially expanded. For Hegel, we might say, "Africa *is* witchcraft." The mouth is open and ravenous and unrestrained. But his remedy is simply a slower tooth and a more ruthless use, a metabolism consuming brain as well as brawn.

Of course, Hegel reads his remediation teleologically. The great chain of being is tipped over on its side and given both historical dynamism and moral import. Spirit wends its way in one ultimate direction only. The culture of the witch is destined, somewhere, to cross the crevasse, face its opposition with mouth closed and eyes alight to the universal truth of reason, seeking escape from the chain. Slavery will deliver spirit from the maw of nature.

But it is not at all clear that Hegel's *telos* exists. What is clear in history is that European rapacity has eaten African substance unremittingly. As noted above, in recent years, Cameroonian culture has articulated a new wrinkle in the practice of *tfu*: witchery leveraging wealth through "the *zombi*." Flesh is devoured in modern mode, not so much in the immediacy of death, but in slow motion, through labor. *Tfu* sacrifice is no longer limited to blood relations, but the necessary linkage between witch and victim can be effected through money alone; it merely requires that the latter wittingly or unwittingly accept the "gift" of the former. Here indigenous knowledge better grasps the real human meaning of the wage nexus than most western economic theory. Wealth is accumulated through *eating* the work of others.

Hegel's philosophy differentiates itself from the supposed foolery of African

witchery in the predication of an absolute divide. Modern metaphysics in Enlightenment mode thinks itself entirely removed from, and innocent of, modernity's
metabolics. But the mask has its mouth open. A third-world country is falling
out in the form of a well-gnawed bone. The European charge of African witchery
itself hides the deepest practice of witchery yet witnessed in history. Metaphysics misrepresents the mouth that consumes. It is rather the preceding historical
"moment"—to continue to use Hegel's peculiar matrix here—of more overt
"theological battle" that, I would argue, more clearly demarcates the character of the competition. Hegel perhaps represents modern witchcraft's greatest
sophistry—which nonetheless remains instructive and brilliant precisely for its
analytical density. But his erudition is given a reverse charge of potency when
it is hooked to the supposedly naïve knowledge of an African question about
power: not "what" is wrong with me, but "who"? Who is behind the demise?
In this sense, witchcraft discourse reverses the "fetishism of commodities" that
Marx so elaborately mapped out in *Kapital*.

African diagnosis applied to European practice asks of modernity, Why do
Africans die early and often (of war, of wanton violence, of AIDS, of disease, of
starvation, etc.) whereas (relatively speaking) Europeans die late and slowly? It expects an answer that is rooted in a subjective intention. African witchcraft culture
suspects early illness and death to be the work of an enemy, not the mysterious
outcome of an arbitrarily discriminating "nature." European belief fetishizes
subjectivity as an "object," explains social condition as individual choice, reads
the "slow death" of impoverished unemployment and the "living death" of wage
slavery as the victim's own failure to compete. To grasp this wild efflorescence
of the impulse to fetishize, it is necessary to go back behind the Enlightenment's
reputed disenchantments to the depth work accomplished in European ritual
activity.

The Theological Moment

The first moment of sustained encounter between European commerce and African culture was profoundly liturgical. From the beginning of the competitive
project of conquest and colonization, the wholesale expropriation and plundering of non-European cultures had to be underwritten in a manner that both
secured its presumed *legitimacy* inside the still broadly shared intra-European
Christian worldview and secured its projected *superiority* inside the cultures of
the colonized. Christian theological categories, of course, supplied the initial
construct, in which the primary question was one of salvation: Are these new
found "creatures" capable of embracing the faith and thus of proving themselves
"human," as Europeans are human? (Omi and Winant; White). Or are they merely
"human-appearing," but in theological truth "only beasts of burden intended
by the Creator for European use?" (Dussel 54–55). The rhetorical debate raged
all around Europe but was never in serious doubt on the ground in the colonies

or in the slave trade. Theological assessment quickly invested itself in epidermal appearances both light and dark. Christian supremacy gave birth to white supremacy. Indigenous religious practice, in both the Americas and Africa, was frequently "divined" as a demonically inspired "black art."

The race discourse that emerges from such a charge of witchcraft, however, gets entangled in its own taunt. African practice and appearance emerge historically as the test case of European liturgy: They present Europe with its most "disturbing" negotiation of difference and consequently bear the most radical forms of theological condemnation. The dark hues of African skin were fairly quickly interpreted in European theological schemas as a "sign"—on the surface of the body—of a heart unwilling immediately to convert to Christ upon hearing the gospel (Bastide). Swarthy appearance signified a "black" heart. "Blackness" as a term, in Spanish or Portuguese (or later Dutch, French, English, etc.), may or may not have been explicitly used in any given instance, but its symbolic implications were made to stick like hot tar. Those implications partook deeply of a theological discourse on the demonic. The initial evaluation of dark skin associated it with an illicit domain of spirits whose character was presumed to be dangerous and aggressive (Bastide).

In comparison with something like contemporary *tfu* discourse, however, early race discourse works surreptitiously. Rather than leveling a charge of *de facto* aggression toward another, it operates its accusation by way of a twofold implication: the imputation of a *threat* of aggression toward another (i.e., the fear that African witchcraft would be turned upon European colonizers) and the imputation of a *fact* of aggression toward oneself (the culpability implied in resisting God, signified in the darkness that has taken over the bodily surface). Along these same lines, witchcraft discourse explicitly imagines (and witch "confessions" sometimes confirm) the use of a poison, charm, spell, and so on, that effects the erosion and dis-ease that finally kills. It implies the mobilization of a materialized form of curse that itself "causes" the cursedness to happen. It is interesting that early European race discourse can similarly be imagined as the mobilization of a curse—in this case, one that in fact *does* become explicitly formalized as just that, in the "Curse of Ham" mythology that European Christianity predicated as the theological explanation for the "darkness" of African skin. But this was a curse with a difference. The predication of implied blackness, in effect, materialized its spell not in an exterior object that eroded well-being but in an *objectification of skin* as a *cursed object*. The discourse itself accomplishes the spell/curse it names so that the flesh can be "eaten" with impunity.

The complex of attraction/fear such a theological predication "knots up together" is a multilayered tangle. It can be teased out as (1) a European perception of "Africans eating each other," (2) a European fear of "Europeans being eaten by their African other," which (3) coagulate together into the European imagination of "blackness as witchcraft" that becomes the rationale for "European consumption of African substance" (in slave and wage labor and plundering of African resources). The effect of such a predication is to lock Africans up in a domain of "blackness eating itself" that displaces awareness of the real history of consumption the projection underwrites and carries out in the first place. It is even tempting to say that, in this complex projection of witchcraft, whiteness bewitches itself, mislabeling western metabolism of Africa as "saving and civiliz- ing," while mythologizing Africans under the cover of a blackness that both hides and effects the "project of devouring" that is the real meaning of whiteness. In this compass, European liturgy and African sorcery constitute a difference not in religious kind but in degree of rapacity. The first frontier of historical encounter between Europe and Africa is a theater of occult combat, a labor of competing witchcrafts, organized by a virulent new discourse of malaise. The "supremacy" of white over black that is made to emerge from the encounter is finally one of appetite.

Over time, after the breakup of Catholic Europe in the Reformation and the resulting bloodbath of the Thirty Years War, Reason is made the watchword of practice in European self-understanding. What began as a theological "discern- ment" of African spirituality as sorcery is buried in Enlightenment categories of Being, taxonomized in the ever-flexing "great chain," even as real chains reinforce the ontology in a ruthless sociology. White theological supremacy, we might say, successfully fetishized "blackness" as a negative power of "possession" and placed it "in" the African body like a magic "spirit chain," rendering it vulnerable and available for sacrifice to the new supposedly "scientific" project of global commerce. Here blackness emerges as a cipher working a mysterious density of significance: As philosophical taxonomy, it explains European supremacy in empirical terms; as theological symbology, it is hidden as the inchoate "felt ter- ror" of witchery.

Whiteness, on the other hand, is increasingly a category of distance and decep- tion, a veritable incarnation of denial, consciousness without a body, eating the body of its chosen witch, while "witching" its own eating "out of mind." It is a mindless eating, understanding itself as a bodiless mind. In the political economy of the modern slave trade and its continuation as the globalizing system of white supremacist capital, its body is the "blackness" it metabolizes as its own white flesh.

Race Discourse as White Witchcraft

What Mills calls, as a critique of modern social contract theory, "the racial con- tract," I am underscoring, out of its historical emergence, as a white witch pact. It creates an in-group of flesh consumers who share a secretive power/knowledge designated, gradually over time and occasionally in experience (when the necessity to specify the contrast irritatingly presents itself) as "whiteness." It is, in fact, on its own terms, a form of "theological blackness" or witchery, rewritten as ontology and anthropology. But this pact operates with peculiarity. In the dissimulation of modern white supremacy, it is racial *discourse* itself that is the witchcraft *practice.* That is not quite the same as saying race discourse is witchcraft "discourse." Race discourse organizes a material object (dark skin) as a spiritual curse/spell/erosion. Compared to indigenous forms of witchcraft practice still extant in Africa, it represents a shift from a nonverbal manipulation of an object for the sake of "sacrificing" and securing the flesh of an other to a *verbal* manipulation effecting the same result. Of course, as discussed above in Bongmba's work, we do not know whether or how actual flesh is consumed in indigenous practice, but only that such may become an accusation/explanation when people die. With white supremacist practice, however, we do know that the flesh *is* consumed (in slave and wage labor), and we know *how* it is secured (by military force, institutional discrimination, cultural normalization, etc.).

While I agree fully with Mills when he argues that we must recognize the historical propensity of the racial contract to rewrite itself to accommodate new needs for its white-identified signatories, and thus must understand that its real payoff is the securing of whiteness over against nonwhiteness, I am *also* arguing that we do not fully appreciate race discourse if we let its bottom-line category of "blackness" disappear in the more general and encompassing term "nonwhite." It is only with respect to Africa that the deep character of racialization as witchery comes clear. It is not merely a matter of whiteness securing its plunder by way of a "firebreak" predicated between itself and nonwhites but the chain of associations put in operation through the category/meaning "blackness." Its first valence was theological and dense with demonic significance. That such numinosity gets hidden in the Enlightenment "turn to reason" does not mean its visceral evocation disappears. A simple glance, for instance, at KKK lynchings reveals the degree to which the entire domain of race, even in the twentieth century, remains a mythic idiom demanding ritual prosecution. It was never enough "merely" (!) to destroy the black body; its imagined threat was dealt with in terms of the "blood sacrament" of castration. The "felt need" was profoundly fetishistic.

Whiteness, under the veneer of its "heavenly" pallor, is a great grinding witch-tooth, sucking blood and tearing flesh without apology. It is interesting that in postcontact Africa the means for detecting and "outing" witches is by way of catching them in a mirror. I would argue that witchcraft itself is the mirror in which whiteness must be caught.

It is also possible to periodize the metaphor historically. Where indigenous practice of witchcraft is understood to involve the consumption of "dead" flesh, the slavery of early modernity (1) opens a new "after-death" prospect: the *zombi* state, the living cannibalization of commercial capital, flesh not so much as food for thought but as gold for trade. In the industrial phase, (2) whiteness shifts its modality of consumption to that of the machine: flesh as "dead labor" in Marx's phrase, the *zombi* rendered bionic, the massive and mysterious transubstantiation of laboring flesh into grinding metal. In so-called "late capitalism" (3), the move is to the modality of information, the postmodern magic of transmogrifying flesh into digit. But at heart the consumption continues to metabolize real muscle.

In sum, modern commerce mobilizes a white death-grin to hide its traffic in "blackened" substance. What is talked about indigenously in the idiom of ritual is routinized and "rationalized" in modern practice—first by way of the shackle, then in the form of gear boxes and axles, and, finally, in postindustrial sophistication, as a mere pixel. The mouth opens ever wider while the packaging and storage of the flesh-to-be-feasted is ever narrowed. In African witchcraft human health is devoured as an object of ritual. In modern race-craft human substance is delineated as an object of discourse. Physical mastication is supposedly overcome in metaphysical matriculation. What has really happened is merely patent: an economy of flesh has been made the flesh of the economy.

Appendix

The depths revealed/concealed in the palimpsestlike operation of the eucharistic sacrament (as a kind of "*Ur*-text" of Christian practice) are adumbrated in the work of historian of religions Charles Long. Long's labor to expose the difference between western and indigenous apprehensions of divinity in the colonial encounter around the globe makes use of Rudolph Otto's experientially oriented phrase for ultimate reality, the *mysterium tremendum et fascinosum*. Otto's concern in the first part of the twentieth century was to try to escape theologically loaded language in doing comparative work on religious traditions around the globe. Otto theorized that cultures across the globe bear witness to an "ultimate mysteriousness" operating in human life that seems to be apprehended in a double experience. It is sometimes alluring and attractive, and other times terrifying and repulsive, and the mystery "irrupts" in such a way that neither experience can entirely be resolved into the other. For Otto, this double formulation captured the essence of Christian as well as non-Christian experience.

But Otto's mantra all to the good, it is arguable that in medieval European liturgy, the second element of this apprehension was gradually repressed. The older premonition of God as not only the great Wooer of Hearts (much less as the great Reason in the Sky later imagined by the Enlightenment), but as also inscrutable and terrifying *Tremendum*, dying in a grotesque execution ritual, had been buried under the surface of the liturgy. For instance, early Christian art shied away from depiction of the crucifixion—perhaps not only because of apologetics (a desire to appeal to educated Roman elites), but also because the "scene of torture" got too close to a more archaic and disturbing intuition: "Sometimes, God seems simply to devour!" (This latter perception could be said to be the basic meaning of the scripture text memorializing Jesus' final scream from the cross:

The God Who Is Devoured in Jesus

(The God Who Devours Jesus)

FIGURE 2

"my God, my God, why have you forsaken me!?" [Mk 15: 33–39]). In the practice of a Christianity that was still outlawed and persecuted prior to Constantine, the eucharistic symbolics would perhaps have mediated something closer to the ambivalence Otto notes in terms of (1) a subtext of God as the Great Precipitous Horror That Devours overlaid with (2) the open text of God As the Great Hero Who Is Willing to Be Devoured.

But by the time Europe emerges, in the high Middle Ages, out of its own "dark night" of threatened extinction at the hands of a highly organized and sophisticated Islam, the text has swallowed the subtext. The ritualized structure of medieval Christian consciousness has "transubstantiated" the threat of the *Tremendum* into the Fascination of the sacramental "body and blood." There is no extant imagery for God grasped as "devourer" that is iconically figured or ritually remembered in the Christian tradition of the scholastics or the reformers. Unlike say, Hinduism's mother-figure, Kali, mainstream Roman and Protestant representations of God present One who is unambiguously "good."

Undoubtedly some of the repression involved in this process of "iconographic domestication" finds its motive force in the recodification of anti-imperial resistance as imperial conformity and the gradual incorporation of a prophetic movement of slaves and peasants into a ruling class hegemony. The ferocious God of Moses and Ezekiel, of John and Jesus, had to be reformulated as the very image of Roman aristocracy. The Backer of Revolting Laborers, the Angry Author of Exilic Upheaval, the Chopper of the Tree of Genealogy, the Closed-mouth Father Watching the Son "Fry" on Cosmic Prime Time was "transfigured" into the soft crumbling bread of bowing believers, the paper-thin host of a blessed adoration. The ideological eclipse of terror and its epiphanies of resistance was a *fait accompli* by the time modernity began "showing" in the womb of Europe.

That bloody birth finds its augury in premodern Spain. Castilian Christian triumph over the Muslim menace in the seven hundred–year-long *Reconquista* of Spain gave rise to a ferocity of selective forgetting. After "eating" its way through Moorish culture and cult, Spanish Christian identity emerges as a modality of occultation. The ambivalent and inarticulate *pathos* that Columbus and crew carry west is rife with passion remembered and unremembered. It is ripe for the ritual grotesqueries of the slavery it will underwrite. Analysis of such by way of Otto introduces an interesting caveat into the canon of European colonization. A certain "seductive" longing masks a practice of "terrible" severity.

But it is Long who most compellingly conjures the consequence. Long takes up Otto's aphorism and breaks open its binarism on the hard rock of colonial violence to underscore a radical difference of experience between Europe and its others (Long, *Significations*).

Western culture, in this perspective, lives its mythology of itself in the mode of *fascination*—a relentless quest of curiosity violently crossing and crisscrossing the surface of the globe in search of conquerable and exploitable space, an equally relentless (and profoundly interrelated) resolve to reengineer nature into ever-more-fascinating surfaces of consumption. (It is interesting in this regard to think not only of Kant's eighteenth-century metaphysical assertion that we can only ever "know" the phenomenal exteriority of things, not their noumenal essences, but indeed, today as well, the shift in economics to the marketing of the mere sign of an object—the Nike swoosh or the Hilfiger insignia—as its "real" value) (Long, *Significations*).

The rest of the globe, in the process of "undergoing" westernization—of being violently remade "in the image of" Europe *for* Europe—has been made to experience its utter contingency under the sign of a swiftly descending and completely overwhelming *Terribleness* (Long, *Significations*). It is this latter experience—the unpredictable and inscrutable advent of a depth of disaster that entirely ruptures native categories of local cosmology—that Long comprehends as *Tremendum* (Long, *Significations*). Reality experienced as Terror, as Indecipherable Nightmare, as the Mystery That Shatters—pushes indigenous cultures into a labor of "knowing" that is unlike anything the west has had to fathom. Native practice ends up having to negotiate—not empirically, but mythically—the cosmos itself as now a form of irresistible violence, a kind of All-Consuming Maw (Long, *Significations*). In the Christian category of "God" that said populations are increasingly forced to embrace, Divinity must be combated and conciliated as Devouring Opacity.

Long is clear—like Otto—that sudden epiphanies of radical and incomprehensible "terror" (a sudden uncanny sense of "coming apart," a fear of insanity, a "dread" of dismemberment, etc.) are not peculiar to oppressed populations. He notes that modern western literature regularly circumambulates disturbing "returns" of the contents of repression (Long, *Significations*). But it is his argument that such experiences *are* peculiarly *figured* in western expression—they are comprehended as patently "individual" and are dealt with either psychotherapeutically or turned into acclaimed aesthetic productions of "mad" genius (Long, *Significations*). In modernized societies, the intuition of dissolution is no longer ritualized and worked through in a communal theatrics (Long, *Significations*). Neither is it given expressive shape in a manner that implicates the real history of violence that it references (Long, *Significations*).

For the West	:	Reality Is Fascinosum	:	Divinity as What Is Devoured
(For the Rest)		(Reality Is *Tremendum*)		(Divinity as Devouring)

FIGURE 3

In Longian terms, then, the entire postcolonial global situation could perhaps be said to reflect a profoundly occulted structure.

The way such a construct signifies on race is ribald. Or perhaps, better said, the way race articulates (and articulates with) such an organization of experience is prodigal. The cross-coding represents a veritable Gordian knot of implication and confusion. The postcolonial complex is thick with delirium. Whiteness is a fantasyscape; blackness is deep night. White is fascinated with devouring. Black is a gnawed bone of terror. Whiteness is the unconsciously cannibalistic predilection to eat "God"; blackness is the posttraumatic stress syndrome of being eaten by "God." Which "which" is really witch?

> I should finally like to see us develop a body of studies devoted to the religious situation of contact. I am not here referring to what is called syncretism. I would include that kind of meaning in my definition, but I intend the situation of contact itself as a religious mode.... I have suggested studies of this kind so that we might begin a new kind of discourse in the study of religion. The anticipations for a science of religion, a *Religionswissenschaft,* have not been fulfilled; ... But is a "science" in the enlightenment sense the proper receptacle of these meanings? I am suggesting that the human science that would be the proper receptacle will develop when the shadows surrounding the interpreter and his culture as "otherness" are made a part of the total hermeneutical task. Our goal would then not be a science, but a serious human discourse. (Long, "Chicago Tradition")

> The goal of this inquiry is an attempt to substitute the opposite of colonialism as an alternative set of meanings of thought for what was the reigning content and style of thought of the cultures of European colonizers. I shall, rather, seek to raise the issue of thinking out of some of those relationships, reciprocities, and meanings that were attested to but hidden and obscured during the long period of colonialism.... Eliade's work is unique among works of this kind, for instead of explaining originary constitution as only an internal ordering of consciousness, he always relates this constitution to something other than itself. The thematic structure and style of primordiality is woven through this work as the locus for originary forms.

> In an analogous manner I shall attempt to raise the issue of the constitution of religion and human consciousness but instead of seeking for an arena of primordiality I shall locate this arena within the time and space of the formation of the new extra-European cultures, the new mercantilism and the ensuing relationships that took place during the modern period of imperialism and colonialism.

> My paradigm for this mode of procedure is a phenomenon that was discovered and named within the structures of the present human sciences; it is the cargo cult.... I choose the cargo cult as a paradigmatic basis for the "origin" of a modern meaning of religion for several reasons. First of all, as a religious phenomenon it presupposes and takes place within a colonial setting. Second,

it occurs precisely because of an assumed relationship between the colonizers and the colonized. Third, it is a new creative event and interpretation from the side of the colonized. Fourth, European manufactured goods are central meanings in their rituals. Fifth, the cargo cultists through their rituals attempt to bring about new modes of human constitutions (to make new beings who are neither Melanesian nor Europeans). If colonialism is over we must make sense of religion in terms of the meaning and constitution of humanity over the last five centuries—a humanity that is what it is because of the long duration of colonialism. The "double consciousness" made famous by W. E. B. DuBois is indicative of the structure of a modern consciousness that must come to terms with the facts of this epoch. It is my hope that such a procedure will allow for another analysis of the history of colonialism as a reservoir for the data of religion and give specification to the known but unspoken languages of relationship and reciprocities that took place during the tragic and ambiguous period of colonialism. (Long, "Towards a Post-Colonial Method," 5)

The initial period of European colonization (from 1492 to 1830, according to Pagden) focused largely on conquest of Amerindian land and enslavement of African bodies as the labor force necessary to make that land "productive" for European purposes (Pagden). It was underwritten largely by theological discourse (Omi and Winant). The second period (overlapping the first, from roughly 1730 to 1945) focused on colonial takeover of Asia, Africa, and the Pacific and relied more upon Enlightenment rationale for its legitimacy (Omi and Winant; Pagden). The theological map was gradually succeeded by a metaphysical one that invoked Aristotle and the Greeks in support of its apology for slavery and supremacy (West, *Prophesy Deliverance*). Enlightenment brilliance—surprise, surprise!—found ontological ground for racial hierarchy in redeployment of an ancient neo-Platonic schema as a scientific taxonomy and a moral script (Mills; West, *Prophesy Deliverance*).

Hegel gave it metaphysical density in a more indirect form. "African *Geist*," for him, is a modality of sorcery, the habit of devouring flesh without a second thought. But if such is the perception, its object could hardly be limited simply to other Africans. Hegel does not say as much: Enlightenment thought in Europe presumed itself much too sophisticated—and too well armed and too far removed—to worry about becoming itself a target of witchcraft. But colonial administration on the ground in the colonies reflects a more ambivalent posture.

consciousness	:	black eating black
(unconscious)		(black eating white)
consciousness	:	Europe saving Africa from black eating black
(unconscious)		(black eating white / white eating black)

FIGURE 4

It coupled Enlightenment disdain with the more equivocal and protective "hedge" of criminalization. This later colonial response would seem to encode something of the earlier theological predication of real danger.

If the feared "eating" is allowed to signify in relationship to psychopathology as well as genetics, the evidence is clear. This symbolic structure might well be imagined in terms of a surface perception masking a deeper projection.

Works Cited

Anderson, Victor. *Beyond Ontological Blackness: An Essay on African American Religious and Cultural Criticism.* New York: Continuum, 1995.

Bastide, Roger. "Color, Racism, and Christianity." In *White Racism: Its History, Pathology, and Practice,* edited by B. N. Schwartz and R. Disch. New York: Dell, 1970. 270–85.

Bongmba, Elias Kifon. *African Witchcraft and Otherness: A Philosophical and Theological Critique of Intersubjective Relations.* New York: State University Press of New York, 2001.

Crick, Malcolm. "Recasting Witchcraft." In *Witchcraft and Sorcery,* edited by Max Marwick. London: Penguin, 1970. 343–64.

Dussel, Enrique. *The Invention of the Americas: Eclipse of "the Other" and the Myth of Modernity.* New York: Continuum, 1995.

Eze, Emmanuel Chukwudi, ed. *Race and the Enlightenment: A Reader.* Cambridge, Mass.: Blackwell, 1997.

Fanon, Frantz. *Black Skins, White Masks.* Trans. C. L. Markmann. New York: Grove Press, 1967; repr., New York: Grove Weidenfeld, 1991.

Fields, Karen. *Revival and Rebellion in Colonial Central Africa.* Princeton, N.J.: Princeton University Press, 1985.

Foucault, Michel. *Power/Knowledge: Selected Interviews and Other Writings, 1972–1977,* edited by C. Gordon. Trans. C. Gordon et al. Brighton, U.K.: Harvester, 1980.

Gilroy, Paul. *The Black Atlantic: Modernity and Double Consciousness.* Cambridge, Mass.: Harvard University Press, 1993.

———. *There Ain't No Black in the Union Jack: The Cultural Politics of Race and Nation.* London: Hutchinson, 1987; repr., Chicago: University of Chicago Press, 1991.

Gramsci, Antonio. *Prison Notebooks.* New York: Columbia University Press, 1992.

Haymes, Stephen N. *Race, Culture, and the City: A Pedagogy for Black Urban Struggle.* Albany: State University Press of New York, 1995.

Hegel, G. W. F. *Lectures on the Philosophy of World History.* Trans. H. B. Nisbet. Cambridge, U.K.: Cambridge University Press, 1975.

Herskovitz, Melville. *The Myth of the Negro Past.* Boston: Beacon Press, 1958.

Jumanne, Monifa A. *Affirming a Future with Hope: HIV and Substance Abuse Prevention for African American Communities of Faith.* Atlanta: International Theological Center, 2001. 2.38–2.40.

Long, Charles. "A Look at the Chicago Tradition in the History of Religions: Retrospect and Future." In *The History of Religions: Retrospect and Prospect,* edited by Joseph M. Kitigawa. New York: Macmillan, 1983. 87–104.

———. *Significations: Signs, Symbols, and Images in the Interpretation of Religion.* Philadelphia: Fortress Press, 1986.

―――. "Towards a Post-Colonial Method in the Study of Religion." *Religious Studies News* 10.2 (May 1995): 4–5.

Marks, Morton. "Uncovering Ritual Structures in Afro-American Music." In *Religious Movements in Contemporary America,* edited by Irving I. Zaretsky and Mark P. Leone. Princeton, N.J.: Princeton University Press, 1974. 60–134.

Mills, Charles. *The Racial Contract.* Ithaca, N.Y.: Cornell University Press, 1997.

Mudimbe, V. Y. *The Invention of Africa: Gnosis, Philosophy, and the Order of Knowledge.* Bloomington: Indiana University Press, 1988.

Murphy, Joseph M. *Santeria: African Spirits in America.* Boston: Beacon Press, 1993.

Omi, Michael, and Howard Winant. *Racial Formation in the United States: From the 1960s to the 1990s,* 2d ed. New York: Routledge, 1994.

Otto, Rudolph. *The Idea of the Holy: An Inquiry into the Non-rational Factor in the Idea of the Divine and Its Relation to the Rational.* Trans. John W. Harvey. London: Oxford University Press, 1950.

Pagden, Anthony. *Lords of All the World: Ideologies of Empire in Spain, Britain, and France, c.1500–c.1800.* New Haven, Conn.: Yale University Press, 1995.

Spencer, Jon Michael. *The Rhythms of Black Folk: Race, Religion, and Pan-Africanism.* Trenton, N.J.: Africa World Press, 1995.

Thompson, Robert Farris. *Flash of the Spirit: African and Afro-American Art and Philosophy.* New York: Vintage Books, 1983.

Welsing, Frances Cress. *The Isis Papers: The Keys to the Colors.* Chicago: Third World Press, 1991.

West, Cornel. "Black Culture and Postmodernism." In *Remaking History,* edited by B. Kruger and P. Mariani. Seattle Bay Press, 1989. 87–96.

―――. *Prophesy Deliverance! An Afro-American Revolutionary Christianity.* Philadelphia: Westminster Press, 1982.

West, Cornel, and hooks, bell. *Breaking Bread: Insurgent Black Intellectual Life.* Boston: South End Press, 1991.

White, Hayden. *Tropics of Discourse: Essays in Cultural Criticism.* Baltimore, Md.: Johns Hopkins University Press, 1978.

CHAPTER 11

"Blacks Who Had Not Themselves Personally Suffered Illegal Discrimination": The Symbolic Incorporation of the Black Middle Class

Derrick E. White

A major consequence of the civil-rights movement was the increase of the black middle class. This class has become a subject of intense debate over the last twenty years, and several scholars have studied the relevance or irrelevance of this group. Recently this population has received a significant amount of academic and popular attention. Henry Louis Gates noted in his PBS Frontline Special, "By 1990, the black middle-class, perilous though it might feel itself to be, had never been larger, more prosperous, nor more relatively secure" (PBS, *Two Nations*). Many activists have criticized this class for its lack of commitment to social justice. Martin Luther King Jr. described many in the black middle class as being "detached spectators rather than involved participants in the great drama of social change" and "more concerned with 'conspicuous consumption' than about the cause of justice" (King 131). In addition, scholars of the civil-rights era blame the black middle class and its self-interest as a central cause in the failure of the black Freedom Struggle (Reed; West). Before this class could maneuver in its self-interest, intellectual space had to be created within the conception of America for their inclusion. This space was the result of the dialectical process of the demands for civil rights during the black Freedom Struggle and the nation's attempt to direct and control the direction of the civil-rights movement. The state attempted to control the movement through the explicit use of political languages that labeled the black middle class as exemplary and emblematic of the American experience.

Much of the scholarship about the black middle class has been from a sociological perspective, attempting to classify the composition of this class—behaviorally and economically. These studies have attempted to discuss the black middle class as a purely "objective" category. While not denying the fact that the phenomenon of the black middle class exists objectively based on sociological data such as income and wealth, I plan to expand the examination of this class by also looking at it primarily as a political idea and using "objective" markers, such as occupation and income, of the black middle class as points of reference. Specifically, this essay is looking at how the political language about the black middle class has been used to bisect the black population according to class. In trying to understand the changing relationship between the state and blacks since the 1960s, scholars have analyzed race and class as well as their intersections to explain the transformation that has occurred since the 1960s. As Stedman Jones notes, however, "historians have looked everywhere except at the changes in the political discourse itself to explain changes in political behavior" (21). It is the political discourse surrounding the black middle class that, I believe, can begin to explain the post-1960s relationship between the state and blacks.

The sociological definitions of the black middle class focus on behavior and economics. Income has been the barometer upon which the status of the black middle class has hinged; according to contemporary economic standards, a $32,000 to $50,000 annual income frames middle-class status.[1] My definition hinges on the social perception of the black middle class. William Muraskin's work on Prince Hall Freemasonry believed in defining the black middle class according to "social perception not 'objective reality.'" He continued, "If those blacks who think of themselves as middle class believe their value system is not shared by members of the lower class—who are lazy, drunk, and dirty—and if those middle class blacks act in line with that perception, this is enough to build a definition" (12–13). In addition, for the nature of this project, if whites perceive middle-class blacks as having a different value system from lower-class blacks, this too is an important component of the definition. This project is not debating the existence or size of the black middle class, but the *idea* of a black middle class and how the idea functions in the public discourse.

Andrew Hacker's *Money* discusses the formation of middle-class status. He asks why people who make $14,000, $15,000, or $16,000 do not see themselves as poor. He argues the success of the American economic system is that it allows most people to see themselves as "haves" as opposed to "have nots" even if they earn an income barely above minimum wage. Hacker believes American symbolism, such as welfare, allow the poor to be dysselectedly marked. The most important function of these symbols, however, as scholars Hacker and Michael Katz point out, is to define who is *not* poor. It is the historical economic narrative of the American Dream and the centrality of middle-class status that accompanies it that precipitate certain actions. This historical narrative, according to Richard Waswo, "determine[s] how we act in it" (541). By examining the political languages with the perception of the black middle class, one can begin to understand how the symbolic incorporation, how the narrative of the American Dream and its individualism, comes to include the black middle class, even if only in a token manner, and has allowed for some blacks to be included in the concept of America.

My use of political languages is borrowed from J. G. A. Pocock's essay "Languages and Their Implications," where he argued that the historian could understand political situations by identifying "the 'language' or 'vocabulary' with and within which the author operated and to show how it functioned paradigmatically to prescribe what he might say and how he might say it" (25). In addition, political languages "will present information selectively as relevant to the conduct and character of politics, and it will encourage the definition of *political problems and values in certain ways and not in others*" (*Virtue* 8; emphasis added). The political languages such as "bettering one's condition," "social mobility," "integration," or "separation" function within paradigms that prescribe and proscribe what may and may not be advocated.

A major consequence of the civil-rights movement was the reduction of biological definitions of race. As a result, the political languages of Americanness were widened to include the black middle class. The Moynihan Report exemplifies this shift when it identified the class structure within the black community and categorized the black middle class as different from the majority of the black community, specifically in terms of family structure. Consequently, the black middle class became increasingly associated with whiteness. The marker of difference for the black middle class was not income but the stability of black middle-class families versus that of black lower-class families. Moynihan stated, "There is considerable evidence that the Negro community is in fact dividing between a stable middle-class group that is steadily growing stronger and more successful, and an increasingly disorganized and disadvantaged lower-class group" (51–52). The black middle class was stable because its family structure mirrored that of white America; it was "more patriarchal and protective of its children than the general run of such families" (75). In the end, the report suggested that the extreme isolationism of the black lower classes, from white America and the black middle class, was due to the pathological nature of black lower-class families.

The 1970s witnessed white scholars using Moynihan's arguments in claims of reverse discrimination. Nathan Glazer's book, *Affirmative Discrimination,* was one of the first to promulgate this argument. First, Glazer locates the shift in the meaning of affirmative action, from the uplift and ideal of equal opportunity to quotas and ideal of equal results. He stated, "Until then [pre-1970s], affirmative action meant to seek out and prepare members of minority groups for better jobs and educational opportunities. . . . But in the early 1970s affirmative action came to mean much more than advertising opportunities actively, seeking out those who might not know of them, and preparing those who might not yet be qualified. It came to mean the setting of statistical requirements based on race, color, and national origin for employers and educational institutions" (196–97). This shift to the political language of results coincided with a shift in the analysis of the EEOC and Civil Rights Commission to focus on the results as proof of nondiscrimination rather than on the process of hiring and promotion (Glazer).

The shift to equality of results defined along racial lines was, to Glazer, a subversion of American principles. Affirmative action, according to Glazer, "threatens the abandonment of our concern for individual claims to consideration on the basis of justice and equity, now to be replaced with a concern for the rights for publicly determined and delimited racial and ethnic groups" (197). In addition, the abandonment of "individual claims" ignored the success of the black middle class. They, who Glazer felt were the main beneficiaries of affirmative action, were gaining individual opportunities under the guise of group claims. Consequently, Glazer believed the policy was ineffective because of the perceived success of the black middle class, who had or could succeed without it, and he considered the policy "questionable" because it failed to "reach in any significant way the remaining and indeed most severe problems involved in the black condition" (69–70).

The 1980s culminated in the resurrection of conservative ideology in American politics. Ronald Reagan and his landslide presidential victory over incumbent Jimmy Carter led the "revolution." Reagan's victory signaled the end of the dominance of the liberal ideals of the Democratic party, which began with Franklin D. Roosevelt's New Deal. As governor of California, Reagan was a staunch opponent of civil-rights policy, and he carried this philosophy directly into the White House.

The Reagan era represented an era of civil-rights retrenchment, and for most black people this meant that their economic and social situation worsened. The black middle class, however, maintained their relatively fragile position and in fact demonstrated some growth (Edsall and Edsall 233–34). An examination of Reagan's attack on civil-rights policies will demonstrate how he built upon the isolation of the black middle class from the rest of the black populace created during the 1960s and 1970s and incorporated, at least symbolically, the black middle class into American society.

The elimination of affirmative action became a top goal of the Reagan administration. The attack on affirmative action under the ideology of conservative egalitarianism, using the basic principles of American equality to protect unequal racial and economic distribution, exploited the difference between individual rights and group rights. Reagan and the conservative egalitarian ideology attempted to recognize only individual rights. The focus on individual rights relied on the logic of classic liberalism, in which "the individual—and not the family, community, or the state—is the singular unit of society, and that the purpose of societal arrangements is to allow the individual the freedom to fulfill his own purposes—by his labor to gain property, by exchange to satisfy his wants, by upward mobility to achieve a place commensurate with his talents" (Bell 425).

From the beginning of his presidency, Reagan made the individual the focus of social policy. In his inaugural address, Reagan stated, "Freedom and the dignity of the individual have been more available and assured here [United States] than in any other place on earth" (*Speaking* 63). The administration saw affirmative action as a quota system that violated the presumed individual nature of America society. Reagan believed that "the quota can be used, actually, as an instrument of discrimination, not to cure it" ("Remarks" 110). With the firm belief in individual rights, the Reagan administration began to see equal opportunity as the only method for realizing the "American creed" of individualism. Reagan's attorney general, William French Smith, stated "that the civil rights laws were intended to guarantee individual rights, not group results" (Dugger 203).

A result of redefining rights in individual terms was the coinciding redefinition of victims that this process created. The Reagan administration argued that affirmative action and its necessary goals and timetables forced out white employees who did not commit any acts of discrimination. "White firefighters and police officers—some with more than ten years of service—were furloughed while black and Hispanic employees with as little as two years' seniority were retained," said U.S. solicitor general, Rex E. Lee (qtd. in Dugger 203). This idea of reverse discrimination, which was the focus of intellectuals such as Nathan Glazer and the *Bakke* case, now had the concrete support of a conservative presidency and the Justice Department.

In several Supreme Court cases during the 1980s such as *Firefighters Local Union No. 1784 v. Stotts* (1984), the high court legally reinforced the status of the individual and defined a new set of victims, whites. Unlike the *Bakke* case, which eliminated quotas but maintained affirmative action, the cases in the 1980s tried to eliminate affirmative action altogether. The main line of attack was to shift the burden of proof of discrimination. This shift went from the effects of discrimination to the intent to discriminate. This shift made it much more difficult to prove discrimination (Dugger 210).

The 1984 Supreme Court case *Wygant v. Jackson Board of Education* represents all the elements of conservative egalitarianism that the Reagan administration used in the attack on affirmative action. In 1972 the Jackson, Michigan, school board signed a pact that stated that any future layoffs were to be based on seniority. Subsequently, in a new pact, also in 1972, the board stated, "at no time will there be a greater percentage of minority personnel laid off than the current percentage of minority personnel employed at the time of the layoff" (120). The school board created the new pact to ensure that minority personnel would be in proportion to minority student population.

The lower court ruled against the plaintiff Wygant on the basis of the idea of the effect of discrimination. The lower court held that "there is a sound basis for concluding that the minority under representation is substantial and chronic and that the handicap of past discrimination is impeding access [and promotion] of minorities." (120). Moreover, the lower court believed the minority teachers were role models to minority students (121).

The Supreme Court reversed this claim by focusing on the individual, intent to discriminate, and redefining whites as victims. In the *Wygant* case, individual rights exceeded the group rights of minorities. The justices argued, "one hundred and twenty years after the end of slavery government may still advance some and suppress others not as individuals but because of the color of their skin" (124). The justices continued, "Laws granting preferences to members of enumerated minority groups are also far from benign in practical effects. Such preferences inevitably harm innocent individuals" (139). In fact, the Court suggested that discrimination against minorities was coincidental. "When government provides compensation to individual victims, government is not itself making or implementing a racial classification. The victims compensated may all be members of the same racial or ethnic group, but this is merely because the guilty party's unlawful behavior was defined by race" (146). The Court concluded, "past discrimination against some individuals would not support a *categorical* racial and ethnic preference such as that contained in the Jackson agreement" (148). Thus, the court ruled that only the individual matters.

In focusing on the individual instead of the group, the Supreme Court also shifted the burden of proof, from effects of discrimination to intent. In overruling the lower court's decision, the Supreme Court measured discrimination on the intent to discriminate. The *Wygant* case provides several examples. The justices argued that the Fourteenth Amendment "was intended to assure the equality before the law of all persons, of whatever race or group. . . . [T]herefore any governmental action based on race or national origin bears the heaviest possible burden of justice." (124). As legal scholar Kathleen Sullivan noted, "The Justices sparred about just what evidence would suffice to support an informal conclusion that one had discriminated in the past. The plurality opinion suggested 'sufficient,' 'convincing,' and 'strong' evidence as the benchmarks . . . while Justice O'Connor called a 'firm basis' enough. . . . None of the Justices would require those who would implement affirmative action voluntarily to make 'formal findings' that they had discriminated in the past" (159). Therefore, by eliminating the use of discriminatory effects and not requiring "formal findings," the Court drastically reduced affirmative action initiatives and the ability to prosecute cases of discrimination against blacks (except for extreme cases such as the 1996 Texaco case).

In shifting the burden of proof from effects of discrimination to intent to discriminate, the Court believed that compensation should be "directed to those who have actually suffered discrimination" (*Wygant* 124). Consequently, whites became the primary victims of discrimination because of affirmative action policies. The justices argued that since "the Equal Protection Clause protects personal not group rights, a measure cannot be fairly characterized as a remedy for a violation of equal protection unless it provides relief to an individual who was personally victimized by discrimination" (Edsall and Edsall 187).

The corollary to this argument was that blacks had to become nonvictims. "The core issue of race-based affirmative action, the issue of compensation for historic discrimination," according to Thomas and Mary Edsall, "was reformulated; those blacks who had not themselves personally suffered illegal discrimination were to be considered by government as uninjured by the legacy of discrimination, and were to be redefined as 'non-victims'" (187). In attempting to promote this change in the discourse of affirmative action, the Reagan administration employed the services of black conservatives and their "independent brilliance" (Reagan, *Speaking*, 163).

The main support for this characterization of blacks as nonvictims was the perceived success of the black middle class. The perceived success of this class dissolved the equation of black with victim (Steele). The *Wygant* case used the perceived success of the black middle class as a reason to make blacks nonvictims. The justices asserted, "it is one of the ironies of racial preferences that those who benefit are the most advantaged. Many minority group members and some minority groups as a whole have now surpassed the residual category of 'whites' in income, education, and other measure of success" (*Wygant* 145). Thus, affirmative action was providing "preferential benefits for individuals not shown to have suffered from any past discrimination; preferential medical school admissions for members of minority groups that were already *overrepresented* in the student body; and preferential treatment for minority businessmen whose economic resources and opportunities clearly exceeded those of the average citizen" (*Wygant* 137). Consequently, in the attack on affirmative action, the black middle class was represented as the main beneficiary of affirmative action, and thus blacks as a population group could now be redefined as victimizers and not victims. With the redefinition, the perceived growth in the black middle class allowed blacks as a population group to be judged on an individual basis and therefore subject to the American Dream.

While the Justice Department whittled away at affirmative action, the use of code words began a new type of redefinition. Code words are "phrases and symbols which refer indirectly to racial themes, but do not directly challenge popular democratic or egalitarian ideals" (Omi and Winant 123). At the heart of the use of code words has been the discourse on crime.

Reagan used the rhetoric of law and order by focusing on drugs and the criminalization of drug use. The "war on drugs" campaign evolved out of anti-street-crime rhetoric espoused by Barry Goldwater, George Wallace, and Richard Nixon. Reagan increased the budgets of internal police organizations, such as the Drug Enforcement Agency (DEA), the Customs Department, and the Department of Defense while cutting the budgets of rehabilitative organizations such as the National Institute on Drug Abuse. These internal police organizations began to enforce the antidrug rhetoric aimed at drug dealers and, after 1986, casual drug users. With the proliferation of crack cocaine and the media's focus on the young black dealers and users that Marc Mauer's *Race to Incarcerate* notes had become news under the rhetoric of the "war on drugs," the perception that the drug epidemic occurred only in America's inner cities became the norm. The race-neutral language used by the government did not replace the media's visual images of blacks as the enemy, which increased in frequency by 300 percent during the "war on drugs" (Mauer 171–77).

The call for law and order in an era of decreasing crime rates was based on the racial perception of criminals. David Garland concludes, "it is clear enough that criminal conduct does not determine the kind of penal action that a society adopts. . . . [I]t is not 'crime' or even criminological knowledge about crime which most affects policy decisions, but rather the ways in which 'the crime problem' is officially perceived and the political positions to which these perceptions give rise" (20). The perceived culprit of the high rates of crime were young inner-city blacks. The "crimes of the poor were . . . used as evocative symbols of their undeserving and dangerous nature" (Beckett 11). George H. W. Bush's use of Willie Horton in the 1992 presidential campaign affixed a black face on the race-neutral language of crime. In the end, the "ideologically produced fear of crime" served "to render racism simultaneously more invisible and more virulent" and the war on inner-city blacks resonated firmly with white voters (Davis 269).

The redefinition of the role of government toward the black poor, and the racial undertones of crime in America, defined a majority of black life purely in these underclass themes. The simultaneous use of the reverse discrimination epistemology and code words represents how the political languages on race reflect the dialectical process of the rhetorical and physical divergence between the black middle class and the postindustrial poor/jobless black. This divergence represents the symbolic incorporation of the black middle class.

The question remains: What does the black middle class as political language mean for our present cultural system in the postindustrial society? The answer is that it represents a continuation of the racial contract, in which the terms of the contract have been slightly altered. The political language of the black middle class symbolizes the current evolution of the governing code of symbolic life and death, the binary opposition between the optimal conception of Man and its negation—the nonvalued conception that represents the organizing principle found in all cultures. For example, in feudal Europe symbolic life was represented by the clergy, because of their closeness to God in part due to their celibacy—the avoidance of the "sinful flesh"; whereas the laity was associated with symbolic death in part because of their relationship to the "sinful flesh" (Wynter, "Ceremony," 20–37). Jacques Le Goff identified the schism between the pure and the impure in stating, "The church became a society of bachelors which imprisoned lay society in marriage" (102). Within the cultural system of America, the categories of free/slave and white/black have served to form the parameters of symbolic life and death. The civil-rights era modified the white/black absolutes and allowed for the modest incorporation of the black middle class. The philosophical positions of Charles Mills and Sylvia Wynter provide insight into the importance of the symbolic and partial incorporation of the black middle class into the American cultural system.

Charles Mills's *Racial Contract* proposes an alternative philosophical ground, departing from the tradition of social contract theorists such as Immanuel Kant, John Locke, Thomas Hobbes, and Jean-Jacques Rousseau. The racial contract has moral, political, and epistemological dimensions that explain "how society was created or crucially transformed" (10). The initial terms of the racial contract represented the cultural system that W. E. B. DuBois termed the "color line." The policies of slavery and segregation served, according to Sylvia Wynter, as "icon[s] of an ostensibly pre-selected genetic value differential between *human heredity variations,* the representation of *eugenic descent* on whose basis the global middle classes legitimate their ontological hegemonic social status" ("No Humans Involved," 51–52). Through the coalescing of other status markers, European/ non-European (geography), civilized/barbarian (culture), and Christian/non-Christian (religion), the idea of race (white/nonwhite) manifested itself within the western cultural system. Thus, the problem since the fifteenth century has been the problem of the color line.

The terms of the racial contract, however, are constantly evolving, and the ascension of the political discourse on the black middle class represents a contemporary shift, a shift that has ended the formal existence of the racial contract based on "eugenic descent," best represented by Jim Crow, lynching, and slavery. Mills states, "The scope and terms of the social contract has been formally extended to apply to everyone, so that 'persons' is no longer exclusively coextensive with 'Whites'" (73). There has been an expansion of what Helen Fein calls the "sanctified universe of obligation," that "circle of people with reciprocal obligations to protect each other whose bonds arose from their relation to a deity or other sacred source of authority" (4). This sacred universe has shifted from terms in which being human and American were solely determined along the white/black variant to the transracially middle classes and its negation, the postindustrial jobless of the inner cities, primarily of black and brown descent.

The discourse of "individualism" and "equal opportunity," as espoused by state authorities, has led to the inclusion of the black middle classes within this realm of obligation—even if only secondarily behind white women and other minorities (Wynter, "No Humans Involved"). This represents a transformation from the white/black cultural system to one between the jobholders, including the black middle class, and the black nonjobholders. This new "multicultural" cultural system of jobholders and jobless is, in part, a result of the political language of the black middle class (Wynter, *Do Not*). A discourse on class that has shifted from an internal black community discourse, which addressed the responsibility of the black middle class, to a discourse that was used in the justification of the claims of reverse discrimination, such as in the *Wygant* case. Race, in this new form, has allowed the black middle class to represent a trend "toward a limited expansion of the privileged human population through the 'whitening' of the previously excluded group in question" (Mills 78). The cultural belief is that the black middle class exists but is not a threat. It must be remembered, however, that this shift to the jobholder/jobless variant of the cultural system has not completely replaced the white/black cultural system, just added a new dimension. The incorporation of the black middle class into the sanctified realm is only partial, because, as the O. J. Simpson trial exemplified, the realm can at any moment revert to the biologically defined contours of "race."

The new dimension created by the shift to ostensibly middle-class terms has transformed the idea of race. Western culture constructed the idea of race, prior to the dynamism of the 1960s, on biological terms. Thus, the western cultural system was built upon the terms of the perceived inferiority of *all* blacks and the superiority of *all* whites. Since the revolution of the 1960s, however, a by-product of which was the growth of the black middle class, the cultural organizing principle of race has been reshaped from the rigid biological definition to a less rigid "metaphysical" (nonbiological/nonphenotypical) definition of race. The civil-rights movement of the 1960s represented a crisis to the eugenic model or, in Kuhnian terms, paradigm, in which the shift to the multicultural variant was a coping mechanism to save and maintain the racial contract. Consequently, as Wynter states, the "category of owners/jobholders are, of whatever race, assimilated to the category of 'whites,' the opposed category of nonowners, and the nonjobholders are assimilated to the category of the 'young Black males'" ("No Humans Involved," 53). As Jeremy Rifkin notes, the idea of being a jobholder is a measure of self-worth to the point that being jobless represents a symbolic death (195). People who have the dual outcast status as being poor/jobless and black now serve the function that all blacks served before the 1960s—the Conceptual Other, the position in which the order knows itself.

Describing the shift from phenotypical definitions of race to metaphysical ones should not be seen as a plea for "multiculturalism" but for a more textured understanding of race, one that begins to negotiate the affect of class and one that recognizes the racial contract as best describing our present cultural system. The black middle class's values have been equated with those of the dominant white community, while the black lower class's values are seen as the cultural artifacts of all black people, an inherently racist position. For example, the Moynihan Report argued that black lower-class family structure was highly unstable, whereas the black middle-class family, like the white family, was very structured and stable (51). In addition, the discrimination that many members of the black middle class face and the resultant anger, as depicted in Ellis Cose's *Rage of a Privileged Class,* stem from the contradiction between the rhetoric of black middle-class incorporation into the previously denied realm of obligation and the perception of black life as solely defined by the dysselected values associated with the black lower classes. The American public perceives the black middle class as an exception in comparison to most of the black population; in fact, the political language about the black middle class is one of normalcy—"just like whites." As one of Joe Feagin and Melvin Sikes's respondents stated, "They [white coworkers] don't see you or me and say this is a talented human being. . . . No, they say 'He's black, but' or 'She's black but.' There's an exception. So to be black and be [a] successful contributor is to be an exception to what white folks see in other black folks" (163–64). The "other black folks" are the postindustrial poor in our ghettos, shantytowns, and "Third Worlds." This population group has the black faces of Rodney King, Latasha Harlins, Abner Louima, and Amadou Diallo. Therefore, while the state's racial rhetoric does not include the black middle class, it does assign a black face to the "underclass," and this has become necessary in order to advance the philosophical constructs of the racial contract.

The racial contract, both past and contemporary versions, are maintained through force and ideology. The slave catchers, lynch mobs, and police departments supplied the force during the course of black history. The state-sanctioned and state-supplied force is the most obvious sign of the racial contract; it is, however, the ideological coercion that directly relates to the political language of the black middle class (Mills 83–89).

In 1933 Carter G. Woodson recognized the ideological dimensions needed to preserve the racial contract. He stated, "The problem of holding the Negro down is . . . easily solved. When you control a man's thinking you do not have to worry about his actions" (xii). Moreover, the racial contract is an epistemological contract, one that structures behavior. Woodson queried, "Why not exploit, enslave, or exterminate a class that everybody is taught to regard as inferior?" (3). We as a culture have not answered this question. The black middle class has been incorporated through the political language of "equal opportunity" and "color-blind society," yet their inclusion is reflective of the exclusion of postindustrial poor/jobless blacks. This cultural exclusion of postindustrial poor/jobless blacks has led to the Rodney Kings, Amadou Diallos, and Abner Louimas and the categorization of young black males as "NHI"—No Humans Involved—and young black females as "welfare queens."

This shift in the racial contract has created such confusion that we do not know whether race is declining in significance or whether we live two nations—white and black or black middle class and black underclass. Many black intellectuals have failed to understand this nuance within the cultural system. Moreover, there is an uneasy silence in understanding the linkages between the incidents of police brutality (Rodney King and Abner Louima), the prison-industrial complex, postindustrial society, and the dominance of the economic ethic. It is within the present logic of the cultural-specific goal of "material redemption" that postindustrial poor/jobless blacks are seen as less than human—thus exploitable and expendable. So much so, that political cries to control crime function as a command to eliminate blacks of this undeserving category (Wynter, "No Humans").

The racial contract is the defining structure for western (now global) culture.

Although the dynamism of the 1960s altered the black/white variant of eugenic descent, the hybridly eugenic and multicultural version of the racial contract needs a similar movement in order to complete the cultural transformation begun in the 1960s. The first step must be to understand the effects of systems of classification, of which the political language on the black middle class is a part.

Woodson made an epistemological break in recognizing the link between the misrepresentation of blacks and whites and the subsequent effect on their behaviors. The political language on the black middle class represents the metaphysical variant of race, such that the destructive force aimed at all blacks is now focused (primarily) on the postindustrial poor/jobless, exemplified by the Rodney King, Abner Louima, and Latasha Harlins incidents. A potential starting point for any substantial cultural transformation must be the recognition that under the founding premise of the racial contract, Man (the cultural construction of the western *episteme*) has been equated with the universal (and therefore not culturally bound) determinants of symbolic life (whites and the multicultural middle classes). As Wynter notes, however, at no time has Man been isomorphic with the Human. An alternative paradigm could transform the racial contract, but the transformation must begin from the perspective of the postindustrial poor/jobless because their liminality has the potential to transform (Legesse 271). It is the perspective of the NHI that can begin the transformation of the postindustrial society, just as the perspective of blacks transformed society in the 1960s. The first step in the transformation is a cultural systemic analysis that would "have to engage both in a redefinition of the relation between the concrete individual men and women and the socializing process of the systems of symbolic representations generated from the codes that govern all human purposes and behavior" (Wynter, "1492," 47). This is the mission for a new generation of scholars.

Note

1. This definition of middle raises the issue about popular use of the term and the statistical analysis. Many people who make more than $50,000 claim middle class status. In a survey by the National Center for Opinion Research 71 percent of those with incomes above $75,000 call themselves middle class and 36 percent of those earning $15,000 a year call themselves middle class, although they are just above the poverty line. *People Like Us: Social Class in America.* Public Broadcasting System (PBS) <www.pbs.org/peoplelikeus/resources/stats.html>.

Works Cited

Beckett, Katherine. *Making Crime Pay: Law and Order in Contemporary American Politics.* Oxford, Eng.: Oxford University Press, 1997.

Bell, Daniel. *The Coming of the Post-Industrial Society.* New York: Basic Books, 1973.

Cose, Ellis. *The Rage of a Privileged Class: Why Do Prosperous Blacks Still Have the Blues?* New York: HarperCollins, 1993.

Davis, Angela Y. "Race and Criminalization: Black Americans and the Punishment Industry." In *The House That Race Built,* edited by Wahneema Lubiano. New York: Pantheon, 1997. 264–79.

Dugger, Ronnie. *On Reagan: The Man and His Presidency.* New York: McGraw-Hill, 1983.

Edsall, Thomas Byrane, and Mary D. Edsall. *Chain Reaction: The Impact of Race, Rights, and Taxes on American Politics.* New York: W.W. Norton, 1991.

Feagin, Joe, and Melvin Sikes. *Living with Racism: The Black Middle Class Experience.* Boston: Beacon Press, 1994.

Fein, Helen. *Accounting for Genocide: National Response and Jewish Victimization during the Holocaust.* New York: Free Press, 1979.

Garland, David. *Punishment and Modern Society: A Study in Social Theory.* Chicago: University of Chicago Press, 1990.

Glazer, Nathan. *Affirmative Discrimination: Ethnic Inequality and Public Policy.* New York: Basic Books, 1975.

Hacker, Andrew. *Money: Who Has How Much and Why.* New York: Scribner's, 1997.

Jones, Stedman. *Languages of Class: Studies in English Working Class History 1832–1982.* Cambridge, Eng.: Cambridge University Press, 1983.

Katz, Michael. *The Undeserving Poor: From the War on Poverty to the War on Welfare.* New York: Pantheon, 1989.

King, Martin Luther Jr. *Where Do We Go from Here: Chaos or Community?* Boston: Beacon Press, 1968.

Legesse, Asmarom. *Gada: Three Approaches to the Study of an African Society.* New York. Free Press, 1973.

Le Goff, Jacques. *The Medieval Imagination.* Chicago: University of Chicago Press, 1988.

Mauer, Marc. *Race to Incarcerate.* New York: New Press, 2001.

Mills, Charles. *The Racial Contract.* Ithaca, N.Y.: Cornell University Press, 1997.

Moynihan, Daniel. *The Negro Family: The Case for National Action.* Washington: U.S. Department of Labor: Office of Planning and Research, 1965.

Muraskin, William A. *Middle Class Blacks in a White Society: Prince Hall Freemasonry in America.* Berkeley: University of California Press, 1975.

Omi, Michael, and Howard Winant. *Racial Formation in the United States: From the 1960s to the 1990s.* 2d ed. New York: Routledge, 1994.

Pocock, J. G. A. "Languages and Their Implications." *Politics, Language, and Time: Essays on Political Thought and History.* Chicago: University of Chicago Press, 1989. 3–41.

———. *Virtue, Commerce, and History: Essays on Political Thought and History, Chiefly in the Eighteenth Century.* Cambridge, Eng.: Cambridge University Press, 1985.

Public Broadcasting System (PBS). *People like Us: Social Class in America.* <www.pbs .org/peoplelikeus/resources/stats.html>. Broadcast September 2001. Accessed 12 May 2005.

———. *The Two Nations of Black America.* <http://www.pbs.org/wgbh/pages/frontline/ shows/race/etc/gates.html>. Broadcast 10 February 1998. Accessed 12 May 2005.

Reagan, Ronald. "Remarks and Question-and-Answer Session at the 'Choosing a Future' Conference in Chicago, Illinois." In *Affirmative Action and the Constitution.* Vol. 2, *The Supreme Court "Solves" the Affirmative Action Issue, 1978–1988,* edited by Gabriel J. Chin and Paul Finkelman. New York: Garland, 1998. 110.

———. *Speaking My Mind.* New York: Simon and Shuster, 1989.

Reed, Adolph L., Jr. "Black Particularity Reconsidered." In *Is It Nation Time? Contemporary*

Essays on Black Power and Black Nationalism, edited by Eddie S. Glaude Jr. Chicago: University of Chicago Press, 2002. 39–66.

Rifkin, Jeremy. *The End of Work: The Decline of the Global Labor Force and the Dawn of the Post-Market Era.* New York: Tarcher/Putnam, 1996.

Steele, Shelby. *The Content of Our Character: A New Vision of Race in America.* New York: Harper Perennial, 1990.

Sullivan, Kathleen M. "Sins of Discrimination: Last Term's Affirmative Action Cases." *Harvard Law Review* 100.1 (November 1986): 78–98.

Waswo, Richard. "The History That Literature Makes." *New Literary History* 19.3 (Spring 1988): 541–64.

West, Cornel, "The Paradox of the African American Rebellion." In *Is It Nation Time? Contemporary Essays on Black Power and Black Nationalism,* edited by Eddie S. Glaude Jr. Chicago: University of Chicago Press, 2002. 22–38.

Woodson, Carter G. *The Mis-Education of the Negro.* Washington, D.C.: Associated Publishers, 1933.

Wygant v. Jackson Board of Education, Amicus Curiae Brief. In *Affirmative Action and the Constitution: Volume 2—The Supreme Court "Solves" the Affirmative Action Issue, 1978–1988,* edited by Paul Finkelman. New York: Garland, 1998. 112–49.

Wynter, Sylvia. "The Ceremony Must Be Found: After Humanism." *Boundary 2* 12.1–3 (Spring/Fall 1984): 19–70.

———. *"Do Not Call Us Negroes": How "Multicultural" Textbooks Perpetuate Racism.* San Francisco: Aspire Books, 1990.

———. "1492: A New World View." In *Race, Discourse, and the Origin of the Americas: A New World View,* edited by Vera Lawrence and Rex Nettleford. Washington, D.C.: Smithsonian Institution Press, 1995. 3–52.

———. "No Humans Involved: An Open Letter to My Colleagues." *Forum N.H.I: Knowledge for the 21st Century* 1.1 (Fall 1994): 46–73.

CHAPTER 12

Modernity, Persons, and Subpersons

Charles W. Mills

Mainstream narratives of modernity represent it as characterized by the triumph of moral egalitarianism. The Age of Revolution and the Age of Enlightenment are also supposed to be the Age of Equality. Thus the crucial texts of the period, whether political or scholarly, trumpet human equality—ostensibly unqualified—as a foundational principle. "We hold these truths to be self-evident," Thomas Jefferson ringingly asserts in the famous opening lines of the American Declaration of Independence, "that all men are created equal," and this is echoed thirteen years later in the *liberté, égalité, fraternité* of the French Revolution. It is not, of course, that the ideal of human equality had never been put forward before—after all, Stoicism proclaimed it, and so, in a somewhat different fashion, did Christianity. But equality in the epoch of the Greco-Roman slave states could never become a general principle, while equality in the eyes of God, on the day of judgment, was never intended to contradict the justifiable social divisions of *this* world, as the Catholic Church's underwriting of the feudal order testifies. What marks the modern period is that egalitarianism, and the corresponding ideals of equal rights and freedoms, are taken to become the *dominant* norm, and to do so within the *secular* sphere. Thus the orthodox narrative of modernity provides a periodization in which the ascriptive hierarchies of the ancient and medieval epochs—patrician and plebeian, lord and serf—are contrasted with the unqualified "men," the "persons," of the modern period. Moral egalitarianism—equality of moral status—is then taken as the norm and as constituting the basis for juridical and political egalitarianism, equality before the law and equality of citizenship.

   In this narrative, the leading moral and political Western philosophers of the period—Thomas Hobbes, John Locke, David Hume, Jean-Jacques Rousseau, Immanuel Kant, G. W. F. Hegel, John Stuart Mill, Karl Marx—are represented as the theoretical spokesmen for equality and advocates for competing moral/political visions ramifying from it. The original egalitarian formulations are historically most closely linked to contractarian liberalism and the natural rights tradition.

As one author writes about contractarianism in general: "The emergence of the notion of the social contract is hence linked intimately with the emergence of the idea of the equality of human beings" (Forsyth 37). But the specificity of this connection is contingent. Equality is supposed to be a general axiom, independent of these commitments, and thus to be found also in the proto-utilitarianism of Hume, and the later developed utilitarianism of Mill, where the felicific calculus is founded on the principle that each one counts for one. So while deontological/rights-based and consequentialist/welfare-based liberalisms may disagree on other issues, they are united on liberal equality. Even Hobbes's conventionalist ethic, which makes moral status derivative of comparative threat advantage, is egalitarian. And the same is true for other Western political theories more ambiguously related, or outright hostile, to the liberal tradition: Rousseau's radical republicanism, Hegel's communitarianism, Marx's communism. Normative equality is their starting point. So though these writers will go on to fight about numerous other issues—whether this equality is at bottom a deep equality of moral standing or merely equality of threat; whether equal individual rights or collective group welfare is the appropriate value foundation; whether the sovereign should be absolutist, constitutionalist, or the united and transformed citizenry themselves; whether individuals are best thought of as presocial atoms or as socially constituted beings; and whether their equality is compatible with class society or systematically undercut by material relations of class exploitation—the *fact* of this equality is itself an unquestioned truism. It serves as the framework, the overarching conceptual picture, within which other debates can take place, since *this* debate has been settled. Thus it tacitly imposes a certain conceptual and normative logic, pointing us away from certain areas of inquiry, indeed almost foreclosing the question of their legitimacy. As Will Kymlicka writes, in the opening of his introduction to political philosophy, "the idea that each person matters equally is at the heart of all plausible [modern] political theories" (Kymlicka, *Contemporary Political Philosophy,* 5).

This narrative, this framing paradigm, is a very powerful and influential one; indeed, it is hegemonic. What I want to argue in this chapter is that it is profoundly misleading, deeply wrong, that it radically mystifies the recent past, and that it needs to be confronted and discredited if our sociopolitical categories are to be true to the world they are supposed to be mapping. Three decades of feminist scholarship have done much to demonstrate the political gender exclusions implicit in the ostensibly neutral "men." But the counternarrative of *racial* subordination is not, at least within philosophy, as well developed, nor is the whiteness of "men" inscribed on the concept's face in the same way as their masculinity is. So even when racism is conceded, and discussed, it tends to be within the official framework of egalitarian assumptions, generating a language of "deviations," "anomalies," "contradictions," and "ironies." It is (reluctantly) admitted that these theorists may have been racist, but this concession is not taken to challenge the logic of the basic framework itself. Since equality is the globally dominant norm, the normative default mode, racism has to be a deviation. Thus one speaks of the "irony" of Jefferson's having been a slaveholder, or the "contradiction" of the need for black Jacobins to carry out a separate Haitian Revolution (James). We would find it absurd, clearly counterfactual, to describe the ancient or medieval periods as characterized by egalitarianism, since the whole point about the social systems of these periods is that inequality is the rule. Yet we do not find it equally absurd to conceptualize the modern period as basically one of equality.

What I am arguing for, then, is a reconceptualization of our narrative of modernity, a fundamental paradigm shift in how we think about liberalism, personhood, and egalitarianism. I am suggesting that racism is most illuminatingly seen as *a normative system in its own right,* to be thought of in the same terms and in the same conceptual space as the familiar normative systems of ancient and medieval class hierarchy. I will argue that there was a category in European thought for people of color as less-than-full persons, as what I have called elsewhere "subpersons," and that this inferior metaphysical standing justifies their differential normative treatment (*Blackness Visible* and *Racial Contract*). So it is not that Hobbes, Locke, Hume, Kant, Hegel, Mill, Marx, and others meant their theories of moral and political egalitarianism to apply in the same way and with full force to all humans, to which application their racist statements were lamentable deviations. (Rousseau's environmentalism makes him a trickier case, and so I will exclude him.) Rather, I am suggesting, we need to see their racist statements as part of the *same* theory as their egalitarian statements and to recognize that their moral, juridical, and political prescriptions, and their philosophies of history, follow different rules for whites than for nonwhites. So instead of seeing these theorists as spokesmen for equality *simpliciter,* we need to start seeing them as spokesmen for a racialized *white* equality. And instead of seeing the Age of Modernity as the Age of Equality, we need to start seeing it as the Age of Global White Supremacy, the age in which whites, being metaphysically and morally superior to all other races, are teleologically destined to rule over them.

* * *

The insight that racism should itself be conceptualized as a theory of personhood, with implications for the normative, is not new. Sojourner Truth is supposed to have asked, "And ain't I a woman?" (See Painter 1996.) W. E. B. DuBois pointed out that for white racist thought, blacks were a "*tertium quid,*" "somewhere between men and cattle" (*Souls of Black Folk* 122), and Frantz Fanon stated that "the black is not a man" (*Black Skin, White Masks* 8). In one of the classic texts of anti-imperialism, Jean-Paul Sartre explicitly argued that "there is nothing more consistent than a racist humanism. . . . On the other side of the ocean there was a race of less-than-humans" (26). But, at least until recently, there has been little systematic exploration in philosophy of the ramifications of this idea, and such work as has been done—for example, in the writings of Enrique Dussel, David Theo Goldberg, and Lucius Outlaw—has mostly been from the perspective and with the vocabulary of Continental philosophy, the discourse of First World Self in relation to Third World Other. In the analytic mainstream, which is obviously the crucial location for the goal of influencing debate in the profession, far less has been written, though with recent and forthcoming anthologies this is beginning to change.[1]

This neglect is all the more striking since, with the decline of utilitarianism's stature in recent decades, and the resurgence of Kantian "deontological liberalism," it is precisely the language of personhood that is now all-pervasive. The concept of *persons*—entities who, by virtue of their characteristics, are protected by a certain normative armor of rights and freedoms, entitled to be treated in a certain way—has become the central pillar of contemporary moral discourse. Thus debates about abortion are often fought over the actual or potential personhood of the fetus; animal rights theorists charge that restricting full moral concern to human persons is speciesist; and issues of metaphysical and political autonomy, of freedom of the will and citizenship rights, are discussed in terms of what personhood demands.

But what characterizes these discussions is a Eurocentrically ahistorical view of personhood and its prerequisites. Humanness is not necessary for personhood, because of the possibility of intelligent aliens. But (adult) humanness *is* generally taken as sufficient, or at least strongly presumptively sufficient, for personhood, apart from possible exceptions like the brain-dead. So white moral and political philosophers tend to write as if, apart from these kinds of exceptions, moral equality can be presupposed for humans (not merely normatively, as an ideal, but factually, as an accepted norm). And I want to challenge and disrupt this framework of assumptions by formally introducing the concept of a "subperson" (*Untermensch*)—referring to those humans who, though adult, are, because of their race, deservedly *not* treated as full persons—and arguing that this expanded conceptual apparatus better tracks the actual recent global history, and the actual views of the canonical Western moral/political philosophers, than the conventional account and its standard terms.

In approaching this issue, I am going to draw on a contemporary debate in American political theory, since I think that, with appropriate adjustments and modifications, the terms of the debate can be mapped onto, and illuminate, the corresponding positions in political philosophy. In a landmark 1993 article, later expanded into a prizewinning book, *Civic Ideals*, Rogers Smith argues that the dominant conceptualizations of the American polity in the literature have been fundamentally misleading. Citing the work of Alexis de Tocqueville, Gunnar Myrdal, and Louis Hartz as emblematic, Smith points out that the dominant framing of the United States has been as an egalitarian liberal democracy, for which racism and racial exclusion have been an "anomaly." In large measure because of the centrality to their analysis of European class categories, commentators have been blinded to the fact that "the relative egalitarianism that prevailed among white men (at first, moderately propertied white men) was surrounded by an array of fixed, ascriptive hierarchies, all largely unchallenged by the leading American revolutionaries" (Smith, *Civic Ideals,* 17).

Smith emphasizes that it is not that these theorists have altogether ignored the history of racial oppression (Native American expropriation, African slavery, Jim Crow, etc.), but that they have conceptualized it in a misleading way, one that leaves intact the mainstream picture of the polity. Tocqueville, for example, "treated racism as mere prejudice, ignoring the burgeoning scientific racism in Jacksonian America," and even though "he correctly saw racism as prevalent throughout the nation," he still wrote in "unqualified terms about America's supposedly egalitarian conditions" and relegated "blacks and Native Americans to the status of tangents in a final chapter" (Smith, *Civic Ideals,* 21–22). Myrdal's famous book, *An American Dilemma,* was focused precisely on racism, and—with the help of a research team that included many leading black social scientists—provided massive documentation of the systemic subordination of blacks across the country in all spheres of social, political, and economic life. And he conceded that "far from being an exceptional or marginal phenomenon, moreover, the nation's racial ordering . . . affected virtually all aspects of American life." But again, when it came to the question of how this subordination should be *conceived* (for example, in his introduction to the book), he framed it in terms of a violation of the liberal egalitarian American ideals that white citizens were, nonetheless, still thought of as endorsing, giving rise to the tragic dilemma of the title (Smith, *Civic Ideals,* 23).

So racism and white supremacy are not thought of as rising to the level of the ideological and political; rather, they are "prejudices," hangovers from the premodern. As Smith comments, it then becomes possible, remarkably, to represent as an egalitarian liberal democracy a country in which for most of its existence people of color were subordinated, whether enslaved, expropriated, segregated, disenfranchised, or deprived of equal socioeconomic opportunities. And what makes this feat of evasion possible is, in part, the ignoring of the facts, but in addition, and more important, the *mapping* of the conceptual terrain in such a way that the facts are deprived of their proper significance. This history of domination is not framed, as it should be, as an account of a white-supremacist political system, in which some citizens are superior to others. And the beliefs justifying this rule are not seen, as they should be, as the ideology of white supremacy but demoted to the status of "prejudice," the "nonrational," "interest-driven deviations." Smith points out that these racist traditions "provide elaborate, principled arguments for giving legal expression to people's ascribed place in various hereditary, inegalitarian cultural and biological orders, valorized as natural, divinely approved, and just." But later writers in the Tocquevillian mode read "egalitarian principles as America's true principles, while treating the massive inequalities in American life as products of prejudice, not rival principles" (*Civic Ideals* 18, 27). Smith's move is therefore to contrapose to the mainstream "anomaly" view what he calls the "multiple traditions" view, which recognizes racism and white supremacy as alternative political and ideological traditions in their own right within the political culture. So it is not that there is one liberal egalitarian tradition, with racism as an anomaly. Rather, there are multiple traditions. Another position, in the spirit of Smith's, but more radical, is the "symbiosis" view, which would claim that actually racism *is* the dominant tradition, and that liberal egalitarianism has been racially inflected from the start.[2]

Now what I want to suggest is that, writ large—that is, transferred to the global stage—and writ high—that is, elevated to the level of abstraction appropriate to philosophy—these terms can assist and elucidate the present debate. For modernity in philosophy is standardly presented in analogous terms (though obviously, since philosophy is a nonempirical discipline, with even less attention to the history of racism): as introducing personhood and liberal equality as the global norm, for which racism is the anomaly. And what I want to argue for is a reconceptualization of the philosophy of modernity along "multiple traditions" or "symbiosis" lines. My own preference is for the "symbiosis" view, but the important thing to recognize is that, whichever of these is chosen, the anomaly view is utterly inaccurate as a characterization both of the United States and of recent global history.[3] As Matthew Frye Jacobson comments about the United States, but I would claim with more general validity: "Exclusions based upon race and gender did not represent mere lacunae in an otherwise liberal philosophy of political standing; nor were the nation's exclusions simply contradictions of the democratic creed. Rather . . . these inclusions and exclusions formed an inseparable, interdependent figure and ground in the same ideological tapestry" (22–23). And this, I am claiming, is the story of modernity itself. The idea of a person is linked with that of a subperson as figure and ground, symbiotically related.

The formal demarcation and specification of the concept of a subperson, then, is meant to force recognition of this reality, by encapsulating, in an analytic philosophical framework, the *non*anomalous, but rather symbiotic, relation between liberalism and racism. Liberalism historically—though not, in my opinion, as a matter of conceptual necessity—has been racialized, so that in reading the classic liberal theorists as if they were making race-neutral pronouncements we are anachronistically misrepresenting them. Because of the delusionary self-image of the profession, the same language Smith criticizes—the language of "deviation," "anomaly," "contradiction"—is routinely used in discussing Enlightenment philosophers' sexist and racist remarks. And it is just as misleading. We need to reread these texts with the realization that what we are being presented with are different aspects of the same theory. As Catherine Wilson comments in the introduction to her recent anthology, *Civilization and Oppression:* "Sexism and ethnocentrism are not personal quirks that crop up in the philosophical population like a penchant for coffee-drinking or backgammon. They are articulated and elaborated theories, pulled together from the floating beliefs and half-beliefs of the surrounding culture and personal experience and given shape and logical structure, enabling them to be developed and transmitted, and ensuring that they will be so" (18). Instead of seeing them as "contradictions," then, "accessory political curiosities, cut off from [the philosopher's] main doctrine," we need to recognize them as "form[ing] a complementary whole" (22).

Now for sexism, the material context that undergirds this complementary relationship is, of course, the household, the sexual division of labor, and the relation between those who legitimately inhabit the public sphere and those confined to domesticity. Since this context goes back thousands of years, sexism is far older than racism, and so structures premodern as well as modern political thought. The material context for racism, on the other hand, is modern European expansionism and the growth of empire. Uday Singh Mehta points out that liberalism is "coeval" with empire, though this relationship "has scarcely been considered in recent times by political theorists" (4–5), and while in theory liberalism is self-consciously universalist and cosmopolitan—"transhistorical, transcultural, and most certainly transracial" (51)—in actuality it has been marked by "the systematic and sustained political exclusion of various groups and 'types' of people" (46). But if political theorists have scarcely considered these exclusions, philosophers have been almost totally negligent. The accounts of the development of liberalism in the mainstream literature are resolutely internalist, usually ignoring altogether this fact and its theoretical implications. But once liberalism and modernity are examined from a global rather than Eurocentric perspective, it becomes obvious that its vaunted egalitarianism, cosmopolitanism, and universalism are really meant to extend only to (male) Europeans at home and abroad: the population of full persons.

The failure to recognize these exclusions, though certainly underpinned by the ahistoricity of analytic philosophy, has also, I believe, been facilitated by a certain kind of semantic slippage. "Persons" as prescriptive, normatively loaded (how humans *should* be treated) tends to slide over into "persons" as descriptive (how humans *have* been treated). The egalitarian moral truism that all humans should be treated as persons is projected backward to become the unconscious assumption that all humans have been treated as persons, or that where they have not, this has been an anomaly. The reality that there were entire categories of humans systematically seen by the theory as *less than* persons is obfuscated by the term itself. Indeed, this is well illustrated by the Kymlicka quote cited earlier, which is either tautologous, analytic—if "person" means "human entitled to equal moral treatment"—or radically false, if "person" just means "human."

Because of the whiteness of the profession, the amnesia—particularly bad in philosophy, though widespread in other disciplines also—about the history of racism and imperialism, and the absence of an alternative narrative of modernity, an easy elision between "humans" and "persons" is facilitated, and the distinctive conceptual and moral issues raised by the experience of those humans *not* treated as persons because of their race are not confronted, or even recognized as existing.

"Person" then is really a technical term, a term of art, referring to a status whose attainment requires more than simple humanity. Mehta argues that liberalism presupposes a political anthropology: "the exclusionary basis of liberalism does, I believe, derive from its theoretical core, and the litany of exclusionary historical instances is an elaboration of this core. . . . behind the capacities ascribed to all human beings exists a thicker set of social credentials that constitutes the real bases of political inclusion" (48–49). And these social credentials are generally out of the reach of non-Europeans, nonwhites, who are covered by a different set of categories, the category of the "savage" and the "barbarian." No less than "men" or "person," then, these need to be seen as technical theoretical terms adverting to a peculiar ontological/moral/political status that legitimates their possessors' exclusion from the rights and freedoms enjoyed by whites. White women in the household were not originally meant to be included in the "men" of liberal theory; we are all now self-consciously aware of this because of the excavationary and revisionary work of feminism. But neither were nonwhite savages and barbarians meant to be included, either in the "men" or the "persons." Writing about the United States, but with more general applicability, Lee Baker points out: "Between the middle of the eighteenth century and the dawn of the twentieth century, science played an important role in establishing the 'fact' that savages were racially inferior to members of civilized society. . . . [and thus] Negroes and Indians were . . . not worthy of citizenship or freedom" (13–14). *Social* equality was impossible because of natural *racial* inequality (Baker 36). It is not at all a matter of "contradictions," internal inconsistencies, but of a consistent exclusivist white egalitarianism which is now, in contradiction to the actual historical record, being denied. Moral and political equality had racial prerequisites.

The concept of a subperson, then, formally registers this *actual* division in modern Western political theory, and by its overt presence, and the set of implications and ramifications its introduction establishes, illuminates an architecture *already there* in these theories but currently obfuscated by the illusory inclusiveness of "persons" read backwardly as race-neutral. Subpersons are humanoid entities who, because of deficiencies linked with race, lack the moral status requisite for enjoyment of the bundle of rights and freedoms appropriate for persons. Writings that currently seem irrelevant, remarks that seem like throwaway lines, comments that seem puzzlingly inconsistent with (what we have been taught is) the "theory," are no longer marginalized but integrated into a theoretical whole. We then realize that far from this being a perverse or bizarre hermeneutics, a poststructuralist or deconstructionist or other interpretatively relativist technique, we are simply doing what should have been done all along: standard textual exegesis in which the text is approached in its historical context with corresponding sensitivity to the actual contemporary denotation and scope of the terms at the time. It is in fact the orthodox commentators who have been guilty of ignoring the textual evidence, and projecting into these terms an ahistorical nonracial inclusiveness they were never meant to have.

Putting this simply, the contrast between the orthodox "anomaly" view of racism and the "symbiosis" view I am advocating can be represented as follows. Let T be the (egalitarian) moral/political theory of the philosopher in question; p stand for person; and sp for subperson. Mainstream commentary is basically saying that

> For philosopher P:
> T asserts egalitarianism for all p, where p is race-neutral.
> Racist statements are then an exception, and not part of T.

And what, by contrast, I am recommending as an interpretive framework is

> For philosopher P:
> T asserts egalitarianism for all p, where whiteness is (generally) a necessary condition for being a p.[4]
> T asserts nonegalitarianism for sp, where nonwhiteness is (generally) a sufficient condition for being an sp.
> Racist statements are then part of T, not an exception.

On both views, racism can be admitted—the charge is not that mainstream views cannot concede racism. The crucial question is *how* they frame it, whether as anomaly/contradiction, et cetera, or as an integral/symbiotic part of the theory.

It will be appreciated, then, that this semantic innovation, so simple to describe, would, if adopted, quite radically transform our view of modern Western moral/political philosophy. We would have to start thinking of these theorists, and their theories, quite differently from how they are presented in the standard textbook. This does not rule out, of course, a sanitized reappropriation and retrieval of their theories. But it would have to be explicitly acknowledged that that *is* what we are doing, that we are not reading them as they intended. So it is not that liberalism and egalitarianism, abstract L and E, were historically meant to extend to everybody. Rather, we would need to talk about racialized liberalism and racialized egalitarianism, RL and RE. Racism would then emerge, as it should, as a normative system in its own right—indeed, as the *actual* normative system obtaining for most of the modern period. And just as the hierarchical ideologies of the ancient and medieval world were multiply tiered, with different standings (of class) for different sets of human beings, we would be forced to acknowledge that (actual, historical) liberalism also is a two-tiered ideology, with a different status assigned to, and correspondingly differentiated norms prescribed for, whites and nonwhites. The orthodox narrative of modernity would have to be rewritten; the orthodox cartography of the political would have to be redrawn.

Apart from being—unlike the present narrative—true to the actual historical record, and so demanding implementation on those grounds alone, this transformation would have the great virtue of uniting the conceptual spaces and periodization times of the white political and the nonwhite political. As emphasized at the start, the mainstream narrative orients us toward certain players, certain dates, in keeping with a macro-picture of global history in which an egalitarian modernity triumphantly succeeds the hierarchical ancient and medieval epochs. So there is a segregation of events, an apartheid of the historical calendar, a color coding of concepts. Textbooks provide an account of the history of Western political philosophy that moves smoothly from Plato to John Rawls without dealing with race, as if, in the modern period, Western theorists were proclaiming their egalitarian views as applicable to everybody. The views of known racist theorists—Joseph de Gobineau, Houston Stuart Chamberlain, Adolf Hitler—are usually excluded from these accounts, and the racism of Enlightenment theorists is not highlighted or even mentioned. The West is constructed in such a way that racism and white racial domination have been no part of the history of the West, and the normative superiority of whites to nonwhites, justified by these theorists, has been no part of that history. We have a history of the official political proscenium with a certain cast of actors (Whigs and Tories; liberals and conservatives; socialists, anarchists, and fascists), and these other players (abolitionists, anti-imperialists, Pan-Africanists . . .) seem to be on a different stage, a stage so oddly related to the familiar one that it hardly seems political at all. Similarly, we are all familiar with 1776 and 1789 as crucial dates for human liberation: the American and French Revolutions. But how many of us would be able to come up unassisted with the date of the Haitian Revolution or the end of New World slavery?

Imagine a standard textbook account of Locke's "Second Treatise." It will be at pains to situate Locke as a Whig spokesman in an ideological and political conflict with the quasi-feudal views of Sir Robert Filmer's patriarchal Toryism. Locke will be portrayed as the modernist advocate of egalitarianism as against intrinsic subordination, of liberal parliamentarianism as against absolutism and the divine right of kings, and his proclamation of the equality of all men in the state of nature will be central to that portrayal. But these same textbooks will say nothing about *racial* hierarchy, and Locke's role in justifying Native American expropriation and countenancing African slavery. The battle of white men for political egalitarianism is recognized as a political struggle; the battle of people of color for political egalitarianism is not. So these same Western theorists will not be represented—as they (usually) are—as defenders of colonialism and exponents of global white supremacy, a political system in which whites rule despotically over people of color. A mystified account of political philosophy complements a mystified account of recent world history, in which the central role of imperialism and racial domination has been either sanitized or written out of the record altogether.

I now want to consider some of the objections that might be raised to this conceptual recommendation.

The Objection of Overstatement

First, it might be objected that I am vastly overstating the extent of racism in the period, so that it could not have had the far-reaching conceptual implications I am imputing to it. The problem here is a failure of historical memory that is no mere ordinary forgetting, but rather a willed amnesia (not on the individual but the sociocultural level). Writing in 1971, Leon Poliakov suggested that the aftermath of the Third Reich had created a taboo around certain subjects, so that investigators into fascist and racist ideologies "display[ed] no inclination to look into the remote past when searching for origins. . . . Anti-racism has been promoted to the rank of a dogmatic orthodoxy. . . . This has produced a self-censorship, to a great extent retroactive, by authors of all kinds, but particularly historians who, often without knowing it, try to reinterpret the history of modern thought under this influence. *It begins to look as if, through shame or fear of being racist, the West will not admit to having been so at any time,* and therefore assigns to minor characters only (like Gobineau, H. S. Chamberlain, etc.) the role of scapegoats. A vast chapter of Western thought is thus made to disappear by sleight of hand" (5; emphasis in original). Similarly, in his study of race in international affairs, Frank Füredi argues that until recently "race was a central category in international relations," with doctrines of "the superiority of the white races" (1) being taken for granted by all shades of political opinion. The international system was "run by white states," "a global framework where double standards were institutionalised and ideas and diplomatic practices reflected the differential treatment of races" (20). So even though "white solidarity had more the character of an informal convention than a formal principle," it did nonetheless produce a "considerable degree of unity" even among European adversaries once they were dealing with the colonial world (32). Füredi points out that the historical literature today rarely discusses the fact that at the 1919 post–World War I conference in Versailles, a proposal from Japan to include "the equality of races" in the League of Nations Covenant was strongly rejected by the Anglo-Saxon nations. Indeed, as late as 1941, "the [British] Foreign Office had come out unambiguously against the proposal for publicly supporting the principle of racial equality" (14).[5]

But with the colored colonial world pressing for change during and after World War II, the old racial order could no longer be maintained—at least in its explicit guise. There would be a shift to a "racial pragmatism," not a principled antiracism, but a policy by the West of avoiding explicit racist discourse in order to preempt racial conflict. In this intellectual atmosphere, the past was sanitized and whitewashed, so that whereas in reality "the principle of racial equality had few intellectual defenders in the 1930s," by the postwar period the "volte-face" on race was so rapid and complete *that it was not recognized as such* by later theorists: "Some writers in the 1960s assumed a lengthy antiracist tradition and asked why there had been such a delay in implementing these principles in terms of civil rights. . . . [T]he previous longevity of anti-egalitarian and racist sentiments can and was easily lost sight of" (Füredi 15). A revisionist history was created, which continues to shape moral, political, and philosophical discourse today, one that makes racism marginal, an "anomaly" in the history of the West, rather than what it actually was, a central structuring norm. For the reality is, in the words of George Mosse, that "racism as it developed in Western society was no mere articulation of prejudice, nor was it simply a metaphor for suppression; it was, rather, a fully blown system of thought, an ideology like Conservatism, Liberalism, or Socialism, with its own peculiar structure and mode of discourse" (ix), indeed "the most widespread ideology of the time" (Mosse 231).

The Objection of Cognitive Hierarchy

Second, it might be argued that even if racism were widespread, it could not have had this conceptual impact because as irrational "prejudice," it does not rise to the level of a developed worldview. But as the Mosse quote indicates, this conceptualization of racism as "prejudice" is itself a contestable political move, itself part of the problem.[6] As I will discuss in greater detail below, what is being proposed is a partitioning of the ideational terrain between principles/theories, which occupy the conceptual high ground, and racist beliefs, demoted to a lower cognitive status. But as Rogers Smith has pointed out with respect to the United States, in reference to a comparable move on the part of Gunnar Myrdal, this partitioning was refuted by Myrdal's own research. Racist beliefs were not "merely matters of bigoted ignorance" but supported by the biological sciences, backed up by "hierarchical racial theories" of great prestige, so that white supremacy, in Myrdal's own words, could "not be denied high qualities of structural logic and consistency" (Smith, *Civic Ideals,* 23). Racism is best seen, as Mosse insists, as an ideology, or a family of ideologies (in the broad sense that includes both academic and folk beliefs),[7] making fundamental descriptive and normative claims about human beings (what they basically are, what in consequence they're basically entitled to), and as such it is indeed in the same conceptual space as the liberal principles and theories usually stipulated to be raised above it.

The Objection of Anachronism

On a different note, it might be argued that scientific racism is a comparatively late theoretical development, and that earlier Enlightenment theorists would not have been influenced by it and in some cases would not even have had the concept of race to work with.

I would make two related moves here. First, I would emphasize that I am working with a broad concept of racism, not one limited to "scientific" racism. So for me, theological views that explain black inferiority, for example, in terms of Africans' descent from Ham's accursed son Canaan, or "commonsense" secular explanations that attribute it to innate qualities of an unknown and as yet untheorized kind, still count as racism. My justification is the moral/political focus of my concerns: however the inferiority of people of color is explained, the bottom line is that it grounds and justifies the denial to them of equal moral standing. It is because of their inferiority that they are not moral equals, and so antiegalitarianism in public policy is mandated.

Similarly, I would argue, even if the theorist does not always have a developed concept of race in the modern sense, he is often utilizing a category that can be seen as either a conceptual equivalent or a conceptual precursor. Here I would follow the lead of writers like Audrey Smedley, David Stannard, and others, who argue that a concept can be in formation in popular consciousness long before its developed critical articulation by intellectuals. Thus Smedley describes race as a "worldview" (7), "a sociocultural phenomenon" (7), which has been "from its inception, a folk classification" (25), "a way of categorizing what were already conceived as inherently unequal human populations" (26). Similarly, Stannard writes:

> As for the idea that racism proper did not and could not emerge until the rise of an "explicit and rationalized" pseudoscientific ideology regarding the term "race" itself, as Richard Drinnon has remarked, this "is roughly equivalent to saying . . . the practice of birth control waited upon Margaret Sanger to coin the term" . . . [N]either skin color distinctions nor pseudoscientific ideas of biological determinism are *necessary* criteria for the categorization and degradation of people under the rubric of "race." Even a glance at the standard etymologies of the word ("the outward race and stocke of Abraham"; "to be the Race of Satan"; "the British race"; "that Pygmean Race"—to cite some sixteenth- and seventeenth-century examples) clearly shows that the term "race" was in widespread use in Britain to denote groups of people and classes of things marked by characteristics *other* than color well before it was used exclusively in that way, and centuries before it had grafted upon it the elaborate apparatus of biological and zoological pseudoscience. . . . In sum, there is little doubt that the dominant sixteenth- and seventeenth-century ecclesiastical, literary, and popular opinion in Spain and Britain and Europe's American colonies regarding the native peoples of North and South America was that they were a racially degraded and inferior lot—borderline humans as far as most whites were concerned. (274, 278)

So even if no developed theory of scientific racism was available at the time, even if—as has been claimed for Hobbes and Locke, for example—they did not explicitly use the concept of race, this does not imply, given my framework, that they were not working with its equivalent ("savages") and its pejorative presuppositions.

The Objection of Variations in Degrees of Racism

Another objection might be that, even if widespread racism is conceded, it would be mistaken to assume that *all* Western political philosophers of the modern period were racist, and/or to the same degree, and in the same respects, and for all nonwhites. But my position does not imply this (though it does imply that *most* were racist—the exceptions are few, and it is important, in light of the aforementioned sanitization of the record, not to ignore this fact). Sometimes, apart from simple ignorance of writings not part of the familiar canon, the judgment of innocence is based on the inference that because a particular thinker, say, opposed slavery, or genocide, or colonialism, or complained about the ill treatment of nonwhites, that this necessarily makes him nonracist. But this is to set the bar very low indeed. To begin with, one could oppose some of these policies (for example, slavery, colonialism) for other than moral reasons, for example, economic ones. But in addition, even a *moral* opposition does not necessarily imply a belief in nonwhite moral equality. In the same way that one can oppose cruelty to animals without seeing animals as normatively equal to humans, one can oppose certain kinds of policies regarding nonwhites without considering them equal. (In the United States, for example, most white abolitionists saw blacks as inferior even while they agitated for their freedom.) There are varieties and degrees of racism, and it would be a mistake to infer from the absence of one variety, or the absence of extreme degrees, to the absence of other varieties, or the absence of milder degrees. The bottom line for me is moral inequality, and it is a straightforward logical point that there are far more ways to be *un*equal than there are to be equal.

Relatedly, the concept of a subperson is meant to be broad and flexible enough to cover a whole range of possibilities, corresponding to these varieties and degrees of racism. Unequal moral status can extend from zero to just below equality, but all of these positions are nonetheless statuses of inequality. In addition, it is not being claimed, nor should it be thought, that all people of color were treated the same, and held exactly the same status. Subperson is a useful umbrella term, but it has to be subdivided. Traditionally, as earlier noted, there have been intra-racial hierarchies in the subordinated groups, with "barbarians" being distinguished from simple "savages," and Asians (Indians, Chinese), for example, standardly ranked above Native Americans, Africans, and Australian Aborigines. Moreover, because of the variety of theoretical frameworks used to justify racism, there will be a wide range of conceptions: theological racism (the three main racial groups recognized at the time—whites, yellows, blacks—as descendants of Noah's three sons—Japheth, Shem, and Ham) (on this point, see Poliakov) versus scientific racism; polygenesis versus monogenesis; more biologistic versus more environ-mentalist accounts, et cetera, not to mention the internal varieties within all these. One could be inferior because of being a nonhuman animal, because of being an entity intermediate between nonhuman animals and humans (the "missing link"), because of being humans of an inferior separate genesis, because of being humans of the same genesis but marked by an evolutionary backwardness, and so forth. The concept of a subperson is meant to be a simplifying concept aimed at tracking this status of moral inferiority, and so it abstracts away from other differentiations. But once that is given, there will be a tremendous number of ways in which one can be a subperson, and in other contexts these distinctions will obviously be important.

Nor am I claiming that a "smoking gun" can always be found in the form of unequivocal and explicit racist statements on the part of these theorists. Some-times they will be present—indeed, as with Kant, there will be entire smoking arsenals, which still seem to go unnoticed by mainstream philosophy—but in other instances the case has to be made more indirectly. For example, it may be via inference to the best explanation: the thesis that, on the basis of the author's seeming inconsistencies, contradictions, double standards, racism seems the most reasonable explanatory hypothesis. The point is that such interpretive moves are, in other contexts, a perfectly legitimate and standardly employed technique in the repertoire of critical commentary on a theorist, so that they cannot be ruled out of court here because the conclusion is uncongenial to the establishment image of the theorist.

The Objection of Common Humanity

Another kind of objection takes a different tack. Even if, it may be conceded, rac-ism among these theorists was widespread, even if a "symbiosis" analysis is more accurate than an "anomaly" analysis, nonetheless it is still a mistaken conceptual move to suggest that people of color were seen as subpersons. For as long as they were seen as human, then they would have been viewed as persons.

The first response is to point out that, as cited above—particularly for blacks, Native Americans, and Native Australians—people of color were in some cases *not* seen as fully, or at all, human. There was sometimes genuine uncertainty about where they should be located in taxonomies of the humanoid, whether the premodern Aristotelian apparatus of medieval thought and the Christian Great Chain of Being, or the later evolutionary hierarchies of social Darwinism. Mark Cocker reminds us that "as late as 1902 a member of the Commonwealth Parlia-ment in Australia felt able to announce that 'There is no scientific evidence that the Aborigine is a human being at all'" (13). Moreover, in polygenetic theories, their separate creation made it possible to concede they were human while still categorizing them as an inferior species *of* humans.

But even with the triumph of monogenesis, the resources of social Darwinism and other theories of innate human differentiation provided a basis for
demarcating varieties of human. To a certain extent, this objection simply begs
the question, by assuming—in contradiction, as I argue, to the historical record—that "humanity" is a sufficient condition for "personhood" and, in the
framework of present-day (in theory, anyway) racial egalitarianism, ruling out
the possibility of *degrees* of humanity. "Person" (or, more usually, "man"), as
used by these theorists, is a technical term, a term of art, linked, according to the
theorist in question, with the ability to appropriate the world efficiently, to rise
above heteronomous determination, to achieve intellectual maturity, to make
history, and so forth. Mere biological membership in the human species is not
sufficient for accomplishing these feats; a certain level of sociocultural achievement is the additional prerequisite (often linked with other biological markers),
and the result turns out to be European.

Moreover, the case of gender provides a good illustration of what such emaci-
ated "personhood" would amount to, even if conceded, and how hollow it would
be. By the biological criterion, women are nominally "persons" for Kant, yet, as
feminists have pointed out, they are explicitly denied full citizenship, forbidden
to own property, to pursue an intellectual life, et cetera (see Kleingeld; Mendus;
Schröder). So if personhood is supposed to be a robust notion linked with moral
egalitarianism, and a bundle of moral rights and freedoms that translate into
juridical and political equality, what is this Pickwickian "personhood" worth?
Clearly, it is purely formal, titular, not substantive. And if gender inequalities
evacuate (white) female personhood of real content, the case is even more extreme
for people of color.

The Objection of Theoretical Quarantining

Finally, let me conclude with a particular set of objections increasingly being
raised in the light of recent scholarship on philosophy and racism, which has
made it more difficult for mainstream writers to proceed as before. "X," it will
now be conceded, "had racist views. But these views do not affect X's *theory*." So
a kind of theoretical quarantining is implemented, a conceptual *cordon sanitaire*
is installed, which supposedly protects X's theory. There is a brief discussion in
the introduction, or an endnote, and then business proceeds briskly just as before.
So if we think in terms of a conceptual mapping of the philosopher's discourse,
there is (a), on the one hand, the Theory (morally egalitarian), and (b), on the
other hand, views assigned some lower epistemic category—if not quite what
X thought when he was having a bad day, at least not something that rises to
the level of the Theory: unthinking prejudice, bigotry, preconception, and the
like. So the Theory is egalitarian and is taken to be unaffected by these views,
protected by the *cordon sanitaire*. Some ground has been conceded, but the basic
line is still being held.

Now there are three possible ways of defending this move: one can claim that the egalitarian Theory (henceforth T) is what X *actually* thought, and the racist views do not affect T because of being (by some criterion) in a different epistemic space; one can claim that T represents the *essence* of X's views; and one can claim that T can be *reconstructed* as a sanitized version of X's views. But each of these moves faces problems of its own.

The first would seem to be the most vulnerable, since it runs up against the obstacle of what X *actually* said. Nevertheless, it will be argued that these racist remarks do not rise to the status of a theory, and as such should be taken as over-ridden by T (construed as egalitarian and nonracial). In the light of my discussion above, however, we immediately appreciate that the obvious reply should be to ask by what non-question-begging, noncircular criterion this determination of inferior epistemic status is made. It cannot be supported by simply invoking T's apparent race-neutrality as manifested in its vocabulary of "men" or "persons," for, as I have argued, the very question is whether we have independent reason to believe people of color are numbered among those persons. (In other words, hu-manness is being taken, without argument, as sufficient for personhood—which is precisely what is at issue.) Nor can it be supported by the general claim that racism can *never* rise to the level of a theory, for this assertion has already been rejected. Nor can it be assumed that the brevity of the racist remarks in question demonstrates that no theory is being elaborated, for in some cases the philosopher may simply be appealing to the common wisdom. If X made pronouncements about nonwhites that are in seeming contradiction to his general pronounce-ments about "men"/"persons," then we do have to entertain the possibility that he did not mean "men"/"persons" to include them. The case for exclusionary white personhood becomes more plausible if a developed account is given of why nonwhites are inferior, but even without such an account the possibility needs to be considered, rather than be ruled out a priori. Thus we need to learn to read, and to *see*, these texts differently. We need to be on the lookout for the aside, the throwaway, the seemingly casual remark, the offhand comment, whose significance lies in that very casualness—the making of a set of assumptions that, when unpacked, reveal a world of difference. In these seemingly marginal remarks are often contained distinctions that go to the center of the theorist's thought and that demonstrate its whiteness.

The second is a fallback to another line of defense. The idea here turns on a subtle distinction—of the kind a J. L. Austin would have been happy to parse—be-tween what X *actually* said and what X *really* or *essentially* meant. So we are to assume that there is a gap between the two, and that when X (actually) denied the equality of nonwhites, he (really) meant something else. Sometimes this might be phrased in terms of X's *essential* views—he said this, but essentially he meant that. But again, the problem here should be obvious. What non-question-begging reason is there to think that X did indeed mean something else, not-p, when he said p, unless it is the aprioristic principle that X could not really have been a racist? Moreover, there is an ambiguity in "essential." It could mean "essential" for the utilitarian purpose of *our* use (we, later, nonracist philosophers), or it could mean "essential" by criteria intrinsic to the theory itself. The first shades over into option three, to be discussed below. The second has the problem of articulating an independent noncircular rationale for what is deemed incidental and essential in the theorist's own eyes. The fact that *we* do not take X's racist views as essential to his theory does not prove that *he* did not.

Finally, the third alternative faces the simple challenge that—however useful it may be—it does not represent X's actual views. Suppose, for example, that the claim of several recent commentators is correct: that Kant did not think of non-whites as full persons. Then to reconstruct a theory in which all persons should be treated with respect, and for which "persons" extends to nonwhites, cannot be said to be Kant's theory. Whether it is an admirable theory, or a useful theory, or a theory we should endorse, is not the point—these are all separate questions. The point is that it is not *Kant's* theory. Some of the crucial terms—respect, the kingdom of ends, the categorical imperative—are the same, but insofar as "persons" is not the same, does not have the same denotation, it cannot be said that it is Kant's theory. Now one can enclose it in scare quotes and claim that it is still in some sense "Kantian," but for the specific purpose at hand—that of determining what Kant actually thought on the question of racial egalitarianism—this is clearly inaccurate. So while this is possible as a reconstructive move, developing a usable theory for contemporary audiences, the aim of asserting that this was X's *actual* theory has been abandoned.

My claim is, then, that if we read these theorists and take their references to "men" or "persons" in a race-neutral way, we will in fact be misrepresenting them and distorting their theoretical intentions. Since this is exactly what has been done by generations of commentators, and continues to be routinely done today, it means that in crucial respects we have a fictive picture of the content and significance of modern Western moral and political philosophy. The deployment of my "revisionist" vocabulary—in scare quotes, since I am claiming that this is just a formalization of what these philosophers actually thought—then makes explicit what they were really arguing for.

The Symbiosis of Racism and Egalitarianism in Four Modern Philosophies

I now want to turn to the concrete illustration of what I am contending is this symbiotic relationship in the work of Hobbes, Locke, Kant, and Mill. The discussion of each will necessarily be brief, but the virtue of analyzing all four is that most of the main tendencies in modern Western liberal political theory are covered: contractarian versus utilitarian liberalism; realist versus moralist accounts; and autonomist versus proprietarian views of the self. (A similar analysis could be done of Hume, Hegel, and Marx, and would, I claim, produce comparable results, though there is no space to undertake this in an already overlong essay.) These four thinkers are all regarded within the discipline of philosophy as crucial spokesmen for Enlightenment modernity, and, in somewhat different ways, for equality. What we need to examine is how the traditional account of their views needs to be modified once we recognize that a dichotomized logic, whether explicit or implicit, can be argued to be at work in their texts, and that the same egalitarian rules which specify one set of norms and a certain history and prognosis for persons specify a different set of rules and a different history and prognosis for subpersons. Moreover, since moral equality is at the normative heart of the liberal-democratic polity (Hobbes is, of course, not really a liberal), and the normative theorization of it, ramifying through the legislative branch and the functioning of the state, a moral *in*equality will be similarly all-encompassing in its practical and theoretical ramifications. So to repeat my earlier point: It is not just a matter of demonstrating that these *theorists* were racists, which by now is presumably no longer that controversial a contention, but of demonstrating what continues to be resisted by establishment commentators, that their *theories* were racist.

Hobbes

Let us begin with Hobbes, who represents the realist position in contractarianism and political theory more generally. As Will Kymlicka points out, there are two strains within the social contract tradition, one that takes people to have an independent moral standing aside from the contract and one that derives people's moral standing from conventional agreement and comparative threat advantage (see Kymlicka, "The Social Contract Tradition"). Hobbes is, of course, the famous exponent of the latter approach. But though people's moral status is derivative rather than foundational for Hobbes, it turns out, nonetheless, to be the same, that is—ostensibly—equal. Moreover, this egalitarianism, though based on factual realities rather than original parity of moral status, is absolutely pivotal to the text. Thus in the famous thirteenth chapter of *Leviathan*, which has been the subject of so much secondary literature, Hobbes begins by stating that, "Nature hath made men so equall, in the faculties of body, and mind," that nobody so physically dominates others that he cannot be killed, if necessary "by confederacy with others," while mentally, the equality is even greater, since "Prudence, is but Experience; which equall time, equally bestowes on all men, in those things they equally apply themselves unto" (*Leviathan* 86–87). Similarly, in the earlier *De Cive* (*On the Citizen*), he asserts that "therefore all men are equal to each other by nature. Our actual inequality has been introduced by civil law" (26). So Hobbes, no less than the other theorists, is (apparently) an egalitarian, and the anti-Aristotelianism that permeates *Leviathan* manifests itself here in his opposition to the claim that "Master and Servant were not introduced by consent of men, but by difference of Wit." Against any notions of natural Aristotelian hierarchy, then, Hobbes emphasizes in his "ninth law of Nature" (the conventionally agreed-upon norms that are to govern the society) "*that every man acknowledge other for his Equall by Nature*" (*Leviathan* 107; italics in original). So from this equality springs both the threat of the state of war and the potential for avoiding it, since the rational agent will eventually realize that a policy of constrained maximization of interests is the best long-range strategy for promoting his welfare. Hence the rationally mandated covenant to transfer the Right of Nature to the sovereign, and to agree upon laws of nature which will bind all and hence benefit all.

And yet the text seems to contradict itself, both upon the literalness of the bellicose state of nature and the equality of the "men" within it. In reply to the question of whether there really ever was "such a time [or] condition of warre as this," Hobbes says, "I believe it was never generally so, over all the world." Yet he then goes on to add the qualifier, "but there are many places, where they live so now": "For the savage people in many places of *America,* except the government of small Families, the concord whereof dependeth on naturall lust, have no government at all; and live at this day in that brutish manner, as I said before" (*Leviathan* 89).

As a result of this textual ambiguity, the Hobbesian state of nature has been judged by some to be hypothetical and by others to be actual. One well-known Hobbes scholar, Bernard Gert, asserts flatly that Hobbes "shows that he knew that no person was ever actually in the state of nature" (167), while Macpherson says, "Civilized men would see the need to get out of this condition [the state of nature]. Hobbes knows that they never have been in it: savage peoples he believes are in it, but civilized people only approximate to it in times of civil war" (Introduction to *Leviathan* 41).

Now, as I have argued elsewhere (*Racial Contract*), the simple resolution of the puzzle is to recognize, as Macpherson does, that for Hobbes "men" need to be subdivided into two categories, the civilized and the savage. Hobbes's generalization in the next paragraph—that "there had never been any time, wherein particular men were in a condition of warre one against another"—contradicts what he has just said only if *men* is read inclusively. Once it is recognized that he is talking, in effect, about "civilized" men here (though without a developed concept of race), the mystery vanishes.[8] And so does the illusion of a race-neutral equality. In this one sentence—so easy to read through, to pass by, to ignore, in the huge text of *Leviathan*—I suggest, we have the statement of the *non*universality of Hobbes's vaunted egalitarianism. Even were this sentence isolated in the Hobbesian corpus, it would suffice to show that Hobbes was not really talking, at the beginning of chapter thirteen, about *all* men. And in fact, as Richard Ashcraft pointed out more than thirty years ago, in an essay that needs to be rediscovered by contemporary philosophers working on race, the reference is not singular. Hobbes makes similar claims in *De Cive* and *De Corpore Politico:* Ashcraft comments, "Clearly, Hobbes' definition of the state of nature was explicitly intended by him to be associated with the 'brutish' and 'savage' life of the Indians" (153–54).

What are the implications of what Hobbes is saying? We have *just* been told a few paragraphs earlier that all men are roughly equal in their abilities, particularly their cognitive ones. We have *just* been told that all men will have had the experience, and hence the prudence, to learn from their history. And yet, without any seeming awareness of contradiction, Hobbes now casually cites Native Americans as men still in a state of nature, who have apparently *not* been able to take the necessary steps, and develop the "prudence," to leave it. The natural inference—how could it be any clearer?—is that *Native Americans do not have what it takes to leave the state of nature.* But since we saw at the beginning of the chapter that "all men" are roughly on a cognitive par, and since we know that "we" (we Europeans, we white people) *have* left the state of nature, the obvious conclusion is that, insofar as Native Americans are "men," they are men of a different and inferior sort—savages. So they deservedly occupy a category of their own: in my recommended vocabulary, they are "submen," or, updated for gender, "subpersons."

It is not, then, that we are being presented with an internally contradictory text, in which Hobbes takes back what he said only a few sentences before. (Think how implausible this would be. It is not that philosophers, even prominent ones, do not contradict themselves. But to contradict yourself not hundreds of pages later, but in the space of a paragraph?) Rather, we are being presented with a *consistent* text, in which Hobbes—the materialist theorist of humans as a particular kind of animal, whose book begins with chapters on various human cognitive functions—proceeds on the basis that claims made about, and rules generated on the basis of, entities having one kind of nature will naturally have to be modified for entities having *another* kind of nature. For this is not the only citation of Native Americans in *Leviathan.* In the third part that hardly anybody reads, Hobbes, in his defense of absolutism, argues against those who "maintain, that there are no grounds, nor Principles of Reason, to sustain those essentiall Rights, which make Soveraignty absolute." Such people argue: "For if there were [such principles], they would have been found out in some place, or other; whereas we see, there has not hitherto been any Common-wealth, where those Rights have been acknowledged, or challenged. Wherein they argue as ill, as if the Savage people of America, should deny there were any grounds, or Principles of Reason, so to build a house, as to last as long as the materials, because they never yet saw any so well built" (*Leviathan* 232). The image is doing double, or even triple, duty. Native Americans' inability—as savages—to build long-lasting habitations is cited as concrete illustration of their incompetence, and their mistaken extrapolative induction from their own incompetence to the general impossibility of such houses illustrates their cognitive deficiencies. But in addition their unbuilt *mate-*

rial house also represents their inability to build—to conceive of, to go through the requisite train of reasoning and covenanting for—the *metaphorical* house of government. The only "government" they can create is the *sub*political one of the family, which requires only "natural lust," an "endeavour" we share with animals. Since Hobbes elsewhere distinguishes rational desires and emotional desires (see Gert), the natural inference is that Native Americans' deficiencies undermine their development of the former. But it is the former, "our long-term desires for real goods" (Gert 163), that ultimately propel us out of the state of nature.[9] So the distinctively human level of rationality required for creation of the political, and for departure from the state of nature, is not something Native Americans have. As Ashcraft points out, "men are not recognizably different from other animals by virtue of divine creation (which may leave them, as the 'savages of America,' still in the state of other animals, i.e. the state of war); they become different only because they themselves *create* a political society" (157).[10]

Once this fact is faced without evasion, it will be seen that it necessarily ramifies throughout the rest of Hobbes's text, even if Hobbes himself does not spell out the implications. (This is why it is a mistake to infer from the brevity of these passages to their insignificance.) The ahistorical, amnesiac reading backward into these books from present-day liberalism of an unqualified, race-independent category of colorless "men" or "persons" distorts authorial intent, gets what they're saying wrong, misrepresents their thought. *We* may be talking about people in general; *they* were not. Their humans—when all were seen as human—were divided into categories, with different conclusions about each group. *Leviathan* was famously thought of by Hobbes as constructed on the "geometric" Cartesian model of science, as a body of rigorous deductions from initial premises. Like one toppling domino at the start of a chain, then, this rereading should trigger a set of implications that necessarily transform our understanding of the text once we recognize that there are some humans who occupy a *different* category. The laws of nature, the legislation passed, the functioning of the sovereign, must then all be different when dealing with such humans, because these moral/juridical/political prescriptions and policies have all been predicated on equi-rationality and equality of threat advantage. If rationality is diminished, it becomes a different story. What are we—we who are smart enough to leave the state of nature—to do with those who are not?

In that same chapter where American savages are cited as poor house builders, Hobbes has a paragraph on colonialism. (It must be remembered that the Virginia Jamestown settlement had by then [1651] been in existence for several decades.) In order to prevent idleness at home, "the multitude of poor, and yet strong people still increasing, they are to be transplanted into Countries not sufficiently inhabited [the notion of emptiness and underpopulation was, of course, a standard colonial characterization of North America]: where neverthelesse, they are not to exterminate those they find there; but constrain them to inhabit closer together, and not range a great deal of ground, to snatch what they find; but to court each little Plot with art and labour, to give them their sustenance in due season" (*Leviathan* 239). This brief passage is fascinating for a number of reasons. To begin with, there is Hobbes's explicit antiexterminist injunction. Why should it even have been necessary to say this? What does it reveal about the views and practices of the times that it was even necessary to voice such a prohibition? And the answer, obviously, is that genocide *was* a real option, and had been carried out by the Spanish in Mexico and South America in the previous century, giving rise, through Bartolome las Casas's widely translated *Devastation of the Indies,* to *la leyenda negra,* the black legend, of Spanish atrocity (see Stannard, *American Holocaust*). Hobbes opposes genocide (though that "neverthelesse" would bear further examination), but, in a characterization that anticipates Locke, represents the Indians as nonsedentary nomads, hunters and gatherers, who must be taught European agriculture. (The machinery of forgetting is already in place—the fact that the Jamestown settlement survived only through Native American agricul-tural education and assistance to the starving and ignorant Englishmen is already being erased in European thought.) Moreover, they must be "constrained" to do this—Hobbes thus takes for granted that the implanted colonial government has legitimate power over them. What justifies this? Why is no detailed rationale given? The reason, I submit, is that the rationale is so obvious it does not even need to be spelled out. Savages, whose cognitive deficiency is proven by their inability to leave the state of nature, should not just be killed outright. But they do not have the right to continue to occupy valuable lands needed by European immigrants, whose state of nature was merely hypothetical, and who are now going to transform the *actual* American state of nature, thereby making possible industry, culture of the earth, navigation, building, transportation, knowledge of the earth, timekeeping, arts, letters, society, and ending the solitary, poor, nasty, brutish, and short lives of the natives (*Leviathan* 89).

Native American savages, then, must be forced into a relationship of some kind with the civilized polity, and not killed. So Hobbes is a comparative liberal. But insofar as a certain ground-floor level of rationality, and the need to control one's impulses on a day-to-day basis, is essential to one's functioning as a good citizen, it becomes questionable how successful such an incorporation will be for those whose rationality is inferior and who cannot learn from experience. Unable to participate equally in the building of the house of the Commonwealth, they may pose a standing threat to its security and survival as reluctant neighbors or coerced residents. Given the ruthlessness of the Hobbesian absolutist state toward its *own* citizens when they transgress the rules, does it seem unreasonable to argue that in consistency, the job of Leviathan may be the elimination of those threatening, by their very presence, a return to the state of nature? Remember that for Hobbes the bottom line is prevention of the worst possible alternative, the fall back into the state of war, whether civil war or "that dissolute condition of masterlesse men, without subjection to Lawes" (*Leviathan* 128) and here we have a whole group of humanoids who, by their very nature, live in that savage way, and have difficulty recognizing the rules in the first place.

At the very least, then, Hobbes justifies colonial encroachment on and expropriation of native lands. And if he balks at genocide, it may be only provisional. Native Americans are represented as inferior beings, subpersons, and thus a standing threat to the civilized polity. Ashcraft goes on to point out that the impact of Hobbes's book was to shape English perceptions of Native Americans for centuries to come. If *Leviathan*'s recommended absolutism had no influence on internal political policy in the Western states themselves—as commonly pointed out, it functions more as a provocation, a challenge to be refuted in political theory (like skepticism in epistemology), than a guidebook—it *did* have a major influence on what we need to start thinking of as the *other*, unacknowledged "external" polity of European domination of the non-European world, of global white supremacy. The opposition of European civilization and native savagery, which would be a central rationale of the colonial and later imperial enterprise, was not invented by Hobbes, but his work would constitute one of its most powerful and long-lasting formulations.

Locke

We turn now to John Locke. Unlike Hobbes the absolutist, Locke is central to the liberal-democratic mainstream: the celebrated Whig champion of property rights, limited government, parliamentarianism, and the right to revolt against despotic rule. Whereas Hobbes's (putative) moral egalitarianism is conventionalist, derivatively based on equal human capacities to threaten one another, Locke's is foundational. As he states in the "Second Treatise": "To understand Political Power right, and derive it from its Original, we must consider what State all Men are naturally in, and that is, a *State of perfect Freedom* to order their Actions. . . . A *State* also *of Equality*, wherein all the Power and Jurisdiction is reciprocal, no one having more than another" (269). Thus he is the spokesman for a principled opposition to the ascriptive hierarchy of Sir Robert Filmer's Tory patriarchalism (*Patriarcha*). Property is the normative concept most central to Locke's universe, being used to denote both legitimate possessions and rights. We own ourselves; we own our bodies and our labor; we appropriate the world by mixing our labor with nature; and others are duty-bound to respect our property rights and our rights as our private "property."

But if Locke is the theoretical champion of proprietarian liberalism, he is also, as James Tully reminds us, a *colonial* theorist, though in political philosophy this connection is usually ignored. He "was one of the six or eight men who closely invigilated and helped to shape the old colonial system during the Restoration," played a policymaking role in the Carolina government (including taking a hand in writing their 1669 *Fundamental Constitution*), and had investments in the slave-trading Royal Africa Company (Tully 168). Thus Locke's theoretical and practical writings directly concerned two groups of nonwhites, Native Americans and Africans. And in both cases, it can be argued—though admittedly more controversially in the second case—it is clear that they could not have counted as equal "persons" for him.

NATIVE AMERICAN   The Native American case is clear-cut (but for a defense of Locke, see Uzgalis, "Inconsistency"), and, as Tully points out, is the subject of a huge body of literature outside philosophy. Like Hobbes, Locke characterizes Native Americans as still being in the state of nature, though a late stage. Since Locke's state of nature, unlike Hobbes's, is not intrinsically warlike, this is less of an indictment for Locke than it is for the earlier theorist. But it does, nonetheless, inevitably say something about their development: These are not people who have reached the stage of instituting the commonwealth, civil society. As Tully comments, "Amerindian political organization is disregarded . . . thereby dispossessing Amerindian governments of their authority and nationhood and permitting Europeans to deal with them and punish them on an individual basis" (178).

Moreover, their activities *in* the state of nature also leave much to be desired. God may have given the world to "mankind in common," but in the light of the divine imperative to earn a living by the sweat of your brow, he gave it preeminently to "the Industrious and Rational." Indeed, these are virtually "co-implicative," since reason is demonstrated by the recognition of natural law, and natural law mandates that we appropriate the world through mixing our labor with it. The "freedom" in the state of nature, then, is not *license,* but constrained by obligations of various kinds, among which is economic productivity.

Now Locke believes not merely in the labor theory of property, but, as with most of the British political economists, the labor theory of value. He says that 90 percent, or perhaps even 99 percent, of the value of manufactured goods comes from labor; their natural base is worth only a tiny fraction of the final total. So refusal to mix one's labor with nature, or doing so in a desultory way, leaves the world far less valuable than, counterfactually, it *could* be if such mixing were taking place. Insofar as Native Americans are negligent on this score, then, they are falling short of their natural-law duty to improve the world and add value to it. Moreover, since they are singled out as a *group*—it is not a matter of *some* Native Americans being stigmatized, but the group as a whole—this is a general characteristic of them. Locke's proviso forbids an appropriation of the world that results in "enough and as good" not being left for others, and "waste and spoilage" resulting. The usual examples cited are attempts to monopolize some natural good, for example, the only water source for miles around, and the wasteful nonconsumption of actually appropriated goods, for example rotting deer carcasses, baskets of putrid apples, and the like. But equally important, arguably, are examples of incompetent or inefficient appropriation that do not add enough value to leave "enough and as good" for others, while—through the blocking of the superior methods of the more "industrious and rational"—generating "waste and spoilage" of *counterfactual, potential* goods: the virtual goods that could have been produced, but cannot now be. In other words, if a given plot of land could generate 100V of value if efficiently utilized, and because of Native Americans' (putatively) inferior techniques, only 1V has been generated, then 99V of potential value has been wasted.

The Lockean injunction to appropriate the world thus leads naturally to the *ex*propriation of those in occupation of certain sectors of the world who are not making proper use of it. What seems like a theory of general application to *all* peoples, with uniform colorless norms and prescriptions, turns out to have sharply differentiated consequences for *some* people. But mainstream philosophy does not highlight this distinction. Tully comments, "The fact that the chapter (ch. 5: 'On Property') is organized around a contrast between Europe, where appropriation without consent is not permitted because political societies exist, and America, where appropriation without consent is permitted because it is a state of nature, is rarely mentioned. That the argument justifies European settlement in America without the consent of the native people, one of the most contentious and important events of the seventeenth century and one of the formative events of the modern world, is normally passed over in silence" (173). In effect, then, Native Americans, by virtue of their deficient appropriation, lose the moral status of equality that the opening chapters announce all people to have. And again, I would claim, this should not be seen as an inconsistency, but a corollary of their subpersonhood. Locke provides us with a normative theory of what is required of persons as self-owning proprietors, and the efficient, value-adding appropriation of the world is one of the key prerequisites. Insofar as Native Americans fall short of these requirements, they can legitimately be treated as less than full persons. And in fact the Lockean argument, directly, or somewhat modified, would become the central justification for displacing native peoples in North America, Australia, and parts of Africa. The land was deemed "vacant," *terra nullius, vacuum domicilium*, consistent with a moral/juridical doctrine that denies personhood to certain kinds of humans.

AFRICANS   The more controversial case is African slavery, because here one has not a developed textual rationale whose implications have been ignored by philosophers, but a textual silence, or a seeming inconsistency with the actual text. In *Two Treatises of Government*, Locke opposes slavery except under tightly specified conditions: that it must come about through a just war, for example, the enslavement of the defeated prosecutors of a war of aggression, and it must not extend to the hereditary enslavement of wives and children (see Locke, *Second Treatise*, chapter 16, "On Conquest"). Clearly, the Atlantic slave trade massively violated both these stipulations. Yet, as noted, Locke himself had earlier had investments in the slave trade, and either wrote, or had a large hand in writing, the Carolina Constitution, which enshrined hereditary slavery.

How is this apparent inconsistency to be explained? There is a large literature on the subject, which Wayne Glausser, in a survey article from fifteen years ago, divided into three main categories: (1) Locke's participation in slavery as "a deviation from his theory," "an unfortunate but minor lapse"; (2) Locke's participation as justified by a "tortured logic"; (3) Locke's participation as "part of the fabric of Lockean philosophy, however embarrassing that might be for modern admirers of one of the founding liberals" (199).[11]

As one would expect, I am most sympathetic to the third alternative. A "deviation" so great is hardly plausible (and would, of course, not remotely be "minor"), especially since, as Jennifer Welchman points out in an article, Locke was intimately familiar with the details of American slavery, since "most of the correspondence conducted by the Council [of Trade and Plantations] passed over Locke's desk" (72). The logic of the second set of theories is indeed tortured, requiring, for example, that Locke seriously believe the captured Africans were themselves the aggressors; moreover, it would not explain his countenancing of hereditary slavery. The third set includes different variants, one being the representation of Locke as a "bourgeois theorist" for whom "protections against enslavement are less fundamental . . . than provisions for capitalist growth" (Glausser 211). But this seems to me to underestimate the role of morality, even in the degraded role of moral rationalization. Bourgeois theorists no less than other theorists need to feel morally in the right about what they are doing, and it is difficult to believe that such inconsistency with Locke's own liberal principles (if conceived of as universalist and race-neutral) could simply have been ignored by Locke. No less orthodox a Marxist than Friedrich Engels argued that, even for bourgeois law, "in a modern state, law must not only correspond to the general economic condition and be its expression, but must also be an *internally coherent* expression, which does not, owing to inner contradictions, reduce itself to nought" (Tucker 762–63), and I would suggest that this holds true for bourgeois morality also.

So the explanation in terms of racism (the other variant of the third group), which, for one reason or another, would exclude blacks as inferior humans from the *Second Treatise* prohibitions, seems most convincing to me, though admittedly there is no smoking gun. (And indeed, in a recent article ["The Same Tyrannical Principle"], one of Locke's stoutest defenders, William Uzgalis, goes so far as to argue that the *Second Treatise* was intended in part as a *condemnation* of African slavery.) Jennifer Welchman has developed an ingenious argument linking the African case to the Native American case, which has the virtue of not multiplying theories needlessly. She contends that sub-Saharan Africa no less than North America was seen as a state of nature by Locke, and people's natural rights in the state of nature can be lost by inappropriate behavior. Because of their tolerance of tribal warfare, "each [African] tribe violated their duty to act for their own and others' preservation and thus forefeited their natural rights." Moreover, she thinks this move has the resources to explain his endorsement of the enslavement of children, since "once slavery exists it is no longer the case that human beings subsequently born are all 'creatures of the same species and rank. . . .' Henceforth they are born as members of one *species* but two *ranks,* right-bearing human persons and non-right-bearing human property. The term 'man' no longer denotes any human being, but only those human beings who are persons. Children born to non-persons are neither the children of men nor entitled to claim rights natural to men" (Welchman 80). Obviously, this distinction, and these conceptual moves, would fit perfectly with my own analysis. The controversy can by no means be regarded as settled, of course—the scholarly verdict is still unrendered. But I would claim that in the absence of overtly damning texts, inference to the best explanation is the required interpretive technique, and by comparison with Glausser's other two alternatives, the category of a subperson—whether through natural initial exclusion from a humanity defined as white, or through disqualifying behavior in the state of nature—provides the most elegant solution to the problem.

Kant

We come now to the crucial case of Kant.[12] In a sense, Kant is perfect for my thesis, because of the combination of his absolute centrality (with the rise to hegemony of "deontological liberalism") to contemporary moral and political theory and the detailed explicitness of his writings on race. Within my revisionist framework, far from its being a terrible irony, or a shocking contradiction, that the theorist sometimes honored with the status of the father of modern moral theory is now also being credited as the father of modern racism, it is wonderfully *appropriate,* a perfect *vindication* of my claims. For in my framework of "symbiosis" rather than "anomaly," it is only fitting that the philosopher who provides the richest account of personhood for the Age of Egalitarianism should also provide the richest account of subpersonhood for what is also the Age of Global White Supremacy. Once the conventional framework is inverted, and the conceptual barriers breached, so that we start conceptualizing racism as an alternative normative system, which has in fact been the *real* normative system, then what would originally have seemed oxymoronic suddenly becomes pleonastic. If personhood is raced, then *of course* there will be a different set of rules for persons and for subpersons. What else would one, in consistency, expect?

Kant's reputational commitment to moral egalitarianism is presumably so celebrated as to need no extensive gloss. As Roger Sullivan writes, "Kant's is an ethics of the people, of moral egalitarianism. . . . Respect is an attitude due equally to *every* person, *simply* because each is a person, a rational being capable of moral self-determination" (197). We see here the ambiguity I have tried to expose in the term *person.* If *person* is already tacitly morally normed, then as a statement of Kant's views (or anybody's), this is tautologous ("Respect is an attitude due equally to every human who deserves equal respect"); but if *person* just means "human," it becomes far more questionable, and, I would in fact say, as a statement of Kant's own position, simply false. Feminists have long argued that the use of generic, gender-neutral language in discussing Western philosophers' moral/political views is misleading, and in the case of Kant, this judgment seems particularly true. Consider Hannelore Schröder's blistering indictment of the implications of Kant's assumption of natural female inequality:

> These irrational, yet for Kant self-evident premises, serve him as a basis for the legitimation of two quite different relations. First, relations of "Mensch zu Mensch," which must be translated here as male to male [I would, of course, substitute "white male"], where contractual relations are based on freedom, equality, and reciprocity, through which only males are persons and citizens. Second, relations between these patriarchal citizens and their subjected women (noncitizens). The men are at the same time lord and master over reified female human beings (*verdinglichte Menschen*) where legal relations are based on total lack of freedom and lack of rights securing the injustice of male dominance imposed on women whom God and Nature wish to see, once and for all, as nonpersons and noncitizens. . . . So this is the legal double status of women as object and yet as person, which is completely illogical and self-contradictory. . . . So Kant gets entangled in a chaos of self-contradictions. Claims he makes in one sentence are contradicted in the next. . . . Women are both things and persons. . . . Such beings have no end of their own. So he reduces half of the human population as means to the ends of his sex. This is taking his categorical imperative *ad absurdum,* canceling it himself. (285, 287, 294, 296)

I would claim that this argument goes through even more forcefully and dramatically for race, since people of color do not even have the functional status within the white household—albeit a secondary status—that white women have, so they can die off (not an abstract possibility by any means, as we will see below) without disrupting (indeed, perhaps, facilitating?!) the functioning of the white polity. Unlike the case of Locke, Kant's racism is explicit, needing no inferential reconstruction. Moreover, it is not a matter of a few incidental remarks but a full-blown and elaborate theory. Emmanuel Eze's important essay ("Color of Reason") of a few years ago brought to a North American philosophical audience the shocking news—shocking only to philosophers, since it had long been known by historians and anthropologists—that Kant was one of the central figures in the birth of scientific racism. In fact, Robert Bernasconi suggests that "if any one person should be recognized as the author of the first theory of race worthy of the name, it should be the German philosopher Immanuel Kant" (Bernasconi, "Who Invented," 14), discounting the claims of more familiar candidates such as Carolus Linnaeus, George-Louis Buffon, and Johann Friedrich Blumenbach. Kant's lectures and writings on anthropology and physical geography (usually ignored by philosophers) provide a detailed account of a racialized human nature classified into four categories—white Europeans, yellow Asians, black Africans, red Amerindians—who are hierarchically related to one another.

Eze summarizes Kant's conclusions. These peoples, these races, are all human, but human nature is mere raw material. The task of humanity is to develop "moral nature, or rational character, which constitutes humanity proper." And it turns out that not all peoples, not all races, are equally up to the task: Non-European "people lack the capacity for development of 'character,' and they lack character presumably because they lack adequate self-consciousness and rational will. . . . [The Amerindian], the African, and the Hindu appear to be incapable of moral maturity" (Eze, "Color of Reason," 114–15). Why is this? Eze quotes Kant:

> The race of the [Amerindian] cannot be educated. It has no motivating force, for it lacks affect and passion. . . . The race of the Negroes . . . can be educated but only as servants (slaves), that is they allow themselves to be trained. [Eze points out that, from what Kant says elsewhere, it is clear that "training" means physical punishment, flogging with a split bamboo cane, which will be more effective than a whip in causing the Negro the requisite degree of pain.]. . . . [The Hindus] can be educated to the highest degree but only in the arts and not in the sciences. They can never achieve the level of abstract concepts. . . . The Hindus always stay the way they are, they can never advance, although they began their education much earlier. (Eze, "Color of Reason," 116–17)

As Eze concludes: "It is, therefore, rather predictable that the only 'race' Kant recognizes as not only educable but capable of *progress* in the educational process of the arts and sciences is the 'white' Europeans. In an important single sentence, Kant states: 'The white race possesses *all* motivating forces and talents *in itself.* . . .' For Kant, then, skin color encodes and codifies the 'natural' human capacity for reason and rational talents" (Eze, "Color of Reason," 117–19).

The point made earlier that *humanity* is not sufficient for full *personhood* is thus made explicit here. As feminists have claimed with gender, I would suggest that it is ludicrous, given this characterization of nonwhites (particularly Native Americans and blacks), to think that they could be full persons in a Kantian theory. How could the morally ineducable (Native Americans), the natural slave (Africans), be anything but subpersons, especially in a theory for which autonomy is the central notion? Insofar as "personhood" has implications for moral standing, juridico-political treatment, and location in a theory of history, how could humans with these traits be covered by the same set of normative rules as whites? Obviously—I would claim—Kant's theory, not just his ethics, but his normative political theory, his cosmopolitanism, and his theory of history, must all be color coded. Yet this conclusion has been tacitly denied by generations of past commentators who have written as if "person" is race-neutral and is now overtly denied by those contemporary commentators who erect a conceptual wall between his now-impossible-to-deny racism and his theory.

Allen Wood's recent book, *Kant's Ethical Thought,* for example, begins by saying that "Kant's views about gender and race offend us not merely because we now see them as false . . . but rather because we see them as demeaning to the *human dignity* of women and nonwhites." But he goes on to insist that "the most influential philosophical articulation of these values is Kant's theory of moral autonomy, grounded in the dignity of humanity as an end in itself" and claims that Kant "conspicuously declines to infer from [his] racialist beliefs . . . that there is any difference in the human rights possessed by different peoples" (Wood 5, 7). Similarly, Louden's *Kant's Impure Ethics* draws a contrast between Kant's *theory* and Kant's *prejudices,* denying that the latter should be taken to modify (what we think of as) the former: "Kant's writings do exhibit many private prejudices and contradictory tendencies. . . . But Kant's theory is fortunately stronger than his prejudices, and it is the theory on which philosophers should focus. We should not hide or suppress the prejudices, but neither should we overvalue them or try to inflate them into something they are not. . . . The prejudices are not centrally connected to the defining features of his theory of human moral development" (105, 177).

I would argue that these commentators are guilty of the question-begging dichotomization earlier discussed, in which the Theory is held aloft from contamination by vulgar (and *sub*theoretical) prejudice, when in fact the racism is part of the Theory, and this can be ignored only by reading its terms in a race-neutral way that is controverted by Kant's other writings. Wood cites as evidence of Kant's racially inclusive vision of human rights that he condemned slavery and European colonialism. But in fact, Bernasconi ("Kant As an Unfamiliar") argues in another connection (not in reply to Wood) that he condemns only the *cruelties* of slavery—that split bamboo cane presumably doesn't count, just a standard instructional tool—while he never condemns the institution itself. And indeed if you believe that some people are natural slaves—"Americans and Blacks cannot govern themselves. They thus serve only for slaves" (qtd. in Bernasconi, "Kant As an Unfamiliar," 152)—what other vocational training is possible for them? How could people incapable of self-government have the full panoply of rights of full, self-governing persons? Similarly, Bernasconi argues that Kant is really against the more vicious forms of colonialism, not colonialism as a practice (Bernasconi, "Kant As an Unfamiliar"). And in his recent book, *Achieving Our Humanity,* Eze suggests that a principled condemnation of colonialism as such is not available to Kant, given his theoretical commitments, since Europeans are governed by law while non-Europeans still exist in the state of nature (see chapter 3, 77–111). So whereas Wood chooses to place greater theoretical weight on the apparent condemnations, a case can be made for the reverse: that in adjudicating which position should "give way" in seemingly contradictory writings, it is the elaborated theory of racial inferiority (which is, of course, denied the status *of* a theory by Wood) that should be taken to trump such passages.

Finally, Kant's vision of the ultimate destiny of the globe has not been sufficiently publicized. Kant had no fear of a black, or any other kind of nonwhite, planet, since it turns out that "all races will be extinguished . . . only not that of the whites" (qtd. in Bernasconi, "Kant As an Unfamiliar," 159). Kant does not shed any tears over this prognosis—if he does not condone it, he does not condemn or deplore it either—since history is made only by whites, so that history will go on regardless. But he does not go into detail about how he expects this extinction to come about. The theory of "dying races" was put forward and extensively discussed in the nineteenth century, in both pre- and post-Darwinian versions. Patrick Brantlinger points out that it provided a convenient obfuscation of genocidal policies; the obvious reasons for which, say, Native Americans or Native Australians were "dying out"—that they were being *killed* both directly and indirectly!—were mystified into an intrinsic biological weakness, an inability to compete. So this is an interesting eighteenth-century anticipation of what would later become a routinely discussed possibility. If, as Mark Larrimore has suggested, Kant regarded nonwhite races as an example of natural "waste," then such a development could arguably be seen as positive. But whatever the ultimate judgment on this particular question, I think it should be clear that considerable strain is involved in concluding that Kant's (presanitized) theory can accommodate equal treatment for nonwhites. As with Locke, the final scholarly jury is still out, requiring a comprehensive analysis of the racial writings. But I suggest that here also the result will be that people of color turn out to be not *Menschen,* but *Untermenschen.*

Mill

We conclude by leaving the contractarian tradition and considering John Stuart Mill. The standard critique of consequentialist liberalism for decades has been, in Rawls's famous words, that "Utilitarianism does not take seriously the distinction between persons," so that, unlike deontological, rights-based liberalism, individuals' rights are subject to the calculus of welfare maximization (Rawls 27). So personhood, it is claimed, is not as securely and foundationally lodged in the normative apparatus of the theory as with the contractarians. But utilitarians would, of course, challenge this characterization, and in any case Mill's *On Liberty* is unquestionably a great paean to individual self-realization.

Yet there are those lines in chapter 1 right after the statement of the harm principle where, after insisting on the individual's "absolute" independence and "sovereignty" over matters concerning himself, Mill casually and offhandedly asserts that "this doctrine is meant to apply only to human beings in the maturity of their faculties," not children, those "still in a state to require being taken care of by others," nor, for the same reason, "those backward states of society in which the race itself may be considered as in its nonage": "Despotism is a legitimate mode of government in dealing with barbarians, provided the end be their improvement, and the means justified by actually effecting that end. Liberty, as a principle, has no application to any state of things anterior to the time when mankind have become capable of being improved by free and equal discussion" (*On Liberty* 13–14).

So easy to read through and miss the significance of—as generations of liberal-arts students throughout the Western world studying this universally assigned text have doubtless done—unless, as noted, you have a background theory contextualizing Mill's remarks and showing that they are *not* casual and offhand after all. No less than with his contractarian fellow-liberals, Mill's "individuals" are not "humans" *simpliciter,* but racially divided, with different rules applying to different subsets. As several recent commentators have reminded us—Mehta, Parekh, Souffrant—Mill the famous liberal and champion of individual liberty was also Mill the employee of the East India Company. He was a colonial official and a theorist of colonial rule, who never intended his domestic pronouncements to be extended without qualification to the colonies. But as with Locke and Kant, Western commentators who have noticed these remarks have generally framed them in the language of "inconsistencies" and "anomalies." In a recent book, Souffrant characterizes such accounts as "aberration theories," since they claim that "Mill's work on intervention and his tacit support of the colonization of one group by another are inconsistent with his overall philosophy" (5). By contrast, Souffrant insists

> Mill's Utilitarianism does not contradict his interventionist posture in international affairs. . . . [H]e would permit the qualified intervention of a more civilized group in the affairs of uncivilized others. . . . Advocates of the second aberration theory [Souffrant identifies several varieties] assume that Mill's ban against encroachment is universal and that it applies to the international environment as well as the domestic. But in Mill's eyes, the immature [such as barbarians] are exempt from the protection of the principle of liberty and open to intervention . . . [W]hen Mill speaks of individuality, he is referring to an attribute of mature individuals, human beings who have been brought up within the confines of particular societies. Mature individuals enjoy having had a formative period contributing to their maturity. . . . He believes furthermore that in his time individuality is an attribute exclusive to the European nations. (5–6, 8, 54–55)

As we have seen before, then, there is an anthropology underlying seemingly transparent and straightforward claims about "humans" or "individuals," which either overtly or in effect racializes the criteria for full enjoyment of personhood. Mehta comments that the obvious contrasts between Lockean and utilitarian liberalism should not blind us to the common "anthropological basis of [their] universalistic claims" (48, n. 2). Mill's theory makes it possible to reconcile liberalism at home and in the white settler states with despotism abroad in the nonwhite colonies, because of the different levels of maturity of the respective populations. India as a civilization is "infantilized," seen as analogous to a child that is not ready to direct its own affairs. So the justifiable lack of freedom is both individual and national, micro and macro; as with the other theorists, normative inegalitarianism for individuals has ramifications on the political level. As Mehta points out, Mill's comments in *On Liberty* have their larger echo in a chapter in *Considerations on Representative Government,* "a revealing document on the increasing relevance of cultural, civilizational, linguistic, and racial categories in defining the constituency of Mill's liberalism":

> Mill . . . divides colonized countries into two classes. The first of these classes is composed of countries "of similar civilization to the ruling country; capable of and ripe for representative government: such as the British possessions in America and Australia" [in other words, white settler states]. The other class includes "others, like India, [that] are still at a great distance from that state." Mill goes on to celebrate England's realization that countries in the first class must be the beneficiaries of "the true principle of government," namely representative government. . . . Regarding the second class of countries—countries with a population whose civilization, culture, language, and race were different from the British—Mill's attitude is strikingly different and his recommendations correspondingly so. Not only is Mill opposed to dismembering colonialism, he is equally opposed to these countries['] being internally democratic. . . . He goes on: "Such is the ideal rule of a free people over a barbarous or semi-barbarous one." (70–71)

Thus Mehta concludes, with Souffrant, that there is no "inconsistency" or "aberration" here: Rather, "it is by reference to utility that Mill comes to the view that representative institutions are appropriate for Europe and its predominantly white colonies and not for the rest of the world. *The bracketing of India, among others, is not therefore the mark of an embarrassing theoretical inconsistency,* precisely because at the theoretical level, the commitment to representative institutions is subsequent, and not prevenient, to considerations of utility" (73, my emphasis). In effect, "under conditions of backwardness or for children, the principle of liberty would sanction behavior that would be contrary to utility maximization. Under such conditions alternative norms are required to remain consistent with the progress associated with utility" (Mehta 99). What I have characterized, following the political science literature on race, as "anomaly" theories of racism are thus as mistaken at the more abstract level of political philosophy as they are in political science; rather, a "symbiosis" analysis is the appropriate one.

So we get Mill wrong if we treat his "individuals" as colorless, and his consequentialist principles as applying in the same way to all adult humans. Mill's praiseworthy progressiveness on gender did not extend to race. His defense of freedom in the white world becomes a defense of despotism for people of color in the colonies, not because—the deontological versus utilitarian debate—"person" is subject to welfare maximization but, more fundamentally (in the sense of a premise common to *both* sides of the liberal debate), because he did not see people of color as full persons in the first place. He shared with his theoretical adversaries a vision of nonwhites as humans not fully human, not fully mature and capable of directing themselves. Both on the individual and on the political level, nonwhites were in effect subpersons for him.

* * *

By looking at these four theorists, then, I believe I have shown—admittedly more controversially in some cases than in others—how radically misleading orthodox philosophical narratives of modernity are. The vaunted egalitarianism of the modern world is really color coded, reserved for whites. Humanness is not presumptively sufficient for personhood but requires additional achievements. Whether because of inability to do long-term prudential calculations, inferior and inefficient appropriative skills, heteronomous exclusion from full moral educability, or mental immaturity, nonwhites are denied the status of full persons. Thus the wide differences between these theorists' versions of egalitarianism and liberalism (except Hobbes) masks a common commitment to European superiority and European domination. Insofar as our textbooks, encyclopedia summaries, journal articles, and classroom presentations continue to depict them as if they were arguing in a racially inclusive fashion, insofar as we continue to utilize the framework of "anomaly," "contradiction," and "inconsistency" in talking about their racism, we are fundamentally misrepresenting their thought and blinding ourselves both to the real architecture of their theories and the corresponding real architecture of the world their theories helped to bring about and rationalize. We are also endorsing a fictive moral/political topography. For taking the presumptive normative personhood of all humans, independent of race, as *already* accomplished—part of the moral/political territory—profoundly distorts the actual moral economy of the past few hundred years. The political struggles around race, conquest, slavery, imperialism, colonization, segregation; the battles for abolition, independence, self-government, equal rights, first-class citizenship; the movements of aboriginal peoples, slaves, colonial populations, black Americans, and other subordinated people of color; and the texts of all these movements, vanish into a conceptual abyss papered over by the seemingly minor, but actually tremendously question-begging, assumption that all humans are and have been acknowledged as equal persons. The formal recognition of the category of the subperson not only brings these embarrassing realities into the same discursive universe as mainstream Western political theory, but it overturns the sanitized and amnesiac assumptions of that universe by forcing the admission that—at its foundational origins, its modern genesis—*this category was its own*, that Western political theory's liberalism, humanism, and egalitarianism were all racialized: all white.

Notes

Different and (obviously) much shorter versions of this paper have been presented at various conferences. I would like to mention the following three in particular: First, the British Radical Philosophy Group's conference "Philosophy and Race," held at the Senate House, University of London, 6–7 November 1998. Second, the conference "Racism and the Challenges of Multiculturalism," organized by the philosophy department of Rhodes University, Grahamstown, South Africa, 25–27 June 1999, where it was presented as the opening plenary session. (I would like to thank the department in general and Thomas Martin in particular for the invitation, and to express my appreciation to the South African government's National Research Fund for financing my trip.) And third, the interdisciplinary conference "Race in the Humanities," sponsored by the University of Wisconsin–La Crosse, 15–17 November 2001, where it was one of the keynote addresses. (I would like to thank Jana Braziel and Joseph Young in particular for the invitation.)

1. See, for example, Babbitt and Campbell, eds., *Racism and Philosophy;* Boxill, ed., *Race and Racism;* Eze, ed., *Race and the Enlightenment;* Valls, ed., *Race and Racism in Modern Philosophy;* Ward and Lott, eds., *Philosophers on Race.*

2. For a discussion of the "anomaly" and "symbiosis" views, see Hochschild, *The New American Dilemma,* especially chapter 1.

3. The problem with the "multiple traditions" view is that it carries the connotation that these two "traditions" are, if not equally influential, at least roughly on a par with one another. One may also get the image of two traditions fighting it out and alternating in power. But both these pictures are quite misleading as characterizations of the American polity. It is not the case that periods of white supremacy have alternated in U.S. history with periods of nonracial power sharing that would make whites and nonwhites equal players. (When blacks were given some power, for example, during Reconstruction, whites continued to hold the reins.) Nor has it, until comparatively recently, been the case that periods where racist views were dominant have alternated with periods where antiracism has been dominant. Rather, throughout most of the history of the republic, most whites have held racist views.

So, if one tradition has been hegemonic throughout the period in question, only weakly challenged by the other, surely it is more accurate to represent this as symbiosis. In other words, for most whites there has been no tension between different "traditions," since liberalism has been racialized from the start, so that its values hold fully only for the white population.

4. The qualification is necessary because of a point of *dis*analogy between gender and race—that while there is only one subordinate gender, there are several subordinate nonwhite races, and their respective statuses may differ over time and from one theorist's writings to another's. So while blacks and Native Americans are fairly consistently seen as subpersons in racist theory, some Asians (Indians, Chinese) have on occasion been judged to be almost equal to whites.

5. See also Penny M. Von Eschen, *Race against Empire.*

6. For a critique of the analysis of racism in terms of personal prejudice, see Goldberg, *Racist Culture,* 90–116.

7. See Shelby's recent, very thorough discussion, "Ideology, Racism, and Critical Social Theory."

8. And though I am not saying he intended this reading, Gert's assertion also becomes true, since Amerindian savages are *not* persons.

9. See, for example, Hampton, *Hobbes and the Social Contract Tradition.*

10. As can be seen, I endorse Ashcraft's reading. For a contrary view, see Lott's important essay, "Patriarchy and Slavery in Hobbes's Political Philosophy." In this essay, Lott criticizes me for "racializing" (in *The Racial Contract*) the "dichotomy of 'savage' and 'civil'" in Hobbes, suggesting that Hobbes's use "was influenced more by his study of the classics" (71–72), and that his later reference (*Leviathan* 459) to the "ancient Philosophers" of India, Persia, Chaldaea, and Egypt contradicts my claim that he was committed to European superiority. Moreover, Lott argues, "According to Hobbes, although Native Americans are not philosophers, they have a basic capacity to reason" ("The Savages of America, are not without some good Morall sentences; also they have a little Arithmetick, to adde, and divide in Numbers not too great: but they are not therefore Philosophers": *Leviathan* 459). So the real problem is not their racial inferiority but the lack of the leisure time that would be afforded by civil society. I think Lott makes some good points here, and a more detailed reply will have to wait for another occasion. But briefly: (1) His gloss of my position on page 71 ("White men from civilized societies encounter nonwhite 'savages' who inhabit the state of nature") gives the misleading impression that in the passage referred to (*The Racial Contract* 13) I was implying that *all* nonwhites were to be characterized as savages in a state of nature, whereas on the same page I go on to differentiate the case of nonwhites conceded to be *in* societies, though inferior ones ("barbarians"). And in my discussion of Hobbes in the book (64–67), I do limit the discussion to the case of Native Americans as examples of nonwhite "savages," who would be in a separate category from the "philosophical" nonwhites he mentions. As emphasized above—see note 4—the status of various nonwhite races is not always the same. (I do concede, however, that on occasion in the book I make generalizations inconsistent with this differentiation.) (2) I would claim that when used about people in the *modern* period, "savage" *is* indeed either racialized, or at least a very close conceptual precursor to race. In her "English Ethnocentrism and the Idea of the Savage," Smedley points out (*Race in North America* 52–61) that the category first crystallized in mass English consciousness as a result of the sixteenth–seventeenth-century conflicts with the Irish, whom some theorists have seen as the first racialized group, "incapable of being civilized," "something less than human" (see, for example, Allen, *The Invention of the White Race*).

"To document and confirm the growing beliefs about the unsuitability of Irishmen for civilization, many of the Englishmen pointed to the experiences of the Spanish with New World natives. They cited Spanish practices of exterminating Indians . . . as justification for policies of killing Irish men, women, and children. . . . In the English collective consciousness, 'the savage' was thus a kind of composite of these streams of negative ideas and images. . . . The savage came to embody all of those repulsive characteristics that were contrary and opposed to English beliefs, habits, laws, and values. . . . [S]uch attitudes were more strongly felt by Englishmen and were instrumental in molding the [English] cognitive perceptions of other conquered peoples in the New World as well as later in the Middle East, India, Burma, South Asia, and Africa. They became important subthemes to the ideology of race and in the characterization of racial differences" (Smedley 61).

It seems to me difficult to believe that Hobbes would *not* have been strongly influenced by such perceptions and associations in his decision to use the term, and so I would question Lott's charge of overracialization (3). Finally, in response to Lott's claim that Hobbes sees Native Americans as different only because of "social development and environmental influences," not intrinsic inferiority, I would raise this simple challenge: Why, then, are they still in the state of nature? Why have they *not* developed a society that would give them the necessary leisure to become "philosophers"? The horrible "environment" of the state of war described in *Leviathan,* chapter 13, is the consequence of *human* behavior, not extra-human factors. Therefore, since all humans are (supposedly) equal, why have *these* particular humans not been able to pursue the prudential, natural law–mandated imperative to create a sovereign and end the state of war? They may have a "basic capacity to reason," but it would seem that it does not attain the minimum threshold necessary for leaving the state of nature. So I would suggest that Lott's reply only defers the question to another level.

11. My discussion below follows Glausser.

12. For a far more detailed statement of this argument, see my "Kant's *Untermenschen*" in Valls, ed., *Race and Racism in Modern Philosophy.*

Works Cited

Allen, Theodore W. *The Invention of the White Race.* Vol. 1. New York: Verso, 1994.

Ashcraft, Richard. "Leviathan Triumphant: Thomas Hobbes and the Politics of Wild Men." In *The Wild Man Within: An Image in Western Thought from the Renaissance to Romanticism,* edited by Edward Dudley and Maximillian E. Novak. Pittsburgh, Pa.: University of Pittsburgh Press, 1972. 141–81.

Babbitt, Susan E., and Sue Campbell, eds., *Racism and Philosophy.* Ithaca, N.Y.: Cornell University Press, 1999.

Baker, Lee D. *From Savage to Negro: Anthropology and the Construction of Race, 1896–1954.* Berkeley: University of California Press, 1998.

Bernasconi, Robert. "Kant As an Unfamiliar Source of Racism." In Julie K. Ward and Tommy L. Lott, eds., *Philosophers on Race: Critical Essays.* Malden, Mass.: Blackwell, 2002. 153–54.

———. "Who Invented the Concept of Race? Kant's Role in the Enlightenment Construction of Race." In Robert Bernasconi, ed., *Race.* Malden, Mass.: Blackwell, 2001. 11–36.

Boxill, Bernard, ed., *Race and Racism.* New York: Oxford, 2001.

Brantlinger, Patrick. "'Dying Races': Rationalizing Genocide in the Nineteenth Century." In Jan P. Nederveen Pieterse and Bhikhu Parekh, eds., *The Decolonization of Imagination: Culture, Knowledge, and Power.* London: Zed Books, 1995. 43–56.

Cocker, Mark. *Rivers of Blood, Rivers of Gold: Europe's Conflict with Tribal Peoples.* London: Jonathan Cape, 1998.

Du Bois, W. E. B. *The Souls of Black Folk.* New York: Signet Classic, 1969.

Dussel, Enrique. *The Invention of the Americas: Eclipse of "the Other" and the Myth of Modernity.* Trans. Michael D. Barber. New York: Continuum, 1995.

Engels, Friedrich. *The Marx-Engels Reader,* 2d ed. Edited by Robert C. Tucker. New York: W. W. Norton, 1978.

Eze, Emmanuel. *Achieving Our Humanity: The Idea of the Postracial Future.* New York: Routledge, 2001.

———. "The Color of Reason: The Idea of 'Race' in Kant's Anthropology." In Emmanuel Eze, ed., *Postcolonial African Philosophy: A Critical Reader.* Cambridge, Mass.: Blackwell, 1997. 103–40.

————, ed., *Race and the Enlightenment: A Reader.* Cambridge, Mass.: Blackwell, 1997.

Fanon, Frantz. *Black Skin, White Masks.* Trans. Charles Lam Markmann. New York: Grove Press, 1967.

Filmer, Sir Robert. *Patriarcha and Other Writings,* edited by Johann P. Sommerville. New York: Cambridge University Press, 1991.

Forsyth, Murray. "Hobbes's Contractarianism: A Comparative Analysis." In David Boucher and Paul Kelly, eds., *The Social Contract from Hobbes to Rawls.* New York: Routledge, 1994. 35–50.

Füredi, Frank. *The Silent War: Imperialism and the Changing Perception of Race.* New Brunswick, N.J.: Rutgers University Press, 1998.

Gert, Bernard. "Hobbes's Psychology." In Tom Sorell, ed., *The Cambridge Companion to Hobbes.* New York: Cambridge University Press, 1996. 157–74.

Glausser, Wayne. "Three Approaches to Locke and the Slave Trade." *Journal of the History of Ideas* 51 (1990): 199–216.

Goldberg, David Theo. *Racist Culture: Philosophy and the Politics of Meaning.* Cambridge, Mass.: Blackwell, 1993.

Hampton, Jean. *Hobbes and the Social Contract Tradition.* New York: Cambridge University Press, 1986.

Harris, Stewart. *It's Coming Yet . . . An Aboriginal Treaty within Australia between Australians.* Canberra, Austral.: Aboriginal Treaty Committee, 1979.

Hobbes, Thomas. *Leviathan.* Rev. stu. ed. Ed. Richard Tuck. New York: Cambridge University Press, 1996.

————. *On the Citizen,* edited and translated by Richard Tuck and Michael Silverthorne. New York: Cambridge University Press, 1998.

Hochschild, Jennifer L. *The New American Dilemma: Liberal Democracy and School Desegregation.* New Haven, Conn.: Yale University Press, 1984.

Jacobson, Matthew Frye. *Whiteness of a Different Color: European Immigrants and the Alchemy of Race.* Cambridge, Mass.: Harvard University Press, 1998.

James, C. L. R. *The Black Jacobins: Toussaint L'Ouverture and the San Domingo Revolution,* 2d ed. New York: Vintage, 1963.

Kleingeld, Pauline. "The Problematic Status of Gender-Neutral Language in the History of Philosophy: The Case of Kant." *Philosophical Forum* 25.2 (Winter 1993): 134–50.

Kymlicka, Will. *Contemporary Political Philosophy: An Introduction.* Oxford, Eng.: Clarendon Press, 1990.

————. "The Social Contract Tradition." In Peter Singer, ed., *A Companion to Ethics.* Malden, Mass.: Blackwell, 1991. 186–96.

Larrimore, Mark. "Sublime Waste: Kant on the Destiny of the 'Races.'" In Wilson, *Civilization and Oppression,* 99–125.

Locke, John. *Two Treatises of Government,* edited by Peter Laslett. New York: Cambridge University Press, 1988.

Lott, Tommy. "Patriarchy and Slavery in Hobbes's Political Philosophy." In Julie K. Ward and Tommy L. Lott, eds., *Philosophers on Race: Critical Essays.* Malden, Mass.: Blackwell, 2002. 63–80.

Louden, Robert B. *Kant's Impure Ethics: From Rational Beings to Human Beings.* New York: Oxford University Press, 2000.

Macpherson, C. B. Introduction to *Leviathan,* edited by C. B. Macpherson. New York: Penguin Books, 1968.

————. *The Political Theory of Possessive Individualism*. Oxford, Eng.: Oxford University Press, 1962.

Mehta, Uday Singh. *Liberalism and Empire: A Study in Nineteenth-Century British Liberal Thought*. Chicago: University of Chicago Press, 1999.

Mendus, Susan. "Kant; 'An Honest but Narrow-Minded Bourgeois'?" In Ellen Kennedy and Susan Mendus, eds., *Women in Western Political Philosophy*. New York: St. Martin's Press, 1987. 21–43.

Mill, John Stuart. *Considerations on Representative Government*, edited by Currin V. Shields. Library of Liberal Arts, No. 71. New York: Liberal Arts Press, 1958.

————. *On Liberty with The Subjection of Women and Chapters on Socialism*, edited by Stefan Collini. New York: Cambridge University Press, 1989.

Mills, Charles W. *Blackness Visible: Essays on Philosophy and Race*. Ithaca, N.Y.: Cornell University Press, 1998.

————. "Kant's *Untermenschen*." In Andrew Valls, ed., *Race and Racism in Modern Philosophy*. Ithaca, N.Y.: Cornell University Press, 2005. 169–93.

————. *The Racial Contract*. Ithaca, N.Y.: Cornell University Press, 1997.

Mosse, George L. *Toward the Final Solution: A History of European Racism*. 1978. Madison: University of Wisconsin Press, 1985.

Myrdal, Gunnar. *An American Dilemma: The Negro Problem and Modern Democracy*. 2 vols. New Brunswick, N.J.: Transaction, 1996.

Outlaw, Lucius. *On Race and Philosophy*. New York: Routledge, 1996.

Painter, Nell Irvin. *Sojourner Truth: A Life, a Symbol*. New York: W. W. Norton, 1996.

Parekh, Bhikhu. "Liberalism and Colonialism: A Critique of Locke and Mill." In Jan P. Nederveen Pieterse and Bhikhu Parekh, eds., *The Decolonization of Imagination: Culture, Knowledge and Power*. London: Zed Books, 1995. 81–98.

Pieterse, Jan P. Nederveen and Bhikhu Parekh, eds. *The Decolonization of Imagination: Culture, Knowledge and Power*. London: Zed Books, 1995.

Poliakov, Leon. *The Aryan Myth: A History of Racist and Nationalist Ideas in Europe*. Trans. Edmund Howard. London: Heinemann, 1974.

Rawls, John. *A Theory of Justice*. Cambridge, Mass.: Harvard University Press, 1971.

Sartre, Jean-Paul. Preface to *The Wretched of the Earth*. Trans. Constance Farrington. New York: Grove Weidenfeld, 1968. 7–31.

Schröder, Hannelore. "Kant's Patriarchal Order." Trans. Rita Gircour. In Robin May Scott, ed., *Feminist Interpretations of Immanuel Kant*. University Park, Pa.: Pennsylvania State University Press, 1997. 275–96.

Shelby, Tommie. "Ideology, Racism, and Critical Social Theory." *Philosophical Forum* 34.2 (Summer 2003): 153–88.

Smedley, Audrey. *Race in North America: Origin and Evolution of a Worldview*. Boulder, Colo.: Westview Press, 1993.

Smith, Rogers M. "Beyond Tocqueville, Myrdal, and Hartz: The Multiple Traditions in America." *American Political Science Review* 87 (1993): 549–66.

————. *Civic Ideals: Conflicting Visions of Citizenship in U.S. History*. New Haven, Conn.: Yale University Press, 1997.

Souffrant, Eddy M. *Formal Transgression: John Stuart Mill's Philosophy of International Affairs*. Lanham, Md.: Rowman & Littlefield, 2000.

Stannard, David E. *American Holocaust: The Conquest of the New World*. New York: Oxford University Press, 1992.

Sullivan, Roger J. *Immanuel Kant's Moral Theory.* New York: Cambridge University Press, 1989.

Tucker, Robert, ed. *The Marx-Engels Reader.* New York: W.W. Norton, 1978.

Tully, James. "Rediscovering America: The *Two Treatises* and Aboriginal Rights." In G. A. J. Rogers, ed., *Locke's Philosophy: Content and Context.* Oxford, Eng.: Clarendon Press, 1994. 165–96.

Uzgalis, William. "'An Inconsistency Not to Be Excused': On Locke and Racism." In Julie K. Ward and Tommy L. Lott, eds., *Philosophers on Race: Critical Essays.* Malden, Mass.: Blackwell, 2002. 81–100.

———. "'. . . The Same Tyrannical Principle': Locke's Legacy on Slavery." In Tommy L. Lott, ed., *Subjugation and Bondage: Critical Essays on Slavery and Social Philosophy.* Lanham, Md.: Rowman & Littlefield, 1998. 49–77.

Valls, Andrew, ed., *Race and Racism in Modern Philosophy.* Ithaca, N.Y.: Cornell University Press, 2005.

Von Eschen, Penny M. *Race against Empire: Black Americans and Anticolonialism, 1937–1957.* Ithaca, N.Y.: Cornell University Press, 1997.

Ward, Julie K., and Tommy L. Lott, eds., *Philosophers on Race: Critical Essays.* Malden, Mass.: Blackwell, 2002.

Welchman, Jennifer. "Locke on Slavery and Inalienable Rights." *Canadian Journal of Philosophy* 25 (1995): 67–81.

Wilson, Catherine. "Introduction—Social Inequality: Rousseau in Retrospect." *Civilization and Oppression.* Ed. Catherine Wilson. *Canadian Journal of Philosophy,* Supplementary Volume 25. Calgary, Alta.: University of Calgary Press, 1999. 1–30.

Wood, Allen W. *Kant's Ethical Thought.* New York: Cambridge University Press, 1999.

CONTRIBUTORS

Matthew Abraham is an assistant professor of English at the University of Tennessee at Knoxville, where he teaches courses in rhetoric and composition, specializing in civic and political rhetoric. Abraham's scholarly interests include critical race theory, critical legal studies, rhetorical theory, and composition theory, and he is currently writing a book entitled *The Rhetoric of Resistance and the Resistance to Theory: Controversial Academic Scholarship in the American Public Sphere,* which examines the scholarly and public interventions of such controversial figures as Lani Guinier, Edward Said, and Norman G. Finkelstein. More recently, Abraham's scholarly work has turned to the Palestinian Intifada and its rhetoric of resistance. Abraham received the 2005 Rachel Corrie Courage in Teaching Award.

Molefi Kete Asante, professor and chair of Africana studies at Temple University, is an internationally known scholar of Afrocentric theory. As chair of Africana studies at Temple University, Asante began the first doctoral studies program in the United States for African American studies. Asante's scholarship has provocatively challenged conventional thinking and radically shaped the direction of African American studies. Foremost among his scholarly works are *The Afrocentric Idea; Afrocentricity; Kemet, Afrocentricity, and Knowledge; Malcolm X as Cultural Hero and Other Afrocentric Essays; Classical Africa; African American History: A Journey of Liberation; The Negotiation of Cultural Identity; The Painful Demise of Eurocentrism: An Afrocentric Response to Critics; The Egyptian Philosophers: Ancient African Voices from Imhotep to Akhenaten;* and most recently, *Scream of Blood: Desettlerism in Southern Africa.*

Gatsinzi Basaninyenzi is an associate professor of English at Alabama A&M University, where he teaches African American literature, literary theory, and composition. Basaninyenzi's dissertation comparatively analyzed the influence of black aesthetics in the novels of John Oliver Killens, William Melvin Kelley, Ishmael Reed, and Alice Walker. Basaninyenzi has also taught at Simpson College, Solusi University (Zimbabwe), and Oakwood College.

Jana Evans Braziel is an assistant professor of English at the University of Cincinnati, where she teaches Caribbean, diasporic, and hemispheric American literatures. She writes articles for *Small Axe; Callaloo; Comparative American Studies;*

Women and Performance; Meridians; feminism, race, transnationalism; Journal of Haitian Studies; Popular Music and Society; A/B; Tessera; Journal x; Studies in the Literary Imagination; and the *Journal of North African Studies.* She has also co-edited two collections: *Theorizing Diaspora: A Reader* and *Bodies Out of Bounds: Fatness and Transgression.* Most recently, Braziel completed *Rethinking the Black Atlantic: Race, Diaspora, and Cultural Production in Haiti and Haiti's 10th Département,* which forms a critical rejoinder to Gilroy's theorizations of the black Atlantic by focusing on Haiti and Haiti's diasporic extraterritorial "tenth department."

Azfar Hussain is a visiting professor of ethnic studies at Bowling Green State University. He has also taught in the Department of Comparative Ethnic Studies and in the English Department at Washington State University as Postdoctoral Blackburn Fellow. He has published—in both English and Bengali—nearly a hundred academic, creative, and popular pieces, including translations from Bengali, Hindi, Urdu, Sanskrit, and Arabic. He has written on a wide range of topics such as Native American poetics and politics, critiques of postmodern-poststructuralist-postcolonial theory, Marxist political economy, third-world literatures, and global racism and imperialism. In addition to editing and guest-editing numerous issues of journals and magazines, Hussain has co-edited a two-volume reader titled *Reading about the World.* He is currently working on several books.

S. Lily Mendoza is an assistant professor of culture and communication at the University of Denver, Colorado. She is the author of *Between the Homeland and the Diaspora: The Politics of Theorizing Filipino and Filipino American Identities.* Some of her areas of interest are critical intercultural communication; cultural translation; the politics of representation; and postcolonial, transnational, and diasporic studies.

Charles W. Mills, Distinguished Professor of Philosophy at the University of Illinois at Chicago, works in the general area of radical political theory. He has written numerous articles and book chapters and has published three books: *The Racial Contract, Blackness Visible: Essays on Philosophy and Race,* and *From Class to Race: Essays in White Marxism and Black Radicalism.* He is currently working on two book projects, a collection of Caribbean essays titled *Radical Theory, Caribbean Reality,* and a collaboration with Carole Pateman tentatively titled *Contract and Domination.*

James W. Perkinson holds a joint appointment as associate professor of philosophy and religious studies at Marygrove College and associate professor in ethics at Ecumenical Theological Seminary. He is currently on leave and lecturing at the University of Denver. He has written *White Theology: Outing Supremacy in Modernity* and *Shamanism, Racism, and Hip-Hop Culture,* as well as articles in *Social Identities,* the *Journal of Religion, History of Religions, Cross Currents,*

Nova Religio, and *Semeia.* His interests include race theory, postcolonial studies, Afro-diaspora religious experience, liberation and black theologies, and cultural practice as political resistance. He is a performance poet working in inner-city Detroit and Denver.

Alexis Shotwell is a Ph.D. candidate in the History of Consciousness program at the University of California, Santa Cruz. Her work addresses racial formation, nonpropositional knowledge, individual transformation and the role communities play in such change (particularly in Nova Scotia), personal narratives, and liberation.

Derrick E. White is an assistant professor in history at Florida Atlantic University. He was a dissertation fellow at the University of California–Santa Barbara in 2003–4. His article "'Liberated Grounds': The Institute of the Black World and Black Intellectual Space" will appear in *"We Will Independent Be": African American Place-Making and the Struggle to Claim Space in the U.S.,* edited by Leslie Alexander and Angel David Nieves.

Joseph Young is an associate professor of English at the University of Wisconsin–La Crosse, where he teaches African American literature and composition. Young has publications on Oscar Micheaux (*Black Novelist As White Racist*) and Richard Wright ("Phenomenology and Textual Power in Wright's 'Man Who Lived Underground'") and is currently working on two books: one exploring literary slave revolts, titled *Broken Fetters and Heroic Slaves,* and an edited collection titled *Erasing Public Memory: Race, Aesthetics, and Cultural Amnesia in the Americas,* co-edited with Braziel.

Robert Young, an assistant professor of English at the University of Alabama–Tuscaloosa, teaches and researches in contemporary African American literary and cultural theory, contemporary social theory, and materialism. Building intellectually on articles published in *Cultural Logic, Callaloo, Alethia, Negotiations, Red Orange,* and *Bridges,* Young is currently completing a book titled *Signs of Race in Poststructuralism: Toward a Transformative Theory of Race.* An article of his on Langston Hughes recently appeared in the *Langston Hughes Review.*

Tony Zaragoza is on the faculty of Evergreen State College. His area of study is the political economy of racism. Zaragoza completed his Ph.D. in American studies at Washington State University, and his dissertation examines the history of labor and technology in the apple industry and the effects of the industry's changing demands on agricultural communities, rural poverty, and manifestations of racism. Originally from northwest Indiana's industrial working class, he hopes his work will contribute to organizing on the basis of equality and liberation for all across racial lines, geographical spaces, and national boundaries.

INDEX

Louima, Abner, 207–8
lower-class blacks, 198
Lubiano, Wahneema, 45, 62
Lumpenproletariat, 137–41
lynchings, 189

Mamdani, Mahmood, 126
Mandel, Ernest, 144
Manichean allegory, 12
Manifest Destiny, 76
Marable, Manning, 31
Marx, Karl, 24, 33, 42–45, 55, 61, 128, 130–31,
133–42, 144, 186, 189, 211–13, 229, 248, 251
Marxism, 24, 33–35, 38, 40, 42, 44–45, 62,
128–29, 134, 138–39, 144, 254
Mauer, Marc, 203–4, 209
McGary, Howard Jr., 45
mechanisms of repression and control, 157
Mendoza, S. Lily, 13, 18, 24–25, 155, 164, 168–70,
172, 254
"metabolic violence," 25
Million Man March, 35, 150
Mill, John Stuart, 27, 173, 211–13, 228, 242–44,
250
Mills, Charles W., 1–2, 5–6, 8, 12, 14, 16, 18,
20–21, 26–27, 31, 36–38, 45, 61–62, 67–69,
71–72, 74, 77–79, 89, 92, 174, 182–83, 188–89,
194, 196, 205–7, 209, 211, 250, 254
minorities, 74
modernity: domination inherent to and violence of, 186, 197; European modern philosophy, race, and, 211, 213, 216–18, 220, 229,
245; Europeanness and, 80; globally diverse
experiences of, 175–76; race as constitutive
of, 2, 18, 27, 42, 211, 213, 216–18, 220, 229,
245; slavery and, 189; white supremacy and,
182–83, 185
Moynihan, Daniel Patrick, 83, 199, 206, 209
Moynihan Report, The, 199, 206
Mudimbe, V. Y., 175–76, 196
multiculturalism, 33, 58, 153, 206
Muraskin, William, 198, 209
mutatis mutandis, 185
myth, 126, 195, 248, 250

nation, 30, 91–92, 144, 195, 209–10
National Institute on Drug Abuse, 203
naturalness, 25, 77, 156, 165
Navarro, Atoy, 170–71, 173
New Deal, 200
new humanism, 153
Newtonian logic, 158
nonpropositional, 20, 46–49, 51–54, 57, 59–61,
255

nonpropositional knowledge, 48–49, 52, 57,
61, 255
normativity, 156
Notes on the State of Virginia (Jefferson), 97

Omi, Michael, 4, 18, 47, 60, 62, 183, 186, 194,
196, 203
"the oppressed," 2, 10, 14, 78, 141, 145–46, 151,
153
"the Other," 94, 115, 118, 141, 148, 195, 248
Other Side of Racism, The, 150, 154
Otto, Rudolph, 9, 28, 190–92, 196

pedagogy, 173, 195
people-of-colorism, 153
phenotype, 153
philosophy of force, 95
planetary humanism, 11, 19
Plato, 148, 220
Pocock, J. G. A., 199, 209
political correctness, 148
political economy: class blindness and, 37;
of colonialism, 127–31, 133–34; Engels on,
136, 143n6; Fanon on (as political epistemology), 130, 131, 133–43; global political
economy of capitalism, 128; of labor, land,
language, and the body, 142; Marxist political economy, 254; of modern slave trade,
188; postcolonial theory, race, and, 41; poststructuralism and, 8; of race, 8, 17, 24, 37, 41,
43, 127–31, 133–34; "racial contract" (Mills),
international law and international political economy, 89
postcolonial academy, 170
postindustrial, 190, 204–5, 207–8
post-Marxism, 19, 40
postrace, 19, 40
poststructuralism, 8, 33, 127
power: "biopower" (Gilroy), 15; Black Power,
8, 183; class and power relations, 75; colonial discourse as apparatus of, 156, 167;
colonialism, national middle class and, 137;
commerce, wealth, power, and repression,
106; commonsense (Gramsci) and, 60;
dominant power relations, 86; economic
power, 137, 149, 166, 181; European colonialism, gender, and, 176; European power, 181;
fetishizing of, 184; Foucauldian conceptualizations of, 156; Frederick Douglass and
language as, 94; hegemony (Gramsci) and
consent to, 156; implicit forms of knowledge and, 51; interpellation and imposition
of European colonial power structures
in colonized territories, 167; John Locke

on, 234; labor and, 133, 135–36; law, legal, system, and will to power, 73, 75; "multiple traditions," American polity, and, 246; political power, 149; possession and, 186, 188; power and disenfranchisement from, 95; power, land, labor, language, and global subaltern bodies, 142; "power over nature" (Hegel), 183; and privilege, 14, 182; production relations and power relations, 128–29, 131–32, 134; race as constitutive in material, political, and social forms of, 4; race, theory, and, 7; "racial contract" (Mills), color-blindness, and, 14; social contractualism, "racial contract" (Mills) and, 77; relations of, 107; state apparatus and state/political power, 41, 58–59; subjectivity, bodies, and, 15, 27; supernatural power, 103; theory and power structures, 159; Thomas Hobbes and naturalization of European colonial power, 233; Title VI, *Sandoval* case, and rescinding of power, 86; *tfu* as, 177–80, 182; Tutsis, Hutus, and colonial racial-power structures, 23, 124; *umoja*, collective, and, 150; "veiled majoritarianism," and, 68

Pratt, Mary Louise, 163, 173
prehistorical, 148
protocols of reading, 130
pure politics, 73

race: and academic disciplines, 1, 5, 18, 26; and aesthetics, 11, 94–126; and Affirmative Action, 197–210; Althusserian theorizations of, 44n1; analytical category of, 3, 11, 128; and anticolonial struggles, 8; and anti-essentialism, 6; and anti-race discourses, 7, 11, 150; and asymmetrical social relations, 38, 46; and biased interpretations of the law and legal discourses, 4, 18, 21; as biological or psychological essence, 5, 9, 79, 87, 94, 97, 114–26, 199, 206; and biological reductionism, 5, 9, 14, 79, 87, 94, 97, 199, 206; as "blank" (spectral), 128; as collective national identity, 150; as commonsense (Gramsci), 4–5, 18, 20–21, 46–62, 223; as constructed by and implicated in European colonialism, 6, 80, 155–96; and continental modern philosophy, 211–51; critical race theory and, 3, 6, 9, 16, 18, 21, 28, 67–68; critiques of "racial contract" by Goldberg, 67–68; cultural amnesia about, 1, 28; as cultural construct, 4, 150; and David Horowitz, 89n8; death of the concept of, 4; denials of, 3–4, 21; de-ontologizing of, 12–13; and discrimination, 86, 199; discursive formations of, 4; and 18th

century continental philosophy, 211–51; and essentialism, 6, 9–10; as fixed or unchanging category of uncomplicated belonging, 97, 174–96, 211–51; as formative within thought, 3, 26; and Foucauldian theoretical blindspot, 15, 27; and Frantz Fanon, 127–44; as genetically determined classification with presumed intrinsic epistemological interpretations, 5, 79, 87; as a globally operative or deployed regime of power, 7; "grammatical" reading of (Goldberg), 38; as ground of possibility, 4; the Hima as, 22–23, 114–26; as historical category, 5, 97; Howard Winant and theorizations of, 4, 38, 47; and hybridity, 39, 42–43; and identity politics, 15; ideological dimensions of, 32–45, 55, 58; as illusion, 4, 8, 58, 151; and Immanuel Kant (Kantian thought), 238–42; as implicit knowledge, 20, 60–61; and indigenous ritual, 25, 175; and inequalities of wage labor, 38; institutionalized foundations of (systemic forms of), 1, 18, 21; and international division of labor, 38; and Jim Crow, 14, 35–36, 76, 81–83, 205, 215; and John Locke (Lockean thought), 234–38; and John Stuart Mill, 242–45; juridical analyses of, 21, 65–93; and knowledges, 1, 18, 26; legacies of within the Americas, 3; and liberalism, 39; and literary genres, 7, 94–126; as malleable category, 4; a mark of foundational exclusion, 4; material consequences of, 3; and material, political, social, intellectual, and academic consequences of, 5, 27, 75–93, 197–210; and middle-class, 34, 137, 197–210; and miscegenation, 181; and mixed-race, 17, 181; and modernity, 18, 80, 211; modern representations of, 12, 80; and "multi-modal" (Gilroy), 38; and nationalism (fascism), 89n9; and 19th century racialized sciences, 6, 22–24, 94, 114–26, 223; as nonexistent, 4–5, 8, 21; as nonpropositional, 51, 61; and objectivity, 5; as ontological category, 5, 14, 97, 174–96, 211–51; and oppression (exploitation), 32–33, 36, 38, 46; and Pan-Africanism, 10; as part of Marxian economic base, 32; and personhood, 214, 238; as a point of differential knowledge, 4, 14, 27; political economy of, 17, 24, 37, 41, 43, 127–31, 133–34; and postcolonial theory, 41–43; "post-race" (Gilroy), 19, 40, 153; poststructuralist deconstructions of (within academics), 3, 5–6, 8–9, 17, 19, 33, 38; as a "powerful durability," 56; premodern constructions and uses of, 223; as

truth, 6, 34, 48–49, 72, 119, 156, 177, 185–86
Tutsi, 22–24, 114–15, 119, 121–25
Tutsis, 5

Uncle Tom, 99, 104, 109, 111, 113
underdeveloped, 31
United Kingdom, 149, 152
United States: African American cultural experience in, 20; African American scholars in, 149–50; anti-miscegenation laws in, 71; the black church in, 25, 175; black power activism in, 183; *Brown v. Board of Education,* cold war, and anti-communist ideology in, 68; colorblindness in race discourses of, 46; constitutional language and race in, 70–71; Constitution of, 75; cultural racism in, 21; Frederick Douglass as abolitionist orator in, 95; homophobia and contact sports in, 51; Henry Highland Garnet in, 112; imperialism in the Philippines and, 160–61, 170; international law and, 89; *Korematsu v. the United States,* 70; legal system and racial oppression in, 66; "new racism" in, 91; political and legal apparatus of, 86; race and egalitarian liberal democracy in, 214; race and War on Drugs in, 83; race post-9/11 and Patriot Act in, 79; racialized hierarchies in, 218, 222; racially-divided electorate in, 63; racial minorities and the Supreme Court in, 73; racism among economic and political elite in (Lubiano), 44; rhetoric of freedom in (Reagan), 200; slave revolts in, 98; white abolitionists and racism in, 224; white supremacy in, 84, 152, 216

"veiled majoritarianism," 21, 64, 68–69, 71–72, 86

Wallace, George, 203
war, 22, 29, 62, 68, 70, 76, 83, 92, 95, 171–72, 209, 221, 249
War on Drugs, 22, 83, 92
War on Terror, 14
Waswo, Richard, 198, 210
Weber, Max, 79–80, 89, 92
Welsing, Frances Cress, 182, 196
West: and academic disciplines as Westernized, 155–73, 175, 192; Afrocentricity as a critique of, 145–50; Christianity and Western civilization, 23, 120; and Christianity as a Western institution, 106, 120; colonialism and, 10; and contact with aboriginal cultures, 25, 179, 192; dichotomized notion of

the West and the rest, 174–75; and erasure of white racial domination in Western history, 220–22, 239, 243; and Eurocentricism among Western scholars, 146, 175; and imperialism, 13; and liberation discourses, 8; and Manifest Destiny, 76; and "metabolic violence," 175, 179, 188, 192; and racialization of history, 22; relation to proslavery constructions of Western history, 98; and slave revolts in the Western hemisphere, 98; and slavery in the Western hemisphere, 111; and universalist conceptualizations of knowledges, 25, 177; and Western aesthetics, 11; and "Western analytic" (Anglo-American philosophical tradition), 48; and Western Christian myths of origins, 175, 190; and Western cultural system as racialized, 205–7; and Western domination of indigenous cultures, 155–73, 175, 179, 190, 192; and Western *episteme,* 208; and Western feudalism, 98; and Western hegemony, 147–50; and Western legal and political systems, 73; and Western mores, 107; and Western notion of Marxist political economy, 138, 183; and the Western notion of the a-ontological nature of blackness, 105; and Western philosophers, 211, 214, 219–20, 224, 228, 239; and Western philosophy, 51; and Western political states, 234; and Western political theories, 212, 218, 220, 224, 228, 245; and Western traditions, 24; whiteness, Darwinian epigenesist, and, 6; and white supremacy, 149; and white supremacy in Western literature, 153, 192
West, Cornel, 7, 30, 38, 151, 153, 175, 183, 194, 196–97, 210
Western academy, 146
Western hegemony, 147
Western science, 147
When Victims Become Killers, 114, 126
White supremacy: challenges of abolitionism, antilynching, and civil rights movements to, 84; challenges of black nationalism to, 152; eugenic insistence of, 80; as institutionalized within the U.S., 246n4; modern "Age of Equality" as Age of Global White Supremacy, 213, 215, 220, 234, 238; nexus of law, capitalism, and white supremacy, 75–86; as political system, 216, 222, 234; as related to "*veiled majoritarianism*" and structural dimensions of U.S. law, 69; relation to Christian supremacy, 187; relation to fear of difference and xenophobia, 187; relation